Presidents and Democracy in Latin America

This new textbook provides students with a comprehensive and accessible introduction to the presidents and presidential leadership in Latin America. Unlike other texts, *Presidents and Democracy in Latin America* integrates both political analysis and major theoretical perspectives with extensive country-specific material.

Part One examines the developments in recent years in Latin American presidentialism and identifies different characteristics of society and politics which have influenced Latin American governments. The personalization of political life and of presidential government help to illustrate the character of Latin American politics, specifically the type of political career of those who occupied the presidential office, the leadership style of these presidents and the type of government which they led.

Part Two studies two presidents in each of six countries in the region which reflect the broad trends in the political and electoral life: Argentina, Brazil, Chile, Colombia, Mexico and Peru. Each case study first provides the biographical background of the president; it outlines the political career of the president both inside and outside of a party, including at the local level; the popularity of the president at the time of the presidential election is given, as well as the mode of selection of the candidates (selection by party leaders only, by party members or by a primary). The relation of the president with the government or ministers, especially if there is a coalition government, is detailed.

This textbook will be essential reading for all students of Latin American politics and is highly recommended for those studying executive politics, political leadership and the state of democratic governance in Latin America.

Manuel Alcántara is a Full Professor at the University of Salamanca and Professor Emeritus of FLACSO Ecuador. His field research concerns parliament elites in Latin America, parliamentary performance in Latin America and democracy and elections in Latin America. His most recent books include *El oficio de político* (2012) and *Sistemas Políticos de América Latina* (2013, 4th edition) and, as editor, *Procesos políticos y electorales en América Latina (2010–2013)* (2013) and *Selección de candidatos y elaboración de programas en los partidos políticos latinoamericanos* (2013).

Jean Blondel is a Professor at the European University Institute, Florence, Italy. He became a Professor of Political Science at the EUI in 1985 and was an External Professor from 1994 to 2000. Professor Blondel set up the Department of Government at the University of Essex in 1964 and co-founded the European Consortium of Political Research. He was the winner of the Johan Skytte Prize in Political Science for 2004. He has been awarded *honoris causa* doctorates from the University of Salford, the University of Essex, the University of Louvain-la-Neuve, the University of Turku, the University of Macerata (2007) and the University of Siena (2008).

Jean-Louis Thiébault is Professor Emeritus and former Director (1997–2007) at the Institute of Political Studies, Lille, France. He has co-edited with Jean Blondel, *The Profession of Government Minister in Western Europe* (1991); with Gérard Marcou, *La décision gouvernementale en Europe (Belgique, Danemark, France, Pays-Bas et Royaume-Uni)* (1996); with Gérard Marcou and François Rangeon, *La coopération contractuelle et le gouvernement des villes* (1997); and with Jean Blondel, *Political Leadership, Parties and Citizens: The Personalisation of Leadership* (2009). He has also published 'Book review: Alain Rouquié, A l'ombre des dictatures. La démocratie en Amérique Latine,' *Etudes Internationales*, XLI(3), 2010, 413–415; 'Des économies émergentes ou des marchés émergents: le développement politique avec ou sans la démocratie,' *Revue Internationale de Politique Comparée*, 18(1), 2011, 9–52 and 'Comment les pays émergents se sont-ils développés économiquement?' *Revue Internationale de Politique Comparée*, 18(3), 2011, 11–46.

Presidents and Democracy in Latin America

Edited by
Manuel Alcántara, Jean Blondel
and Jean-Louis Thiébault

NEW YORK AND LONDON

First published 2018
by Routledge
711 Third Avenue, New York, NY 10017

and by Routledge
2 Park Square, Milton Park, Abingdon, Oxon, OX14 4RN

Routledge is an imprint of the Taylor & Francis Group, an informa business

© 2018 Taylor & Francis

The right of Manuel Alcántara, Jean Blondel and Jean-Louis Thiébault to be identified as the authors of the editorial material, and of the authors for their individual chapters, has been asserted in accordance with sections 77 and 78 of the Copyright, Designs and Patents Act 1988.

All rights reserved. No part of this book may be reprinted or reproduced or utilized in any form or by any electronic, mechanical, or other means, now known or hereafter invented, including photocopying and recording, or in any information storage or retrieval system, without permission in writing from the publishers.

Trademark notice: Product or corporate names may be trademarks or registered trademarks, and are used only for identification and explanation without intent to infringe.

Library of Congress Cataloging-in-Publication Data
A catalog record for this book has been requested

ISBN: 978-1-138-08207-6 (hbk)
ISBN: 978-1-138-08209-0 (pbk)
ISBN: 978-1-315-11266-4 (ebk)

Typeset in Times New Roman
by Florence Production Ltd, Stoodleigh, Devon, UK

Printed and bound by CPI Group (UK) Ltd, Croydon, CR0 4YY

To Chantal, Estelle, Aline, Lena and Camille
Jean-Louis Thiébault

Contents

List of Figures	ix
List of Tables	xi
Contributors	xiii
Acknowledgments	xvii

PART I
Presidentialism and Political Capital in Latin America — 1

1 Politics in Latin America in the Past Third of a Century (1978–2015) — 5
   Manuel Alcántara

2 Presidential Leadership in Latin America — 23
   Jean-Louis Thiébault

3 The Character of the 'Government' in Latin American Presidential Republics — 55
   Jean Blondel

4 Political Career Trajectories and Social Backgrounds: Latin American Presidents in Comparative Perspective (1978–2015) — 73
   Manuel Alcántara, Mélany Barragán and Francisco Sánchez

PART II
Personal Power and Institutional Constraints: Case Studies — 89

5 Mexico: Zedillo and Calderón: The Challenges of Governing under Adversity — 93
   Marisol Reyes

6	Colombia: Political Leadership in a Turbulent Environment: César Gaviria and Álvaro Uribe Vélez *Javier Duque*	117
7	The Singularity of Peruvian Politics and the Role of Presidential Leadership: The Cases of Alberto Fujimori and Alan García *Martín Tanaka and Jorge Morel*	145
8	Presidential Leadership in a Robust Presidency: The Brazilian Case *Magna Inácio*	167
9	Menem and Kirchner: The Two Faces of Peronism? *Mario D. Serrafero*	205
10	Chile: Continuity and Change in Presidential Government: Patricio Aylwin and Ricardo Lagos *Carlos Huneeus*	231
11	Conclusion	255
	Index	263

Figures

4.1	Impeached former presidents	85
6.1	Evolution of César Gaviria's popularity, 1990–1994	132
6.2	Favorable image of Álvaro Uribe Vélez, 2002–2010	133
8.1	Approval rating of the administrations of FHC and Lula by term month—Brazil, 1995–2010	176
8.2	Evolution of the level of popularity and of the National Consumer Confidence Index	176
10.1	Presidential approval in Chile, 1990–2016	239

Tables

4.1	Presidencies and presidents in Latin America, 1978–2015	76
4.2	Family in politics	77
4.3	Position held by relative in politics	78
4.4	Highest academic degree	78
4.5	University degree	79
4.6	Political careers in Latin America	80
4.7	First and last political positions	83
4.8	Age at arrival to presidency	84
4.9	Number of positions before presidency	84
4.10	Second-term presidents	84
4.11	Way out of politics and political capital profitability	85
8.1	Voter preference during electoral years for Brazilian presidents—1994, 1998, 2002 and 2006	175
8.2	Use of communication outlets by Brazilian presidents—1995–2010	178
8.3	Electoral results and performances of the presidents elected in 1994, 1998, 2002 and 2006	181
8.4	Number of provisional measures issued per year by the presidents—Brazil, 1988–2007	184
8.5	Coalitions in the Brazilian government, 1995–2010	186
8.6	Party discipline in the administrations of FHC and Lula by party—Chamber of Deputies, 1995–2010	194
8.7	Support of the government coalition for the executive's legislative agenda—Brazil, Chamber of Deputies, 1995–2010	195
8.8	Frequency of united and divided votes of governing coalitions per presidential term—Brazil, 1995–2010	195
8.9	FHC and Lula's party activity prior to their presidencies	203
9.1	Ministers and ministries	220
9.2	Reasons behind ministers' departures	220

Contributors

Manuel Alcántara is a Full Professor at the University of Salamanca and Professor Emeritus of FLACSO Ecuador. His field research concerns parliament elites in Latin America, parliamentary performance in Latin America and democracy and elections in Latin America. His most recent books include *El oficio de político* (2012) and *Sistemas Políticos de América Latina* (2013, 4th edition) and, as editor, *Procesos políticos y electorales en América Latina (2010–2013)* (2013) and *Selección de candidatos y elaboración de programas en los partidos políticos latinoamericanos* (2013).

Mélany Barragán holds a PhD in Political Science from the University of Salamanca. She also serves as researcher of the Project of Parliamentary Elites in Latin America. Her research focuses on elites, political parties and electoral systems, with a specialization in federal systems. Among her recent publications are: 'El estudio de las élites parlamentarias en América Latina: pasado, presente y futuro' *(Revista Andina de Estudios Políticos)*, 'Repensando la profesionalización de los políticos' *(Revista Iberoamericana)* and 'Consecución de mayorías legislativas en América Latina: una revisión crítica' *(Revista de Derecho Electoral).*

Jean Blondel is a Professor at the European University Institute, Florence, Italy. He became Professor of Political Science at the EUI in 1985 and was an External Professor from 1994 to 2000. Prof. Blondel set up the Department of Government at the University of Essex in 1964 and co-founded the European Consortium of Political Research. He was the winner of the Johan Skytte Prize in Political Science for 2004. He has been awarded *honoris causa* doctorates from the University of Salford, the University of Essex, the University of Louvain-la-Neuve, the University of Turku, the University of Macerata (2007) and the University of Siena (2008).

Javier Duque is a political scientist, professor at the Universidad del Valle, Colombia, and author of numerous articles and several books, including: *Corrupción, organizaciones criminales y accountability*, Programa Editorial Universidad del Valle, Bogota; *La Construcción de una comunidad académica. La Ciencia Política en Colombia 1968–2013*, Universidad del Valle y Ministerio Nacional de Educación, Colombia; *Las cortes y el presidente*, Oveja Negra, Bogota; and *Políticos y partidos en Colombia. Los liderazgos partidistas durante el Frente Nacional Prolongado 1974–1986*, Oveja Negra, Bogota.

Carlos Huneeus is a Professor at the Facultad de Derecho of the University of Chile. His research has focused on public opinion, authoritarian regimes, democratization and presidentialism. He is author of several books, including *La Unión de Centro Democrático y la transición a la democracia en España, Chile, un país dividido, The Pinochet Regime, La guerra fría chilena, Gabriel González Videla y la ley maldita* (2009) and *La democracia semisoberana, Chile después de Pinochet* (2014) and is co-editor of *Eduardo Frei Montalva: un gobierno reformista. A 50 años de la 'Revolución en Libertad'* (2016).

Magna Inácio is an associate professor at the Universidade Federal de Minas Gerais. She is currently carrying out research on presidents and presidencies with a focus on the dynamic of multiparty cabinets and its impacts on executive–legislative relations and internal organization of the Executive branch. Her research interests include coalition governments, the institutional presidency, and parliamentary elites in Brazil and Latin America. She has co-edited the books *Legislativo Brasileiro em Perspectiva comparada* (with Lucio Rennó) and *Elites Parlamentares na América Latina* (with Anastasia, Mateos and Mendes) and published articles in several journals such as *Journal of Politics in Latin America, Brazilian Political Science Review* and *America Latina Hoy*.

Jorge Morel has a Master's degree in Social Sciences from the Graduate Institute of International and Development Studies (Switzerland). His research interests are social policies and border policies.

Marisol Reyes is a Lecturer in political science and international relations at Tecnológico de Monterrey, Mexico. She holds a PhD in Political Behavior from the University of Essex, United Kingdom. Dr. Reyes has a Master's degree in Latin American Studies from Georgetown University, United States and a BA in International Relations from the National University of Mexico. Her research has focused on Mexican and Latin American electoral systems, citizens' political engagement, and gender and politics. She is coauthor of the books: *Las Revoluciones Necesarias para América Latina* (ITESM, 2011); *Testimonios y Reflexiones del Proceso Electoral Federal 2012* (IFE, 2012); and *Women in Academia: Crossing North-South Borders* (Lexington Books/ Rowman & Littlefield, 2015).

Francisco Sánchez is a Professor Titular of Political Science at the University of Salamanca and Deputy Director of the Institute of Iberoamerica at the University of Salamanca and FLACSO España. He previously worked as a researcher at Institut Für Iberoamerika Kunde Hamburg. He is the author (with Manuel Alcántara and Mercedes García) of *Funciones, procedimientos y* *escenarios: un análisis del Poder Legislativo en América Latina* (2005 AECPA Prize) and of *¿Democracia no lograda o democracia malograda? Un análisis del sistema político del Ecuador*.

Mario D. Serrafero is a Professor of Political Science at Universidad de Buenos Aires and Senior Researcher at The National Scientific and Technical Research Council. He received his PhD in Law from the Universidad de Buenos Aires and his PhD in Political Science from the Universidad Complutense. He is the author of several books, including *Exceptocracia ¿confín de la democracia?* (Lumiere, 2005) and *Reelección y sucesión presidencial* (Belgrano, 1997) and co-editor of *Estudios presidenciales. Perspectivas y casos en América Latina* (L&G, 2015).

Martín Tanaka has a PhD in Political Science, from FLACSO Mexico. He is Senior Researcher at the Institute of Peruvian Studies (IEP) and Full Professor at the Pontifical Catholic University of Peru (PUCP). He has recently published 'Agencia y estructura, y el colapso de los sistemas de partidos,' in Torcal (coord), *Sistemas de partidos en América Latina* (Anthropos, 2015), and 'The Future of Peru's Brokered Democracy' (with Carlos Meléndez), in Abente and Diamond (eds), *Clientelism, Social Policy, and the Quality of Democracy* (Johns Hopkins University Press, 2014).

Jean-Louis Thiébault is Professor Emeritus and former Director (1997–2007) at the Institute of Political Studies, Lille, France. He has co-edited, with Jean Blondel, *The Profession of Government Minister in Western Europe* (London: Macmillan, 1991); with Gérard Marcou, *La décision gouvernementale en Europe (Belgique, Danemark, France, Pays-Bas et Royaume-Uni)* (Paris: L'Harmattan, 1996); with Gérard Marcou and François Rangeon, *La coopération contractuelle et le gouvernement des villes* (Paris: L'Harmattan, 1997); with Jean Blondel, *Political Leadership, Parties and Citizens: The Personalisation of Leadership* (London: Routledge, 2009). He has also published 'Book review: Alain Rouquié, A l'ombre des dictatures. La démocratie en Amérique Latine,' *Etudes Internationales*, XLI(3), 2010, 413–415; 'Des économies émergentes ou des marchés émergents: le développement politique avec ou sans la démocratie,' *Revue Internationale de Politique Comparée*, 18(1), 2011, 9–52 and 'Comment les pays émergents se sont-ils développés économiquement?' *Revue Internationale de Politique Comparée*, 18(3), 2011, 11–46.

Acknowledgments

We owe particular thanks to the Universidad de Salamanca, the Instituto de Iberoamerica and The Project of Parliamentary Elites in Latin America (PELA) —'Las elites parlamentarias y el consenso de las "commodities" en América Latina,' financed by the Ministry of Economy and Competitiveness Ref: CSO2015–64773-R—and to Octavio Amorim Neto and the Fondacion Getulio Vargas, Rio de Janeiro, to Miguel Jerez Mir and the Universidad de Granada, to Cristina Ares and the University of Santiago, and to Xavier Coller and the Universidad Pablo de Olavide, Sevilla. Special thanks to Mélany Barragán for her patient editorial work.

Part I
Presidentialism and Political Capital in Latin America

Latin American governments have been influenced by two main characteristics of society and politics. They are primarily the result of the important part played by individuals in social and political life. Latin American societies have been markedly affected by inter-personal relationships in the villages and rural communities where substantial practices of patronage and clientelism have long prevailed; with the extension of the right to vote, elections were deeply influenced by these practices. The impact of personalities on the political life of Latin American countries has continued to this day, and remains substantial despite increased urbanization. Latin American voters have continued to choose personalities over party programs. Political culture has been strongly influenced by this personalization of social and political life.

The second main characteristic of Latin American governments has been the adoption of the presidential system. Influenced by the work of the founding fathers of the American republic, Latin American countries set up institutions drawn largely from the US constitutional model. Nonetheless, Latin American presidents represent another type of executive. In the United States, there is a president, but there is no government. Latin America has a large number of presidential regimes characterized by a high degree of consistency and similarity. They constitute a type of intermediary regime comprising many elements of presidential regimes, but also few features of parliamentary systems with coalition government integrated by a sufficient number of parties to ensure a majority in congress. For almost twenty years, Brazil has been considered an extraordinary case of 'coalition presidentialism', and Bolivia's political regime between 1985 and 2005 was defined as 'parliamentarized presidentialism.' This explains why the president's leadership is important and has an impact on the nature of government. The key feature of the popular election of the president has been the inherent tendency of Latin American countries to emphasize the role of personalities in politics.

The analysis presented here takes into account the specific characteristics of Latin American polities from the early 1990s. These characteristics are in the first place economic. Latin America experienced a series of economic crises during that period, being one of the most 'volatile' parts of the world economically: regional indicators such as the gross domestic product, exchange rates and budget deficits were roughly two or three times more 'volatile' than those of developed countries. On the other hand, since the beginning of the twenty-first century, the region has experienced marked economic growth and substantial social progress: Asian demands for commodities and for agricultural products, which constitute the main part of Latin American exports, have grown strongly. The income from that trade has greatly stimulated regional economies and helped to strengthen monetary reserves. Economic growth has indeed benefited the poorest citizens of the region. There has been a reduction in poverty and a significant decline of economic and social inequalities. Governments spend more money than previously to help the poor and improve health, education and housing for low-income segments of the population and, as a result, the percentage of the population living above the poverty line has risen sharply: in 2010, a third of Latin Americans belonged to the middle class, compared with 17 percent in 1990. Yet these changes have not prevented Latin America from being markedly affected by violence. A long list of factors accounts for this violence, such as the persistence of inequalities, youth unemployment, organized crime, and weak institutions of justice and security.

There are also aspects specific to Latin American politics. In the 1990s, democracy spread across the region, except in Cuba and Venezuela, while Colombia and Mexico experienced marked political violence, the state being unable to maintain order and public security. The militarization of these countries often led to abuses in terms of human rights without preventing the spread of violence. Democratic development also meant that the number of regularly held free and fair elections increased. The number of political parties and the growing ideological polarization were also a sign of strong political pluralism. Institutional mechanisms have also been used to resolve conflicts, while military coups have ceased to occur and the new democratic regimes have proven able to solve political crises as they occurred.

Yet Latin American democracy still faces problems. First, there persists some degree of 'illusion' about what elections can achieve: many countries remain in a hybrid zone, on the road to democratic consolidation, as if the electoral process was sufficient to establish democracy. Second, what has been called 'delegative democracy' has tended to spread. Moreover, personalization and concentration of political power have resulted in a degree of 'turbulence' in Latin American democracies. The fall of the Soviet Union and the end of the Cold War also led to difficulties. Meanwhile, the period was marked by the implementation of a 'Washington Consensus,' which became central to economic policies in the region, despite some variations among the countries concerned.

Thus, two main characteristics (the personalization of political life and the adoption of presidential government) provide some explanation of the character of Latin American politics, specifically regarding the personality type of those who have occupied the presidential office, the leadership style of those presidents, and the type of government that they led.

Chapter 2 examines the conditions in which presidential leadership takes place in Latin America. That leadership is strongly influenced by the institutional context resulting from the presidential form of government. Additionally, there are three other strong sources of influence over presidents: their personal skills, the social and political relations that they hold and their personal reputation.

Chapter 3 examines the nature of presidential government in Latin America. Its differences from presidential government in the United States are highlighted, where, instead of a cabinet, the ministers (the 'secretaries'), are individually and separately dependent on the president. In Latin American presidential government, there is a range, from governments wholly dominated by the president to governments which are coalitions and are at least partly collegial.

Chapter 4 seeks to identify trends, patterns and differences in terms of profiles based on the levels of education and family backgrounds of Latin American presidents from 1978 to 2015, including those who were popularly elected and those who replaced popularly elected presidents who had died or resigned. The political careers of these presidents, both before they came to office and after leaving it, are also examined. During the period under consideration, only three women were elected presidents. Presidents tend to be drawn from an urban context, except in Brazil. In the case of most, family members had previously held political office. Presidents tend to have had a university education, mainly in law. They also had pursued a long political career before becoming president.

1 Politics in Latin America in the Past Third of a Century (1978–2015)

Manuel Alcántara

Latin America's transition to democracy, a period that stretches from the 1978 elections in the Dominican Republic to those held in El Salvador in 1994, has been followed by the full consolidation of electoral democracy, with leaders elected competitively, freely and, for the most part, without corruption. This period is unprecedented in the region's history, not only due to its length but also because, despite the very different models of political development adopted by individual countries, its key features are common to the vast majority of Latin American nations (Alcántara, 2008 and 2013).

The advent of democracy and its subsequent development were a consequence of different causes: on the one hand, a clear effort to redesign institutions in order to guarantee new political regimes after transitions and, on the other hand, the existence of new leadership. The end of dictatorships and military governments allowed the emergence of new elites, and presidents became fundamental pieces of the political system. Presidentialism along with old phenomena like 'caudillismo' and populism reinforced the role of the presidency.

Although each country's transition was crucially influenced by its particular history, the Venezuelan presidential elections of 1998, from the perspective of hindsight and given the events that have since occurred, should probably be considered a key dividing point from the late 1970s to the middle of the second decade of the twenty-first century.

From 1998 onwards, not only did Latin American countries gradually begin to form two blocs, with some espousing the form of political action referred to as 'Bolivarian,' but elements that, albeit not necessarily new, were important in defining the nature of the political struggle were also more explicitly incorporated into the Latin American political agenda. Understanding these processes and explaining the political struggle requires paying attention to who holds power. In that sense, Latin American politics offers wide heterogeneity of leaderships: professional politicians, outsiders and populists are just a sign.

This chapter examines the different periods into which Latin American politics between 1978 and 2015 can be divided. It is based on matters of a political-institutional nature, and of political economy combined with different kinds of leadership. The chapter concludes that there are sufficient grounds for thinking that 2016 may have marked the start of a new political cycle which, despite institutional consolidation, raises questions about the advance of democratic representation.

Recovery of Democracy and Neoliberal Victory in the 1990s

The Third Wave: Democratization Arrives in Latin America

Latin America's processes of democratization in the 1980s were unprecedented both in their intensity and reach. They were intense in that, despite the constraints discussed below, countries that took the democratic road did not abandon it and, in an historic milestone, distanced themselves from a return to authoritarianism. Moreover, democratization affected the vast majority of the countries of the region, except Cuba: there was no precedent when almost the whole of Latin America had embraced democracy at the same time. Although democracy was restored in the Dominican Republic and Ecuador in the second half of the 1970s, it was not until the 1980s that it became generalized. In the 1990s, however, the optimism that had prevailed at the beginning of that decade began to be widely questioned. A bitter-sweet sensation predominated in analyses of a situation that permitted very divergent appraisals of the results, with a positive view (which was not groundless) pitted against a negative view backed by equally solid and verifiable results (Diamond et al., 1999).

The positive interpretation of democracy's performance drew on arguments of four kinds. The first cited a generally positive mood in the region, given the advances achieved by all countries, except Colombia,[1] Venezuela,[2] Peru[3] (at least in 1992–2000), and Guatemala.[4] The second argument points to the indisputable fact of the number of elections that took place, mostly in a clean manner, with respect for the rules and with a quite high level of competition.[5] Turnout was also more than acceptable, with a regional average of over 60 percent.[6] Thirdly, it is important to note the existence of clear and free competition between the political parties that serve as the channels for political representation. Both the level of ideological polarization and the number of parties, with a regional average of around 3.6, clearly testify to pluralism, with an ideological spectrum including parties that had historically been excluded from the system (Alcántara, 2004). The fourth set of arguments points out that, throughout this period, institutional mechanisms (rather than force or discretional decisions by a single group, as had historically been the case) were used to handle conflicts and to advance direct political participation. One key example of this was the way in which the region handled the economic crisis it suffered in the 1980s due to the exhaustion of the state-centric matrix and its replacement by a neoliberal model.[7] The new democratic regimes also demonstrated their ability to deal with different political crises correctly.[8] Further evidence to this effect is provided by the processes of political reform in very diverse spheres that took place within political regimes through standard mechanisms they themselves had established.[9]

Similarly, the most solid 'authoritarian enclaves'[10] that had persisted in Latin American political regimes were gradually eliminated.[11] Finally, some countries increasingly introduced mechanisms of direct democracy such as plebiscites and referendums.[12]

The negative view of Latin American democracy's performance was, in turn, based on four elements, which, it has been argued, reflected the region's dysfunctionality. The first of these had to do with the so-called *electoral fallacy* (Karl, 1986) according to which elections are virtually the only expression of democracy in Latin America. Due to a complex history of frequent violations of electoral practice, and a legacy of discrediting the reviled *formal democracy*, the emphasis on election processes, necessary for any constituent process, was such that they completely filled the democratization agenda. As a result, the region left behind authoritarianism but only a small number of countries successfully consolidated their passage to democracy, whereas the vast majority remained in a hybrid zone 'on the way to democratic consolidation' (Alcántara, 1991 and 1992) and persisted in the electoral fallacy, with free elections coming to be seen as a sufficient (as well as necessary) condition for democracy. The Latin American countries 'on the way to democratic consolidation' established 'democratic procedures yet have certain difficulties in passing the threshold of consolidated democratic systems [. . .] The legacy of the transition, institutional ineffectiveness and the fluctuating credibility of the system's virtues' (Alcántara, 1992: 220), as well as the traditional personalization patterns, are the key features of countries in this category.

The second negative argument has to do with the spread of *delegative democracy* (O'Donnell, 1994). This is one of the most useful categorizations for analyzing the meaning of democracy in those Latin American countries that had completed their transition, but where consolidation remained a distant prospect. Delegative democracy existed in a good number of Latin American countries where weak political institutions were unable to constrain the unlimited power of executive governments elected by voters mobilized by clientelistic ties or by a candidate's personal, rather than programmatic, appeal, all in a context of weak parties that were, moreover, rejected by citizens. The absence of mechanisms of control and horizontal accountability, together with government by decree (by a president determined to enshrine the will of the people) and an authority based on personal charisma and the support of some expression of popular mobilization, rather than the institutionalized organization of preferences, are the principal characteristics of delegative democracy. What was new in this very widespread expression of democracy in Latin America (Diamond, 1999: 38) was not so much its poor institutionalization and partly autocratic nature but rather its persistence over a decade or more, in an international and regional context obsessed with maintaining the facade of democracy at any cost, which generated enormous pressure against its replacement.

The third negative argument arises from the fact that, in Latin America as a whole, both the degree of delegation and its impact on democracy had changed (Diamond, 1999: 39). However, its principal effects, such as personalism,

8   *Manuel Alcántara*

concentration of power and weak political institutions, have been key causes of turbulence and of the poor quality of democracy, with resulting cynicism and political apathy by Latin Americans (Alcántara, 1998).

Finally, the fourth and theoretically more complex argument refers to obstacles to the success of democratic consolidation that were a result of the priority given during much of the 1990s to the shorter-term aim of *governability* (Alcántara, 1994*)*. This is referred to in a special section below. In any case, these negative arguments represent a chiaroscuro vision in contrast to the positive aspects of Latin America's political development in the last quarter of the twentieth century.

The International Context: The Fall of the Wall, the Washington Consensus and the Emergence of a New World Order

Other factors of an exogenous nature also had equally important effects around the region in the last decade of the twentieth century. Firstly, the fall of the Berlin Wall, with its effects on the world of Soviet socialism and the disappearance of a symbolic reference point for sectors of the left. In Latin America, the events of the autumn of 1989 contributed decisively to the pacification of Central America. The 'Communist threat' disappeared from the national security agenda of the US Department of State to be gradually replaced by other issues, led by drug trafficking and subsequently terrorism but also including migratory flows, the environment and free trade. Events in Europe were followed in late 1992 by the election in the United States of President Bill Clinton, a Democrat. This marked the end of 12 years of Republican government during which, particularly during President Ronald Reagan's first administration, US policy towards Latin America had focused obsessively, and with an important symbolic component, on events like the Sandinista Revolution.

Secondly, this period brought the consolidation, albeit with nuances depending on the country, of the Washington Consensus (Williamson, 1994: 26–28) as the central pillar of the economic policies adopted in the face of the crisis of the so-called Popular National state model that had developed gradually over the previous half-century. With its focus on liberalization and balanced fiscal budgets, the Washington Consensus implied unrestricted implementation of a gradual but firm process of liberalization of the economy, emphasizing the free movement of capital, deregulation—with the inevitable trend towards large private monopolies in key sectors—and privatization. This process greatly eroded the public sector while its alleged lack of transparency represented an inexhaustible source of corruption and poverty, and inequality increased.

The Nineties: Political Changes and Institutional Reforms

After Alberto Fujimori's coup in Peru in 1992, an event that can be considered a watershed in this first post-transitional period, Latin America entered a new age in which, having left behind the black-and-white world of military authoritarianism or sultanism that existed prior to the 1980s, it became engulfed in a complex process with many nuances and differences among countries.

In the 1990s, Latin American countries sought to rewrite their constitutions, for different purposes. These political reforms, sometimes implemented simultaneously in the same country, fall into six main groups. The first and most important group, designed to ensure the executive's predominance over the political system, included measures such as the introduction of presidential re-election in Argentina, Brazil, Peru and Venezuela,[13] marking a break with the policy of non-re-election that has existed in Mexico since the 1930s, as well as the lengthening of the president's term in Bolivia and Venezuela. This increased presidential powers over the legislative agenda and caused the paralysis of the legislature's most important forms of control (Morgenstern and Nacif, 2002), such as its ability to impeach presidents[14] or other top government officials.

Secondly, there were measures that sought to weaken the legislature, which lost its central role in the political game due to a trend towards single-chamber parliaments. Examples of such measures include the constitutional reforms implemented in Peru in 1993 and in Venezuela in 1999.

A third group of measures sought to improve operational aspects of elections and boost their legitimacy. These were basically of four types: improvement of electoral administration in order to ensure reliable results;[15] the introduction in more countries of a second round in presidential elections in order to enhance the winner's legitimacy (Molina, 2000); the incorporation into the constitution (or the relevant legislation on political parties) of mechanisms of internal democracy, both in their functioning and in the selection of candidates (Alcántara, 2001); and timid steps towards greater control of political spending, combined with a gradual increase in state funding.

The fourth group of measures, related to the introduction of the neoliberal model, redefined the state's role in the economy and in relation to property rights.[16] The fifth group, which marked a continuation of the trend towards political and administrative decentralization seen in the previous decade, sought to increase the efficiency of government and to bring it closer to citizens (Jordana, 2001) through the popular election of local authorities[17] and through an increase in the powers of existing local bodies.

Finally, the sixth group included constitutional reforms for purposes that ranged from the creation of bodies to organize, administer and oversee the judiciary, or the state legal defense service, to recognition of a country as multicultural and multiracial (as, for example, in Ecuador's constitutional reform in 1998).

Economic Collapse and the Emergence of Populism

Throughout the 1990s, the historical weakness of the Latin American state deepened. Its longstanding lack of a monopoly of legitimate violence, of control over its territory,[18] of efficient administrative apparatus, and of a citizenry imbued with civic and republican values and subject to universal rights and fully capable of exercising them (Méndez et al., 1999) was compounded by the Washington Consensus. As indicated above, this implied fiscal austerity in the form of spending limits accompanied by privatization of public assets, liberalization of markets, and deregulation, all of which eroded the state's already limited operational capacity. In general terms, the state ceased to be able to implement public policies designed by the government in a bid to achieve certain programmatic objectives in line with the demands and needs of Latin American societies.

A new type of populism, which had been thought to be in decline and persisted only in a relatively small number of countries, emerged with the appearance of formulas that favored demobilization and anti-political behavior maintaining strong personalization patterns. The populism of Carlos S. Menem in Argentina, strongly strengthened by the political machine of the historic Justicialista Party, or that of Abdalá Bucaram in Ecuador, supported by the Roldosista Party, were of a different nature to the populism of Alberto Fujimori in Peru. Fujimori sought to distance his government from politics, disdaining the social and/or political mobilization that could have been mounted through some movement or party. Instead, Fujimori expressly renounced such mobilizations, and depoliticized all the other political bodies. In this way, he undermined the role not only of Congress and the Supreme Court, reducing them to their minimum expression, but also of municipal governments whose role was reduced to the technical administration of projects. In between these two extremes, Hugo Chávez in Venezuela initially positioned himself as a populist critical of the previous political class; however, faced with the particracy of the time, he eventually created his own apparatus for mobilization and strengthened the institutional structure, to which he looked for support without abandoning his personalism or emotional rhetoric abounding in mythical references heavy with the symbolism that imbued his political actions.

During the 1990s, Latin America also lost weight internationally. Its heterogeneity, diverse interests and disperse leadership have always been a problem, preventing the region from speaking with a single voice and resulting in inconsistencies and even contradictions in its positions, thus giving an impression of weakness in international forums.[19] In addition, the fall of the Berlin Wall deprived important sectors of the left of a reference point and reduced the support received from this source to a minimum. At the same time, because Washington no longer feared that its 'backyard' could fall into enemy hands, the region lost weight in international organizations where its traditional alignment with the United States had given it some limited 'blackmail' leverage. In this context, attention shifted to Eastern Europe, with its political and economic transitions and the outbreak of the conflict in the Balkans. Moreover, Latin America continued to lose weight in the international economy, as a result of the collapse of the economic model it had established half a century earlier, along with the greater dynamism of the Southeast Asian economies and the attention required by sub-Saharan Africa, with its more dramatic need for aid. Although Latin

America's formal institutional ties with northern hemisphere countries led to the first Summit of the Americas in 1994 and, five years later, the first European Union–Latin America and Caribbean Summit, these events produced only limited results.[20] In the international agenda on drug trafficking and migration, the only two issues able to produce an impact in and a certain response from the United States[21] and the European Union, Latin America warranted barely two lines.

Political Change in Latin America in the Twenty-first Century

From Chavist Neopopulism to Regional Polarization

The neoliberal policies that had caused real social trauma and inspired very strong popular mobilization, principally in Argentina and Bolivia, as well as Ecuador—which also suffered enormous political instability with seven presidents in barely ten years—helped to bring to power governments which, albeit differing in nature, corresponded to the model of 'rentier populism' (Mazzuca, 2013). This model drew on the precedent established by Chávez in Venezuela since 1999, a year that represented an inflection point for the entire region with respect to its political development over the two previous decades. The model gained strength in Venezuela after Chávez overcame a coup and oil strike against his government. Moreover, this group of countries, with their shared plebiscitary hyperpresidentialism and strong leadership, adopted a common language and a pattern of solidary regional action. In defense of the so-called twenty-first-century socialism, the governments of Argentina, Bolivia, Ecuador and Venezuela, followed by Nicaragua, adopted common strategies. These gradually formed a new political group with some ties to the government of Brazil, after President Lula da Silva took office in 2002, along with Uruguay, following the victory of the left-wing Frente Amplio in 2004 and, to a lesser extent, Paraguay, after the victory of Fernando Lugo in 2008. This new situation provided a powerful argument for the region to establish for the first time a reasonably heterogeneous foreign policy in a bid to increase its limited international weight.

Twenty-first century socialism—a name used almost exclusively to refer to the Venezuelan case; in Ecuador, the term "citizen revolution" is used—brought together classic features of the Latin American left such as anti-imperialism (or, in other words, anti-Americanism), rhetoric about the great fatherland as the culmination of Bolívar's dream of regional unification, and pressure for equality. However, it also incorporated some half dozen elements characteristic of the region's populist tradition. Among those were: the charismatic and messianic *caudillo* who implied not only intensely emotional rhetoric but also indefinite re-election and concentration of power; the central role of the rentier state in economies based on extraction of natural resources; constant evocation of the *nacional popular* tradition and its role as subject of history; an overwhelming tendency to control information in order to 'protect' its freedom against large media business groups; recourse to systematic manipulation of elections in favor of the incumbent; and, in some countries, denunciation of racist and discriminatory conduct on the part of the white minority.

Despite the process's very weak institutional framework, electoral practice was never brought into question. In formal terms, this model has been seen principally in Venezuela, Ecuador and Bolivia in the assumptions of the so-called neoconstitutionalism,[22] as opposed to classic liberal constitutionalism. Concern about third-generation rights, recognition of the multicultural and multinational nature of Latin American countries, and the incorporation of criteria of participative democracy (but also re-election in favor of the supreme leader, often without limit, and measures that increase the weight of presidentialism) gradually became more generalized (Nolte and Schilling-Vacaflor, 2012).

Differences among Countries

In 2015, the region could be usefully divided into three groups of countries. This was the result of a combination of factors, some relating to the definition of political action in institutional terms, and others of an identity-ideological nature (Alcántara and Tagina, 2013). Despite the significant differences that still exist within each group, there are sufficient grounds for considering them blocks with a certain level of internal consistency. These differences are arguably a result of the various national experiences during a diffuse period, between approximately 1998 and 2003. During this time, some countries—but, in a key explanatory factor, not all—became convinced that the Washington Consensus had not only failed to reduce inequality in the region, among the highest in the world, but had also failed to contribute to their economic growth. There was, in addition, an assortment of new, proactive leaders in Evo Morales, Rafael Correa, Daniel Ortega and Cristina Fernández, backed by strong processes of social mobilization, all of whom introduced political reforms of differing weight, such as the drastic constitutional reforms in Ecuador and Bolivia or the partial constitutional reforms of Nicaragua and Venezuela.

The Latin American countries included in this block do not have a common denominator, either institutionally or ideologically and, indeed, various interpretations by the left in power in the region have identified at least two subgroups. Increasingly, other authors like Dabène (2012) argue that the idea of "two lefts" is reductionist and superficial. In general, the two subgroups are considered to be one that is populist (and further to the left) while the other is more social democrat. However, these distinctions have not taken into account, for example, the broad multi-party coalition governments seen in Chile which, although headed by two Socialist presidents, Ricardo Lagos and Michelle Bachelet, have included parties far from the left. Similarly, the governments of Lula da Silva and Dilma Rousseff in Brazil included, starting with their vice-presidents, center and even right-wing forces.

In a further significant difference, the possibility of eliminating limits on presidential re-election has not arisen in Chile, Brazil or Uruguay.[23] On the other hand, constitutional mechanisms of the classic liberal rule of law were not eliminated in the bid to limit democratic pluralism, maintaining the balance of powers and avoiding any hint of executive interference in the judiciary or electoral bodies. However, these three countries have implicitly accepted and validated the form of political action seen in the countries that make up the hard nucleus of the Bolivarian axis—Bolivia, Ecuador and Venezuela—where the obsession with indefinite presidencies soon made itself felt.

This second division implies that, as of 2015, there was—with the peculiarities indicated above—a bias in numerical terms towards the center-left, with a group of countries formed by Argentina, Bolivia, Brazil, Chile, Costa Rica, Cuba, Ecuador, El Salvador, Nicaragua, Venezuela and Uruguay in opposition to a group formed by Colombia, the Dominican Republic, Guatemala, Honduras, Mexico, Panama and Peru.

When Chávez was diagnosed with cancer, however, this situation began to change—a process that accelerated after December 8, 2012, when Chávez explicitly left his vice-president Nicolás Maduro in charge of the Bolivarian process before returning to Havana to continue his treatment, and that culminated on March 5, 2013, the official date of his death. After Chávez, two new circumstances contributed to produce ever more acute polarization in Venezuela. Given the impossibility of transferring charisma, leadership of the Bolivarian process is undergoing a complex reconfiguration because Maduro[24] lacks the leadership exercised by his predecessor, not only in terms of charisma but in political skill. History demonstrates the complexity of such a situation, and the need for a certain time to elapse or for solid leadership to be established. However, Venezuela's economic situation in 2015, with runaway inflation, an enormous fiscal deficit and scarcity of basic products, as well as very high crime levels, suggested that time was running out. This also had evident repercussions for the rest of the region, without a leader able to unite the different sensitivities that arise both from factors related to the personalities of the other national leaders and the momentum of the imposition of a model validated by twenty-first-century socialism.

Chávez's charisma, which worked so well among his peers, is sorely lacking, and Maduro's anointment by the late president has not helped much. Moreover, the end of the region's economic boom has prevented financial rescue operations such as those carried out by Chávez when he bought the debt of Argentina, Bolivia and Uruguay at critical moments during the early years of this century, perhaps with the help of other countries that may have included China (Bonilla and Milet, 2015). Similarly, Venezuela's current financial situation means that it has had to reduce the assistance provided to Caribbean countries through the Petrocaribe alliance.

This new situation has, in any case, served to confirm once again the heterogeneity of Latin America. Although a shift to the left has indeed occurred, especially in the south of the region, this had a dual component that resulted in important differences reflected not only, as indicated above, in response to the failure of neoliberalism but also in the culmination of a political electoral cycle where changes of power were a natural consequence of this failure (Cameron and Hershberg, 2010). This has given rise to processes seeking social change, based on an important transformation of the political elite, who are generating their own mystique by creating new myths or reinterpreting old ones—Bolívar— while engineering a new message. In addition, processes of institutionalization of different types in Colombia and Paraguay[25] have achieved significant successes both socioeconomically and politically in experiences that are clearly more to the right, while the government of Peru has shown marked ambiguity. After 20 years of center-left government, Chile had a brief experience with right-wing government before returning to the center-left at the beginning of 2014.

Chile and Colombia—after overcoming the personalism of President Álvaro Uribe and launching peace talks with the guerillas—are two examples of notable institutional maturity in contrast to the complex situations of Paraguay and Peru (the former suffering from volatilized political parties and the latter from marked oligarchic ossification). Mexico is a case apart with the return to power of the PRI which, at the start of its new administration, is laying the foundations for great and far-reaching national agreements. Complementing this, Central America has seen the consolidation of government by the left in El Salvador and, in Costa Rica, the election of a new center-left option. All these cases testify to the gradual appearance of different models, as discussed in the first part of this chapter.

The Quality of Democracy Issue

This vision of democracy in Latin America and its recent evolution serves as a basis for examining the factors that may be behind this situation. As regards the groups of countries discussed above and the evolution of the quality of democracy in the years since 2008,[26] the different variables into which democracy can be broken down would appear to give convincing results about its performance. In fact, six aspects stand out and can be taken as lessons derived from the empirical evidence. Two relate to the sphere of the state, whereas the others involve the poor quality of inter-institutional accountability, inequality, the oligarchic structure of the media, the weakness of political parties and party systems and the doubtful quality of the professionalization of politics.

The problems related to the dynamics of the state itself, strongly questioned at one time by neoliberalism, appear to be consequences of serious failings in the rule of law, not only in areas such as corruption, lack of public safety and weak protection of economic and social rights, but also in the state's inability to confront internal violence. The state is, in addition, perceived as being very inefficient, with an administrative capacity constrained by the precariousness of a public administration that lacks both professionalization and independence. Moreover, this has been aggravated by the chronic fragility of the security forces and, in general, the state's inability to exercise a monopoly of legitimate violence.

The institutional framework seeks to provide a new answer to constitutional development by creating bodies to implement mechanisms of horizontal accountability in line with more successful experiences in other countries, sometimes with the explicit incentive of help in setting them up. However, weak personnel training and institutional capture by hegemonic projects that have already spread around the region render these inefficient, transforming them into mere decorations of the official project, unable to exercise real supervision or enforcement.

The lacerating economic inequality that makes Latin America the world's most unequal region also conspires against the quality of politics. Inequality is, however, not only economic—it also has an ethnic component in that indigenous and Afro-descendant sectors remain highly marginalized, while gender inequality, both socioeconomical and cultural, constitutes a further problem (UNPD, 2014). The fact that the region had four women presidents simultaneously, albeit only for a few months, does not negate the subordinate political role that they still play in executive government, 35 years after the start of the region's transition to democracy, although their participation in other political arenas has been growing (Caivano and Marcus-Delgado, 2013).

The oligarchic structure of the media in countries with a weak political opposition means that they take on the latter's role, challenging the hegemonic political power. Even where the situation is different, the media have an all-powerful presence when it comes to anointing presidential candidates and keeping them in the public eye during campaigns. Further evidence of a power struggle in which public opinion is subordinated to politics is also seen in laws through which the political power attempts to gag the press, in the creation of public communications networks, and in the sometimes interminable 'sabatinas' (presidential addresses) which all the media are obliged to broadcast in real time (Tello, 2013).

The weakness of some countries' political parties and party systems means that they have been relegated to a secondary role, replaced by candidates who act autonomously with no respect for party discipline or positions. This is particularly clear in Panama and Guatemala. We also find party movements under personalistic leaders that are not transparent as regards their funding or their lack of internal mechanisms for selecting leaders and candidates, and which offer no clarity as to how their programs are drawn up (Alcántara and Cabezas, 2013). This situation has its roots in the institutional mechanisms of presidentialism, the widespread phenomenon of the personalization of election campaigns, and the erosion of society's trust in political parties.

Finally, it is also important to take into account the quality of the region's political leaders. One issue to which very little attention has been paid is the professionalization of politics (Alcántara, 2012). Some politicians in Latin America have insufficient experience and training and, in the absence of effective mechanisms of control and transparency, live encapsulated in the political system. On the other hand, for the sake of the quality of politics, they should be subject to evaluation before taking office, while in office and after leaving it. In this context, the creation of independent agencies to report on their records of accomplishment and to monitor their performance emerges as an imperative that would certainly benefit the quality of the system.

The New Political Cycle

In 2014 and 2015, Latin America's extremely diverse nations held ten presidential elections, marking the culmination of a political cycle that had begun a decade earlier. The common denominator of these elections was the return to power of the incumbent government. Only in Costa Rica, Panama and Guatemala was there a change of power, with the election of new political options. In Bolivia, Brazil and Colombia, the existing presidents were re-elected and, in Argentina, El Salvador and Uruguay, the government parties received a new term, while, in Chile, there was a sort of 'interrupted continuity.'

Over the past decade, there were few changes among the region's leaders, as illustrated by the photographs of presidential summits where the differences in faces are minimal. This was the case for the Kirchners, Evo Morales, Rafael Correa, Daniel Ortega and, until his death, Hugo Chávez. There were also presidents who obtained two terms including Lula da Silva, Leonel Fernández and, at the time of writing, Michelle Bachelet, Juan Manuel Santos, Dilma Rousseff and Tabaré Vázquez. There are four principal reasons for this continuity.

Firstly, this period coincides with the region's economically 'winning decade' during which it was deeply affected by the international financial crisis only in the year 2009. Increased demand for raw materials (minerals and agricultural products), the rise in their prices (particularly oil), and the earlier structural reforms which meant a healthy financial system all gave the region the fiscal surpluses that allowed it to increase public and, particularly, social spending.

Secondly, the presidentialism that had prevailed since 1994 gained strength through constitutional reforms that opened the way to the re-election entirely, of presidents.[27] Only Mexico and Panama continue to forbid re-election and these were joined by Colombia where, after permitting re-election under Uribe, again outlawed the possibility in 2015. However, Mexico has approved the re-election of legislators.

A third reason has to do with the serious deinstitutionalization being experienced by political parties, with resulting autonomy for candidates. This is particularly apparent in the Andean countries as well as in Guatemala, Panama and Paraguay and, in some cases, Brazil.

Finally, as indicated above, it is important to bear in mind that Latin America is currently experiencing a political epoch the likes of which it has never seen before. Since the 1980s, as a general average, all the region's countries with the exception of Cuba have been living through a period in which, without interruption, democracy is the only plausible legitimate option. Leaders are chosen in regular, free and competitive elections whose results are largely accepted by voters and independent international observers. As a result we can talk about generational waves aligned with demographic cycles. However, one generational cycle is now poised to make way for the next.

In this context, 2015 was a year of transition. Towards the end of the year, Argentina and Guatemala held presidential elections, while legislative elections took place in El Salvador, Mexico and Venezuela. Argentina may be the watershed that most clearly marks the emergence of a new cycle, because the Kirchner family, which initially took power in 2003, was succeeded by a political figure with a profile very different from the center-left Kirchnerism that had held power for 12 years. Moreover, public opinion points to a need for politicians to address issues to which they have until now paid scant attention. These issues in themselves represent a script for the period now beginning.

In line with the principal concerns expressed by public opinion (LAPOP, 2014) as well as the conclusions of international organizations (UNPD, 2014) and scholars (Zechmeister, 2014; Millet et al., 2015), these issues include violence, corruption, inequality and poverty. Over the past decade, violence has become systemically embedded in Mexico in a sinister spiral of drug trafficking in connivance with different arms of the security forces and local political groups. In addition, violence makes everyday life extremely difficult in many Central American cities such as San Pedro Sula in Honduras or San Salvador, as well as in some South American capitals such as Caracas. Only the possible success of peace talks between the Columbian government and the FARC and FLN guerrillas offer some hope of a positive change.

Corruption, the scourge of most democracies, has also recently reared its head in Brazil and Chile, two countries that, in the recent past, were held up as models. In Brazil, the problem resides principally in the giant state oil company Petrobras, while in Chile multiple metastases have emerged indicative of a political class that feels immune from punishment. In Guatemala, corruption has also meant that neither the president, Otto Pérez Molina, nor his vice-president were able to complete their terms and, a few months before those terms ended, found themselves in prison awaiting trial. Despite the reduction in inequality and poverty achieved over the past 25 years, when some 60 million Latin Americans rose from poverty into the middle classes, these two scourges continue to seriously limit the region's development.

The systemic nature of these two problems implies a complexity calling for instruments that have been discussed for years. Now, however, with relative political stability and three decades' experience of confrontation between neoliberal and populist solutions, the region is in a position to actually deploy them. The first urgent task is to address the matter of fiscal weakness, because many Latin American countries continue to obstinately ignore the need for reforms to increase tax revenues. Although significant progress was achieved in this field during the economic boom, current practices do not suffice.[28] By increasing pressure and revenues, it would be possible to advance not only the implementation of redistributive policies but also the building of essential state structures that are still lacking. These range from a professionalized public administration recruited independently on merit and skills—so glaringly absent in Latin America—to professional and responsible state security services with a monopoly of legitimate violence, not forgetting the state's fundamental leadership in matters of welfare, where education should be paramount in order to ensure the necessary development of human capital. A final issue that needs to be discussed is the establishment of a style of politics different from caudillist presidentialism that would make it feasible to reach broad national agreements of a clearly inclusive nature.

Notes

1. Columbia was engulfed in a climate of chronic political violence, with actors of different types challenging a state unable to impose a monopoly of legitimate violence. The guerrillas, the so-called paramilitaries and drug traffickers had total freedom of action, often prevailing over the state.
2. Venezuela saw how the Social Democrat government of President Carlos Andrés Pérez, which took office in 1989, had awakened a violent popular movement against economic policies that were presented as the only realistic way to address the severe damage suffered under the old state-centric model in the wake of the 1983 economic collapse but at odds with election promises of immediate prosperity. Heavy repression of the popular movement, inconsistencies in relations between Pérez and his party, and a worsening of the country's external financial situation due to a new drop in oil prices triggered a crisis that lasted through 1992 and included two attempted coups that represented the first intervention of the armed forces in Venezuelan politics in 30 years, and that almost brought down the government. Its weakness was clear when, only a few months later, Pérez was impeached and forced out of office, resulting in a crisis of so-called traditional politics that was to culminate five years later when former coup leader, Colonel Hugo Chávez, took office. A populist leader, his political platform brought together new markedly anti-political sectors with others from the old minority left.
3. Peru, engulfed in an escalation of terrorist violence that approached paroxysm, as well as the consequences of a serious economic crisis that resulted in hyperinflation, had elected a practically unknown politician, Alberto Fujimori, in 1990, in an election in which his rival was Mario Vargas Llosa, a very popular novelist but also an inexperienced politician. Fujimori represented a 'non-political' option against the classic actors of a left that, although fragmented, was one of the most powerful in the region, along with the no less omnipresent APRA party and important Christian Democrat sectors of the center-right. Lacking legislative support, and beset by a judiciary with which he felt uncomfortable, Fujimori opted for authoritarianism. With the support of the armed forces, traditionally active in Peruvian political life, he dissolved Congress in April 1992, purging judges and regional governments and embarking on an extremely personal form of politics under which, bowing to international pressure, he retained a certain institutional framework. However, after drawing up a new political constitution the next year, Fujimori's government rendered meaningless any democratic expression it could have had in formal terms.
4. Although the peace process resulted in important agreements between the state and the guerillas, these agreements were never implemented due to the failure of the plebiscite on their ratification. Moreover, a large part of the (indigenous) population continued to suffer political exclusion, as reflected in Latin America's highest rate of election abstention.
5. The number of presidential elections held from the transition to democracy through to October 2002 is as follows: Argentina (4), Bolivia (5), Brazil (4), Chile (3), Ecuador (7), El Salvador (2), Guatemala (4), Honduras (5), Mexico (2), Nicaragua (3), Panama (2), Paraguay (3), Peru (6), Dominican Republic (7) and Uruguay (4).

Colombia, Costa Rica and Venezuela are not included because elections have taken place there without interruption since the 1950s. Out of the 61 elections indicated (some of which required a second round), important procedural irregularities were reported only in those in the Dominican Republic in 1994 and Peru in 2000, and these were, in any case, re-held (in the Dominican Republic in 1996 and in 2001 in Peru). A similar level of legitimacy is also seen in elections of other types, with important examples including Peru's Constituent Democratic Assembly in 1992 and its constitutional plebiscite in 1993. Out of some one hundred elections that took place in Latin America in the 1980s and 1990s, irregularities occurred in only 4 percent.

6 Although voting is compulsory in almost all Latin American countries, the penalties for abstention are often irrelevant and have little dissuasive effect.

7 Stokes (2001) analyzes the way in which the first democratically elected presidents reneged on their election platforms and implemented far-reaching economic reforms.

8 The destitution, through one form of impeachment or another, of Presidents Fernando Collor de Mello in Brazil, Carlos Andrés Pérez in Venezuela, Raúl Cubas in Paraguay and Abdalá Bucaram in Ecuador, without causing a breakdown of the system, demonstrates the correct functioning of institutions. This is also borne out by the solution of the Guatemalan Congress to the crisis triggered by President Jorge Serrano. Ernesto Samper was also impeached but was cleared of the charge of having received drug-trafficking money for his presidential campaign. Similarly, the political crises that affected executive branches of government were resolved with notable smoothness without a breakdown of constitutional order. This was the case for the processes to replace Presidents Jamil Mahuad in Ecuador, Alberto Fujimori in Peru and Fernando de la Rúa in Argentina, all of which occurred in 2001, the year in which instability in the region reached its highest level in recent times, and of the solution of the crises caused by the failed coup in Paraguay against Juan Carlos Wasmosy in April 1996 and against Hugo Chávez in Venezuela in April 2002.

9 During the 1990s, far-reaching constitutional reforms took place in Colombia, Paraguay, Argentina, Ecuador and Venezuela, as well as more limited reforms in Bolivia and Mexico. This occurred in an anti-democratic way only in Peru, where Congress was unconstitutionally dissolved in April 1992, and where not all political forces were represented of a constituent nature in the new one that was elected. Other more minor but no less significant reforms, such as the electoral reforms seen in Uruguay and Nicaragua, were also carried out correctly. All this took place within the institutional framework and regulated by procedures accepted by all the political forces, even in the case of the failed reform to implement the peace agreements in Guatemala.

10 Seen particularly in Chile, these are institutional recourses of an authoritarian nature that remained encrusted in the democratic political regime, and whose elimination was especially difficult in both technical and political terms (Garretón, 1989).

11 Although triggered by external intervention, the 'Pinochet case' had a satisfactory outcome in terms of starting to eliminate these enclaves. This was evident when he was stripped of the legal protection from prosecution he enjoyed as a senator. The task that remained, however, was to eliminate at least the autonomous role of the armed forces and non-elected Senate seats.

12 Between 1978 and October 2002, a total of 30 popular consultations took place in ten countries of the region. Although five of them (Panama in 1983, Uruguay in 1980

20   *Manuel Alcántara*

and Chile in 1980, 1988 and 1989) were under authoritarian regimes, most of the others originated 'from above.' The executive was directly responsible for eleven of the 25 that took place in democracy (Argentina in 1994, Colombia in 1997, Ecuador in 1986, 1994, 1995 and 1997, Venezuela in 2000, and the constitutional reform consultations in Guatemala in 1994, Panama in 1998, Peru in 1993 and Venezuela). Only seven of the 25 originated 'from below' of which six were in Uruguay (two constitutional reforms approved in 1989 and 1994, two that were rejected in 1994 and 1999, and two referendums against ordinary laws in 1989 and 1992). The other seven consultations were on constitutional matters (Brazil in 1993, Colombia in 1990, Ecuador in 1978, Guatemala in 1999, Panama in 1992, Uruguay in 1996 and Venezuela in 1999).

13   In Panama, a constitutional reform bill that would have permitted re-election, presented in 1999 under the government of President Pérez Balladares, was defeated.
14   See note 8 above.
15   The most obvious case is Mexico's transformation of its Federal Electoral Institute into the National Electoral Institute in 2014.
16   One of the most interesting cases is Mexico, since its 1917 constitution, which represented a 'hard' model of a strongly nationalized and state-centered economy, was dismantled in different stages during the 1990s.
17   Columbia's reform in 1989 to introduce popular election of mayors occurred at the same time as the election reform regarding governors in Venezuela. These were followed by constitutional reforms in Colombia, Argentina and Mexico for the election of governors, of departments in Columbia, of mayors in the Federal Capital in Argentina, and for the governor of the Federal District in Mexico.
18   The most obvious case is Colombia, where the state itself has granted a 'clear area' to the guerillas and different non-state actors control nearly 40 percent of the national territory. However, it also applies to Peru, Brazil and, to a lesser extent, Mexico. In the first two, drug cartels and wood traffickers impose their law in the absence of the state, while, in Mexico, the Zapatista guerillas have a sanctuary in the Sierra Lacandona that inhibits state action.
19   At the beginning of the twenty-first century, Latin America had leaders of the stature of Fernando H. Cardoso, Fidel Castro, Hugo Chávez and Vicente Fox, whose heterogeneity and differences in leanings, personality, ideology and party ties were evident.
20   Despite the boost to relations between the European Union and Latin America when Spain and Portugal joined the former in 1986, the share of the region's trade accounted for by the EU dropped from 20 percent in 1980 to 15 percent in 2000. A mere 4.7 percent of the EU's imports in 2000 were from Latin America, and only 5.8 percent of its exports were to Latin America, whereas five years earlier those figures had been 5.2 percent and 5.7 percent, respectively.
21   The Plan Colombia is the most obvious example of the 'star product' of the US administration for Latin America.
22   According to this, any constitution seeks to achieve a series of objectives set out in the constitution itself, which is more than a mere form of organization of power or definition of powers. Through some stretching of the concept, the constitution becomes a program with which compliance is compulsory, and which all the powers of state must serve and, if the body by which it was drawn up sought to transform society and political action, this must be respected without question.
23   In Brazil, two consecutive terms are permitted, whereas Chile and Uruguay permit only non-consecutive re-election.

24 Maduro was elected on April 14, 2013 in an election whose results were highly questioned.
25 After an ambivalent period, due to its coalition nature, under the government of Fernando Lugo (2008–2012) with support from the liberals.
26 A period for which data is available from the four surveys used in addition to that of Morlino (2013).
27 The latest were in the Dominican Republic and Honduras.
28 In 2013, tax revenues reached 21.3 percent of GDP, only slightly up on the previous year. However, this represented an increase from 14.4 percent in 1990. Although the gradual growth of tax revenues has enabled governments to raise spending on social programs and infrastructure in recent decades, they remain 13 percentage points below the OECD average of 34.1 percent. There are, however, wide differences in the region, with figures that range from 35.7 percent in Brazil and 31.2 percent in Argentina to 14 percent in the Dominican Republic and 13 percent in Guatemala (ECLAC, 2015).

References

Alcántara, M. (1991). Sobre el concepto de países en vías de consolidación democrática en América Latina. *Revista de Estudios Políticos*, 74, 113–130.
Alcántara, M. (1992). ¿Democracias inciertas o democracias consolidadas en América Latina? *Revista Mexicana de Sociología*, 54 (1), 205–223.
Alcántara, M. (1994). *Gobernabilidad, crisis y cambio*. Madrid: Centro de Estudios Constitucionales.
Alcántara, M. (1998). Política, democracia y valores ante el siglo XXI en América Latina. *Anuario social y político de América Latina y el Caribe, Caracas-San José: FLACSO-Nueva Sociedad*, 67–75.
Alcántara, M. (2001). *Experimentos de democracia interna: Las primarias de partidos en América Latina*. Papeles de Trabajo. Mexico: FLACSO.
Alcántara, M. (2004). *¿Institutiones o máquinas ideológicas? Origen, programa y organización de los partidos políticos latinoamericanos*. Barcelona. ICPS.
Alcántara, M. (2008). *Sistemas Políticos de América Latina (Vol. II. México, los países de América Central y del Caribe)*. 3rd edn. Madrid: Tecnos.
Alcántara, M. (2012). *El oficio de político*. Madrid: Tecnos.
Alcántara, M. (2013). *Sistemas Políticos de América Latina (Vol. I. América del Sur)*. 4th edn. Madrid: Tecnos.
Alcántara, M. and Cabezas, L. (eds) (2013). *Selección de candidatos y elaboración de programas en los partidos políticos latinoamericanos*. Valencia: Tirant lo Blanch.
Alcántara, M. and Tagina, M.L. (eds) (2013). *Elecciones y política en América Latina (2009–2011)*. Mexico: Miguel Ángel Porrúa.
Bonilla, A. and Milet, P. (eds) (2015). *China en América Latina y el Caribe: Escenarios estratégicos subregionales*. San José de Costa Rica: FLACSO-CAF.
Cameron M.A. and Hershberg, E. (eds) (2010). *Latin America's Left Turns: Politics, Policies, and Trajectories of Change*. Boulder: Lynne Rienner.
Caivano, J. and Marcus-Delgado, J. (2013). Las mujeres de América Latina al alza. *Política Exterior*, 118–126.
Dabène, O. (2012). *La gauche en Amérique Latine*. Paris: Presses de Sciences Po.
Diamond, L. (1999). *Developing Democracy: Toward Consolidation*. Baltimore: John Hopkins University Press.

Diamond, L., Hartlyn, J. and Linz, J.J. (1999). Introduction: Politics, society and democracy in Latin America. In L. Diamond, J. Hartlyn, J.J. Linz and S.M. Lipset (eds), *Democracy in Developing Countries: Latin America*. 2nd edn. Boulder: Lynne Rienner Publishers.

ECLAC (2015). *Estudio económico de América Latina y el Caribe 2015*. Santiago, Chile.

Garretón, M.A. (1989). *La posibilidad democrática en Chile*. Santiago: FLACSO.

Jordana, J. (2001). *Relaciones intergubernamentales y descentralización en América Latina: una perspectiva institucional*. Washington: Inter-American Development Bank. Serie de Documentos de Trabajo I-22UE.

Karl, T. (1986). Imposing consent? Electoralism vs. democratization in El Salvador. In P.W. Drake and E. Silva (eds), *Elections and Democratization in Latin America, 1980–1985*. San Diego: Center for Iberian and Latin American Studies, 9–36.

LAPOP (2014). *Latin American Public Opinion Project*. Nashville: Vanderbilt University.

Mazzuca, S.L. (2013). The rise of rentier populism. *Journal of Democracy*, 24 (2), 108–122.

Méndez, J.E., O'Donnell, G. and Pinheiro, S.P. (eds) (1999). *The (Un)Rule of Law and the Unprivileged in Latin America*. Notre Dame: University of Notre Dame Press.

Millet R.L., Holmes, J.S. and Pérez, O.J. (eds) (2015). *Latin American Democracy: Emerging Reality or Endangered Species?* New York: Routledge.

Molina, J.E. (2000). *Los sistemas electorales de América Latina*. San José de Costa Rica: Cuadernos de Capel 45.

Morgenstern, S. and Nacif, B. (eds) (2002). *Legislative Politics in Latin America*. Cambridge: Cambridge University Press.

Morlino, L. (2013). *La calidad de las democracias en América Latina*. Informe para IDEA Internacional. Stockholm and San José de Costa Rica: IDEA and LUISS.

Nolte, D. and Schilling-Vacaflor, A. (eds) (2012). *New Constitutionalism in Latin America: Promises and Practices*. London: Ashgate.

O'Donnell, G. (1994). Delegative democracy. *Journal of Democracy*, 5 (1), 55–69.

Stokes, S.C. (2001). *Mandates and Democracy: Neoliberalism by Surprise in Latin America*. Cambridge: Cambridge University Press.

Tello, M.P. (2013). *Dioses, diablos y fieras. Periodistas en el siglo XXI*. Lima: Fondo Editorial del Congreso de Perú.

UNPD (2014). *Human Development Report*. New York: United Nations Development Programme.

Williamson, J. (1994). *The Political Economy of Policy Reform*. Washington: Institute of International Economics.

Zechmeister, E.J. (2014). La cultura política de la democracia en las Américas, 2014: Gobernabilidad democrática a lo largo de diez años del Barómetro de las Américas-Resumen Ejecutivo. *Perspectivas desde el Barómetro de las Américas*, LAPOP, 108. Nashville: Vanderbilt University. LAPOP.

2 Presidential Leadership in Latin America

Jean-Louis Thiébault

At the center of this chapter, there is an application of the leadership approach studying the conditions and manifestations of presidential leadership in Latin American countries, which are being considered as classic cases of a presidential system (Mainwaring and Shugart, 1997; Mainwaring, 1990). The Latin American case suggests that presidential leadership is in fact strongly shaped by the institutional framework of the presidential regimes. The study of institutions has become an important variable for the issue of leadership. This chapter focuses on the extent to which Latin American presidents really are constrained. Their freedom of action is limited. There is an interaction between the president and the leadership environment where presidents operate. This leadership environment consists of institutions which structure their behavior and constrain their freedom of action. Institutions play a major part in determining how political leadership is exercised, and they are the most important aspect of the leadership process. This chapter deals therefore with the question of the different types of presidential institutional arrangement on the capacities of leadership. The approach is essentially related to institutional leadership (Elgie, 2014; Elgie, 1995). Leadership is a behavioral concept; leaders have different resources; all potential leaders act in context (Helms, 2015). However, institutions do not determine all presidential leadership. Within a given institutional context, different presidents govern by making different choices. The leadership approach constitutes a useful and meaningful concept for better analysis of a president's performance. The study is carried out along three elements of leadership: skills, relations, and reputation (Bennister, Hart, and Worthy, 2014).

The conditions and manifestations of presidential leadership in Latin American countries find their origins in the traditional personal politics in this area. 'Personalismo,' and its variant 'caudillismo,' are deeply rooted and have long dominated Latin American politics. 'Caudillismo' is a system of political and social domination, based on the leadership of a strongman, that arose after the wars of independence from Spain in 19th-century Latin America. The Spanish word 'caudillo' was used to describe the head of irregular armies or the leader of a political faction. These forces were governed through an informal system of paternalistic relationship between people and the leader. The term is also often associated with the military leaders that ruled countries in Latin America at the beginning of the 20th century, when political conditions were unstable. Many 'caudillos' took over the government of a country and were successful in maintaining it, while others faced strong opposition. In the work of some scholars, 'caudillos' have been understood as local Latin American variants of patrons (Lynch, 1992; Wolf and Hansen, 1967), while others authors refer to them as dictators (Hamill, 1992).

The traditional personal politics in Latin America is also employed by military officers who have overthrown civilian governments. They establish military rule, usually led by a single military strongman, but also sometimes by a 'junta' representing the military. O'Donnell (1973) embedded the idea of rule by the military as an institution, from an empirical investigation into the political and economic processes in Argentina between June 1966 and March 1973 and by comparing this case to analogous ones (Brazil after 1964, Uruguay and Chile after 1973, and Argentina (again) after 1976). He intended to advance the understanding of what he labels the 'bureaucratic-authoritarian state' and, based on this understanding, to analyze and critique the characteristics and consequences of this form of rule (O'Donnell, 1973). In distinguishing one-man rule from more collegial military rule, Remmer (1989) emphasizes the dictator's personal control of the military as an indicator of his concentration of power. Geddes (1999 and 2003) distinguishes also 'military regimes,' by which she means rule by an officer constrained by other officers (rule by the military institution), from one-man rule, which she labels 'personalist rule.'

In the complex and contested context of political leadership research, there is the notion that leadership is a behavioral concept, that political leaders have different resources, and that all potential leaders act in context. The center piece of this chapter is an application of this political leadership concept to a case study of six Latin American countries, with a special focus on the leadership of twelve presidents in the last twenty-five years. They are: Carlos Menem and Néstor Kirchner in Argentina; Fernando Henrique Cardoso and Luiz Inacio Lula da Silva in Brazil; Patricio Aylwin and Ricardo Lagos in Chile; César Gaviria and Álvaro Uribe in Colombia; Ernesto Zedillo and Felipe Calderón in Mexico; Alan García and Alberto Fujimori in Peru.

The Acquisition of Presidential Leadership

The acquisition of presidential leadership effectively starts with the way leaders win office. In contrast to the patterns of recruitment in parliamentary systems, where prime ministers emerge from the parliament and as official leaders of the strongest party in the parliament, the recruitment for Latin American presidents is considerably wider (Helms, 2015; McAllister, 2015; Bennister and Worthy, 2015).

Only some of them have experience as parliamentary leaders at the national level: Gaviria, Calderón, Aylwin, Cardoso, and Lula. Gaviria was elected in 1974 into the Chamber of Representatives, of which he was president in the 1984–1985 period. Aylwin was elected in 1965 to the National Congress as a senator. In 1971, he became the president of the Senate. Cardoso was elected to the Senate in 1986 for the Party of the Brazilian Democratic Movement (PMDB), which substituted the MDB (Brazilian Democratic Movement) after Brazilian re-democratization. He helped a group of PMDB parliamentarians to abandon the party in order to create the Brazilian Social Democracy Party (PSDB). Until 1992, he served as leader of the PSDB in the Senate. Lula won a seat in Congress in the 1986 elections with the most votes nationwide. But he refused to run for re-election as a congressman in 1990, busying himself with expanding the Workers' Party organizations around the country.

Most Latin American presidents are the 'natural' and uncontested leaders of their respective parties. Aylwin served seven terms as president of the Chilean Christian Democrats between 1958 and 1989. He led his party during the dictatorship of General Pinochet. In addition to being one of the leaders of the Socialist Party of Chile, Lagos became in December 1983 president of the Democratic Alliance, a force that grouped the majority of the democratic parties opposing the dictatorship of General Pinochet. Gaviria became in 1977 co-chair of the Colombian Liberal Party. García was the leader of the old traditional populist party APRA (American Popular Revolutionary Alliance) when he was elected president of Peru for the first time on 14 April 1985. In Mexico, Calderón was president of the National Action Party (PAN) from 1996 to 1999. In a few decades, PAN's status was transformed from that of a loyal opposition accepting the rules of the authoritarian establishment to a party in government (Loaeza, 2003; Shirk, 2005). Some presidents were only 'party men.' In Mexico, Zedillo was only a member of the dominant party, the Revolutionary Institutional Party (PRI). Between 1929 and 1997, Mexico was a dominant one-party system with an extremely strong executive who governed for a single, six-year term. The recruitment of presidents was particular. The incumbent president personally selected his successor. All presidents of Mexico between 1929 and 2000 were members, but not leaders, of the PRI. The influence on the party is even greater when the president was the founder of his party. This is the case with Lula, who founded the Partido dos Trabalhadores (PT) or Workers' Party on 10 February 1980. It was a left-wing party with progressive ideas created in the midst of Brazil's military government. He was the leader of the Workers' Party from February 1980 to November 1994.

Although enjoying the support of a party is an indispensable power resource for any president, securing the formal position of party leader has not been considered a necessary element in building up the greatest possible political leadership. Some presidents were outsiders (Fujimori, Uribe). In the Latin American countries in which austerity reforms led to a high level of social protests and in which the established parties were not able to represent the demands for a change in economic policies, new political leaders appeared outside the old party system to channel the new demands. In the case of most of these outsiders, a new political party was created. The weakness of the party system led to the rise of outsiders. In Colombia, the guerrilla activity and the drug war were the explanations for the rise of an outsider (Carreras, 2012).

The literature on Latin American presidentialism has not converged to a single and consensual definition of the outsiders. In fact, scholars interested in the rise of political outsiders have tended to study this issue under the theoretical framework of 'populism' or 'neo-populism' (Barr, 2009; Hawkins, 2010; Roberts, 1995 and 2007; Weyland, 1999; Kenney, 1998). Scholars have tended to put together this concept with the notion of 'populist' or 'antiparty politician.' In the context of presidential elections, political outsiders are candidates who have not had a previous career in politics when the campaign starts and/or who participated in the elections as political independents or in association with new parties. Fujimori did not have a political career and competed in presidential elections with a new party. Uribe was a political figure in an already existing party, but he competed with a newly created party, differentiated from the Liberal Party, to which he had belonged for over two decades. He decided to leave the Liberal Party and to present himself as an outsider through his new political movement, Primero Colombia. Based on antiparty and antipolitics discourse, Uribe portrayed himself as a renovating option that would solve the problems that traditional parties had not solved (Wills-Otero, 2014).

The rise of political outsiders has been identified as one of the perils of presidentialism (Linz, 1990). The presidential system made it possible for individuals without previous political experience to create a new party and participate in presidential elections (Mainwaring, 1993). Some scholars have identified two pernicious consequences of the election of political outsiders to the presidency for the quality of democracy in presidential regimes. First, this phenomenon reduces the efficiency of the presidency when leaders without previous administrative or political experience arrive to power. Second, the rise of outsiders favors the development of a personalist style of doing politics.

Another negative effect of the arrival to power of political outsiders is the conflict that this phenomenon generates between the president and the parliament, which often leads to political instability, or even democratic breakdown. In fact, outsiders come to power through a new party that is often nothing more than the electoral organization they used during presidential elections. However, once in power, outsiders have to face the opposition of traditional and institutionalized parties in parliament. This often leads to executive–legislative gridlock or to executive excesses (Linz, 1990). In addition to political and policy impasses, political outsiders are more likely to suffer presidential crises, leading to governmental instability. When the ruling party is small (minority in the parliament) and the president is not able to build a stable legislative coalition, the probability of a presidential interruption increases (Pérez-Liñán, 2007). Outsider presidents are likely to lack connections with traditional parties. As a consequence, their cabinets tend to be constituted of members with very limited previous experience in public administration. Furthermore, outsiders are likely to engage more often in patronage and pork barrel to build temporary legislative coalitions, since they have trouble building stable multiparty coalitions (Siavelis and Morgenstern, 2008).

Leadership Skills of Latin American Presidents

The significance of leadership skills is important analysis of the performance of political leaders. The president's skill and ability to identify goals, mobilize support and contribute to substantive change are widely considered prerequisites to successful leadership. Such skills can be acquired by experience and learning, or rather directly from a leader's personality (Helms, 2015).

The skills of the Latin American presidents operating in the context of multiparty presidential systems have to be more in the field of cooperation and negotiation than in exercising strong leadership and delivering polarizing partisan rhetoric.

The political/policy vision is one of the key indicators of a president's skills. The ability to produce a consistent narrative and to provide a discourse marks an indispensable quality. Some Latin American presidents have tried to develop a powerful vision at the level of domestic politics. Some have also tried to develop a vision in foreign affairs. Such a presidential vision is a central element of the presidential leadership. A vision is understood as a set of deep convictions and articulations about the direction in which policies should develop. A certain visionary element cannot be denied as having formed part of some presidents' leadership resources.

The first decade (or more) of Latin American post-authoritarian politics was generally dominated by right-wing presidents. Following the demise of the Soviet Union, the related economic and social debacle in Cuba, and the demise of guerrilla (or revolutionary) movements in Peru and Colombia, the right-wing presidents Cardoso in Brazil, Aylwin in Chile, Gaviria in Colombia, Zedillo in Mexico but also the neo-populist Presidents Menem in Argentina and Fujimori in Peru developed right-wing policies in a variety of shapes and sizes.

During the era of state-led import substitution industrialization (ISI) in the middle of the 20th century, conservative presidents in Latin America were not necessarily supporters of liberalization of free markets (Schamis, 1999). But over time, these presidents responded to inflationary pressures and balance of payments constraints by liberalizing markets in the late 1980s and early 1990s. This is the period of the 'Washington Consensus.' The political achievement of the adjustment period was economic stabilization, with the absence of inflationary pressures. At the end of the 1990s, Latin America seemed poised to begin a cycle of democratic governance, overseen by a growing number of right-center or technocratic presidents. Former finance minister Cardoso was about to beat out the radical leader Lula for the presidency of Brazil. Cardoso took economic measures, sometimes considered liberal, such as the privatization of many public enterprises, and maintained the economic policy of opening the country to foreign investment. Aylwin in Chile and Gaviria in Colombia were also representatives of this trend. There was also the ascendance of neoliberal technocrats within the PRI in Mexico. Zedillo belonged to a group of technocrats who stressed the open market economic model and NAFTA (North American Free Trade Agreement). He was also a well-known supporter of the 'Washington Consensus' and for that reason the old PRI hierarchy did not like him (Centeno, 1994). In Mexico, the PAN emerged as the democratic alternative to the incumbent PRI. In 2006, Calderón fought for a right-leaning, market-based economic agenda that supported the NAFTA paired with socially conservative values, with greater support among wealthy and middle-class voters (Wuhs, 2014).

One of the great puzzles of the neoliberal reform period is that independent presidents with popular support but no significant party organization (Fujimori in Peru) or presidents with strong organization such as the old Peronist party (Menem in Argentina) also launched market liberalization. These neo-populist presidents played major roles in the process of market liberalization (Roberts, 1995; Weyland, 2003). The result was the decline of established conservative parties in most of the countries, where liberal economic reforms were adopted by neo-populist presidents. They were an attempt to insulate macroeconomic policy making from social pressures and democratic contestation. Neo-populist presidents like Menem in Argentina, and Fujimori in Peru, were re-elected after successively stabilizing economies plagued by hyperinflation. However, none of them were representatives of established conservative parties (Roberts, 2014).

Colombia had some special characteristics. Security issues were seen as a priority by Colombian presidents. During their presence in power, much of the national budget was devoted to reinforcing the army and the police with the aim of confronting armed insurrection and drug trafficking. Colombia has often elected right-wing or center-right presidents for reasons stemming from the political hegemony of traditional parties since their creation in the mid-19th century. The Liberal Party and the Conservative Party appeared as organizations that fundamentally represented the interests of the privileged classes. Until 2002, these two parties won all the presidential elections (Wills-Otero, 2014) but they have since declined. Uribe participated in the presidential election as an independent Liberal candidate, separate from his former party, the Liberal Party. His electoral program was centered on the defeat of the main guerrilla movement, the FARC.

Latin America's turn to the left was, at least partially, a popular reaction against the neoliberal economic policies implemented by presidents in the 1980s and 1990s. It came out of exhaustion from the policies that right-center presidents, parties, and technocrats had championed after Latin America's return to democracy. However, the right has not become irrelevant in the region. Some countries that were governed by right-wing presidents in the 1990s continued to be ruled by right-wing presidents in the 2000s (Colombia), while other countries have turned to right-wing presidents in recent years (Mexico in 2000 or Chile in 2009) (Luna and Rovira Kaltwasser, 2014).

Despite the early dominance of the political right in post-authoritarian Latin America, the political left represented a powerful challenge to right-wing presidents throughout the region. During much of the present century, left-wing parties have taken advantage of the perceived failures of previous presidents to elect political leaders who diverge, often quite significantly, from the political and economic policies of the right-wing parties (Weyland, Madrid and Hunter, 2010; Hershberg and Rosen, 2006). In the 2000s, the landscape has transformed. Starting with Chávez's victory in Venezuela, a wave of leaders, generically labeled 'leftists,' have swept into power in one Latin American country after another. After Chávez, it was Lula and the Workers' Party in Brazil, then Kirchner in Argentina. There was a veritable left-wing push through the region, Colombia and Mexico being the only exceptions (Castañeda, 2006).

There are two types of left-wing president in Latin America. Some focus on social policy (education, anti-poverty programs, health, and housing). In Chile,the Socialist Party has governed for 16 consecutive years, in alliance with the Christian Democrats. This alliance has led to high rates of economic growth; significant reductions in poverty; a deepening of democracy and the dismantling of Pinochet's political legacy. The role of Lagos has been important in the application of social policy. The case of Brazil is not diametrically opposed. Lula followed a moderate economic and financial policy. But he tried to compensate his liberal economic policy by innovation in social policy (Castañeda, 2006). His most important success in this area was the initiative of the 'Bolsa Familia' (Tepperman, 2016).

Presidents of the other Latin American left-wing countries came from another tradition. This populist tradition has always been present almost everywhere in Latin America. These populist presidents were representative of a very different left, always authoritarian. They did pursue social policies for the poor (Juan Peron and Getulio Vargas) but they also created the corporatist structures that have since plagued the Latin American political systems. They nationalized large sectors of their countries' economies. Their justifications for such policies were always superficially ideological (nationalism, economic development) but also pragmatic (Castañeda, 2006).

Perhaps to some extent, the presidents' vision remained spectacular because of their ability to maneuver and constitute parliamentary majorities, although these often remain very heterogeneous, and because also of their communicative skills, another key factor in terms of leadership. Some presidents were notoriously poor public speakers, but good media performers. Menem's vision remains unspectacular. He was a poor public speaker and therefore was not in favor of great mobilizations according to the Peronist tradition. He held his connection with people through media. Press conferences were offered with certain regularity (Guerrero and Marquez Ramirez, 2014; Voltmer, 2013). Kirchner was a poor public speaker and also a poor media performer. He neither debated publicly in the electoral campaigns nor offered press conferences. Kirchner's contact with media was made by a reliable official like the cabinet chief. Kirchner's principal way of communicating was through his presidential speeches. Néstor Kirchner, unlike Menem, avoided television and rarely watched it during his government (2003–2007).

Presidents' key skills clearly lay in the field of party management. One of the most important elements that reinforce presidential leadership is the president's ability to properly manage relations with his own party. The president must be able to either coordinate or impose a solution that is satisfactory to everyone. Some became chairs of their parties well before winning the presidency, and they were sometimes the founding fathers of the party organization. They knew their party with its complex territorial structures, and the personnel in charge at the various levels. And they made ample use of their knowledge and their widespread intraparty contacts, not hesitating to circumvent the formal chains of command if an issue mattered to them in terms of a particular policy or, more often, if it secured their power status within the party. Their particular leadership strategies within their parties was no doubt a key source of power. One of the best examples is in Brazil. The characteristics of the Brazilian Social Democracy Party (PSDB) as a weak and decentralized organizational structure, its absence of extra-electoral activities, the low participation of its members, and the lack of democratic institutions to veto the decisions of party elites conferred an ample margin of action for Cardoso with respect to running the government. The PSDB's original parliamentary party comprised 8 percent of the members of the Chamber of Deputies, growing to only 12 percent of the deputies when the party achieved the presidency (Inacio and Llanos, 2015).

Presidents overwhelmingly tend to have weaker ties to their parties than do prime ministers in parliamentary systems. They are more likely to pursue policies that differ from the goals of the party line (Samuels and Shugart, 2010). Presidential policies are very often decoupled from their party's preferences (Amorim Neto, 2006; Cheibub, Przeworski, and Saiegh, 2004; Shugart and Carey, 1992). Presidents have good reasons not to feel bound by the programs of their parties. These reasons are both political and institutional. Unlike prime ministers, presidents are elected independently from parliamentarians. The electoral bases of presidents and parliamentarians are not only separate, but often different. It is not rare that substantive variations occur between the percentage of votes in favor of the president and votes in favor of parliamentarians (Samuels and Shugart, 2010). Faced with a much wider constituency, in separate elections and with different electoral rules, presidents must necessarily appeal to a wider electorate. In the majority of countries with a presidential regime, presidents do not give priority to the representation of local interests, which may explain the divergence from the political positions of parliamentarians (Alcántara, García Montero, and Sanchez Lopez, 2005; Marenghi and García Montero, 2008). This main difference in voting patterns is usually cited to explain why the political priorities of the presidential party can only offer a poor indicator of the president's political priorities once the president is in power (Wiesehomeier and Benoit, 2007).

Presidents' exceptional skills are also reflected at the level of coalition management. Keeping together a coalition for many years is a major achievement. Particularly in Latin American multiparty presidential systems, coalition building is common as a means to secure successful legislative outcomes (Amorim Neto, 2006; Cheibub, Przeworski, and Saiegh, 2004; Negretto, 2006). Presidential leadership in Latin America takes place under the conditions of coalition government. In coalition building, the president's role is dominant. His central function as *formateur* gives parties less direct influence over the benefits of office, as compared to parliamentary systems (Samuels and Shugart, 2010). Presidents must be reasonably skillful in managing the relationship between the coalition parties.

In the early 1990s, the critique of presidentialism (Linz, 1990) was widely influential, and the coexistence of presidentialism with multipartism was viewed as a particularly 'difficult combination.' Multipartism was expected to exacerbate the 'perils of presidentialism' by increasing the probability of deadlock between president and parliament, promoting political polarization, and making interparty coalition building difficult to achieve (Mainwaring, 1993). Yet multiparty presidentialism had come to stay. Since the beginning of the 1980s, among the six selected Latin America countries, only one country (Mexico) has had single-party government. Four countries (Brazil, Chile, Colombia, and Peru) have coalition governments, while the last (Argentina) has had coalition governments at least some of the time. In Latin America, the phenomenon of coalition governments has been named coalition presidentialism (Pereira and Melo, 2012; Pereira, Power, and Raile, 2011; Raile, Pereira, and Power, 2011; Chaisty, Cheeseman, and Power, 2014). This unanticipated outcome has raised questions about how presidents have managed these coalitions. Government coalitions in presidential systems have in fact proven unexpectedly functional and durable (Cheibub, Przeworski, and Saiegh, 2004) while becoming the predominant form of democracy in Latin America. Presidents have the capacity to distribute government portfolios. These ministerial posts are strategic resources available to presidents (Martínez-Gallardo, 2005). Equally, a president's perception of the parliament as being 'workable' or 'recalcitrant' (Morgenstern and Cox, 2001) may lead the president to use cabinet appointments strategically to achieve his or her policy goals (Amorim Neto, 2002 and 2006; Inacio, 2013; Davila, Olivares Lavados, and Avendano, 2013; Carreras, 2013; Camerlo, 2013). Presidents are even more successful in obtaining support when they distribute government portfolios proportionally among coalition members (Amorim Neto, 2002 and 2006; Negretto, 2006). Some authors explain how presidents boost voting discipline and buy additional votes with inducements of a clientelistic nature (benefits for constituencies or a party's basis of support), in order to gather winning government coalitions in presidential systems. Pork is exchanged for votes in multiparty presidential systems like Brazil (Ames, 2001; Pereira and Mueller, 2004). Executives may also redesign the internal structure of the government itself, in ways that resemble the allocation of ministerial posts (Raile, Pereira, and Power, 2011; Pereira and Melo, 2012). The political and ideological heterogeneity of coalition parties force presidents to negotiate with many political actors, in order to create and sustain a legislative coalition that approves a large portion of the president's program.

Brazil represents an ideal case for considering the roles of the president in the use of institutional arrangements and the provision of particularistic or clientelistic goods. Largely because of its open-list proportional representation electoral system and its federal structure, Brazil has a highly fragmented party system (Mainwaring and Shugart, 1997). The institutional tools and resources available to the Brazilian presidents are substantial enough to help correct for minority status and party fragmentation (Amorim Neto, Cox, and McCubbins, 2003). The Brazilian president's toolbox allows for controlling the disbursement of goods to legislators. The president establishes the heterogeneity and size of the coalition and determines the proportionality of partisan representation within the cabinet (Raile, Pereira, and Power, 2011). Patronage has been ubiquitously considered as the single motivation behind partisan political appointments in Brazil, because of cultural and historical reasons. It is striking how some ministries have few political appointments, whereas in other ministries, they comprise almost a quarter of the appointments (Praça, Freitas, and Hoepers, 2011).

Brazil and Chile have emerged as the successful models for governance in Latin America. Each is a multiparty presidential system whose president numbers among the region's strongest. Cardoso (1995–2002) governed in a way that more resembled a parliamentary coalition (Amorim Neto, Cox, and McCubbins, 2003). He rewarded coalition parties with ministerial seats in a highly proportional way (except in his lame-duck final year as president) and sent a relatively small proportion of exchange goods outside the formal coalition. Lula (2003–2009) was dealt a more difficult hand. Given the distribution of seats in the Congress, crafting a large, homogeneous coalition was not possible. Lula's own leftist Workers' Party (PT) exhibited factions with the conservative economic policies the president needed to pursue. These policies required constitutional amendments and a 60 percent supermajority of voting support in the legislature. However, Lula governed during his first year with a minority coalition in the Chamber, a situation further complicated by difficult bargaining conditions in contributing to the 'mensalão' corruption scandal that followed (Pereira, Power, and Raile, 2011). Lula needed to firm up interior support with coalition goods and attract support from opponents with exchange goods. He increased dramatically the number of ministerial portfolios and used the new posts to satisfy factions within the PT. Simultaneously, he sent a large proportion of the pork outside the formal coalition as an inducement for his political opponents. Lula's cabinet became even less proportional upon adding the large PMDB to the coalition with little ministerial compensation in December 2003, though he did keep a much larger proportion of the pork within the coalition after that time (Raile, Pereira, and Power, 2011).

Chile is one of the most advanced democracies in Latin America and has enjoyed the most stable multiparty coalition in Latin America. Democracy was restored with the election of Aylwin (1990–1994), who initiated a succession of four governments of the Concertation of Parties for Democracy (a coalition of center-left parties that had been united in opposition to the dictatorship). For twenty years, the presidency has been under the control of the Concertation, while the opposition had coalesced into an alternative coalition called 'Alianza por Chile.' Competition between these two coalitions dominated contemporary electoral and legislative politics. The stability and unity of Chilean multiparty coalitions had profound implications for the workings of Chilean democracy and, more generally, for an understanding of coalition management in presidential democracies. Given the deep divisions that characterized the Chilean party systems in the period before the military coup of 1973, a bipolar realignment proved to be an impressive break with the past. Aylwin showed remarkable conciliatory skills and exerted firm and decisive leadership. He maintained harmony within the coalition (Alemán and Saiegh, 2007; Carey, 1999; Siavelis, 2009).

Longevity in office is identified as another skill-related dimension of leadership. What this indicator measures is effectively a president's skill to survive the multiple challenges that threaten a fall from power. Strictly speaking, securing a long tenure provides the opportunity for extended leadership performance. But longevity alone is not a guarantee of high ranking. Presidents do not become ever more powerful simply because their tenure lasts longer. Their final term is rarely, if ever, considered to be their most successful in terms of leadership performance and public policy achievements. Lula marked an exception with regard to the latter aspect. It is therefore astonishing that many Latin American presidents have sought a second mandate (and sometimes even a third, in the case of Uribe) and necessarily to modify the constitution, with all the political risks that this change entailed. Most have felt that the duration of a single mandate is insufficient to implement a policy of their own. Many have embarked on such campaigns with no awareness of the negative consequences this could have on their leadership skills.

Latin American presidentialism has been characterized by the election of a single executive for a fixed term of office, and critics of this form of government focused on its resulting inflexibility, particularly as compared to parliamentary government (Linz, 1990). Juan Linz, among others, placed fixed terms at the center of his criticisms of presidential democracy. In addition to other defaults, Linz saw presidential systems as institutionalizing conflict between presidential and legislative powers, leading to deadlock and higher incentives to take extraconstitutional action (Ginsburg, Melton, and Elkins, 2011).

Since the beginning of the 1990s, many presidents through Latin America have successfully amended or replaced their constitutions to facilitate term extensions. The presidents who secured the reforms were subsequently re-elected by large margins. This idea was ratified by the resounding re-election victories won by Presidents Menem in Argentina in 1995, Cardoso in Brazil in 1998, Fujimori in Peru in 1995, and Uribe in Colombia in 2006.

In Argentina, the presidential term lasted six years and immediate re-election was forbidden. Menem succeeded in passing an amendment to the constitution and introducing the possibility of the immediate presidential re-election. His long tenure provided Menem the opportunity for extended leadership performance, although his longevity did not translate to success (Levitsky, 2000; Palermo and Novaro, 1996). In Brazil, Cardoso participated actively in establishing a legislative supermajority to support the re-election of the president. The amendment for re-election was approved. Nevertheless, after his re-election, with the devaluation of the currency and the financial crisis that followed, his popularity plummeted. In Peru, Alberto Fujimori's new candidacy in 2000 violated the limit of two consecutive terms demanded by the constitution. He justified his third candidacy by declaring that his first term as president (1990–1995) did not count, because it began under the previous constitution. When a plurality of Peru's Constitutional Tribunal objected to Fujimori's interpretation of his own charter, the president fired the judges. During the 2000 campaign, Fujimori's supporters systematically intimidated opposition candidates, used state resources to pressure the media, and harbored irregularities during the vote count (Carey, 2003).

In 2006, a constitutional change allowed Colombian president Uribe to be elected to a second term, and, not surprisingly, he was. Still not satiated, the president began a campaign in late 2008 for yet another amendment that would clear the way for a third term. A constitutional plebiscite was scheduled. However, on February 26, 2010, the Constitutional Court determined that, in fact, several procedural requirements had been ignored. The referendum was struck down, and Uribe, limited to two terms, left office. He said he accepted and respected the court's decision (Shugart, 2010).

With the appearance of term extensions, Latin America is discovering presidential re-elections and suffering from an acute case of the incumbent's advantage. This exists in all presidential democracies, but in Latin America, it is disproportionately large. Indeed, no incumbents from the twelve selected Latin American presidents have lost bids for re-election. They have won all elections in which they have been allowed to run (Fujimori and Menem, in 1995; Cardoso, in 1998; Fujimori, in 2000; Lula and Uribe, in 2006). This record makes 'incumbency' the variable that best predicts electoral outcomes in Latin America (Corrales, 2012).

There are several reasons for the success of incumbents. One perennial explanation for the incumbent's advantage is of course the idea that many Latin Americans tend to develop personal attachments toward presidents. Another explanation may be the institutional advantages enjoyed by incumbents. They have advantages because they are known by their regular presence on radio and television. They have a network of relations in the various sectors of public life, including trade unions, employers, the army, and the police. They can manipulate state institutions, state resources, and public opinion (Corrales, 2012). In Latin America, where presidential power has fewer institutional constraints and there are fewer and weaker check-and-balance procedures, incumbents are more difficult to defeat (Navia, 2014).

The interruption of the term of an incumbent president is a sign of the weakening authority of that president. A presidential interruption is an incident in which the president leaves, or is forced to leave, office before the end of the constitutional term (Marsteintredet and Berntzen, 2008; Valenzuela, 2004; Pérez-Liñán, 2005). There have been many types of presidential interruptions in Latin America. The first is a coup, which is an undemocratic dissolution of the presidency often supported by military force. Fujimori's 'autogolpe' in Peru in 1992 was a clear case of democratic breakdown, but not a case of presidential interruption.

Latin America has had long experience with military intervention in politics (Stepan, 1988; Hunter, 1995). Non-constitutional transfers of power have been very often the result of military actions, and military coups have occurred across our panel of Latin American countries. The 1964 Brazilian coup led to the overthrow of President Goulart by the military. In Peru, a military coup led to what became known as the Revolutionary Government of the Armed Forces (1968–1980). The 1973 Chilean coup was a watershed event in the history of that country. The 1976 Argentine coup was a right-wing coup that overthrew Isabel Peron on March 24, 1976. In her place, a military junta was installed that remained in power until December 10, 1983. And these cases are only those that involved the military (Dix, 1994). In the last couple of decades, Latin America has seen an even larger number of presidential replacements before the end of their constitutionally prescribed terms that have not involved military intervention (Pion-Berlin and Trinkunas, 2010). Some of these were conducted within the bounds of the constitutions (e.g. impeachments, resignations), but most were triggered by extraconstitutional factors (e.g. massive street protests demanding presidential exits).

There is one case of an interrupted presidency due to successful impeachment in our panel of Latin American countries (Brazil 1992). It may be seen as proof that the constitutional rule is available for solving conflicts between the executive and the legislature in presidential systems (Pérez-Liñán, 2007 and 2005). Impeachment is difficult to use, which explains why only one of the successful presidential interruptions resulted from impeachment procedures (Hochstetler and Samuels, 2011; Hochstetler and Edwards, 2009; Marsteintredet and Berntzen, 2008; Hochstetler, 2006).

There are also some situations in which a president resigns, during popular protests, or under constraints. Some cases of presidential resignation have been triggered by protests in the streets (Argentina 2001), others by corruption scandals (Peru 2000). Direct popular pressure is the factor causing these interruptions (Hochstetler and Samuels, 2011; Hochstetler and Edwards, 2009; Marsteintredet and Berntzen, 2008; Hochstetler, 2006).

The Particular Importance of Relations Between the Presidents and Other Political Actors in Latin America

In presidential regimes, presidents are more likely to have complex relations with a larger number of actors at different levels of the system. The particular importance of these relations is well captured in assessments that describe the president's leadership style as relying essentially on personal contacts rather than institutional means. Developing and maintaining close relationships with decision makers at various levels, at home and abroad, in fact provides one the principal resources of a president. These relations are likely to extend beyond his or her own party, and beyond the institutions politically controlled by that party. Relations with the political opposition are important. But almost all the relations between the president and public opinion are of major importance in presidential regimes, and in terms of authority and power they tend to be somewhat central. In presidential regimes, presidents invariably depend strongly on their public popularity.

The party organization is often the most important network of power relationships, united in the hands of the president. One of the essential elements of the president's leadership must be his ability to manage the presidential party. He must be able to maintain control over his party using personal contacts in order to facilitate the accession to the party leadership of a man (or woman) with his confidence and to monitor the process of nominating candidates for parliamentary elections. In Brazil, Lula succeeded in setting up party leaders who were very close to him and who were among the founders of the party with him: Dirceu (1995–2002), Genoino (2002–2005), Berzoini (2005–2006 and 2007–2010), and Dutra (2010–2011).

The president's ability to run the presidential party depends on the nature of that party. During the 1990s and the first years of the 2000s, the sharp electoral decline of parties that traditionally integrated the Latin American party systems and the rise of new parties or popular leaders with large electoral appeal led to significant changes within those party systems (for example, in Argentina, Brazil, Colombia, Mexico). The president's control over the organization of his party is firmer when he is himself one of the founders. On the other hand, when the party is an organization composed of strong national or local structures and several factions or currents, the control of the president is reduced. Moreover, the party is sometimes shaken by intense competition caused by the process of nomination of the candidate for the presidential election, and the elected president has difficulty restoring a certain level of unity and consistency.

Alongside party organizations, parliamentary party groups are also extremely important networks of power relationships in the hands of the president. Presidents in Latin America typically have the right to initiate legislation, providing a high degree of direct control over policy outcomes (Shugart and Carey, 1992), and presidents often make almost unilateral policy decisions. The interaction between presidents and parliamentary party groups remains important, because it shapes the character of relations between presidents and assemblies and largely determines the ability of presidents to turn a legislative program into policy (Shugart and Mainwaring, 1997). At one extreme (Mexico), when the president has the support of a majoritarian parliamentary party, his policy objectives may not differ from those pursued by his party. The Mexican president long controlled the highly centralized PRI's organization. Over time, however, modernization weakened the corporatist and clientelist organizations through which the president had ensured political control (Langston, 2006). At the other extreme (Brazil), when presidentialism is combined with multiparty systems, the policy objectives pursued by presidents may differ from those pursued by his party. Presidents' parties tend to fall far short of a majority in congress. In Brazil, parties always suffer from scarce resources and weak professionalization. Party labels are often diffuse. Many parties are little more than personalistic tools for their leading figures. The Brazilian case gives the example of presidents weakened by the fragmentation of the party system.

Another manifestation of a president's leadership is his capacity to appoint loyalists to key ministerial posts. The power to appoint and fire a minister is one of the most important assets available to the president in presidential systems. At the outset of a term, cabinet appointments allow the president to form a government that reflects his or her policy goals. The importance of government formation in presidential regimes shows that majority status, partisan composition, and portfolio allocation of cabinets reflects the policy-making strategies of a president (Amorim Neto, 2006; Raile, Pereira, and Power, 2011; Alemán and Tsebelis, 2011; Negretto, 2006). However, the importance of appointments as strategic resources for presidents goes well beyond government formation. In fact, an average of 60 percent of all cabinet appointments that Latin American presidents make happen throughout the president's term. Some scholars also argue that these ministerial replacements reflect a second crucial way in which presidents use appointments as a way to adapt to unforeseen shocks throughout their term in office (Martínez-Gallardo, 2014). This strategic use of appointments is especially important for reinforcing presidential leadership. Cabinet changes can provide embattled presidents a 'safety valve' with which to adjust to changing political and economic circumstances (Mainwaring and Shugart, 1997). Appointments are an explicit political strategy that presidents can use to face such unpredictable challenges. Cabinet changes allow presidents to modify policy by changing the individuals in charge of making policy. They often follow economic crises or scandals like the 'mensalão' bribery scandal in Brazil that led to the exit of Lula's cabinet chief in 2005, or changes in the partisan balance of powers brought on by an electoral triumph or defeat. Presidents use appointments strategically throughout their term (Praça, Freitas, and Hoepers, 2011; Camerlo and Pérez-Liñan, 2014). They form governments that reflect their new policy making strategy and this choice depends on the strength of presidents relative to the legislature (Amorim Neto, 2006). The proper use of these appointments provides testimony to the leadership quality of presidents.

A president's relationship with the general public is complex and never easy. A president becomes popular from the moment when his political action is regarded by citizens as successful. Popularity entails that the president receives some approval from the population and that those satisfied are more numerous than those who are dissatisfied. Because of the weakness of the Latin American parties in the recruitment and governing process, presidents who were not party leaders, or who were contested within their own party, have had to compensate with strong personal popularity. Personal popularity is no doubt a valuable resource for the president, as it helps to transform office-related authority into political power.

Most of the Latin American presidents were very popular during the first part of their presidency, but had a low level of popularity at the end of the term. This was the case for Cardoso. His popularity remained at similar levels during the first term, oscillating between 30 and 45 percent. However, the situation changed after re-election. Exhibiting a declining trend in 1998, his re-election year, Cardoso began his second term with an approval rate that corresponded to half of that achieved in 1994. In Mexico, at the beginning of Zedillo's government in August 1994, Mexicans generally approved of his mandate. However, in December 1994, his popularity dropped dramatically. The most compelling explanation for this change was the criticism leveled at him after he decided to devalue the Mexican peso. Calderón started his mandate implementing a new public security strategy that involved deploying the military to fight organized crime. This decision gained the support of the population. In 2009 the president's popularity started to decrease. This loss can be explained by the increasing number of civilian casualties and an alarming number of 'disappeared' people due to the war on drugs. Public opinion has concentrated its attention on the outcome of policies towards organized crime and public security.

Some Latin American presidents were more and more popular over time. Lula operated under great presidential popularity, and presidential authority and style contributed to this result. Lula's popularity, measured as percentage of voters who evaluated the president's performance as either great or good, remained at similar levels during the first term, oscillating between 30 and 45 percent. In the final year of his administration, 2010, Lula's popularity reached its peak, with an 80 percent approval rating among voters.

Popularity is often the result of very strong links between the president and the people. Presidents use this appeal to the people to win more voters. The personal ability to attract a large part of the electorate is more important than loyalty to an ideological line. It is in Latin America that populism has had the greatest and most enduring influence. It began as an attempt to ameliorate the social dislocations caused by industrialization and urbanization. In Latin America it became an urban movement. Its heyday was from the 1920s to the 1960s, as industrialization and the growth of cities got under way in the region. It was the means by which the urban masses (the middle and working classes) were brought into the political system. In Latin America, where trade unions were weak, that job was accomplished by populist leaders. These included Getulio Vargas, who ruled Brazil in various periods in 1930–1945 and 1950–1954; and Juan Peron in Argentina and his wife, Maria Eva Duarte de Peron, better known as Eva Peron or Evita.

The populist leaders sought a direct link with the masses. They led personal rather than well-organized parties. Populists saw elections as the road to power, but they also relied on mass mobilization, on getting their followers out into the streets, but they were often less than democratic in their exercise of power. There are many common threads. One is nationalism. The populist national culture is against foreign influences. While their discourse was often anti-capitalist, they made deals with some capitalists. They rallied their followers against two enemies: the landowners and the foreigners, almost all Americans. They supported a bigger intervention by the state in the economy, and they granted social benefits to workers. Some scholars have characterized 'economic populism' as involving a dash for growth and income redistribution while ignoring inflation, deficit finance and other risks (Dornbusch and Edwards, 1991). Such policies have been pursued not just by populists of the past. In a milder form, they have been followed by Kirchner, Argentina's Peronist president. In fact, there is nothing inherently left-wing about populism. Many of them favored corporatism rather than individual rights and the pluralism of liberal democracy. Other scholars have seen populism as a technique of political leadership more than an ideology. They have applied the term to such free-market conservatives as Peru's Fujimori and Argentina's Menem who, in different ways, sidestepped interest groups and made direct appeals to the masses.

Populism brought mass politics to Latin America, but its relationship to democracy was ambivalent. Populists crusaded against corruption, but often engendered more. In the 1960s, populism seemed to fade away in Latin America. Its revival showed that it is deeply rooted in the region's political culture (Conniff, 1982 and 1999). One big reason for the persistence of populism is the extreme inequality in Latin America. Yet populism has done little to reduce income inequality. A second reason for its persistence is the wealth of natural resource of many states of Latin America. Presidents such as Menem or Kirchner in Argentina have benefited from rises in the price of commodities, which has ensured the prosperity of these countries to develop generous spending programs for economic and social policies favorable to the whole population. But the subsequent downturn and low prices on commodity markets have led to years of stagnation and indebtedness, putting an end to the popularity of presidents and greatly reduced their leadership.

The two Argentine presidents here discussed, Menem and Kirchner, were excellent examples of different types of populism. Menem was pragmatic and in this case he was authentically 'Peronist.' Regarding his institutional ideas, he saw the presidency as a place of personal power and himself as a principal actor in the political system. Kirchner went back to the classical ideas of 'Peronism' regarding the state and became the clear option for the working class. He represented the opposite face of the neoliberal approach of Menem. Kirchner managed political power as the historical 'Peronist' leaders had traditionally done.

Menem represents one of the most characteristic leaders in a political culture in which personalism and 'caciquismo' surpass other types of authority. But his style was also connected with one of the principal components of the 'Peronist' movement: the charismatic element. Although there are many interpretations of 'Peronism' (Germani, 1978; Di Tella, 1997), very few studies have outlined its charismatic aspect. During his rise to the presidency, Menem appeared charismatic to ordinary people. His personal style, his references to the Peronist past, his discourse, and his close relationship with the people were identified with the traits of a charismatic leader. Yet Menem's links with his followers were not as important as the intimate relationship with the people built by Peron in the 1940s. But Menem personified one of the features of the complex identity of 'Peronism.' His ascent took place at a time of intense social and political unrest (Arias, 1995).

The Reputation of the Latin American Presidents

Presidents enjoy a certain reputation, positive or negative. This reputation depends on their effectiveness, and their ability to carry out their program. It depends on their ability to resolve the challenges faced by their government. But presidents are more or less constrained by the weight of institutions. They must be able to rely on a majority in parliament or congress. In presidential systems in Latin America, presidents rarely have a majority to govern. In those countries where the personalization of power is strong, they are often seen by public opinion as having great power over public policy. However, presidents face institutional constraints, which are often underestimated by public opinion. The reputation of presidents is measured by opinion polls that provide the level of satisfaction felt by public opinion with respect to their policy. Satisfaction refers to the conjectural appreciation of the political action of presidents. It is different from popularity, which is more a measure of the legitimacy of presidents combining both their personal image traits and their political responsibility. The level of satisfaction makes it possible to situate the reputation of presidents. The stronger the satisfaction, the greater the reputation. Latin American presidents who receive a high percentage of satisfaction are presidents who have a high reputation. Lula is the best example.

Reputation is measured not only at the level of public opinion. Presidents operate in a political environment that includes other actors within the country and abroad. Latin American presidents usually have a strong influence within their party, of which they most often control the leadership and have often founded (for example, Lula, Cardoso, Fujimori, Uribe). Nevertheless, the presence of several factions or strong personalities inside the party can tarnish their reputation. Presidents are sometimes in a position where they have to fight to impose their point of view on a recalcitrant party. In Argentina, the hostility of former president Duhalde was a factor of reduction of the reputation of Kirchner. Similarly, the reputation of Gaviria has suffered greatly from the influence exerted by former president Samper in his own party, the Liberal Party. The strategy of Uribe, leaving the Liberal Party to create his own party to avoid hostile opposition to his political program, was the sign of a very strong ability to build or strengthen reputation.

Latin American presidents have benefited from the disruption of party systems that weakened the opposition parties. The fragmentation of Latin American party systems has often led to a proliferation of opposition parties with no real grip on the policy followed by the president. The danger, however, can come from outsiders, who are able to reduce the president's reputation by personal actions and efficient communication. This was the case with Fujimori, before the conquest of the presidency at the end of the term of Garcia. The presence of strong personalities in the opposition can lead to the reduction of the reputation of the president. Opposition from traditional political parties (Radical Civic Union, URC in Argentina; National Action Party, PAN in Mexico; Brazilian Social Democracy Party, PSDB in Brazil) has remained strong. The different presidential candidates of these parties sometimes became highly active opponents. However, the lack of credible opposition personalities is likely to give presidents the opportunity to be and to remain a leader in the future. Presidents can enjoy the performance of their functions to provide a robust reputation of leadership. The role of presidents within their party and their reputation among their peers as key actors in political life cannot be reversed easily.

Latin American presidents operate in a political environment that includes leaders abroad. However, they generally have a low international audience. Only one of them has benefited from a strong positive reputation abroad: Lula. The participation of three Latin American presidents (Argentina, Brazil, and Mexico) in the G20 provided them with a somewhat stronger audience than their colleagues. But its impact was low on the reputation of those presidents, except Lula.

What is important is the ability of presidents to overcome political and institutional constraints that hamper their actions and affect their reputation. Latin American presidents have several institutional means to overcome these constraints. The successful use of these resources can lead to a strengthening of the reputation of these presidents. These institutional means are essentially decrees, and the right of veto.

In Latin America, presidents have a wide range of powers to improve their ability to govern. Much Latin American legislation is the result of the initiative of the presidents. They can also use institutional resources to overcome the hostility of parliamentarians, such as decrees that carry the force of law, as well as partial or total veto. The essential legislative power that is constitutionally attributed to Latin American presidents is the right of veto. The modalities are varied (total or partial veto, delays, means offered to the parliament to fight the presidential refusal to promulgate the law as is). Nevertheless, the very existence of such a weapon gives the executive a well-founded means of managing conflicts with the parliament to the president's own advantage. This power allows one to appreciate the significant differences in the reputations of presidents throughout the political systems of Latin America (Shugart and Carey, 1992). Some presidents can achieve success through the wise use of their veto power. They then succeed in rejecting a law which does not suit them, or which represents a policy contrary to that of their program. Their success reinforces their leadership and demonstrates their ability to resist opposition pressure. On the other hand, some presidents are not able to defeat the resistance of their opponents. They have not managed to prevent passage of a law. Their failure lowers their reputation and confirms their inability to develop their leadership.

In many Latin American presidential systems, the making of decrees plays an important role in policy making (Carey and Shugart, 1998; Ferreira Rubio and Goretti, 1998; Schmidt, 1998; Crisp, 1998; Power, 1998). It strengthens the ability of presidents to overcome the absence of a majority in parliament or congress. However, abuse of the power of decree is also a sign of the weakness of the presidents who use it and demonstrates the reduction of the presidential leadership. The reputation of the presidents suffers greatly from this diminution. But there are also states of emergency. In nearly all Latin American presidential systems, emergency powers allow the president to suspend civil liberties and take direct command of local agencies in times of unrest (Shugart and Carey, 1992).

Latin American presidents have difficulties in putting through an agenda. This presidential incapacity can tempt them to rule largely by decree. In this way, stalemates between presidents and parliaments can lead to 'decretismo.' This was typical of Colombia during the National Front years and later, with the country being under state-of-siege for 75 percent of the time from 1958 to 1989. 'Decretismo' has been used to characterize regimes such as that of Menem in Argentina (Ferreira Rubio and Goretti, 1998; Palermo and Novaro, 1996).

Latin American presidents have also various political means to overcome these constraints. These political means are essentially the outcome of coalition agreements or means of political patronage. The composition of many governments in Latin America results from deals negotiated by the president and party leaders. This composition is very close to that of coalition governments in parliamentary regimes. A mixed selection (partisan and non-partisan) of cabinet ministers are therefore characteristic of a co-optation cabinet. The presence of party politicians results from a political agreement between the president and certain parties. But there is also appointment resulting from private agreements between politicians and the president, and that does not involve their party leaders (Amorin Neto, 2006).

The best examples of an agreement among more than one political party and a partisan selection of ministers are given by the two Chilean and Colombian presidents. In Chile, the two presidents, Aylwin and Lagos, took the coalition parties into account when they named or fired ministers, preserving a certain percentage of proportionality with their number of seats in the parliament. The uncertainty of the democratic transition after Pinochet provided greater incentives for portfolio-sharing arrangements (Siavelis and Baruch, 2014). These two Chilean presidents were craftsmen of the implementation of a policy of conciliation organized by the leaders of the two major Chilean parties, the Socialist party and the Christian-Democratic party. Their reputation stems from their ability to form coalition governments that respect the proportionality of the parliamentary force of the two coalition parties.

From 1958 to 1986, Colombia was governed by a National Front power-sharing system between the Conservative Party and the Liberal Party. After this period, the Colombian governing arrangement experienced some difficulties. Colombian politics has become more pluralist (Hartlyn, 2008). Gaviria's government (1990–1994) was based on the representation of the Liberal Party factions. Although a vast majority elected him, the Liberal Party had majorities in Congress, and he could have put together a government with his party; but Gaviria preferred to distribute power among diverse forces. This was the result of various factors. First, he did not have a unified party to back him, but rather a federation of factions and interests led by diverse national leaders. Second, no government party existed; Gaviria had no partisan powers, given that he did not act as a party chief; his popular base and his legitimacy were quite weak, because the vast majority of Colombians had not voted for him, a rupture in the country's traditional bipartisan predominance.

The best example of a mixed selection of cabinet ministers is provided by the role of Uribe in Colombia. Uribe is also perhaps the clearest example of the personality politics phenomenon: he left the Liberal Party to create the Colombia First movement, with which he became president in 2002. Despite the existence of a coalition, the nomination of the government remained a largely separate process handled by the president. Most cabinet members during this time could be considered 'independents' or technocrats despite their formal association with a political party, maintaining only a loose connection to their parties in parliament.

The failure to come to an agreement with the parties and the choice of a partisan or mixed (partisan and non-partisan) selection of ministers were also characteristics of the presidencies of Cardoso and Lula (Amorim Neto, 2006; Praça, Freitas, and Hoepers, 2011). However, these two presidents differ in the way they mobilized political resources to form their coalition governments. The level of political affiliation of the members of the government, through the distribution of ministerial portfolios to the parties present at the congress, increased in both governments, corresponding to more than 60 percent of ministerial posts. But in the government of Cardoso, this trend was less strong, due to a significant presence of non-partisan or technocrat ministers. The situation changed in the Lula government, with almost 80 percent of portfolios controlled by political parties.

Patronage is the power of appointing people to ministerial or administrative positions in a discretionary manner. A small number of these appointments are justified as a way for presidents to assemble a circle of ministers and civil servants who share a common agenda and are not exclusively party members. A president may decide to appoint people on the basis of their skills, or to appoint people without previous linkages to the ruling party, or both (Sorauf, 1959; Müller, 2006; Kopecký and Mair, 2012).

The successful use of these institutional and political means can lead to a strengthening of the reputation of presidents and success in the implementation of public policies that address the major problems of a country. The reputation of a president gains if they can fulfill their electoral promises. In this case, the president's reputation becomes important. But it often happens that the performance of the president in terms of public policy is considered unconvincing. Some Latin American presidents had the ambitions to diminish an economic and financial crisis (Lula, Cardoso, Zedillo, Calderón, Menem, and Kirchner) and to reduce the influence of drug cartels (Calderón, Gaviria, and Uribe).

In Mexico, Zedillo's economic policy demonstrated a high degree of coherence throughout his term of office. His qualities as an administrator and his competence in addressing the complex problems of the Mexican economy enabled him to make effective decisions to stabilize the country's finances (Ai Camp, 1996). In the same way, Calderón was consistent in his management of the Mexican economy. He had successes in the area of economic policies, while many other presidents had failed, not understanding how to manage an economic downturn.

The performance of some presidents in terms of economic policy is considered less than entirely convincing. In Argentina, Menem took office in 1989, during a great economic and political crisis. He successfully implemented liberal measures, but the country suffered several years of stagnation because of the low prices of commodities. By opting for debt to try to pull the country out of stagnation, Menem led Argentina to the serious economic crisis of 2001. The Menem presidency also resulted in a serious deterioration of social equity.

The performances of two of these Latin American presidents (Calderón in Mexico and Uribe in Colombia) in seeking a reduction in the influence of drug cartels in their countries stand in contrast. Calderón started his mandate implementing a new public security strategy that involved deploying the military to fight organized crime. This decision gained the support of society. Nevertheless, an increasing number of civilian casualties and an alarming number of 'disappeared' people due to the war on drugs decreased popular backing for Calderón's management of this crisis. In Colombia, Uribe's priority as president was to contain or defeat the armed groups in the country. Unlike all his predecessors since 1982, who tried to carry out peace processes, Uribe established a policy of confronting the conflict through the military defeat of guerrilla groups. The strengthening of the military apparatus yielded results, and the number of terrorist actions, homicides, and kidnappings diminished.

Conclusions: Variations in Latin American Presidential Leadership

The consideration of leadership through the three factors of skill, relations and reputation helps to demonstrate how leadership is in fact largely determined by the institutional context of the presidential systems, especially in Latin America. Indeed, the conditions of this concept were also determined by the traditional politics of Latin America, marked by the role of personalities.

One president demonstrated exceptional leadership boosted by personal dominance: Lula. His performance was strengthened by his rich experience as founder and president of the Workers' Party. He ran for president three times unsuccessfully, first in 1989, then again in 1994 and 1998. Lula achieved victory in the 2002 presidential election. In 2006 he was re-elected for a second term as president, which ended on January 2011. He is often regarded as one of the most popular politicians in the history of Brazil, boasting approval ratings over 80 percent and, at the time of his mandate, he was one of the most popular in the world. For most of the eight years of Lula's presidency, his particular leadership strategy within the Workers' Party was no doubt a key source of power. The quality of good coalition management was also a main contributor to the strengthening of his leadership. Lula was a good manager of the coalition governments that he was forced to set up to govern. His Workers' Party being a minority in the congress, he was forced to regroup center-right and center-left parties to form a victorious coalition. The quality of his relationship with public opinion was essential to strengthening Lula's leadership. His popularity can be credited in part to Brazil's economic growth. Lula was the first 'common man' to come to power in a very unequal society. His life story echoed that of many Brazilians: a poor boy from the impoverished north-east who made his journey to find a job in the industrial belt of São Paulo. The Lula presidency has had real significance. He demonstrated that the left in Brazil was responsible and modern, not revolutionary. Brazil has made great progress in reducing poverty. Some 29 million Brazilians entered what is termed the middle class between 2003 and 2009. His time in office saw Brazil emerge as an increasingly confident international player. On balance, social democrat presidents like Lula did better than the populist left-wing presidents. However, Lula was plagued by corruption scandals, most notably the 'mensalão' scandal, in his first term.

Some presidents have demonstrated leadership skills arising from good political performance and strong cohesion of the majority coalitions that support them: Aylwin and Lagos in Chile, or Cardoso in Brazil. It is impossible to explain the stability of these coalitions without referring to the various mechanisms of coalition management and the presidents' leadership. Containing contention between the different parties was another key element of their approach to coalition management. These systems were kept running by the presidents' ability to generate support for their governments' policies from all coalition member parties. Most importantly, these three presidents facilitated the transition to democracy following the failure of authoritarian regimes in Chile and Brazil. They did not enjoy the same authority as Lula, but they showed great conciliation and moderation skills during the difficult transition process: the restoration and consolidation of the democratic regimes in Chile and Brazil. Aylwin was the first president of Chile after democracy was restored in 1990. After the victory of the 'no' vote in the referendum of 1986 lost by Pinochet, he participated in negotiations that led the government and opposition to agree on constitutional reforms, thereby making possible a peaceful transition following 16 years of dictatorship. Aylwin was elected president on December 14, 1989, with 55.2 percent of the votes. Although Chile had officially become a democracy, the Chilean military remained very powerful during Aylwin's presidency, and the constitution ensured the continued influence of Pinochet and the military. The good quality of coalition management was one of the main contributions to the strengthening of Aylwin's leadership. At the end of his term, Aylwin had exceedingly high approval ratings. He was successful in the treatment of issues that invariably arise in an immediate post-authoritarian context. In spite of the severe limits imposed on Aylwin's government by the constitution, his government did much to reduce poverty and inequality during its time in office.

In the 1980s, Lagos headed the Concertation coalition in Chile, and he won the 1999–2000 presidential election. Since he failed to obtain an absolute majority, as is required for election to the presidency, a runoff was subsequently held in January 2000 for the first time ever in Chile. Winning 51.3 percent of the vote, he became the new president of Chile. The good quality of coalition management was again a significant factor in strengthening his leadership. During the first year of his term in office, Lagos had to confront a high level of unemployment, in a process that began to revert at the end of 2003. In spite of this, Lagos enjoyed great popular support. As president, he oversaw a national dialogue about the Pinochet dictatorship. He had some success: he created new anti-poverty, health, and housing programs. He finished his six-year term with historic approval ratings above 70 percent. Successful, stable governments were hardly the rule in Latin America, and for a president to leave office more popular than when he entered was even more unusual.

Fernando Henrique Cardoso was elected president of Brazil in 1994 with the support of an alliance of his own Social Democratic Party, the PSDB, and two right-wing parties. Brazil's largest party, the centrist Party of the Brazilian Democratic Movement (PMDB), joined Cardoso's governing coalition after the election. Cardoso won sufficient support for some of his legislative priorities, because his coalition held an overwhelming majority of congressional seats. During his first term, several government-owned enterprises were privatized. The devaluation of the currency was an instrument of monetary policy employed directly after his re-election. His popularity in his first four years, gained through the success of the Plano Real, decreased through his last four years as the currency crisis was followed by lower economic growth and employment rates, larger public debt, growing political dissent, and, finally, an energy crisis. He had problems gaining support for his government priorities in Congress and among people in general. But as a president with a pragmatic and moderate political vision, Cardoso was more successful than the populist right-wing presidents (Menem and Fujimori). Although he claimed to remain a social democrat, his economic policies led people on the left to identify him with neoliberalism.

A third group of presidents demonstrated lesser leadership skills (Kirchner in Argentina, Gaviria in Colombia, Zedillo and Calderón in Mexico). They came to power without having held important positions in the governments headed by their predecessors. They served more as mediators than vigorous party bosses had done. All were second-rank candidates, being elevated due to events that upset or disrupted the appointment of a first candidate. They were unable to show strong authority but muddled through in the face of significant obstacles and divisions. Kirchner served as president of Argentina from May 2003 to December 2007. He won by default with only 22.2 percent of the vote in the first round, when former president Menem (at 24.4 percent) withdrew from the contest. Kirchner's performance was reduced by the fact that he was not the real leader of the Justicialist Party. Argentina had faced a serious economic crisis in previous years, leading to the 2001 riots and the fall of President de la Rua. Argentina's debt default was the largest in financial history, but it gave Kirchner significant bargaining power with the IMF. He was considered at times to be a left-wing president. However, he did not advance classic left-wing policies. He was a 'Peronist' and managed political power as historical 'Peronist' leaders had traditionally done. Kirchner adopted a confrontational style with the main sectors of society: farmers, the Catholic Church, the military, the Congress, the main media, and certain business circles.

In 1990, Gaviria was elected president of Colombia, running as a Liberal Party candidate. In August 1989, Luís Carlos Galán, the Liberal Party presidential candidate, was assassinated by drug traffickers, and so César Gaviria was transformed from former finance minister to front-running presidential candidate. He received 47 percent of the vote, the lowest percentage for a Liberal candidate in the previous five presidential elections. As president, Gaviria led the fight against drug cartels and various guerrilla factions. He sponsored the reintegration of the rebel armed forces into civil society and pushed for the constitutional reforms of 1991.

Zedillo was president of Mexico from December 1, 1994, to November 30, 2000. He was first appointed campaign chief of Colosio, the official candidate of the PRI. After the assassination of Colosio, Zedillo found himself one of the few politicians who could run as the PRI candidate. The beginning of his presidency was marked by the devaluation of the Mexican peso which plunged Mexico into deep economic crisis, although responsibility for the crisis was blamed on the economic management of the Salinas government.

Calderón served as president of Mexico from December 1, 2006, to November 30, 2012. He was a member of the Partido Accion Nacional (PAN), one of the three major Mexican political parties. The 2006 presidential election resulted in a narrow margin of 0.58 percent for Calderón over his closest contender, López Obrador. His presidency was marked by the ignition of the Mexican drug war, which began almost immediately after he took office. By the end of his administration, the official death toll of the Mexican drug war was at least 60,000.

A fourth group suffered from depleted leadership. This group includes Fujimori in Peru, Menem in Argentina, and Uribe in Colombia. These three presidents adopted more-or-less authoritarian behavior, characterized by hostility against or even repression of the opposition. They used exceptional means, such as a state of emergency or government by decree, to implement their economic and social policies, as well as to fight against armed rebellions and drug trafficking. However, these exceptional means did not enable them to achieve the expected results. Their presidencies were characterized by an authoritarian conception of the practice of power and by corruption.

Fujimori was president of Peru from July 28, 1990, to November 17, 2000. He was largely an outsider. The emergence of outsiders such as Fujimori has promoted the development of the personalization of politics, and this trend has led to crises and setbacks, not least in terms of the political success of this president. Fujimori was a controversial figure. Throughout his successive mandates, he built a political strategy aimed at cementing his power. This strategy was based on actions such as: the establishment of a direct and quasi-affective relationship with the most disadvantaged sections of the population, through clientelist practices; the instrumentalization of certain groups of actors, in particular through social programs; and the control of information through surveillance of the media and opponents. Many were killed in the 1980s and 1990s in clashes with the guerrillas of the Shining Path, defeated at the cost of violent repression by the government. The political management of Fujimori remained popular until the late 1990s, when revelations of corruption accelerated the fall of his regime. Fujimori ended his presidency by fleeing Peru for Japan amid a major corruption scandal and allegations of human rights violations.

Menem was elected president on May 14, 1989, with 47.5 percent of the vote, defeating the Radical Civic Union candidate by a substantial margin. His campaign attracted the working class, traditional constituents of the Justicialist Party. Inflation took a turn for the worse, growing into hyperinflation and causing public riots. Outgoing president Alfonsin resigned and transferred power to Menem five months early, on July 8, 1989. The turnaround of the economy by Menem proved to be successful. By creating a currency board, he arrested inflation. He inherited an economy with extensive state controls, and his government privatized nearly all of it. With these economic successes, a large majority re-elected Carlos Menem to the presidency in 1995. His popularity was high, but the quality of his relationship with public opinion was not sufficient to strengthen his leadership. Economic difficulties re-appeared when the dollar began to rise from 1995 onwards in international markets. High external debt also caused mounting problems. Finally, Menem was also an outsider, and the personalization of politics led to crises and setbacks in terms of his political success. His presidency was also tainted by repeated accusations of corruption by opponents. Menem's attempt to run for a third term in 1999 was ruled to be unconstitutional.

Uribe served as president of Colombia from 2002 to 2010. He ran as an independent liberal candidate, having unofficially separated from his former party. Uribe was also an outsider, again promoting the development of personalization. He was elected in the first round of May 26, 2002 elections with 53 percent of the popular vote. Polls consistently showed unprecedented support for Uribe by many Colombians, estimated at around 70 percent after his second year in office. His relative popularity is largely attributed to his administration's successful campaigns against the FARC, and in part to the efforts to begin demobilizing the paramilitary forces. At the same time, he tried to implement macroeconomic measures to stimulate economic growth and reduce unemployment. Uribe enjoyed strong popularity. In 2004, he successfully sought a congressional amendment to the Colombian constitution of 1991 which allowed him to run for a second term as president. The amendment permitting a single re-election was approved by Congress in December 2004. With this amendment, he was re-elected on May 28, 2006, for a second presidential term and became the first president to be consecutively re-elected in Colombia in over a century. He received about 62 percent of the vote, the largest victory for a presidential candidate in Colombian history. As the end of his second term approached, his supporters sought a new amendment that would grant him the right to run for a third term. Congress backed a proposed referendum on the matter, but the Constitutional Court rejected it, further claiming that the law calling for a referendum contained 'substantial violations to the democratic principle' that rendered it unconstitutional. Uribe stated that he would respect the decision. Uribe's presidency was also the subject of numerous controversies relating to relations with narco-trafficking and 'paramilitarism.' The presidential management of Uribe enjoyed wide popular approval. In 2008, Uribe broke the popular-acceptance record in Colombia with 80 percent. However, the reliability of the relevant surveys has been questioned.

References

Ai Camp, R. (1996). The Zedillo legacy in Mexico. *Policy Papers on the Americas*, 8(6), CSIS Americas Program, October.

Alcántara, M., García Montero, M., and Sanchez Lopez, F. (2005). *Procedimientos y escenarios: Un analisis del poder legislativo en America Latina*. Salamanca: Universidad de Salamanca.

Alemán E. and Saiegh, S.M. (2007). Legislative preferences, political parties, and coalition unity in Chile. *Comparative Politics*, 39(3), 253–272.

Alemán, E. and Tsebelis, G. (2011). Political parties and government coalitions in the Americas. *Journal of Politics in Latin America*, 3(1), 3–28.

Ames, B. (2001). *The deadlock of democracy in Brazil*. Ann Arbor: University of Michigan Press.

Amorim Neto, O. (2002). Presidential cabinets, electoral cycles, and coalition discipline in Brazil. In: Morgenstern, S. and Nacif, B. (eds), *Legislative politics in Latin America*. New York: Oxford University Press, 48–78.

Amorim Neto, O. (2006). The presidential calculus: Executive policy making and cabinet formation in the Americas. *Comparative Political Studies*, 39(4), 415–440.

Amorim Neto, O., Cox, G.W., and McCubbins, M.D. (2003). Agenda power in Brazil's Câmara dos Deputados, 1989–98. *World Politics*, 55(4), 550–578.

Arias, M.F. (1995). Charismatic leadership and the transition to democracy: The rise of Carlos Saul Menem in Argentine politics. *Texas Papers on Latin America*, Paper no 95–02.

Barr, R.R. (2009). Populists, outsiders, and anti-establishment politics. *Party Politics*, 15(1), 29–48.

Bennister, M. and Worthy, B. (2015). Going on and on? Tony Blair and Margaret Thatcher: Leadership capital compared. *Social Science Research Network*, March 29.

Bennister, M., 't Hart, P., and Worthy, B. (2014). Assessing the authority of political office-holders: The leadership capital index. *West European Politics*, 38(3), 417–440.

Camerlo, M. (2013). Gabinetes de partido unico y democracias presidenciales: Indagaciones a partir del caso argentino. *America Latina Hoy*, 64, 119–142.

Camerlo, M. and Pérez-Liñan, A. (2014). Presidential approval and technocratic survival. *Social Science Research Network*, June 1.
Carey, J.M. (1999). Partidos, coaliciones y el Congresso Chileno en los años noventa. *Politica y Gobierno*, 6(2), 365–405.
Carey, J.M. (2003). The reelection debate in Latin America. *Latin American Politics and Society*, 45(2), 119–133.
Carey, J.M. and Shugart, M.S. (eds) (1998). *Executive decree authority*. New York and Cambridge: Cambridge University Press.
Carreras, M. (2012). The rise of outsiders in Latin America, 1980–2010: An institutionalist perspective. *Comparative Political Studies*, 45(12), 1451–1482.
Carreras, M. (2013). Presidentes outsiders y ministros neofitos: un analisis a través del ejemplo de Fujimori. *America Latina Hoy*, 64, 95–118.
Castañeda, J. (2006). Latin America's left turn. *Foreign Affairs*, 85(4), 28–43.
Centeno, M.A. (1994). *Democracy within reason: Technocratic revolution in Mexico*. University Park: Pennsylvania State University Press, 1994.
Chaisty, P., Cheeseman, N., and Power, T. (2014). Rethinking the 'presidentialism debate': Conceptualizing coalitional politics in cross-regional perspective. *Democratization*, 21(1), 72–94.
Cheibub, J.A., Przeworski, A., and Saiegh, S.M. (2004). Government coalitions and legislative success under presidentialism and parliamentarism. *British Journal of Political Science*, 34, 565–587.
Conniff, M.L. (1982). *Latin American populism in comparative perspective*. Albuquerque: University of New Mexico Press.
Conniff, M.L. (1999). *Populism in Latin America*. Tuscaloosa and London: University of Alabama Press.
Corrales, J. (2012). The incumbent's advantage in Latin America: Larger than you think. *Vox Lacea*, December 18.
Crisp, B.F. (1998). Presidential decree authority in Venezuela. In: Carey, J.M. and Shugart, M.S. (eds), *Executive decree authority*. Cambridge: Cambridge University Press, 142–171.
Davila, M., Olivares Lavados, A., and Avendano, O. (2013). Los gabinetes de la Concertacion en Chile, 1990–2010. *America Latina Hoy*, 64, 67–94.
Di Tella, T. (1997). Populism into the twenty-first century. *Government and Opposition*, 32(2), 187–200.
Dix, R.H. (1994). Military coups and military rule in Latin America. *Armed Forces and Society*, 20(3), 439–456.
Dornbusch, R. and Edwards, S. (1991). *The macroeconomics of populism in Latin America*. Chicago: Chicago University Press.
Elgie, R. (1995). *Political leadership in liberal democracies*. London: Palgrave Macmillan.
Elgie R. (2014). The institutional approach of political leadership. In: Kane, J. and Patapan, H. (eds), *Good democratic leadership: On prudence and judgment in modern democracies*. Oxford: Oxford University Press, 139–157.
Ferreira Rubio, D. and Goretti, M. (1998). When the president governs alone: The 'decretazo' in Argentina, 1989–1993. In: Carey, J.M. and Shugart, M.S. (eds), *Executive decree authority*. Cambridge: Cambridge University Press, 33–61.
Geddes, B. (1999). What do we know about democratization after twenty years? *Annual Review of Political Science*, 2, 115–144.

Geddes, B. (2003). *Paradigms and sand castles: Theory building and research design in comparative politics*. Michigan: University of Michigan Press.
Germani, G. (1978). *Authoritarianism, fascism, and national populism*. New Brunswick, New Jersey: Transaction Books.
Ginsburg, T., Melton, J., and Elkins, Z. (2011). On the evasion of executive term limits. *William and Mary Law Review*, 52, 1807–1872.
Guerrero, M.A. and Marquez Ramirez, M. (2014). *Media systems and communication policies in Latin America*. London: Palgrave Macmillan.
Hamill, H. (1992). *Caudillos: Dictators in Spanish America*. Norman: University of Oklahoma Press.
Hartlyn, J. (2008). *The politics of coalition rule in Colombia*. Cambridge: Cambridge University Press.
Hawkins, K.A. (2010). *Venezuela's chavismo and populism in comparative perspective*. New York: Cambridge University Press.
Helms, L. (2015). The politics of leadership capital in compound democracies: Inferences from the German case. *European Political Science Review*, 7(3), 1–26.
Hershberg, E. and Rosen, F. (2006). *Latin America after neoliberalism: Turning the tide in the 21st century*. New York: The New Press.
Hochstetler, K. (2006). Rethinking presidentialism: Challenges and presidential falls in South America. *Comparative Politics*, 38(4), 401–418.
Hochstetler, K. and Edwards, M.E. (2009). Failed presidencies: Identifying and explaining a South American anomaly. *Journal of Politics in Latin America*, 1(2), 31–57.
Hochstetler, K. and Samuels, D. (2011). Crisis and rapid reequilibration: The consequences of presidential challenge and failure in Latin America. *Comparative Politics*, 43(2), 127–145.
Hunter, W. (1995). Politicians against soldiers: Contesting the military in post-authoritarian Brazil. *Comparative Politics*, 27(4), 425–443.
Inacio, M. (2013). Escogiendo ministros y formando politicos: Los partidos en gabinetes multipartidistas. *America Latina Hoy*, 64, 41–66.
Inacio, M. and Llanos, M. (2015). The institutional presidency in comparative perspective: Argentina and Brazil since the 1980s. *Brazilian Political Science Review*, 9(1), 39–64.
Kenney, C.D. (1998). Outsider and anti-party politicians in power: New conceptual strategies and empirical evidence from Peru. *Party Politics*, 4(1), 57–75.
Kopecký, P. and Mair, P. (2012). Patronage as an organizational resource. In: Kopecký, P., Mair, P. and Spirova, M. (eds), *Party patronage and party government in European democracies*. Oxford: Oxford University Press, 3–16.
Langston, J. (2006). The changing party of the institutional revolution: Electoral competition and decentralized candidate selection. *Party Politics*, 12(3), 395–413.
Levitsky, S. (2000). The 'normalization' of Argentine politics. *Journal of Democracy*, 11(2), 56–69.
Linz, J.J. (1990). The perils of presidentialism. *Journal of Democracy*, 1(1), 51–69.
Loaeza, S. (2003). The National Action Party (PAN): From the fringes of the political system to the heart of change. In: Mainwaring, S. (ed.), *Christian democracy in Latin America: Electoral competition and regime conflict*. Stanford: Stanford University Press.
Luna, J.P. and Rovira Kaltwasser, C. (2014). *The resilience of the Latin American right*. Baltimore: Johns Hopkins University Press.

Lynch, J. (1992). *Caudillos in Spanish America, 1800–1850*. Oxford: Clarendon.
Mainwaring, S. (1990). Presidentialism in Latin America. *Latin American Research Review*, 25(1), 157–179.
Mainwaring, S. (1993). Presidentialism, multipartism, and democracy: The difficult combination. *Comparative Political Studies*, 26, 198–228.
Mainwaring, S. and Shugart, M. (1997). *Presidentialism and democracy in Latin America*. New York and Cambridge: Cambridge University Press.
McAllister, I. (2015). The personalization of politics in Australia. *Party Politics*, 21(3), 337–345.
Marenghi, P. and García Montero, M. (2008). The conundrum of representation. In: Alcántara, M. (ed.), *Politicians and politics in Latin America*. Boulder: Lynne Rienner, 29–64.
Marsteintredet, L. and Berntzen, E. (2008). Reducing the perils of presidentialism in Latin America through presidential interruptions. *Comparative Politics*, 41(1), 83–101.
Martínez-Gallardo, C. (2005). *Presidents, posts and policy: Ministerial appointments and political strategy in presidential regimes*. Doctoral dissertation, Columbia University, New York.
Martínez-Gallardo, C. (2014). Designing cabinets: Presidential politics and ministerial instability. *Journal of Politics in Latin America*, 6(2), 3–38.
Morgenstern, S. and Cox, G.W. (2001). Latin America's reactive assemblies and proactive presidents. *Comparative Politics*, 33(2), 171–190.
Müller, W. (2006). Party patronage and party colonization of the state. In: Katz, R.S. and Crotty, W.J. (eds), *Handbook of party politics*. London: Sage, 189–195.
Navia, P. (2014). Unbeatable incumbents. *Buenos Aires Herald*, June 17.
Negretto, G. (2006). Minority presidents and democratic performance in Latin America. *Latin American Politics and Society*, 48(3), 63–92.
O'Donnell, G. (1973). *Modernization and bureaucratic-authoritarianism*. Berkeley: Institute of International Studies, University of California at Berkeley.
Palermo, V. and Novaro, M. (1996). *Politica y poder en el gobierno de Menem*. Buenos Aires: Grupo Editorial Norma.
Pereira, C. and Melo, M.A. (2012). The surprising success of multiparty presidentialism. *Journal of Democracy*, 23(3), 156–170.
Pereira, C. and Mueller, B. (2004). The cost of governing: Strategic behavior of the president and legislators in Brazil's budgetary process. *Comparative Political Studies*, 37(7), 781–815.
Pereira, C., Power, T.J., and Raile, E.D. (2011). Presidentialism, coalitions, and accountability. In: Taylor, M. and. Power, T.J. (eds), *Corruption and democracy in Brazil: The struggle for accountability*. Notre Dame: University of Notre Dame Press.
Pérez-Liñán, A. (2005). Democratization and constitutional crises in presidential regimes. Toward congressional supremacy? *Comparative Political Studies*, 38, 51–74.
Pérez-Liñán, A. (2007). *Presidential impeachment and the new political instability in Latin America*. Cambridge: Cambridge University Press.
Pion-Berlin, D. and Trinkunas, H. (2010). Civil praetorianism and military shirking during constitutional crises in Latin America. *Comparative Politics*, 42(4), 395–416.
Power, T.J. (1998). The pen is mighter than the congress: Presidential decree power in Brazil. In: Carey, J.M. and Shugart, M.S. (eds), *Executive decree authority*. Cambridge: Cambridge University Press, 197–230.

Praça, S., Freitas, A., and Hoepers, B. (2011). Political appointments and coalition management in Brazil, 2007–2010. *Journal of Politics in Latin America*, 3(2), 141–172.

Raile, E.D., Pereira, C., and Power, T.J. (2011). The executive toolbox: Building legislative support in a multiparty presidential regime. *Political Research Quarterly*, 64(2), 323–334.

Remmer, K. (1989). *Military rule in Latin America*. Boston: Unwin Hyman.

Roberts, K.M. (1995). Neoliberalism and the transformation of populism in Latin America: The Peruvian case. *World Politics*, 48(1), 82–116.

Roberts, K.M. (2007). Latin America's populist revival. *SAIS Review*, 27(1), 3–15.

Roberts, K.M. (2014). Democracy, free markets, and the rightist dilemma in Latin America. In: Luna, J.P. and Rovira Kaltwasser, C. (eds), *The resilience of the Latin American right*. Baltimore: Johns Hopkins University Press, 25–47.

Samuels, D.J. and Shugart, M.S. (2010). *Presidents, parties, and prime ministers: How the separation of powers affects party organization and behaviour*. New York: Cambridge University Press.

Schamis, H. (1999). Distributional coalitions and the politics of economic reform in Latin America. *World Politics*, 51(2), 236–268.

Schmidt, G. (1998). Presidential usurpation or congressional preference? The evolution of executive decree authority in Peru. In: Carey, J.M. and Shugart, M.S. (eds), *Executive decree authority*. Cambridge: Cambridge University Press, 104–141.

Shirk, D. (2005). *Mexico's new politics: The PAN and democratic change*. Boulder: Lynne Rienner.

Shugart, S.M. (2010). Great news for Colombian democracy! *Fruits and Votes blog*, February 28.

Shugart, M.S. and Carey, J.M. (1992). *Presidents and assemblies: Constitutional design and electoral dynamics*. Cambridge: Cambridge University Press.

Shugart, M.S. and Mainwaring, S. (1997). Presidentialism and democracy in Latin America: Rethinking the terms of the debate. In: Mainwaring, S. and Shugart, M.S. (eds), *Presidentialism and democracy in Latin America*. Cambridge: Cambridge University Press, 12–54.

Siavelis, P.M. (2009). Elite-mass congruence, partidocracia, and the quality of Chilean democracy. *Journal of Politics in Latin America*, 1(3), 3–31.

Siavelis, P.M. and Baruch, H. (2014). Chile: ministerial selection and de-selection. In: Dowding, K. and Dumont, P. (eds), *The selection of ministers around the world*. London: Routledge, 244–263.

Siavelis, P.M. and Morgenstern, S. (2008). Political recruitment and candidate selection in Latin America: A framework for analysis. In: Siavelis, P.M. and Morgenstern, S. (eds), *Pathways to power: Political recruitment and candidate selection in Latin America*. University Park: Pennsylvania State University Press, 3–38.

Sorauf, F.J. (1959). Patronage and party. *Midwest Journal of Political Science*, 3(2), 115–126.

Stepan, A. (1988). *Rethinking military politics: Brazil and the Southern Cone*. Princeton: Princeton University Press.

Tepperman, J. (2016). Brazil's anti-poverty breakthrough: The surprising success of Bolsa Familia. *Foreign Affairs*, January–February.

Valenzuela, A. (2004). Latin American presidencies interrupted. *Journal of Democracy*, 14(4), 5–19.

Voltmer, K. (2013). *The media in transitional democracies*. New York: John Wiley and Sons.
Weyland, K. (1999). Neoliberal populism in Latin America and Eastern Europe. *Comparative Politics*, 31(4), 379–401.
Weyland, K. (2003). Neopopulism and neoliberalism in Latin America: How much affinity? *Third World Quarterly*, 24(6), 1095–1115.
Weyland, K., Madrid, R., and Hunter, W. (2010). *Leftist governments in Latin America: Success and shortcomings*. Cambridge: Cambridge University Press.
Wiesehomeier, N. and Benoit, K. (2007). *Presidents, parties, and policy competition*. Paper presented at the V Congreso Europeo CEISAL de Latinoamericanistas, April 11–14, in Brussels.
Wills-Otero, L. (2014). Colombia: Analyzing the strategies for political action of Alvaro Uribe's government, 2002–10. In: Luna, J.P. and Rovira, C. (eds), *The resilience of the Latin American right*. Baltimore: Johns Hopkins University Press, 194–215.
Wolf, E. and Hansen, E.C. (1967). Caudillo politics: A structural analysis. *Comparative Studies in Society and History*, 9(2), 168–179.
Wuhs, S.T. (2014). Mexico: The Partido Accion Nacional as a right party. In: Luna, J.P. and Rovira, C. (eds), *The resilience of the Latin American right*. Baltimore: Johns Hopkins University Press, 219–241.

3 The Character of the 'Government' in Latin American Presidential Republics

Jean Blondel

In the second and third decades of the nineteenth century, not long after the United States, having become independent, drafted its constitution in 1789, the newly independent Latin American republics became involved in an entirely new process of national development that the US Constitution of 1789 had started. The great majority of these new Latin American republics adopted and thereby contributed to start the spread of the 'presidential system' which had been created under half a century earlier in Philadelphia for the United States.

In fact, these newly independent Latin American countries were the only polities that seemed eager to adopt the US model early in the nineteenth century. The one country of the region that did not follow that trend was Brazil, which had become a parliamentary empire in 1822; that regime lasted to 1889, at which point Brazil became a presidential republic as well. Chile was to subsequently try the model of the parliamentary republic, from the 1880s to the mid-1920s, but the political instability of that system was such that the result was a return to presidential government. Brazil again became parliamentary, this time in a republican context, but for one year only, in 1961–1962: in a popular referendum, moreover, the country affirmed its preference for the presidential republic. Finally, the only contemporary exception was Castro's Cuba, which moved to a communist regime in the late 1950s; however, halfway through certain second decade of the twenty-first century, it is far from certain that the country will never return to the presidential system.

Admittedly, these Latin American presidential republics repeatedly experienced major political difficulties, as the 'regular' constitutional regime was frequently interrupted by coups; there was also a degree of uncertainty, mainly in the early decades after independence, in a number of the newly created Latin American republics, as to whether the US model of the presidential system was to be preferred. Yet, despite many hiccups, and from about the middle of the nineteenth century, each time a Latin American country was to return to constitutional government, typically after a coup, a form of presidentialism was adopted: it was as if that type of government was the one which Latin Americans seemed comfortable with, while elsewhere, especially in Europe, constitutional monarchies, not presidential republics, came to be the norm well beyond the nineteenth century.

The 'Invention' of the Presidential System in the 1789 US Constitution and its Widespread Extension to Latin America Early in the Nineteenth Century

The fact that Latin American countries tended to adopt a kind of presidential system clearly showed that the system that the United States invented at the end of the eighteenth century filled a need in the new republics further South. A number of other republics had previously existed, the most famous having been the old Roman republic, which lasted for centuries: but neither that example nor many other instances set up from time to time, in particular in Italy, were presidential. The United States constitution of 1789 created a novel model of government on the basis of which, for the first time, the national executive was to be in the hands of a single person, referred to as the 'president,' elected by 'the people,' at any rate indirectly, and in office for four years—a term which was then renewable indefinitely by a series of re-elections.

What the American constitution of 1789 did was to establish the principle, then entirely new, that the head of the executive was to be a republican leader, regularly elected, and in charge of the whole executive: he or she was to be the executive, in a domain in which single republican leadership, wherever it took place, had previously been typically held by 'usurpers.' The only form of dominant single leadership which could until then be claimed to have been 'constitutionally regular' was not republican but monarchical; indeed there was a significant tendency for usurpers to endeavor to become kings or, in some cases, emperors.

Moreover, in the historical republics which had been established from time to time, both in the old Roman republic and in its successors, severe limitations were imposed on the duration of the term in which regularly appointed republican leaders could remain or be prolonged in office, while the powers of such leaders were also reduced as a result of the part played by other regularly appointed holders of various offices: thus consuls in the old Roman republic were in office for one year only; they had to wait ten years to be candidates again. They also had to contend with 'praetors' and 'ediles' who had clearly defined powers. It is therefore very difficult, indeed almost impossible to exaggerate the extent to which the presidential republic which emerged from the American constitution of 1789 was truly an 'invention': that constitution made possible (if not certain) regular single and dominant republican rule among national executives.

Why the Presidential System Came at Such an Opportune Moment in the US in the Late Eighteenth Century

Admittedly, the presidential character of the rule 'invented' by the US Constitution of 1789 and which the newly independent Latin American republics were typically attempting to replicate, at any rate in some form, was in large part the consequence of two major socio-political developments which were to alter markedly the conditions under which political behavior was to take place from the late eighteenth century onwards: these two major political developments rendered the occasion in which the American constitutional model had been introduced particularly opportune, first in the Americas and subsequently across the world in the context of the decolonization process.

The first of these two major developments was the gradually increasing pressure for some form of popular involvement in the determination of the way in which national executives were to be appointed, a pressure that coincidentally resulted in the decline of monarchies and especially of traditional monarchies. The second of these two major developments was, mainly from the late nineteenth century and primarily in the West, the massive extension of the scope of state intervention in the 'welfare' of its citizens. The American constitution of 1789 played a major part in furthering the first of these two major developments, as it established, for the first time in an unequivocal manner, that a single head of the national executive was to be chosen by means of a popular election, at least indirectly. The industrial revolution was at the origin of the second key development, as it gradually resulted in national states playing a major part in such matters as national education, employment, working conditions and financial support to be given to citizens after they had retired. Thus the emergence of new ways in which governments came to be organized in, the contemporary world was embedded in, as well as being the political response to, major forms of economic and social change which began to occur in the world from the late eighteenth century.

Presidentialism and the Character of the Group, Collegial or Otherwise, Constituted by Those Who Are in the 'Government'

The presidential system came to play a major part in the contemporary world—a part that has been regarded by many specialists as somewhat negative, as the provocative views on the subject of Fred W. Riggs and Juan J. Linz were to show (Riggs, 1988; Linz, 1990; Linz and Valenzuela, 1994). What was scarcely considered, on the other hand, was the extent to which the character of the group of those within the 'government,' in the strict sense of the word, often embodied in the notion of 'cabinet,' was being affected by the new process. Interestingly, the members of the American convention of 1787–1789 appear to have been conscious of the magnitude of the change they were introducing in this respect, as they refused to recognize, in the constitutional document which they were elaborating, the existence of a 'cabinet' around or even under the president:[1] the ministers (or 'secretaries,' as they were to be known in the United States) were to be hierarchically and also individually and separately dependent on the president; they were not to be colleagues or even full members of the cabinet. These characteristics have not been markedly altered in the American federal government over two centuries during which the American constitution of 1789 has been in force. The status of these secretaries is thus markedly different from that which characterized ministers in other political systems, even if these were monarchies.

Yet, somewhat surprisingly, comparisons between the US secretaries and the members of cabinets in a number of Western European parliamentary systems have not been made, except occasionally to claim that these parliamentary cabinets are becoming 'presidential' (Poguntke and Webb, 2005). There does not seem to have been so far any concerted attempt to investigate empirically whether, in the many other presidential systems in existence in the contemporary world, the situation is basically analogous to that which has prevailed in the United States, except to an extent in the relatively recent context of so-called 'semi-presidential' governments. Thus little is known as to whether there are substantial differences in the degree of collegiality of members of the government in other presidential governments and, in particular, among some, many or all Latin American governments.

This is all the more surprising because, in principle at least, the matter is of some importance with respect to the nature of decision-making by national executives: there would not be a discussion about the extent to which the 'presidentialization' of parliamentary cabinets is taking place if there were not a feeling, in the case of parliamentary cabinets, that these should be constitutionally more collegial than they often are in practice. On the other hand, a sizable amount of literature now exists on the extent to which parliamentary cabinets are remaining collegial; yet no work has so far appeared which suggests that, presidential national executives might be, in some cases, less hierarchical than they are supposed to be. In the case of the American executive, it appears to be accepted as fact that such a move has not taken place, although it is not clear whether such a standpoint follows logically from the character of the executive position held by the American president.[2] Nor is it clear that this should be what occurs (or at least what occurs to some measurable extent) in other presidential systems, of which there are now so many in Latin America and elsewhere.

As a matter of fact, with respect to the internal structure and development of the executive, indeed with respect to many other aspects of the analysis of the characteristics of presidential systems, it is clearly dangerous to generalize primarily, let alone exclusively, about the characteristics of presidential systems on the basis of United States M.S. Shugart and J.M. Carey's 1992 volume on *Presidents and Assemblies* carefully pointed out how the provisions of constitutions of Latin American countries differed from the provisions of the American constitution with respect to the powers given to presidents, for instance. That work concentrated exclusively on the problems posed by the relationship between executive and legislature; however, a field in which there has by now been a substantial amount of analysis going beyond the US–British or US–Western European traditional comparisons; on the other hand, with respect to the characteristics of presidential government in the precise sense of the expression, generalizations continue to be based almost exclusively on what occurs about the US executive in fields such as the internal characteristics of the executive, about which little comparative research has been undertaken either within each or between the two systems of government.

The aim of this chapter is therefore to begin to examine whether 'presidential chief executive dominance' continues to be wholly valid in the presidential governments of Latin America. The question which arises is whether we are not often confronted on the contrary by a markedly more 'nuanced' distinction and whether one should not recognize that we are in the presence of something resembling a 'continuum' in which presidential national executives range from governments wholly dominated by a leader, to governments which are at least partly collegial.

The Internal Characteristics of the 'Government' in the Contemporary World

Major changes in the characteristics of national executives were naturally to have an impact on the way in which the 'governments,' in the precise sense of the term, were both formally constituted and operated in practice: the main contrast, at any rate in theory, was between parliamentary forms of governments and the newly created presidential government of the American constitution of 1789: however, as that type of constitution was adopted, almost universally in the Latin American independent countries which emerged in the early part of the nineteenth century, the scope of presidential government was markedly extended, even though this was in the context of major difficulties encountered by the newly created Latin American countries.

Meanwhile, in the course of the late nineteenth and twentieth centuries, the tendency for the state to expand its role widely in increasing aspects of citizens, welfare, in Western Europe in particular, as was noted earlier, affected decision processes in parliamentary cabinets as it rendered genuinely collegial decision-making increasingly difficult within national executives: yet the formal contrast remained between parliamentary cabinets in which the collegial governmental principle was held and the presidential executive, as it was conceived and practiced in the United States, based on the dominant power and authority of the head of the executive branch, while the cabinet was in reality to be an 'executive machinery.'

Yet, with the extension of the presidential formula to Latin America, in the first instance, some changes in the 'philosophy' of how the executive was to operate in practice was to be expected, if only because the influence of European (parliamentary) governments was likely to be strong among the countries of an area in which European political, social and economic influence tended to be large. This is why the question arises as to whether some accommodation away from the US presidential principle of domination of the whole executive by the president did not occur, even if to a varying extent, from one Latin American country to another.

On the other hand, the extent to which collegial practices were being gradually eroded in European parliamentary systems has been markedly discussed and indeed led to the conclusion that such moves as the growing technicality of the decision-making process was bound to result in some increase over time of the power of many prime ministers. Moreover, the increase in the size of governments, which led to a need for greater coordination among ministers, resulted in turn to a substantial part being played by government committees: this had the effect of diminishing, in practice if not in theory, the extent to which parliamentary governments were remaining collegial.

This trend was countered by a number of structural reasons why, at least in Western European parliamentary governments, moves towards something approaching the domination of the national executive by presidents in presidential governments were not just unlikely, but in effect impossible. This has been so regardless of the increase of the part played by some prime ministers (or by officials appointed to advise prime ministers). A major emphasis has to be placed on these 'structural factors,' because they prevent parliamentary governments from being wholly dominated by their prime ministers: whereas these factors do not obtain in the presidential government as it is constituted in the United States, they may be present, or may play a greater part, in other presidential systems, and in particular in Latin American presidential systems. Two of these structural factors are at the origin of 19 characteristics which distinguish 'pure' parliamentary governments from 'pure' presidential governments, as reproduced in an appendix to this chapter. The extent to which these two broad structural factors fully or only partly obtain in a given executive account for the tendency for said executive branch to be either more collegial or more dominated by the president, being the head of the executive branch.

The main characteristic behind these two structural factors relates to the extent to which the head of the executive, whether president or prime minister, is subjected to particular constraints when selecting the members of his or her 'government.' The American president, both in theory and in practice, even after over two hundred years, is not subjected to any such constraint: he or she may appoint whom he or she thinks fit, subject only to (subsequent) approval by the Senate, an approval or rejection which has not been based in practice on considerations of a political character with respect to the person concerned.

In parliamentary governments, on the other hand, prime ministers are subjected to two structural constraints: these result, in constitutional terms, from the fact that the 'government' (or cabinet) as a body has to be approved by a majority in parliament (or at least must not be 'censored' by a parliamentary majority). To meet that constitutional requirement, the prime minister needs to establish a reasonably harmonious relationship with that parliamentary majority. It is to achieve that result that two structural characteristics must be met: first, the government has to be composed of members who are broadly acceptable to parliament and, second—a point which came increasingly to be a consequence of the previous one—the government must be composed of members who belong to or are at least regarded as acceptable to parties which form part of the government's majority in parliament. From these two requirements follows the consequence that the government is likely to be composed of (or at least include) a substantial number of MPs or ex-MPs, typically drawn from the parties which are expected to support the government in the course of its duration.

Both directly and indirectly, these two requirements reinforce collegiality or at least establish a minimum of collegiality: given that, in parliamentary systems, prime ministers have in practice to appoint at least a number of parliamentarians or ex-parliamentarians as ministers, they are consequently appointing men and women who have known each other for substantial periods. This does not mean that these ministers necessarily like each other; but they will not be 'strangers,' a characteristic which Hugh Heclo found to be the case in American government and which was the title of his 1977 volume.[3] Moreover, the fact that members of these parliamentary cabinets belong to the same or to different parties results in parliamentary governments being clearly either single party or coalition governments.

One must neither exaggerate nor minimize the importance of the two structural factors here mentioned, and which shape the formal characteristics of parliamentary governments. Thus the fact that members are likely to have known each other as a result of having belonged to one body from which they are then appointed, parliament, does not mean that these members will agree with each other. Two points need to be made, however: first, the prime minister will experience some constraint in the choice of his or her ministers; second, the prime minister is likely to have at least some idea of the way in which ministers are likely to react to his or her proposals, while ministers are likely to be aware of the idiosyncrasies of other members of the government.

Moreover, the same kind of conclusion can be drawn in relation to the parties which are to be represented in the cabinet, and to the part played by these parties in 'holding the cabinet together'. In parliamentary governments, ministers are not 'strangers,' to quote H. Heclo, because these ministers have known each other while in parliament, at least in many cases; but they are also, and perhaps typically, prominent players in the party to which they belong: they are party politicians as well as parliamentary members, and the combination of these two positions contributes to making it less likely that a prime minister will have to consider these politicians when the members of his or her cabinet have to be selected. Indeed, these characteristics may determine whether the government in the process of being constituted is to be single party or coalition: in a parliamentary system, the leading politicians from each of the parties in a coalition tend to know each other, whatever feelings they may have towards each other. Conversely, in the United States context, this kind of personal relationship is unlikely to exist, at any rate on a substantial scale, among the members of a given administration: although the members of the executive administration, including the cabinet, may well belong to the same party as the president, party membership and especially party leadership are unlikely to play a major part in considerations when a president selects the secretaries who will be in charge of the various positions in the administration.

The question which therefore arises is whether, in some presidential systems, similar characteristics to those of parliamentary governments do not also come to occur. This may not be the case in the United States, as the holder of the presidency in that country chooses the members of the executive in the way he or she wishes; but, as a consequence, the manner in which the members of the executive will react to each other when in the government is less predictable. Thus there will be greater uncertainty about how members of the government can be expected to work together in a presidential government based on the 'classical' US model. What is therefore in question is whether such unpredictability may or may not have arisen to the same extent in some other presidential systems when presidents have chosen the members of their governments. It might well be that, in Latin America, where the experience of presidential government has extended over a truly long period, relationships between ministers may have more resembled the relationships which can be found in parliamentary governments among ministers than those which can be found in the American national executive.

More generally, the question arises as to whether the factors identified here as being characteristic of parliamentary governments are also to be found in some presidential governments. This is why it is not irrelevant to note that Latin American countries may have been influenced to some extent by the governmental practices of Western European countries in the course of the nineteenth and twentieth centuries. If such influence has played a part, at least some characteristics of parliamentary governments may well be found in some Latin American executives. If Latin American governments appear to combine elements of the 'classical' presidential American government with elements of 'typical' parliamentary governments, one naturally would want to know to what extent such a combination has occurred.

To be comprehensive, the empirical evidence provided by presidential governments other than that of the US government must therefore be systematically examined, if not for the earliest period, at least from the last decades of the twentieth century, when presidential governments in Latin America had become generally 'regular'. A comprehensive analysis of this kind cannot be undertaken in the present chapter, however, as the characteristics of the governments of only two relatively recent presidents from each of six Latin American countries are being explored: yet the empirical evidence provided by the countries concerned shows that there is indeed more than the merely casual indication that at least contemporary Latin American presidential governments are far from being exclusively 'governments of strangers.'

How Far Do Latin American National Executives Differ from the 'Classical' US Presidential Model?

The study of the characteristics of contemporary Latin American national executives is based on the nature of those executives under the last two presidencies completed by 2015 in Mexico, Argentina, Brazil, Chile, Colombia and Peru. There are thus no examples from Central America or the Caribbean islands; only half the South American countries, albeit including the most populous ones, belong to the sample; but with respect to the six countries analyzed, the data provided by academics who studied the composition of the governments under the two presidents selected for these six countries provide a clear indication of the extent to which the composition of these executives varied from the composition of American national executives by being somewhat closer to the 'model' of parliamentary executives.

These variations from the mode of behavior characterizing the American federal executive were provided by answers to 19 questions relating to the composition and behavior of the executives of these six Latin American countries: the answers suggest that there is somewhat greater collegiality within these national executives, and that a minority, if only a minority, of the members of these executives are typically drawn from among ex-members of the national Congress, and that these national executives are composed of parties which may or may not enjoy a majority in Congress. It is also noted that that the electoral programs of these presidential executives may not be based on the kind of detailed policy documents which the concept of program would seem liable to suggest.

Six general characteristics need to be specifically looked into based on the answers given for each of these six countries if a picture is to emerge of the extent to which the behavior of the governments of the countries concerned did vary or not from the American presidential model. These are:

(1) whether presidents had been ministers in previous governments;
(2) whether there is a coordinating minister or even a prime minister;
(3) whether the whole national executive meets, regularly or at least occasionally, as a body;
(4) whether and in what proportion ministers are ex-members of Congress in the countries which are being examined;
(5) whether the governments which are constituted in these countries can be described as being 'party governments' and whether the concept of 'coalition government' is commonly used to account for the type of party composition of these national executives if all the ministers do not belong to one party; and
(6) whether electors are regularly confronted with detailed governmental programs being presented to them.[4]

Had the Presidents Examined in the Study Been Ministers in Previous Governments? (Question 1)

Five of the 12 presidents analyzed here had been ministers under previous presidents. The proportion is high, much higher than in the United States; indeed, there are good reasons accounting for the fact that the proportion of ex-ministers among presidents was not even higher. Both Mexican presidents selected, Zedillo and Calderón, had previously been ministers; this was also the case for one Brazilian president (Cardoso), one Chilean president (Lagos) and one Colombian president (Gaviria).

The fact that neither of the two Peruvian presidents examined here had been ministers previously is due to the fact that one, Fujimori, was a total outsider and had been in a sense politically ostracized, whereas the other, García, elected in both 1985 and in 2006, immediately before and after Fujimori, happened to be the first president to which the long-standing Peruvian party of the Left, the PAP (more commonly known as APRA) hitherto excluded from all the 'democratic' governments in the country, won power on the basis of its unprecedented successes at the polls. Neither Fujimori nor García could have therefore been ministers before becoming president. Nor could President Aylwyn of Chile have been a minister prior to being elected to the presidency, as he came to office immediately after the end of Pinochet's dictatorship, during which ex-Senator Aylwyn had indeed played a prominent part as an opponent of the regime. In Colombia, Uribe was elected president on what might be described as a 'populist' platform that differed markedly from the policies of his predecessors. Finally, in Brazil, Lula, who had so far been a successful trade union leader, could not have been minister in any previous government, as his party, the PT, was precisely the key instrument that enabled Lula to be elected president at the 2002 election.

Only in Argentina is it somewhat surprising that neither of the two presidents examined here, Menem and Kirchner, had been a minister in a previous government, because both belonged to the Peronist party which had been in power under Peron and his second wife, Isabella; but the support which these two presidential candidates enjoyed within their party was obtained at the regional and not at the national level.

Is There a 'Coordinator' in the National Executive Alongside the President? (Questions 2, 3 and 7)

There are marked variations among the countries examined here with respect to the appointment of a government 'coordinator.' Peru is described by the author of the paper dealing with that country as being 'semi-presidential,' presumably as a result of the existence, since 1993, of a 'President of the Board of Ministers': but the holder of that post is not regarded by the author as a 'prime minister.' There is no equivalent position to prime minister in either Brazil, Chile, Colombia or Mexico; but in Argentina, the idea of appointing such a coordinator was discussed and the position of 'chief of cabinet' was set up in 1994 to provide a solution to the problem.

The existence of a less formal coordinator should therefore be raised in relation to the position of the chief of cabinet in Argentina. In Mexico, the Minister of the Interior is said by the author of the chapter on that nation to play just such a part. In Brazil, the position of minister of the 'casa civil' set up by President Lula is regarded as having been designed to provide a degree of informal coordination. As in Peru, the existence of the position of 'President of the Board of Ministers' seemed to suggest that the problem had been solved, and that steps

The Character of the 'Government' 65

toward this end were being taken (except in Colombia, although some discussion of the subject did take place under Uribe); but whether there is an 'increasing' move in the direction of coordination cannot be ascertained on the basis of the data. What might be concluded is that a 'semi-formal' solution to the problem of coordination in these national executive branches has indeed been generally advanced.

Do Ministers in the National Executive Formally Meet as a Government? (Questions 4 and 5)

The answer appears to be 'yes' with respect to the countries analyzed here, but the exact character of the role of these government meetings clearly depends on the wishes of each president. Thus, in Argentina, Menem called meetings of ministers on a monthly basis, but Kirchner discontinued the practice. In Brazil, ministers came to meet in a 'political council,' but the function of that body is said to have been purely advisory. Meetings of a similar character took place in Mexico, but only if the president decided to convene them. The same principle appeared to be applied in Peru, but President García is said to have applied that principle less frequently than Fujimori. In Chile, whereas Aylwyn convened meetings of the 'cabinet council' every two weeks, the practice was not followed by Lagos. Finally, in Colombia, the question of coordination was not resolved under the two presidents examined here, Gaviria and Uribe: only in 2014, under the Uribe's successor, Santos, was the post of 'Minister to the Presidency' specifically established to be responsible for coordination.

A Minority, but not even always a Large Minority, of the Ministers in Latin American National Executives Tends to be Appointed from among Ex-Members of Congress (Question 9)

All presidents, except Fujimori, included a number of ex-members of the legislature being appointed to the executive branch of government, but in all cases these have constituted a minority of the ministers. In Argentina, that proportion was appreciably larger in Menem's cabinets (about a third) than in Kirchner's cabinets (a quarter); in Brazil, the proportion of ex-members of Congress in the two presidential cabinets under examination was around one fifth, whereas in Mexico, there were five ex-members of Congress in Zedillo's cabinets and ten in Calderón's cabinets; in Colombia, ex-members of Congress formed about a fifth of the ministers under Gaviria as well as under Uribe. There is thus a regular practice, at any rate in the countries analyzed here, to appoint a number of top members of the government from among ex-members of Congress, but these remain a minority among ministers in these Latin American governments, in contrast to Western European parliamentary systems, where a majority of the members of cabinets are or have been members of parliament.

'Party Government' is Recognized in Latin American National Executives, but the Phenomenon of 'Coalition-Building' and its Recognition as a 'Regular' Practice Appears to Remain Less Widespread (Questions 10–17)

The notion of 'party government' being a natural characteristic of government in a democratic context is well recognized: this is so to an extent that more resembles European parliamentary cabinets than United States presidential administrations. Moreover, presidents are regarded as having the right to choose (and to force the resignation of) members of their own party who come to ministerial posts.

On the other hand, in the Latin American countries examined here, recognition of coalitions, whether minority or majority in character, does not appear to be universal. This coalition question arose in Mexico from 2000 onwards, when a candidate from the PAN managed to be elected and thus defeat the PRI, the party to which all members of Mexican governments since the late 1920s had belonged (or been associated with). Yet, although a member of the PAN and a member of the PRI received appointments Zedillo and Calderón presidencies respectively, these appointments were not regarded as constituting formal coalitions. At the other extreme, since the return to democratic government in Chile after the fall of Pinochet in 1990, all cabinets have been coalitions and recognized as such by members of the government and by political observers. In Colombia, a degree of uncertainty remained under Uribe as to whether certain of his governments were coalitions: despite the fact that members of various parties came to participate from time to time in his governments, these moves were regarded as informal. Only in the Brazilian case, especially towards the end of Cardoso's presidency and at the beginning of Lula's, was the concept of 'minority' coalitions within the national executive formally recognized as such. Thus coalitions do not appear to be regarded everywhere as constituting a truly 'normal' characteristic of government in Latin America, at any rate in relation to the presidencies examined in this study.

The question of who can force a ministerial resignation also raises some difficulties. Whereas, as was noted earlier, presidents can appoint ministers and appear to have the right to dismiss those who belong to their own party, a further question arises as to whether Congress is also entitled to dismiss ministers, at least on an individual basis, but in a manner resembling what occurs in parliamentary rather than presidential systems: this congressional power seems ostensibly inconsistent with a strict application of the 'separation of powers' principle characterizing the presidential system on the US model. The power to dismiss ministers (on an individual basis) is explicitly given to Congress by the Colombian constitution, and attempts were indeed made on this basis on a number of occasions to 'censure' ministers and force their resignation: none of these succeeded, however.

On the other hand, resignations of ministers, ostensibly on their own volition, have taken place, both in the context of endeavors by Congress to ismiss these ministers and in the context of attempts by presidents to do likewise: yet, in the case of presidents the common practice has been for the ministers themselves to resign and to account for their resignation on personal grounds.

Do Parties Present Detailed Programs at Elections and Do the Media and/or the Academic Literature Discuss the 'Coherence' of the Government? (Questions 18 and 19)

There is seemingly a degree of 'skepticism' about the character and possibly even the practicality of presidential candidates elaborating detailed programs in the context of their own elections, at any rate in the countries examined here. In Brazil, Argentina and Peru, no 'program' as such is said to be recorded. Indeed, strangely enough, given the policy competition between the candidates in Brazil during the Cardoso and Lula presidencies, no answer emerged to the question of whether there was greater programmatic coherence in the context of these elections. In Argentina, Mexico and Peru, it is remarked by the authors of the studies concerned with those countries that discussions have taken place in the media about the character of the programs presented by the presidential candidates, and about the limited specificity of statements made: yet that state of affairs does not appear to have been regarded as constituting a truly major flaw with respect to the character of the presidential electoral processes in the countries concerned.

Based on these findings, can Latin American presidential republics be regarded as having developed an 'intermediate' model between the classical American presidential system and parliamentary government as practiced in Europe?

Latin American government is clearly not parliamentary, if the crucial point of the parliamentary form of government is seen as the principle that the government cannot formally survive unless it has (at least a passive form of) support from the single or lower house of parliament. Even the Colombian formal exception with respect to the possible censure of individual ministers is not fully an exception in this respect, as it concerns merely the right of Congress to censure individuals and not the whole government, let alone to effectively force the entire executive branch to resign.

Still, on the basis of the evidence provided by the characteristics of governmental powers in the six countries analyzed here, it seems that there are substantial variations from the classical United States model. These variations suggest that these (and possibly all) Latin American executives operate, not just on the basis of a series of different arrangements, but perhaps on something like a 'philosophy of government' which is distinct from that of the American executive. Admittedly, if one considers that the key characteristic of the American presidential executive is the fact that the holder of that executive is elected directly by the people, the Latin American executives analyzed here fall in the same category; however, if, as is often suggested, another key principle of the

American form of presidentialism is a clear separation between executive and legislature, that principle appears to be less manifestly recognized in practice in Latin America, even if the methods of appointment and the duration in office of executive and legislature are well separated.

As a matter of fact, among the six countries which have been analyzed here in detail, there is only one, Peru, in which the formal position of 'President of the Board of Ministers' has been constitutionally set up: it was suggested by the author of the paper on that country that Peru no longer has a 'presidential' system but a 'semi-presidential' system of government, presumably due to the existence of a position similar to 'prime minister' and because a key characteristic of the classical (US) formula where the president alone is in charge of the entire executive branch appears to have been abandoned. However, it seems that what characterizes the semi-presidential system is the notion that the government as a whole is politically responsible to parliament, as in Fifth Republic France.

Even if one leaves aside the important but somewhat formal question of the presence or absence of a prime minister among Latin American executives, what emerges is a series of substantial differences in the practice, and to an extent the theory, of the nature of the 'national executive' in the United States and Latin America. These differences amount to the suggestion that there is more of a government, so to speak, in the Latin American countries than in the United States: the question is therefore not whether Latin American countries are not 'presidential' in character, but whether, in contrast to the United States, where the president is the executive, the Latin American 'conception of the executive is closer to the 'collegial' character of parliamentary governments. What is at stake is, that, with respect to the structure of the national executive, the distance between 'parliamentary' cabinet practices on the European model and practices of contemporary Latin American governments is much smaller than between the concept of the US national executive and that of European parliamentary executives.

We have indeed found that this 'distance' between the European executive and the Latin American executive (on the basis of the six countries examined here) is smaller with respect to: a) the proportion of presidents who had previously been ministers; b) coordination arrangements within the executive; c) the tendency to organize meetings of the executive; d) the proportion of parliamentarians among members of the executive; and e) the extent to which the notion of 'party government' had developed in Latin American executives. In all of these cases a marked difference has been observed between Latin American executive arrangements and Western European governmental arrangements, but it was appreciably less marked than differences to the US executive: indeed an impression has emerged that Latin American executives have tended to constitute 'governments' to a greater extent than United States executives have done.

Conclusions

Given that there is less of a 'distance' in Latin America between presidents and the other members of the national executives, at any rate in the six countries studied here in detail, and assuming that the cases of the six countries are representative of other Latin American national executives, it seems permissible to conclude that the national executives of Latin American presidential republics, while remaining fully 'presidential' in character, occupy an 'intermediate' position between those of the United States and of European parliamentary countries. It seems therefore permissible to conclude, if one adopts the rather telling expression coined by Hugh Heclo in his 1977 volume in relation to the US executive, that Latin American executives are unlikely to constitute 'Governments of Strangers,' at least to the same extent as United States national executives might be characterized.

Notes

1. The word 'cabinet' is used in this chapter to refer to what might be described as the 'first level' ministers below the prime minister or president. The juridical difference between the concept of 'cabinet' in presidential and parliamentary systems is well known, but the purpose of this paper is to describe indicators which may help to assess whether reality does truly correspond to the juridical position. It must be pointed out at the outset that this paper considers only the 'cabinet' in both systems and not the 'government' in general. In parliamentary systems, 'governments' have tended to be become much larger than the cabinet itself (in Britain, for instance, the cabinet has about 20 members but the government includes typically over 100, when 'ministers of state' and 'parliamentary secretaries' are taken into account). When it is said that the parliamentary cabinet is 'collegial,' one refers only to the cabinet in the strict sense: there is no collegiality as far as the rest of the government is concerned. Thus the question which is being examined here is exclusively how far 'cabinets' in parliamentary systems differ in terms of their role from 'cabinets' in presidential systems.
2. There is for instance no reference at all to the character of the 'government' (cabinets or otherwise) in the two 'systems' in Lijphart (1992).
3. It may not always have been so. ' "But, sir," Fessenden was resolute, "without going to such an extreme, a united Cabinet that is consulted by you is not an impossibility." "It is, I would have said, a reality." Lincoln was demure. "I realize that there has been much talk to the effect that I am controlled by my 'premier,' Governor Seward, and that I seldom consult the Cabinet on major issues, and so on. . . ." ' (Vidal, 1984). See also, for an academic presentation of the problem, Fenno (1959, especially pp. 9–20). In his book *A Government of Strangers* (1977), H. Heclo strongly makes the point that there is considerable ignorance about the way the US Federal executive functions: 'Despite a host of management and organization studies, Washington exposés and critiques of bureaucracy, very little information is available about the working world and everyday conduct of the top people in government' (p.1). A detailed analysis of the relationship between presidents and the secretaries from Nixon to Clinton has been provided by Warshaw (1996).
4. The question of the extent to which there might be a possible relationship between Latin American presidentialism and Western European parliamentary systems is

70 *Jean Blondel*

referred to in Mainwaring and Shugart (1977) *Presidentialism and Democracy in Latin America*, esp. at pp. 74–75. No detailed empirical basis is presented to support the conclusions which are drawn, however. Meanwhile, only two questions are not specifically dealt with under the six coming rubrics of the paper: one (Q. 6) was related to whether any 'administrative' body which might have come into existence in one of the countries played any 'political' part, as that matter was not positively raised in the answers given in the country reports; the other (Q. 8) was concerned with ascertaining which ministerial positions were regarded as the most important in the government of the country concerned: nothing emerged in the answers which suggested that the positions in question raised any particular problem.

References

Fenno Jr, R.E. (1959). *The President's Cabinet*. New York: Knopf.
Heclo, H. (1977). *A Government of Strangers*. Washington, DC: Brookings Institution.
Lijphart, A. (1992). *Parliamentary versus Presidential Government*. Oxford: Oxford University Press.
Linz, J.J. (1990). The perils of presidentialism. *Journal of Democracy*, 1(1), 51–69.
Linz, J.J. and Valenzuela, A. (1994). *The Failure of Presidential Democracy*. Baltimore: The Johns Hopkins University Press, 3–90.
Mainwaring, S. and Shugart, M.S. (1997). *Presidentialism and Democracy in Latin America*. Cambridge: Cambridge University Press.
Poguntke, T. and Webb, P. (2005). *The Presidentialization of Politics: A Comparative Study of Modern Democracies*. Oxford: Oxford University Press.
Riggs, F.W. (1988). The survival of presidentialism in America. *International Political Science Review*, 9(4), 247–278.
Shugart, M.S. and Carey, J.M. (1992). *Presidents and Assemblies. Constitutional Design and Electoral Dynamics*. Cambridge: Cambridge University Press.
Vidal, G. (1984). *Lincoln*. New York: Random House.
Warshaw S.A. (1996). *Powersharing: White House-Cabinet Relations in the Modern Presidency*. Albany, New York: State University of New York Press.

Appendix: The Nature of 'Governments' in Latin American Presidential Republics

Nineteen indicators designed to determine the nature of the relationship within governments in six Latin American presidential republics.

Nineteen indicators thus make it possible to determine whether 'governments' tend to constitute 'units' alongside and more or less independently from the president of the country. These indicators are:

(1) Whether the president is an ex-minister of the preceding or a recent government.
(2) Whether there is a prime minister; if yes, why such a post was created in that country and whether there have been discussions around the prospect of establishing such a post in other countries.

(3) Where there is no prime minister, whether there is an informal or formal recognition, by both the president and the members of the government, that one minister is in charge of fostering inter-departmental coordination within the government.
(4) Whether there are meetings (formally and/or informally) of the 'full' government and, if so, how often they occur.
(5) Whether there are partial meetings of the government and whether these are chaired by the president or by a specifically nominated minister.
(6) Assuming that all presidents are helped by a presidential staff, how far does the head of that office intervene in the activities of the various departments?
(7) If a minister is in charge of coordination of the government, is there an office at the disposal of that minister and does the head intervene in the activities of the various departments?
(8) What is the number of top-level ministers in each or the two presidencies under consideration for each country?
(9) What is the number and proportion of ex-members of parliament among the ministers in each of the two presidencies?
(10) Is there is formal recognition of 'party' in the composition of the government, for instance by means of stipulating that the 'government' is a 'coalition'?
(11) In the context of one-party governments, does the president choose the ministers?
(12) In the context of coalitions, does the president choose the ministers from his own party?
(13) In the context of coalitions, does the president choose the ministers from other parties than his own?
(14) May the president dismiss the ministers? If yes, give the number of such dismissals for each president and for each presidential term.
(15) Does parliament have the power to dismiss ministers? If yes, give the number of such dismissals for each president and for each presidential term.
(16) Are there are many cases of resignation of ministers during the mandates of each president?
(17) Are there many cases of minority coalitions during each presidential term?
(18) What is the process of elaboration of coalition programs? Did this process lead to a written text and how long was this text?
(19) Whether there have been discussions in the media and/or the academic literature about the degree of 'coherence' of the 'government' (including general discussions, giving the dates concerned), or of the concept of 'party coherence' of the government (going beyond the countries which are specifically analyzed in the current study).

4 Political Career Trajectories and Social Backgrounds

Latin American Presidents in Comparative Perspective (1978–2015)

Manuel Alcántara, Mélany Barragán and Francisco Sánchez

This chapter constitutes an exploratory analysis of the career trajectories and social backgrounds of politicians in Latin America. Building on previous works (Alcántara, Barragán and Sánchez, 2016), the aim of this research is to connect sociodemographic questions with the political career trajectories of Latin American presidents in the late twentieth and early twenty-first centuries. This is an important topic because in presidential political systems, presidents become the main political leaders of their countries. In this sense, the academic literature paid attention to the question of leadership for the first time in 1873. Walter Bagehot, in his classic work *The English Constitution* (2001)—a seminal work in the study of comparative governments—warned that presidential systems gave the holder of power two different functions: on the one hand, a 'ceremonial' role as head of state and, on the other hand, an 'effective' function of chief executive. This double role creates a special aura, self-image and popular expectations that are quite different from those associated with prime ministers in parliamentary systems.

Building a presidential image requires managing diverse forms of capital and particular historical conjunctures. On the one hand, family networks, education and political socialization in the broadest sense are determinant in terms of one's entrance in politics. On the other hand, politicians may have different preferences and opportunities that influence their career trajectory. Finally, they have to consider life after politics, which might be voluntary or involuntary depending on whether they are re-elected or not.

The presidency is the result of a direct election and it demands high levels of political capital, leadership and aggregate authority characterized by three dimensions: skills, relationships and the leader's reputation (Bennister, 2012). These dimensions are the consequence of career patterns and their understanding requires a systematic and comparative approach. Following these principles, this chapter is a proposal for the study of Latin American presidencies analyzing three moments in time—their entrance, development and exit from politics—according to the use of political capital made by these politicians and the impact of presidentialism on their trajectories.

Understanding politicians and political careers in this way would be impossible without integrating an analysis of these three phases. Within the 'path dependency' approach, the entrance phase into politics has been the most analyzed of the three; however, it may be insufficient to understand the larger topic of political careers. It is also insufficient in explaining the incentives, opportunities and disadvantages that all political systems offer. The phases of development and exit also offer important insights into interpreting career patterns and discerning different styles of leadership and types of political capital.

This study follows a line of research started by Alcántara (2012) and assumes two main principles. On the one hand, there is empirical evidence that shows that contemporary political involvement is shaped by an ethos of professionalism. This means that people who make a living from politics spend long periods within that activity, holding different offices.

On the other hand, remaining in politics depends on a classic strategy based on the maximization of one's political capital. Political capital can also help to explain the entrance into and exit from politics after occupying a public office. Political careers and political capital can be then studied as dependent variables but also as independent variables for understanding political systems.

Henceforth, this chapter aims to reflect on political careers and political elites, analyzing Latin American presidencies from 1978 to 2015. It is divided into three parts. First, there will be a brief discussion of the scholarly literature, focusing attention on the links between political capital, leadership and political career patterns. Second, data will be introduced to identify trends, regularities, and differences in terms of politicians' profiles, based on education and family background. Third, we focus on political careers from arrival to the presidency until after departure, before presenting our closing reflections.

Political Careers, Presidentialism and Leadership

In order to analyze the careers of Latin American presidents, this chapter focuses its attention on the importance of political experience and the professionalization of politics, paying particular attention to the differences between presidential and parliamentary careers. In that sense, the first task is to discuss the roles played by professionalization and political capital.

Although scholars sometimes study these as a single phenomenon, there are some differences between them. Whereas the first is the result of years of dedication to politics, the second is a mix of inherent personal skills and experience. However, institutional design influences both processes: presidential and parliamentary career patterns present some marked differences.

As Linz (1994) stated, one of the points to keep in mind when comparing political career trajectories in presidential and parliamentary systems is the way in which party competition is structured, including the relationship between the president, elites and society, and the ways power is exercised. Furthermore, in a prior article, Linz (1990) noted that presidential elections offer the advantage of allowing people to elect the chief executive in an open, direct manner, for a predictable period, thus decreasing party control and manipulation. As such, in presidential systems, becoming president depends on voter support whereas in other forms of government it is linked more to government control, parties and institutions (Pennings, 2000).

In this sense, presidential elections are characterized by a zero-sum game in which there is no hope for changing alliances or expanded bases of support. Instead, the losers must wait four or five years without access to executive power or patronage. In contrast, studies on executive careers in parliamentary systems generally show that those who occupy important positions usually come from the legislature (Dogan, 1979; Gallagher et al., 2001).

In contrast, this does not necessarily happen in a presidential system in which political career trajectories may be markedly different. For example, a presidential systems allow for the existence of outsider candidates, and this is also considered one of their risks. In this vein, the personalization of the presidential candidate can open the possibility that inexperienced people may win the presidency, especially when the party system is weak (Carrera, 2013). Hence, voters may value the personal qualities of presidential candidates and decide to vote based on factors other than party loyalty (Blondel and Thiébault, 2010; Linz, 1994; Suárez, 1982). Therefore, in presidential systems, outsiders with few links to the political class and the established parties can come to power more easily.

In addition to the institutional historical tradition of the region, other particularities of presidential systems must be taken into account to describe the career trajectories of Latin American presidents as well as their profiles. The institutional environment constitutes an important variable to understand trajectories and the roles exercised by leadership and political capital.

Who Have Been the Latin American Presidents Over the Last Thirty Years?

The scholarly literature supports the proposition of the importance of the president in presidential political systems (Alcántara and García Montero, 2011; Mainwaring and Shugart, 1997; Paniagua, 2012). However, there is less information about their sociodemographic characteristics, political capital, leadership, style of government, and their impact on the quality of democracy of their political systems (Alcántara et al., 2016). In this sense, the first thing to note about this literature is that the demographic profile is very similar to that of many legislators and senators (Alcántara, 2012; Martínez Rosón, 2008; Cabezas, 2012; Barragán, 2012).

Since the transitions to democracy in the region began, Latin America has witnessed the arrival of 112 elected presidents and 23 presidents who came to power because an elected president died, resigned or could not complete their term for reasons beyond their control. Some of these presidents were re-elected, so in this period we can analyze 135 presidencies (Table 4.1).

The period analyzed stretches from 1978 to 2015. Presidents elected before 1978 are not included, as this year marks the beginning of the transition to democracy in Latin America. However, because the transition to democracy began in the years after 1978 in many countries, this research does not analyze each of the cases from 1978 onward, but from the year when each country returned to democratic governance.

One of the first characteristics of the data that needs to be mentioned is the gender distribution: 94.6% of the presidents have been men and just 5.4% are women. This can be explained by the predominance of *machismo* culture in the region, in which voters will elect women to the legislature, but prefer to elect men to the most powerful positions in the political system. Consequently, one can argue that there is a masculinization of politics in Latin America.

The question of gender in presidential career trajectories is subject to a large number of variables. Among them are how one enters into politics. Two key aspects are family socialization and education both of which are relevant because they frame political capital. There is evidence that family plays the most important role in socialization. Family is the first institution that shapes an individual's sense of self and personality. It also determines one's position in the social structure, and one's access to different forms of capital: economic,

Table 4.1 Presidencies and presidents in Latin America, 1978–2015

Country	Total presidencies	Elected presidencies	Total presidents	Elected presidents	1st presidency year
Argentina	8	7	6	5	1983
Bolivia	12	9	9	6	1982
Brazil	9	7	6	4	1985
Chile	6	6	5	5	1990
Colombia	10	10	8	8	1978
Costa Rica	10	10	9	9	1978
Dominican R	9	8	7	6	1978
Ecuador	16	9	13	8	1979
El Salvador	7	7	7	7	1984
Guatemala	8	7	8	7	1985
Honduras	10	9	10	9	1982
Mexico	6	6	6	6	1982
Nicaragua	6	6	4	4	1985
Panama	6	6	6	6	1989
Paraguay	8	8	6	6	1989
Peru	10	6	8	5	1980
Uruguay	7	5	7	5	1985
Venezuela	11	7	10	6	1978
N	159	136	135	112	–

Source: Database of the authors.

cultural and social. However, education is also important in the socialization process as it transmits social and cultural values as well as being especially important in terms of determining one's network and connections. Moreover, education promotes certain values and norms.

Research on political socialization notes that there is a direct relationship between growing up in a family interested in politics and the interest of the individual in politics (Hyman, 1959; Lane, 1959; Tedin, 1974). However, the presence of other family members involved in politics is also a good indicator to take into account. The reason for this is that the existence of relatives involved in politics provides political relations that can be capitalized upon as resources of power and leadership. In this vein, 49.1% of the presidents have had family members involved in politics (Table 4.2). This figure may be underreported in the sample due to the disparity of sources.

The influence of family members involved in politics is strong and has an effect on the formation of political capital and leadership. For example, many presidents are relatives of former presidents (Table 4.3). Political dynasties generate political capital in their own right in terms of networks, knowledge and particular skills. Generally, those who are part of a political dynasty inherit power quotas and contacts and are also exposed to the political world at a young age. In political dynasties, familial ties facilitate one's entrance in politics and also increase their chances of occupying a political office.

Besides family socialization, other factors may be decisive in shaping one's political career trajectory, including one's education and contacts. Generally, presidents are well educated, although their academic training is not on balance as advanced as that of legislators. There are also many presidents who did not complete university, which may be explained, at least in part, by the political history of their countries (Table 4.4). Dropping out of university can also be explained by periods spent in exile by some presidents, or the absolute dedication to politics from a young age.

At any rate, university education produces two types of capital: on the one hand knowledge and, on the other, new social and political relationships. It must also be emphasized that Latin American universities are highly politicized, and

Table 4.2 Family in politics (%)

Family in politics	(%)
Father	48.1
Mother	5.6
Husband/wife	7.4
Brother/sister	9.3
Son/daughter	5.6
Uncle/aunt	9.3
Grandfather	3.7
Others	11.0
N	55

Source: Database of the authors.

Table 4.3 Position held by relative in politics (%)

Position	(%)
President	19.2
Legislator	9.6
Senator	1.9
Party officer	9.6
Major	1.9
Governor	9.6
Ministry	12.2
Councilor	1.9
Other	26.4
No position	7.7
N	50

Source: Own elaboration.

Table 4.4 Highest academic degree (%)

Academic Degree	(%)
Primary school	0.9
High school	3.6
Diploma	8.0
Professional training	1.8
College	41.1
Army career	4.5
Master's degree	20.5
PhD	19.6
N	112

Source: Database of the authors.

student movements have had an important role in the political transformations that have occurred in the region. Furthermore, universities are spaces where politicians acquire skills that improve their leadership capabilities as public speakers or leaders of groups.

However, in Latin America, factors such as social and structural economic inequality, difficulties in accessing education and inequalities within the education system prevent social mobility. There are structures of social exclusion in Latin America that can predetermine the life trajectory of individuals and can also hinder the functioning of the political system (Rivas et al., 2010). Furthermore, it is also important to note the role of university education (Table 4.4) in terms accumulating the political capital required to launch a political career, also taking into account that university education is not just a social mobility mechanism (Neelsen, 1975). University education also contributes to political mobility (Best and Cotta, 2000).

Returning to the idea of university education as a sign of status, Ecuadorian President Rafael Correa has a PhD from a North American university and this

Table 4.5 University degree (%)

University degree	(%)
Law	39.2
Political or Social Science	4.9
Philosophy	1.0
Military	5.9
Engineering	16.7
Economics	14.7
Business	4.9
Medicine	4.9
Others	7.9
N	45

Source: Database of the authors.

has been lauded as an important credential. On the other side, Presidents Lula da Silva and Evo Morales were questioned by the most conservative sectors of their respective countries due to their lack of university education. These two different positions reflect the prejudices and elitist view of Latin American politics, as a space reserved only for the university educated or the 'enlightened.'

If it assumed that a politician's skills and abilities are derived from academic studies (Table 4.5), it should be noted that most of the presidents with a university education studied law. The study of law of courses facilitates an understanding of the legal system and of public administration, knowledge that can also be acquired by those who studied political and social sciences. On the other hand, there are a large number of presidents who studied business administration. This reflects the strong connection between politics and business in Latin America and constitutes a feature of presidential leadership in the region. Finally, it is also important to mention that 46.6% of the presidents in the sample studied abroad.

Finally, the variable of the presidents' birthplace was also introduced to analyze whether those who were born in the capital city are predominant amongst those in the study. Due to the heterogeneity of the region, the percentage of those who were born in the capital can help explain if political activity and access to elite circles are centralized or not. The data shows that there is overrepresentation of presidents who were born in the capital city of their country, at 45.5%. This evidence suggests that being born in the capital offers more advantages than being born somewhere else. This information needs to be complemented by noting that all of these presidents moved to the capital to pursue their political or professional career.

The Road to Becoming President: Electoral Careers or Appointed Trajectories?

Before analyzing the presidents' career trajectories in detail, it may be interesting to pay particular attention to the 'outsider' presidents in the sample.

Although only elected presidents have been studied, it is interesting to distinguish among the different ways in which politicians come to politics in Latin America (Table 4.6).

With regard to presidents who are elected without having held any elected political office before the presidency, as it has been mentioned in the theoretical discussion, presidentialism—as an institutional design—cannot prevent the election of outsiders or people with no prior experience in elected office. As Mayorga (1995: 34–35) asserted, presidentialism is close in this sense to Rousseau's conception of direct democracy. In spite of the existence of mediating structures such as political parties, the institutional design doesn't limit the premodern form of understanding politics characterized by a substantial connection between 'the people' and the state. In this sense, presidentialism makes it easier for a president to become the embodiment of the people's will as a leader through direct election.

The combination of charismatic plebiscitarian leadership and its messianic potential is related to the origins of mass politics—a phenomenon to which Weber (1964) paid attention and found an excellent breeding ground for presidentialism. This is a particularly Latin American phenomenon, partly linked

Table 4.6 Political careers in Latin America

	Total	Outsiders	Appointment	Electoral
Argentina	6	–	–	5
Bolivia	9	–	2	6
Brazil	6	–	1	4
Chile	5	–	2	5
Colombia	8	–	1	8
Costa Rica	9	–	–	9
Dominican R.	7	–	1	6
Ecuador	13	1	5	8
El Salvador	7	3	–	7
Guatemala	8	1	–	7
Honduras	10	–	–	9
Mexico	6	–	3	6
Nicaragua	4	–	–	4
Panama	6	2	–	6
Paraguay	6	3	2	6
Peru	8	3	1	5
Uruguay	7	–	–	5
Venezuela	10	1	4	6
N	135	14	23	112

Route of access to politics	(%)
Electoral position	72.6
Appointment position	17.0
Direct to presidency (outsiders)	10.4
N	135

Source: Database of the authors.

to presidentialism. There is no doubt that these political career trajectories would be less common in parliamentary systems of government, the main reason being that parliamentary systems have developed a series of control mechanisms such as, for example, the election of the head of the government by a legislative majority composed by professional politicians. This design generates incentives for achieving merits and acquiring political experience. This is different from presidentialism, where the leader, through a direct election, can win based on their leadership capabilities.

In this sense, it is relevant that 14 of the 112 cases are people who had not held any political office before, whether by elections or appointment. Although none were anonymous individuals and in many cases were party leaders who had tried to reach the presidency previously, they held very limited political and public management experience (Table 4.6).

The phenomenon of outsider presidents has often been explained as something characterizing countries undergoing a political representation crisis. The weak structure of party systems and the lack of trust in politicians can generate what has been called an episode of anti-politics (Mayorga, 1995, Garcia Montero, 2001; Carrera, 2013). In this sense, it seems clear that the quick ascent of politicians with no previous experience is only possible because political institutions have failed—mainly political parties. The explanation behind this phenomenon can be obtained by observation of variables such as the form of party system, country size, economic status and the degree of democratic consolidation.

One of the characteristics of the outsider presidents is their anti-politics discourse and rejection of politicians and the political system as a whole. Their principal distinction from these traditional politicians is that they haven't had a political career, which, in their opinion, gives them a moral superiority over those who 'live' for politics and have not been able to solve citizens' problems. In these cases, the lack of political experience is not a problem because the society is in a crisis situation. This explains the cases of Hugo Chávez, Lucio Gutierrez or Alberto Fujimori.

Experience shows that a significant proportion of these leaders have been involved, before or after their election, in an institutional crisis that has compromised the democratic stability of their respective countries. Chávez in Venezuela and Gutierrez in Ecuador are two similar cases. The first led a military coup against the government of Carlos Andrés Perez in 1992, and the second was the leader of the takeover of Congress that ended with the resignation of Jamil Mahuad in 2000. This group could also include the Peruvian Ollanta Humala, who along with his brother Antauro led a military uprising in the turbulent days at the end of the Fujimori regime.

Another case of a president without a previous political career (and another conflictive presidency) was that of Alberto Fujimori, who could not finish his third term because of the loss of internal and external support due to the flagrant corruption of his regime. The last case of an outsider who could not finish his term as president is Fernando Lugo—but he was a singular case, because he had experience in ecclesiastical politics as a Church leader.

More interestingly, perhaps because they have not been studied to the same degree as others, are the cases of politicians who arrived to the presidency with no previous political experience. There are examples in both Paraguay and Panama, where the presidents came from the private sector, senior management or public administration. One explanation in the case of Panama can be that, due to its own geopolitical characteristics, the private sector and the public are closely linked, with big business being deeply involved in the management of state.

Something similar occurred in Paraguay, despite its strong party system. However, the election of presidents without any previous political career is not limited to the current presidents of Panama (Ricardo Martinelli) or Paraguay (Horacio Cartes). It has also occurred in El Salvador with Alfredo Cristiani and Antonio Sacca.

In these cases, the private business activities of the individuals served as the basis for political leadership. Their economic position as entrepreneurs gives access to relationships that contribute to the accumulation of political capital and building political leadership. Their success in the private sector can also serve as evidence of their management skills.

Since Mayhew's work on the electoral connection (1974), the desire to win elections becomes relevant for the analysis of a political career. Although this theory does not hold up when it is applied to the field of comparative politics, especially in institutional and partisan models, winning elections is still at the core of democratic politics and constitutes a way to understand political leadership.

Although all presidents in the sample won democratic elections when they ran for the presidency, not all have had the same trajectory: some occupied electoral office but some occupied appointed offices (Table 4.7). Their contacts and their political leadership skills do not necessarily come from the electoral side of politics. Thirty-four presidents came into politics through election to the National Congress, and five were senators before their election. This contributes to a model of entry into politics based on the national legislative branch and only equates to ministers in the case of appointment.

If we consider the electoral process as an arena where politicians can accumulate political capital and improve their leadership skills, it is worth noting the role of the governors in federal systems, or mayors in the large cities of small countries. These could be considered as platforms from which to run for the presidency. By occupying such positions, these individuals are at the forefront of national politics and have high public visibility. Moreover, and more importantly, these positions allow them to demonstrate to potential voters the results of a good public management as the main political capital and verifiable example of their leadership.

On the other hand, there is no doubt that having occupied a ministry is the most common springboard to accumulate the necessary political capital and leadership skills to aspire to run for the presidency. It is therefore usual to find ministers who took part in successful governments and occupied highly visible posts in government. These positions catapulted them as key figures in national

Table 4.7 First and last political positions (%)

	First political position	Last political position before presidency
Councilor	4.5	–
Mayor	7.9	2.9
Provincial legislator	3.4	–
Governor	2.2	6.9
Legislator	29.2	29.4
Senator	5.6	11.8
Vice president	2.2	4.9
Constituent legislator	5.6	–
Ministry	20.5	15.7
Public office	5.6	–
Other	10.1	8.8
Without recent position	–	19.6
N	112	112

Source: Database of the authors.

policy and politics and gave them the opportunity to present themselves to the voters as efficient managers.

Mexico is one of the clearest examples of countries with presidents who first served as ministers and as part of the cabinet. Three of the six presidents analyzed in this chapter—Miguel de la Madrid, Carlos Salinas and Ernesto Zedillo—rose to the presidency without having previous experience in an electoral campaign, but by holding the position of Finance Minister in the Ministry of Planning and Budget. It must be emphasized that in Mexico, the presidential candidate nomination was 'handpicked', as the outgoing president typically chose his successor. However, this longstanding pattern was broken with the end of the hegemony of the PRI in 2000, when electoral experience began to weigh more heavily on access the presidency.

The hegemony of the 'Colorado' party, in Paraguay, is similar to the case of the PRI in Mexico. In contrast, in countries with higher levels of political competition—such as Panama, Chile and Brazil—ex-ministers who ascended to the presidency had the support of citizens. In Chile, Lagos was Minister of Education and, later of Public Works, and Bachelet held the Public Health portfolio and the Ministry of Defense before being elected president. This last position was very important, because she was the first female to occupy that ministry in a very traditional country. In Brazil, Dilma Roussef was Minister of Energy and Mines one's Chief of Staff to President Lula.

The duration of one's career and the number of electorally held and appointed positions occupied before ascending to the presidency are other important elements to account for in the acquisition of leadership skills. The first point to remark relates to short careers without much experience. According to our sample, about 40% of the presidents ascended to office before reaching the age of 50. Moreover, in many countries, the Constitution establishes age limits for legislators; in the

Table 4.8 Age at arrival to presidency (%)

Age at arrival to presidency	(%)
<40	5.8
40–50	34.0
51–61	34.0
61–70	18.4
>70	7.8
N	112

Source: Database of the authors.

Table 4.9 Number of positions before presidency (%)

	Appointment positions before presidency	Electoral positions before presidency
None	43.7	35.9
One	29.1	34.0
Two	17.5	19.4
Three	5.8	3.9
Four	1.9	4.9
Five	1.9	1.0
Six	–	1.0
N	98	98

Source: Database of the authors.

case of appointed positions, presumably, these leaders should have more expertise, and as such access to the position should occur later in life.

Re-election, Justice and the Way Out of Politics

After occupying the presidency, politicians often have to make a decision: whether to continue in politics, to retire or to change to a different professional activity. Even when there are incentives in the political system to seek re-election, and if this is permitted, the sample shows that only 13.6% of the 112 presidents tried for a second term, and the explanatory factor is usually the support of the populace of his first term. Table 4.10 shows that 57.1% of these were re-elected.

Table 4.10 Second-term presidents (%)

Re-election	(%)
Yes	57.1
No	42.9
N	14

Source: Database of the authors.

Career Trajectories and Social Backgrounds 85

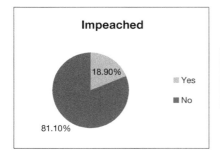

	Impeached
Cleared	38.1%
Not cleared	61.9%
(N)	21

Figure 4.1 Impeached former presidents (%)

What happened to presidents who were not re-elected? Nowadays, 44.1% of former presidents remain in politics and 55.9% have left active politics. In the latter group, the way out of politics was either voluntary or involuntary. When politicians have made the decision voluntarily, they followed one of two different paths: retirement, or moving to another professional activity. Those who did not retire followed different trajectories. Some of them returned to their previous jobs but, for the most part, found a new job or entered into a professional activity closely related to politics. In this sense, the presidency may serve as a step, or a way to build up political and social capital, before entering new activities beyond or related to politics.

Sometimes, former presidents want to continue in politics but find that there are impediments to doing so. Usually, electoral defeat, lack of confidence or disqualification are the main obstacles. However, some of the former Latin American presidents in the sample were impeached or left office early, due to varied situations. As Figure 4.1 shows, 11% of the presidents were involved in

Table 4.11 Way out of politics and political capital profitability

			Mechanism			
			Voluntary retirement	Electoral defeat	Lack of confidence	Impeachment
Political capital profitability	No	– Return to previous job	8	0	1	1
		– Retirement	12	1	2	5
	Yes	– New job	3	0	1	0
		– Activity related to politics	32	1	1	3
		– Capital transfer	2	0	0	1

Source: Database of the authors.

a legal process after their presidency, and 61.9% of these were not cleared during the legal proceedings.

Why is it important to study the pathway out of politics? One of the main reasons is that it allows us to identify and analyze the profitability of political capital. Table 4.11 demonstrates how former presidents' political capital can diminish due to voluntary retirement, electoral defeat, lack of confidence or disqualification. The path of those who used their political capital well in retirement included those presidents who entered in activities related to politics, such as foundations, public presence or as opinion leaders. In other cases, as with Fujimori's daughter or the Kirchners in Argentina, there was a transfer of political capital 'within the family.' Finally, a small group left politics due to illness or advanced age, or returned to their previous job.

Conclusions

Presidentialism has been the historical form of government in Latin America countries since the beginning of independence two centuries ago. This institutional design has been combined with the unrestricted power of presidents, which has provided a way of doing politics 'with presidential dominance.' Consequently, check-and-balance mechanisms have been limited in Latin American presidential systems.

The arrival of democracy in the late 1970s brought with it the transition to the longest democratic period in the region, in terms of direction of the political project and continuity (with Cuba being an exception). Above all, since the seminal work of Linz (1990), there has been much literature analyzing the risks associated with presidentialism and the virtues of parliamentarianism. Yet attention has been focused on institutional design, and not on the actors in political systems. This chapter provides an initial analysis of presidential leadership emphasizing the presidents' political career trajectories.

In this chapter we have not addressed institutional differences across distinct presidential systems according to the various national constitutions, and we have not linked this to the presidents' partisan universe which, in one way or another, is linked to a previously existing party (in the vast majority of cases) or leads to the establishment of new parties or political movements (Fujimori, Chávez and Correa, most prominently). Both aspects represent important avenues for future research.

The empirical evidence accumulated in our database, that cover 18 Latin American countries over the past three decades, show some general characteristics of the region and some general patterns: for example, the overwhelming presence of men versus women as well as the question of 'centralism,' where half of the presidents were born in the capital city. Whereas the presence of women in legislatures of Latin America countries has increased, their presence in the executive is considerably lower. In October 2015, there were only three women serving as elected presidents, and in one important and large Latin American country—Mexico—no woman serves as governor in any of its 32 states. On the other hand, the demographic and economic power of the capital city (Brasilia being the only exception) is the city of origin of half of the presidents.

Latin American presidents also predominantly study law, which is similarly common amongst the legislative Latin American elites; most presidents are university educated and many have also studied abroad. However, data on political experience is less encouraging. Only 11% of presidents have reached the summit of their country's political system without prior experience in elected office. Equally notable in the sample are strong family links in Latin American politics, both in the executive and the legislative branches.

This chapter has attempted to provide a first approach to analyzing presidential career trajectories in Latin American politics and has explored some of the most important sociodemographic characteristics of the presidents in the third wave of the democratization period. Future work should link these variables with other dimensions and issues relating to the quality of democracy. In this sense, one of the greatest challenges is to define 'quality standards' in the performance of these presidents, from the premise that there is a link between the quality of democracy and the quality of politicians (presidents).

References

Alcántara, M. (2012). *El oficio del político.* Madrid: Tecnos.

Alcántara, M. and García Montero, M. (2011). *Algo más que presidentes. El papel del poder legislativo en América Latina.* Zaragoza: Fundación Manuel Giménez Abad de Estudios Parlamentarios y del Estado Autonómico.

Alcántara, M., Barragán, M. and Sánchez, F. (2016). Latin American presidents (1978–2015): a comparative perspective. In: Inácio, M. (ed.), *Presidents and Executives in Perspective.* Bello Horizonte: UFMG.

Bagehot, W. (2001). *The English Constitution.* Cambridge: Cambridge University Press.

Barragán, M. (2012). *¿Qué determina la permanencia en la actividad política?: Un análisis de las élites parlamentarias en América Latina.* Tesis de Máster. Universidad de Salamanca.

Bennister, M. (2012). *Prime Ministers in Power.* London: Palgrave.

Best, H. and Cotta, M. (2000). *Parliamentary Representatives in Europe 1848–2000.* Oxford: Oxford University Press.

Blondel, J. and Thiébault, J.L. (2010). *Political Leadership, Parties and Citizens: The Personalization of Leadership.* London; New York: Routledge Research in Comparative Politics.

Cabezas, L. (2012). *Profesionalización de las élites legislativas en Bolivia, Colombia, Ecuador y Perú.* Tesis Doctoral. Universidad de Salamanca.

Carrera, M. (2013). Presidentes outsiders y ministros neófitos: un análisis a través del ejemplo de Fujimori. *América Latina Hoy*, 64, 95–118.

Dogan, M. (1979). How to become a cabinet minister in France. *Comparative Politics*, 12(1), 1–25.

Gallagher, M., Laver, M. and Mair, P. (2001). *Representative Government in Modern Europe.* 4th ed, London: McGraw-Hill.

Garcia Montero, M. (2001). La década de Fujimori: ascenso, mantenimiento y caída de un líder antipolítico. *América Latina Hoy*, 28, 49–86.

Hyman, H. (1959). *Political Socialization: A Study in the Psychology of Political Behavior.* Glencoe: Free Press.

Lane, R. (1959). Fathers and sons: The foundation of political beliefs. *American Sociological Review*, 24, 502–511.

Linz, J.J. (1990). The perils of presidentialism. *Journal of Democracy*, 1(1), 51–69.

Linz, J.J. (1994). Presidential or parliamentary democracy: Does it make a difference?. In: Linz, J.J. and Valenzuela, A. (eds), *The Failure of Presidential Democracy.* Baltimore: Johns Hopkins University Press.

Mainwaring, S. and Shugart, M. (1997). *Presidentialism and Democracy in Latin America.* Cambridge: Cambridge University Press.

Martínez Rosón, M. (2008). *La carrera política de los parlamentarios costarricenses, hondureños y salvadoreños: selección y ambición.* Tesis Doctoral. Universidad de Salamanca.

Mayhew, D. (1974). *Congress: The electoral connection.* New Haven: Yale University Press.

Mayorga, A.R. (1995). *Antipolítica y neopopulismo.* La Paz: Cebem.

Neelsen, J.P. (1975). Education and social mobility. *Comparative Education Review*, 19(1), 129–143.

Paniagua, J.L. (2012). España: un parlamentarismo racionalizado de Corte Presidencial. In: Lanzaro, J. (ed.), *Presidencialismo y parlamentarismo: América Latina y Europa Meridional: Argentina, Brasil, Chile, España, Italia, México, Portugal y Uruguay.* Madrid: Centro de Estudios Políticos y Constitucionales.

Pennings, P. (2000). The consequences of ministerial recruitment for the functioning of cabinets in Western Europe. *Acta Política*, 35, 86–103.

Rivas, C., Vicente, P. and Sánchez, F. (2010). La educación como elemento de calidad de los políticos latinoamericanos. *Política y Gobierno*, 25(2), 279–319.

Suárez, W.C. (1982). El Poder Ejecutivo en América Latina: su capacidad operativa bajo regímenes presidencialistas de gobierno. *Revista de Estudios Políticos*, 29, 109–144.

Tedin, K. (1974). The influence of parents on the political attitudes of adolescents. *American Political Science Review*, 68, 1579–1592.

Weber, M. (1964): *Economía y sociedad.* Mexico: FCE.

Part II
Personal Power and Institutional Constraints
Case Studies

Personalization and institutionalization of leadership can provide a better basis for the case of presidents in Latin American countries. Taking into account the sociological and political characteristics of presidential governments is an appropriate way to that purpose. Six countries (Argentina, Brazil, Chile, Colombia, Mexico and Peru) have been selected on the basis of two criteria: sufficient size/population, and the state of democracy. All have successfully completed the process of transition to democracy. (Venezuela, while much more populous than Chile, remains a country with a very low level of quality of democracy.) Within each of the six selected countries, two presidents were chosen, reflecting broad trends in the political and electoral life of their countries. Our goal was to select presidents belonging to one of the key political 'families' of the country, grouped under the banner of a political party, or else representative of two particular approaches to the same problem within the same political family. These presidents have exercised their functions either in the 1990s or in the first decade of the twenty-first century. They may be liberal or conservative, left-wing or right-wing populists, socialists or social democrats, leaders of a political party or 'outsiders,' members of parliament or technocrats.

They are:

(1) Carlos Menem (president from July 8, 1989 to December 10, 1999) and Néstor Kirchner (May 25, 2003 to December 10, 2007) of Argentina.
(2) Fernando Henrique Cardoso (January 1, 1995 to December 31, 2002) and Luiz Inacio Lula da Silva (January 1, 2003 to December 31, 2010) of Brazil.
(3) Patricio Aylwin (March 11, 1990 to March 11, 1994) and Ricardo Lagos (March 11, 2000 to March 11, 2006) of Chile.
(4) César Gaviria (September 15, 1994 to September 15, 2004) and Álvaro Uribe (August 7, 2002 to August 7, 2010) of Colombia.
(5) Ernesto Zedillo (December 1, 1994 to November 30, 2000) and Felipe Calderón (December 1, 2006 to December 1, 2012) of Mexico.

(6) Alan García (July 28, 1985 to July 28, 1990, and from July 28, 2006 to July 28, 2011) and Alberto Fujimori (July 28, 1990 to November 22, 2000) of Peru.

In practice, these presidents were all either center-right or center-left leaders. There are no members of the military, no dictators, and no revolutionaries among the selected presidents. Right-wing populist presidents (Menem, Fujimori and Uribe) have been chosen, based on the idea that populists can be either on the right or on the left. García and Kirchner were both chosen as moderate populists, claiming to be an Aprist and a Peronist, respectively; both represent different periods. The selection makes it possible to analyze processes in a consolidated democracy, but not in military regimes or in dominant party systems.

Each case study first provides the biographical background of the president. It outlines the political career of the president both inside and outside of a party, including at the local level; the popularity of the president at the time of the presidential election, as well as the mode of selection of candidates (selection by party leaders only, by party members, or by a primary). The relation of the president with his government or ministers is detailed, especially in cases of a coalition government.

An initial source of personal power of the president is his relationship with a political party and his capacity to build a strong internal leadership within that party. An indicator of personal power of the president is the nature and form of the decision-making structure (collegial or not) of his party, the presence of more or less institutionalized 'currents' or factions, and whether these constitute a more or less organized opposition internal to the party. A third indicator of the personalization of leadership is provided by the manner in which the president resolves internal conflicts within the party, the extent to which the party is guided by the president through a strategy or program, and the extent to which one faction is played against another.

A second source of personal power of the president stems from the ability to receive support from elected officials of the party and from the party in power within the parliament. It highlights the role of the president in the selection of party candidates, in relation to practices of patronage and clientelism, and with respect to the use of public or private resources to become aware of party rebellions and splits.

A third source of personal power lies in the part played by the president in the development of strategies and programs and in the evolution of the ideology of the party, as well the electoral strategy being adopted. A key question is whether the president truly does embody the ideology and strategy of the party.

Yet the president must also use tools to develop ideas and policies in relation to the outside world, to public opinion and the electorate. The appearance of the president on television and the size of audiences are important. The use of political communication (advertising and marketing) is becoming increasingly important, given the presence of many advisers in communication alongside the president, especially as regards opinion polls. The level of popularity can thus be monitored and help to determine the sectors of public opinion on which the chief executive can rely.

5 Mexico: Zedillo and Calderón

The Challenges of Governing under Adversity

Marisol Reyes

Although presidentialism has largely been regarded as the backbone of the Mexican political system and decision-making process (Carpizo, 2002), since the 1990s, the great concentration of power in the executive branch has reached a point of oversaturation. The political transition overturned an electoral system no longer able to uphold the single party model it had sustained for more than 70 years. The new rules and institutional arrangements intensified electoral competition, broadened the political spectrum, and redistributed power among new and old actors. In this context, two presidents with different political foundations, Ernesto Zedillo from the Revolutionary Institutional Party (PRI), and Felipe Calderón from the National Action Party (PAN), experienced the common challenge of holding their mandates during periods of profound change. Both political figures not only faced the struggle of establishing their governments during episodes of severe political crisis that damaged their legitimacy, but were also forced to react promptly to the rapid swings experienced in an unstable international economy.

The political sources of presidentialism in Mexico (Weldon, 1997) have been changing in the last two decades; hence, comparative studies can explain the transformation of leadership, political behavior, and personal traits in both figures.

Following the basic sociological, institutional, and attitudinal analytical categories covered in the cases analyzed elsewhere in this book, this chapter addresses salient features in the administrations of Ernesto Zedillo (1994–2000) and Felipe Calderón (2006–2012). The study begins by describing relevant aspects of their political careers and professional experience in government. Subsequently, it draws on the nature of their relations with their respective parties and the political context in which their elections took place, principally analyzing the differences in style and approach to leadership. This chapter also studies their decision-making processes, as well as their relationships with the mass media and the management of their image and popularity. Finally, it analyzes the relationship between the presidents and their cabinets, Congress and the judicial branch.

Two Administrations in Times of Adversity

Mexico's transition towards democracy has not followed a steady pattern and has in some periods it experienced episodes of critical crisis. In particular, during Zedillo and Calderón's first years in office, disturbing events affected the legitimacy of their governments.

In the case of Ernesto Zedillo the fundamental difficulty was the exceptional circumstances in which he was endorsed as the PRI's candidate for the presidential elections of 1994. He was perceived as an emergency replacement, chosen abruptly by President Carlos Salinas after the assassination of his first choice, Luis Donaldo Colosio. Weeks before, Salinas's inner-circle had split due to disagreements about the nomination of his candidate. Zedillo, however, remained on Colosio's side, accepting the responsibility of managing the candidate's political campaign until his death. The second event that reduced the importance of the presidential race was the Zapatista uprising that emerged in the south of the country among rebellious indigenous communities in Chiapas (Ai Camp, 1996). Although Ernesto Zedillo won the elections by a significant margin, 20 days after starting his mandate he experienced a significant setback. The Mexican economy fell into a severe recession as a result of the peso's devaluation and the massive withdrawal of foreign investments to safer markets. In 1995, Mexico's GDP declined by 6.2% (Lustig, 1995). The Mexican devaluation, known as 'the tequila effect,' turned into a colossal financial crisis that affected other emerging markets.

Interestingly, under very different circumstances, Felipe Calderón also had important difficulties early in his presidency. His main challenge was the controversy surrounding his victory in the 2006 presidential elections. The narrowness of his triumph over his chief rival, Andrés Manuel López Obrador from the Democratic Revolution Party (PRD), led to speculation about the fairness and transparency of the electoral process, and this led to a battle between party elites (Bruhn and Greene, 2007). López Obrador and his supporters insisted that the result was not valid and that the case had to be taken to the Supreme Court. Finally, the decision to uphold the result brought about one of the longest and most publicized post-electoral conflicts in Mexico (Estrada and Poiré, 2007). In the economic realm, Calderón had to deal with the financial crisis that shook the world in 2008. Mexico was affected because the recession in the United States deeply reduced Mexico's exports to its most important trading partner; at the same time, international investors became extremely risk averse and Mexico stopped receiving the flows of capital it once enjoyed. Between 2006 and 2011 the Mexican economy grew at just 1.6% per year.

Building Two Political Careers: Social Class and Family Background

Atypical of the Mexican political elite, Zedillo and Calderón were both brought up in a provincial middle-class setting. Zedillo lived in Mexicali, the capital of the northern state of Baja California; Calderón was from Morelia, the capital of Michoacán in the center-south. Both politicians grew up in large families supported by hardworking parents who, like many in Mexico's emergent middle class, believed that education was essential to the development and social mobility of their children.

Zedillo studied in public schools to the undergraduate level and won a scholarship to study for his Masters and PhD at Yale University. Calderón attended inexpensive private schools sponsored by scholarships. Years later, when his career was consolidated, Calderón studied a Masters degree in Public Administration at the John F. Kennedy School of Government at Harvard University (Ai Camp, 2011). Despite the socio-economic affinities identified above, a clear difference between these two political careers was the influence that their respective families had on their inclination to engage in politics. The impact of Zedillo's family in his involvement in politics is almost imperceptible. His parents had no connection with or participation in local or national political activities. When Zedillo was very young, his father, a qualified mechanic, made the hard decision to move from Mexico City to Mexicali to seek better opportunities. Notably, this episode is included in Zedillo's official biography to stress his interest in being regarded as a self-made man with 'humble' origins (Presidencia de la República, 1998). Young Ernesto Zedillo showed an early interest in politics, joining and leading students' associations during his college days. Like many youngsters of his generation, the 1968 student protest had a crucial impact on his perception of the country's political situation. He participated in a moderate political group when he was 17 years old, but his real immersion into public life started in his twenties, when he enrolled in the Revolutionary Institutional Party (Ai Camp, 2013).

In sharp contrast with Zedillo's experience, Felipe Calderón's political biography is marked by the strong influence of his family's lineage within the National Action Party (PAN). His main influence and inspiration in politics was his father, Luis Calderón Vega, who is acknowledged as PAN's chronicler and one of its founding fathers and ideologues (Berman, 2006). In numerous articles, documents, interviews, and party discourses, the younger Calderón quotes thoughts and reflections based on the core Christian democratic principles inherited from his father and from his Catholic education. In Calderón's memoirs, written during the 2006 presidential campaign and titled: 'The rebellious son: campaign transcript/El hijo desobediente: notas de campaña,' he describes an upbringing in which religion, party politics, and political activism were the ground rules of his family's life-style. The interplay of those three aspects was influential in Calderón's future personality. Calderón asserts that his first contact with real politics started when he helped in his father's numerous political campaigns. Calderón Senior ran as PAN's candidate in different elections where his party had little chance of defeating the PRI. Calderón Junior has mentioned that one of his more vivid memories of childhood is painting PAN slogans on walls and distributing propaganda while other boys were playing games (Camarena and Zepeda, 2007: 21). Notably, in civil resistance Calderón's family found an effective way to draw attention to issues generally disregarded by public opinion in the 1980s, and this aspect seems to have been a key element that shaped his political profile during his youth. According to Calderón, one of his most affecting memories of these activities is of the national campaign that challenged the results of Chihuahua's 1986 local elections, where PAN alleged lack of fairness and manipulation of the electoral rolls (Calderón, 2006).

Public Administration versus Political Experience

Zedillo and Calderón are near contemporaries, with less than 11 years between them. Zedillo was born on December 27, 1951, and Calderón on August 18, 1962. Both belong to a kind of a mid-twentieth century Mexican baby boomer generation that lived through the social change produced by years of economic stability brought on by the high GDP growth rate (of around 6% annually from 1950 to 1980). They lived through the 'Mexican miracle,' based on the substitution of imports, industrialization, and the oil boom (Santaella, 1998). Both professional trajectories reflect an ambitious aspirational pattern that started in their early years of school, where they stood out among their classmates. Yet the focus of their professional careers, and their practical experience in government, gave them very different sets of skills and professional expertise.

Ernesto Zedillo's foundations were laid in a high-level technical education in economics and finance and effectively built upon by long practical experience in public administration. He graduated from the School of Economics of the National Polytechnic Institute in Mexico and years later pursued an MA and PhD in the same field at Yale. His dissertation addressed Mexico's external public debt. His specialized knowledge of a key and complex problem for the Mexican economy allowed him to return and build a solid career as a researcher in the Central Bank of Mexico between 1978 and 1987 (Ai Camp, 1996). During that time, Zedillo accumulated impressive academic and technical credentials that portrayed him as the new prototype of public officials known as technocrats. They broke up the old tradition of studying law in the National Autonomous University of Mexico to get a prominent position in government, and they replaced it with their specialized knowledge of public administration. However, in parallel with his technical skills, Zedillo's career was jump-started by the resources and opportunities offered through informal ties of friendship made with the new elite that emerged in Miguel de la Madrid's administration, whose dominant trait was their expertise in economics and international finance (Ai Camp, 2013). Ernesto Zedillo's deepest immersion in the top posts of the Mexican public administration took place in 1988, when he was appointed budget secretary under his predecessor, President Carlos Salinas de Gortari. Indeed, since the 1970s, the budget and planning secretariat had become even more prominent than the treasury in furthering the careers of future technocrats (Centeno, 1994). Interestingly, although most conventional analyses stress the important role that local elites played in the recruitment of their own members, Babb (2005) argues that the rise of technocrats is also explained by external factors. After the breakdown of most Latin American economies and the increasing opening of their markets to foreign investors, international banking encouraged the recruitment of 'money doctors.' These were young public officials who were educated in the United States and understood how the financial system functioned. Their main goal was to help open local markets to the international economy. Inside the PRI, Zedillo was perceived as one of the main representatives of this new technocratic generation, with an impulse for the neoliberal reforms that involved the privatization of state-owned enterprises to stabilize the economy by reducing government debt. Equally important was his support in the design and negotiation of the North American Free Trade Agreement (NAFTA). From the perspective of the PRI's nationalistic old guard, neoliberalism was against the fundamentals of the party (López Portillo, 1988). In 1992, Salinas's cabinet was reshuffled and Zedillo was appointed Secretary of Education. In that position, he gained some political experience negotiating with the powerful teachers' union; however, he resigned one year later to join the presidential campaign.

In contrast to Zedillo's technical career, Calderón was raised to be a professional politician. Along with his father's support, his first steps as a 'party-man' were guided by key figures of the contemporary PAN: the spiritual leader Luis H. Alvarez, and the intellectual Carlos Castillo Peraza. He engaged in deep discussions with both and together they reflected on the party's mission, values, and doctrine, influencing their thoughts in official PAN documents (Camarena and Zepeda, 2007). Simultaneously, he traveled to different regions of the country in order to work with PAN's local representatives in strengthening the party. His intense party activism and commitment to the rank and file soon transformed him into one of PAN's youngest emblematic figures (Berman, 2006). Indeed, he was elected President of the National Executive Committee from 1996 to 1999, after being defeated in the Michoacan gubernatorial elections in 1995. The second notable feature of Calderón's political career is associated with his vast experience in the Mexican Congress during the stage in which the legislature gained momentum as an effective space for balancing the power of the executive. His career as a congressman started as a local deputy in the Mexico City Congress in 1988. Later, he was elected deputy in the National Congress from 1991 to 1994. During his time in office, he participated in the trade commission where NAFTA was negotiated. He returned to the same chamber from 2000 to 2003; however, on this occasion he occupied the influential position of party caucus leader. On the other hand, Felipe Calderón's career in Mexican public administration was ephemeral. It began when Vicente Fox won the 2000 presidential elections with PAN. Despite his prominent position within his party, unexpectedly, Calderón's first post was not in the cabinet; instead, he was appointed director of a state-owned development bank. After seven months, he managed to move to a ministerial position as Secretary of Energy, but he stayed there for only one year. Calderón gave up his post on the cabinet when he made public his intention to run for the presidency, without the backing of President Fox (Núñez, 2012).

PRI and PAN: Two Traditions of Party Influence

Zedillo and Calderón's interactions with their respective political parties were marked by times of closeness and distance. In perspective, it is possible to assert that both figures put considerable effort into professionalizing their parties' structures, modernizing their programs, and transforming their elites' conventional behavior.

In many respects, Zedillo represents an atypical case as a detached high-ranking member of the PRI. His party activism started just days before he won the presidential elections of 1994, during a conference organized to evaluate ideas to modernize the PRI. At that event, Zedillo made one of the most astonishing remarks ever expressed by a PRI presidential candidate. He suggested that party candidates should be selected through open primaries and therefore, once in government, the president should keep a 'healthy distance' from the party (Espinoza, 2004). Tensions between Zedillo and his party rose even more in December 1994, when he pressed PRI congressmen to vote for an unpopular 50% increase in the sales tax. A sign that Zedillo had set his mind on his party's democratization appeared early in 1995, when he compelled the PRI leadership to negotiate a major electoral reform with the opposition (PAN, PRD, and the Workers' Party, or PT). His aim was to set the grounds for a fairer and more credible electoral competition, but still-precarious conditions in the political and economic realms forced him to step back and seek his party's support again. He sent a message of reconciliation on the 66th anniversary of the PRI in which he ratified his political alliance with its elites (Zedillo, 1995). The political agreements for electoral reform succeeded in 1996 and one of the most positive outcomes was the creation of a new electoral body, free from the government's control and run for the first time by independent citizens. Yet the distance between the president and his party was not diminished. That same year, the PRI rank and file celebrated their 17th national assembly, in which they welcomed the changes to the electoral system, but also warned about the need to change the 'suffocating neoliberal economic model' (Valentin, 2012: 53). In 1997, the PRI experienced an electoral crisis that deeply discouraged their rank and file. Their party lost absolute control of the Chamber of Deputies, something they had relied on for many years. In parallel, PAN won the governorships of Querétaro and Nuevo León, and the PRD succeeded in Mexico City. While Zedillo perceived that Mexico for the first time achieved the real checks and balances that gave legitimacy to government, the party's old guard resented this and moved out of the president's sphere of influence by instituting a parallel structure within the PRI controlled by state governors (Rodríguez, 2003: 58–59). During the six years of Zedillo's administration, PRI had seven different party presidents; this situation was perceived as a symptom of confusion in the party's identity and ideology, as well as of Zedillo's elusive leadership. Lastly, despite his earlier reservations about meddling in the selection process for the PRI candidate to succeed him, he actively intervened in the design of the rules and mechanisms of this process. In the presidential elections of 2000, the PRI candidate lost for the first time in more than 70 years; this event is regarded as a key moment in the Mexican democratic transition.

In contrast to Zedillo, Felipe Calderón was an early party insider who had the opportunity to follow very closely the complex evolution experienced by PAN. In a few decades, PAN's status was transformed from that of a loyal opposition accepting the rules of the authoritarian establishment (Loaeza, 1974) to the party in government. Calderón's relation with PAN has fluctuated between periods of productive understanding and bitter disputes. Nevertheless, a combination of his family's heritage, his strong knowledge of the regional structures, and his ability to rise to the pinnacle of the party leadership before winning the Mexican presidency, gave him the prestige and moral authority to exert influence upon the party's elite. Felipe Calderón was elected PAN's general secretary in 1993, during the stage in which several of PAN's newly elected local administrations faced a steep learning curve as public policy-makers. He persuaded them of the relevance of avoiding the mistakes of mismanagement and corruption that had eroded the PRI's legitimacy (Vázquez, 2002). After running unsuccessfully in 1995 for the governorship of his home state, the next decisive step in his political career was the contest for PAN's executive post. A year later, Calderón beat the popular Ernesto Ruffo, PAN's first elected governor, in a rather elitist and centralized internal election (Reveles, 2004: 24). Once in the executive position, from 1996 to 1999, Calderón used the motto *Let's take the government, without losing the party* as an appeal to mark a difference in style of government with the PRI. Unfortunately for him, the electoral record of PAN during those years proved that his expectations were not totally attainable. The results of the legislative mid-term elections of 1997 were unsatisfactory, with PAN losing its position as the second party in terms of number of deputies: PAN's 122 seats left the party third, behind the PRD with 125. Furthermore his mentor, Carlos Castillo, obtained a disappointing 15.3% of votes cast in the strategic mayoralty election in Mexico City. Interviews with, and articles by, relevant members of PAN portrayed Calderón as a party leader who skillfully combined orthodoxy with pragmatism (Núñez, 2012: 40–41). In ideological terms, he tried to move the party toward the center on public policy issues and encouraged the professionalization of the party structure at all levels. Yet he was unable to cement the crack that ran through the party, splitting PAN between religious ultra-conservatives and ambitious entrepreneurial newcomers. In the presidential race, PAN headquarters backed the negative campaign arranged by Calderón's spin doctors that eventually damaged the huge popularity that the PRD's López Obrador had gained with the electorate (Portillo, 2012).

Zedillo and Calderón Cross Paths in Politics

Between 1996 and 1999, Zedillo and Calderón's political careers intersected in two events critical to contemporary Mexican politics. The first is related to the negotiation of the cornerstone electoral reform of 1996, and the second involved the enactment of a controversial law to rescue Mexican banks from bankruptcy. In those years, Ernesto Zedillo was president of Mexico and Felipe Calderón was national leader of PAN. The electoral reform of 1996 is considered a watershed in Mexican democratization, because it radically restructured the rules and institutions that had allowed the PRI to control the electoral process. Its main goal was to generate a new system of incentives to make political competition fairer, granting autonomy to the electoral authority and detaching it from the government (Becerra et al., 2000). The negotiation of this reform took approximately two years, and it is one of the few political actions to which Zedillo and his inner-circle dedicated special care and devotion. Even before being formally invested, Zedillo and his political team held informal meetings with the opposition parties to negotiate the bases of the reform. Furthermore, just days after starting his mandate, Zedillo twice visited the Chamber of Deputies and Senate to set the agenda for a broad political agreement with the caucus leaders of all parties represented in Congress (Garrido, 2011: 5). The substantive negotiation process, however, did not take place in Congress; instead, it was conducted by Zedillo's cabinet (specifically, the Secretary of the Interior) and all the party leaders, including Felipe Calderón. This circumstance prompted an intense interaction between both politicians. Zedillo needed the support of PAN's 'loyal opposition' at a time when even the PRI's ranks had turned against him. Calderón, on the other hand, benefited from the new relationship with the executive, empowering his party's position in the bargaining process and allowing him to include topics of strategic importance to his party in the electoral agenda. In November 1996, Zedillo came into ruthless confrontation with his party when, unexpectedly, all the PRI deputies unilaterally approved an electoral reform that excluded all agreements previously reached. PAN declared this action unconstitutional and took the case to the Supreme Court of Justice. Although Calderón publicly vindicated Zedillo and recognized that the PRI's machinery had bypassed the president, the two engaged in a bitter dispute in which both tried to defend their views about the gains and limits of the 1996 electoral reform (Vázquez, 2002: 91).

On the other hand, in 1994, the economic crisis left the Mexican financial system in a critical situation, and the majority of commercial banks lacked the funds to pay their external debts. Two years before finishing his mandate, President Zedillo expressed his concern about a potential new crisis and proposed to Congress a legal framework that involved a bailout program. Controversy arose when the executive declared the banks' loans *de facto* irrecoverable and insisted they be converted into public debt. According to Krueger and Tornell, the amount added up to 552 million US dollars, approximately 16% of Mexico's GDP that year (1999: 26). Colloquially this initiative took the name The Bank Fund for the Protection of Savings (FOBAPROA in Spanish). The proposal was highly unpopular and PAN's membership and congressmen publicly com-plained that the crisis was caused by corruption in the administration of the banks. Calderón, however, discretely bargained with Zedillo, offering the support of his party in exchange for the dismissal of the chief of the Central Bank. In the end, this petition did not succeed, but Calderón's leverage was crucial in obtaining enough votes in Congress to accept Zedillo's law (Camarena and Zepeda, 2007: 37–38).

Elections: Supporters and Opposition

The presidential elections of Zedillo in 1994 and Calderón in 2006 were intricate and controversial. Both involved critical moments of acute social tension and political instability that produced distinctive results. In the presidential election held on August 21, 1994, Ernesto Zedillo obtained 48.6% of the total votes, only two percentage points less than his predecessor Carlos Salinas had achieved in 1988. Yet, outstandingly, the turnout rate surpassed the former election's 66.9% and reached an historic 77.1%. Oddly, Zedillo was the first PRI presidential candidate to win with less than 50% of votes, but at the same time, his election generated the highest level of electoral participation in recent times (Calderón and Cazés, 1996). After Colosio's death, Zedillo was nominated presidential candidate through a stressful process of elimination among Salinas's inner-circle. He was chosen because the most popular members of this select group were unsuitable due to their contentious political backgrounds, or because their candidacies had legal impediments. Zedillo did not have a strong political grouping among the party elite, and his essential supporters were a few members of the small technocratic cabinet. Moreover, the PRI's traditional structure did not support his presidential campaign because, as the leader of the party at that time mentioned, 'there was a reciprocal lack of trust between the candidate and the party' (Pichardo, 2001: 80–81). His limited skills as a professional politician were evident throughout the campaign. In the first presidential debate broadcast by the mass media in May 1994, PAN's candidate, Diego Fernández, easily outperformed him. Neither did Zedillo have the charismatic legacy inherited by the PRD's candidate, Cuauhtémoc Cárdenas, son of the legendary president Lazaro Cárdenas. Instead his public image was rather perceived as 'low profile' (Romero, 2012: 98–101). Analytic accounts of the 1994 election agree that Zedillo's victory is largely explained by the context of political turmoil and social fear following Colosio's assassination and the Zapatista uprising (Ai Camp, 1996). Both events set the conditions for the PRI's electoral strategist to intensively promote a vote against instability and in favor of the *status quo*. In addition, a deceitful official campaign that stressed the capability of the economy enhanced Zedillo's public image as a good economist and administrator (Calderón and Cazés, 1996). The official results of the 1994 presidential elections ranked the PRI in first place with 48.6% of the votes, PAN in second with 25.9%, and the PRD third with 16.5%. Furthermore, the integrity of the election was generally deemed satisfactory and was not challenged. Key factors providing this election a positive image at home and abroad were PAN's up-front acceptance of its defeat, the absence of political violence, and the supportive report crafted by a mission of electoral observers from the United Nations who monitored and analyzed the Mexican elections for the first time (Manaut, 1996).

In contrast with Zedillo's path, Calderón's battle for the presidency was most troublesome. As with many politicians, the first big obstacle that he had to overcome was opposition inside his own party. He competed in a long and intricate primary election in which he had to defeat two powerful pre-candidates: Santiago Creel, the Secretary of Internal Affairs and President Fox's preferred contender, and Alberto Cárdenas, the former governor of Jalisco supported by the party's general secretary, Manuel Espino (Scherer, 2012). Against all odds, Calderón's ability to lobby the rank and file and his influence in the design of a three-stage primary election played in his favor, and he was selected as his party's presidential candidate with 52% of the votes. Although the presidential campaigns officially started in January 2006, two events had ignited the political competition months before. The first involved a total renewal of the councilors of the Federal Electoral Institute (IFE) that had penalized the PRI and PAN with huge fines for exceeding the limits on campaign spending in the 2000 election. The second incident was an acrimonious legal dispute between President Fox and the mayor of Mexico City, Andrés Manuel López Obrador. Fox attempted to bring López Obrador to court in order to end his ambition of running for the presidency. Ironically, this event largely benefited the latter's public image and he took an advantageous starting position as the PRD's incumbent candidate (Lawson and Moreno, 2007). Indeed, at the time PAN nominated Calderón, he was the least well known of the three presidential candidates (Ai Camp, 2011: 154). Calderón's campaign strategy to win the presidency was based on pragmatism. The first stage involved the arrangement of a negative campaign in the mass media that depicted López Obrador as a danger to Mexico (Beltrán, 2009). Its effectiveness helped to increase Calderón's advantage in the polls, although he received severe criticism for its deceitful nature (Volpi, 2006). Calderón also encouraged his party leadership and congressmen to support a law that benefited the two biggest television broadcasters in Mexico, Televisa and TV Azteca, by granting them the concession of the digital frequency spectrum free of charge. In exchange, both networks put him ahead in their polls and delayed the collection of payment for his advertising spots (Camarena and Zepeda, 2007). President Fox also strengthened Calderón's image by placing approximately 462 thousand television commercials three months before the election to suggest that Calderón represented the continuity of PAN's public policies (Reveles, 2007; Portillo, 2012). Finally, an important tactical mistake damaged López Obrador's popularity: he rejected the chance to participate in the first broadcast candidates' debate.

The election was held on Sunday July 2, 2006. That night, the president of IFE announced that the preliminary count system indicated that the difference between the two front-runners, Calderón and López Obrador, was smaller than their statistical margin of error; hence, it was too close to call. Four days later, after running the official district-based ballot counts, the same authority declared Felipe Calderón the winner, but the difference between him and López Obrador was extremely narrow. He obtained 35.8% of the total votes, and his adversary 35.3%. The PRD demanded a full recount of all ballots and its supporters organized a massive protest in the capital that triggered a long post-electoral conflict. On September 5, 2006, Felipe Calderón Hinojosa was declared president by the Federal Electoral Tribunal.

Zedillo and Calderón's Presidential Leaderships

Analyses of presidential leadership in transitional democracies consider the numerous components and traits embedded in the decision-making process used by the executive power (Linz, 1978). In Ai Camp's 1996 study of President Zedillo's first years in office, four viewpoints are explored: the process of making decisions; the manner in which decisions were communicated; the consistency with which decisions were implemented; and the commitment to the administration's policy goals (1996: 3). This preliminary evaluation suggests that Zedillo's economic policymaking showed a remarkable level of consistency through the early part of his administration. His administrative skills and his knowledge of the complex problems of the Mexican economy allowed him to make grounded decisions to stabilize the internal finances, although the communication of those policies—and of his decisions in general—was not always effective (ibid.: 3–4). Not surprisingly, it was in the political arena that Zedillo's leadership experienced the greatest setbacks.

The decentralization of presidential power and reinforcement of the rule of law stand out as the core ideas of the democratization pursued by Zedillo in politics. Evidence of his commitment to both goals is perceptible in his multiple attempts to place himself above party politics. Neutrality in policymaking, however, was unattainable in the changing context of his administration and, ironically, led him to exercise his presidential influence in an erratic fashion and with a discretionary legal framework (Rodríguez, 2003). The president had to intervene in political crises surrounding the resignation of the governors of Chiapas, Guerrero, and Nuevo León from 1994 to 1996. An episode that clearly illustrates the major weakness of Zedillo's leadership was the 1994 conflict that unfolded after the gubernatorial election in the southern state of Tabasco. The PRD pressed the president to remove the elected PRI governor, Roberto Madrazo, charging him with exceeding the limits of campaign expenditure. At that time, Zedillo was keen on the participation of the left in electoral reform negotiations and therefore agreed to use his influence with the local congressmen of Tabasco to force the governor to give up office. In response, the local PRI elite defended their candidate using legal channels—that Zedillo forcefully opposed—and appealed to the Supreme Court. As a result, a further investigation was dismissed and the president lost the case (Eisenstadt, 1999; Rodríguez, 2003).

Like Zedillo, Felipe Calderón faced great leadership challenges at the beginning of his administration. The style of his decision making was shaped by two quite distinctive characteristics. First, he sought to retain the support of the structure and resources of his party, creating his own group inside the PAN and influencing the appointment of national and local party leaders close to his inner-circle. Second, he invested in a strong strategy of mass media advertising in order to legitimize key policies in the eyes of the public. Retrospectively, it is possible to observe a consistent pattern in Calderón's administrative priorities. In the early years of his mandate, 2006 and 2007, he focused on the implementation of social policies like the expansion of health benefits and actions to decrease unemployment. During 2008 and 2009, his main concern was to tackle the effects of the international financial crisis and control the spread of H1N1 swine flu. In 2010 and 2011, the war on drugs reached its climax. Finally, in 2012, he worked on securing political and economic stability in order to assure PAN's continuity in power (Núñez, 2012).

Coincidentally with Zedillo, Calderón was consistent in his management of the Mexican economy. He performed timely and decisive actions reasonably well compared to the leaders of other middle-income nations struggling with a global economic downturn. He coordinated his cabinet to operate different areas of the financial system, restore the normal functioning of the market, and reduce exchange rate volatility (Sidaoui et al., 2010: 296–297). In political terms, Calderón expended time and effort in endorsing several legislative reforms. He holds the record for being the president who amended the most articles of the Constitution since 1917, with 110 articles modified. (He is followed in second place by Ernesto Zedillo, who modified 77.) Some of the most notable amendments involved new rules in the electoral system, the expansion of judicial proceedings for lawsuits allowing citizens to defend themselves against authorities, and stronger human rights. Yet the quintessential policy that overshadowed all Calderón's policies was, without a doubt, the fight against organized crime and the drug cartels.

Analyses of Calderón's decision-making process during the war on drugs agree that his personal leadership style had a great influence on the outcomes. For his detractors, his security policy was originally mismanaged because it lacked strategic planning, resources, and intelligence. Moreover, it has been argued that its main purpose was to restore Calderón's legitimacy after the post-electoral conflict and to gain public support (Aguilar and Castañeda, 2010). Others, however, have argued that under the circumstances of a dramatic deterioration of public security, the weakness of the rule of law, and corruption in the police corps inherited from former administrations, the most feasible option was direct confrontation with the drug cartels despite the high political cost incurred (Chabat, 2010). In 2010, the Mexican government reported that, from December 2006, violence related to drug trafficking had caused more than 28,000 deaths. A group of lawyers and citizens considered that Calderón's war on drugs was a crime against humanity and took the case to the International Court of Justice in The Hague. Calderón's unpopular management of the war on drugs appears to be explained in a letter written by Calderón's political mentor and close friend, Carlos Castillo Peraza, in 1996. He underscored Calderón's struggle to delegate responsibilities to his work-team when he was the National President of PAN. Peraza warned that Calderón's controlling and distrustful nature could deprive him of the support of others, and that he could become isolated doing the job by himself (Peraza, 1996).

Strategies toward the Mainstream Mass Media

Zedillo and Calderón adopted different approaches in their social communication strategies during their respective administrations. Nevertheless, they were both well aware of the relevance of public image in modern politics and therefore kept the mainstream mass media strategically close. This was particularly true for Televisa, the main television broadcast enterprise with the highest audience ratings in Mexico.

In a speech made on Freedom Day in July 1996, President Zedillo publicly articulated a major thesis that guided the relationship of his government with the mass media. He elaborated on the idea that the state should guarantee the basic principle of freedom of information, but at the same time, it should give broadcasting companies the liberty to be regulated by themselves and by the market. Zedillo argued that the audience should not intervene in determining ethical standards, but that it was the companies who should exhibit social responsibility and increase their quality (Trejo, 1997). Zedillo opened a new period of duopoly in the telecommunication sector, epitomized by the powerful titans Televisa and TV Azteca. Zedillo valued the favorable coverage of his presidential campaign by Televisa and at the onset of his administration dedicated special attention to creating a strategic alliance with the company. He participated in a personal and direct way in the consolidation of Televisa as one of the most powerful telecommunication groups in Mexico. Senior officials resigned from his cabinet in order to work with Televisa to clear a significant debt acquired before the death of its founder. Zedillo also used his influence in the financial sector to increase the value of the company's shares and promoted diversification into new markets (Villamil, 2012: 66–68). During Zedillo's mandate, the television broadcaster was reticent about questioning the president's actions or covering scandals such as the events of 1995 in Aguas Blancas, Guerrero, where 17 peasants were assassinated.

Likewise, Calderón pursued a strategic relationship with the owners of the big television enterprises. This started when he was caucus leader of his party in the National Congress and supported a controversial law that favored Televisa's interests. As president, however, Calderón faced new dilemmas that required special support and engagement from the mainstream mass media. He struggled in particular with continual criticism and condemnation from civil organizations about the war on drugs. The president also publicly complained that organized crime activities were more publicized than the government's achievements in eradicating them. In 2010, Calderón was forced to recognize that his own communication strategy had weaknesses because it created confusion and the audience simply did not understand the main goal of his government's security policy (Calderón, 2010). One year later, Televisa and TV Azteca called for the signing of an agreement with smaller media companies to encourage objective coverage of the war on drugs, to avoid interfering in government-led special operations, and to stop interviewing criminals. Finally, it was estimated that, during 2009, the administration of Felipe Calderón spent 501% more on social communication than had been spent by President Fox in the last year of his government (Fundar, 2012).

Performance in Opinion Polls Over Time

Since the late 1980s, opinion polls have proliferated as an instrument for assessing the public image and performance of Mexican presidents. It is noticeable that, in most cases, the state of the economy has been the key issue that directly affects the public perception of presidents. Yet some shocking political events, like corruption scandals, natural disasters, or crimes have proved to have an impact on short-term evaluations (Beltrán, 2009).

Systematic information about Zedillo's public image and performance was collected from two main sources. The first was a technical unit inside the Office of the Presidency that conducted a periodic survey assessing the levels of approval for public policies. The second was the newspaper *Reforma*, which periodically published a study of the president's performance during his six years in office.

A compilation and analysis of the data obtained from both sources indicates that, at the beginning of Zedillo's administration in August 1994, Mexicans generally approved of his mandate; however, in December of the same year his popularity dropped dramatically (Romero, 2012). The most compelling explanation for this change is the criticism leveled at him after he decided to devalue the Mexican peso. Indeed, Zedillo's management of the financial emergency was publicly denounced by former President Salinas as 'the December mistake.' In the end, the escalation of the economic crisis had a powerful effect on both public opinion and living standards. Zedillo reached his lowest point of popularity in May 1995, when just 39% of the public approved of him. Nevertheless, the perception of Zedillo's government had a clear correlation with the state of the economy throughout his administration. When certain macroeconomic indicators like the Gross Domestic Product, inflation, and employment gradually improved, approval for his government increased at much the same pace. In that respect, his popularity rose to 43%, in 1996 to 55% in 1997, to 58% in 1998, and to 62% in the last full year of his mandate, 1999 (Romero, 2012: 39). Over the six years of Zedillo's administration, his public approval averaged approximately 55%—worse than Carlos Salinas's 73%, Vicente Fox's 58%, and Felipe Calderón's 57% (Campos, 2012: 3).

In contrast to Zedillo's experience, Calderón's performance was closely monitored by several private pollsters. Using information from Consulta Mitofsky, Parametría, Buen Día y Laredo, BGC, Ulises Beltrán, and Asocs-Excélsior, it is possible to follow the evolution in public opinion from 2006 to 2012. In spite of the political crisis experienced in the aftermath of the 2006 elections, Felipe Calderón started his mandate implementing a novel public security strategy that involved deploying the military to fight organized crime. This decision gained the support of society; hence, it translated into good evaluations during his two first years in government. His early approval ratings fluctuated between

58% and 61%, but in August 2007 he reached a high point, with support for his administration at 68% (Beltrán and Cruz, 2012; Campos, 2012; Parametría 2012). In 2009, the president's popularity started to decrease, from 65% to 61%. This loss was explained by the increasing number of civilian casualties and an alarming number of 'disappeared' people due to the war on drugs. In that year, the international financial crisis, and the resultant contraction of the US economy, also had an impact on Mexico. Moreover, in October 2009 the president managed to close the public enterprise that had historically provided electricity to the country, sparking a backlash from members of the powerful electricians union who demonstrated for several days in the main boulevards of Mexico City (Buen Día and Laredo, 2012). In 2010 and 2011, pollsters disagreed on Calderón's popularity. Mitofsky indicated a level of approval of approximately 54% to 51%; Buen Día and Laredo, 56% to 54%; and Parametría, 65% to 66%. During that time the public focused on the outcome of policies towards organized crime and public security.

The increase in violence and the inestimable number of deaths deeply perturbed Mexicans. Social policies on health and education were well evaluated, but overall they were overshadowed by the public's perception of insecurity. Finally, Mitofsky reports that at the end of Calderón's mandate he obtained a 50% approval rating. This represented a loss of almost 11 percentage points since 2006. Indeed, Calderón's last year of government was evaluated as worse than the final year of all his three predecessors (Campos, 2012: 16).

Cabinet Formation in Each Government

The relationship between Mexican presidents and their cabinets had been shaped by the peculiarity of three specific institutional features of the political system: the presidency's six-year fixed term; the ban on re-election; and the lack of a vice-president (Weldon, 1997). Although Mexican presidents tend to enjoy considerable autonomy in decision-making, they greatly rely upon the loyalty and competence of their team in the operation of the complex bureaucratic apparatus. Analysis of the formation of Zedillo's and Calderón's cabinets indicates that both presidents were inclined to appoint to the most important posts officials who mirrored their own managerial and professional styles (Alcántara, 2006).

Zedillo showed a clear preference for officials with an academic background in economics, educated abroad, and with experience in economic institutions and agencies like the Mexican Central Bank (Ai Camp, 1995). The ministries of finance, industry, and energy were headed by well-known technocrats. Most of these accumulated cabinet experience in the administration of Carlos Salinas and shared a neoliberal perspective (Rodríguez, 2003).

Zedillo's officials in political positions within the cabinet had a PRI affiliation; however, the tense dynamic of the relationship between the president and his party impacted upon the number of reshuffles experienced in the ministries of the interior and labor (Ai Camp, 1995). Interestingly, Zedillo adopted some innovations in the formation of his cabinet when he appointed a prominent member of PAN to the influential post of Attorney General. This position was critical in sorting out important issues in order to restore trust in Mexican justice. He also included three women in his cabinet, something that was uncommon in previous administrations.

In sharp contrast with Zedillo, Calderón looked primarily to put together a cabinet of renowned members of PAN, each of whom had a good experience of politics—like himself. He predominantly operated his political agenda in coordination with the secretaries of the interior, education, and social development. Most of the individuals who occupied those posts had accumulated experience in PAN's local governments, and some had held relevant positions in Vicente Fox's bureaucracy. Unusually, Calderón also appointed young people from his inner-circle to very important positions in the executive branch. Most of them were part of a group that had worked on his political campaign and had almost no experience of politics or public administration. Probably the most representative figure in this group was his first Secretary of the Interior, Juan Camilo Mouriño. In public interviews, Calderón explained his reasoning by citing a phrase coined by the Czech politician Václav Havel: 'I prefer temporary inexperience over permanent sabotage' (Núñez, 2012).

Overall, Calderón proved to be interested in expanding the professionalization and specialization of PAN's rank and file in public administration at the national level. To this end, he recruited salient local figures from the party that had supported his presidential candidacy during the disputed primaries (Rodríguez, 2011). For economic posts, Calderón was inclined to select independent figures with solid careers in international organizations. To date, Calderón remains the president who appointed the most women to his cabinet, seven in total. Some were appointed to key positions like the ministries of education, energy, foreign affairs, and the post of Attorney General. During his administration, 14 ministries out of 19 were reshuffled at least once. Notably, the ministry of the interior achieved a record number of changes with the substitution of seven ministers, two of which were necessitated by the tragic death of the incumbent in separate airplane accidents.

The Role of the Head of State

The constitutional nature of Latin American presidential systems makes it particularly difficult to differentiate between the roles of the head of state as symbol of the nation and effective chief executive, and as partisan leader fighting to promote his party and its programs (Linz, 1990: 61). In this dilemma, Zedillo and Calderón took different stances based on their own circumstances and personalities. The biographies of both leaders indicate that, whereas Zedillo truly tried to adopt an autonomous style of government beyond the PRI, Calderón was less inclined to do so. Zedillo had the advantage of lacking a close attachment to his party, with his entire career built in the economic bureaucracy. In contrast to the tradition of PRI rulers, his political method of governing was regarded as discrete, inconspicuous, and simple. In his personal analysis on Zedillo's style of government, the historian Enrique Krauze (2000) concluded that he was not an imperial president; rather, he was a republican president. Interestingly, Zedillo did not exercise ostentatious ceremonial powers, either inside the country or abroad. He preferred to hold low-profile negotiations with different political actors who supported his initiatives and helped him achieve his goals. In international affairs, his personality was logical and practical. This aspect created an aura of responsibility that contrasted with conventional Latin American leaders and helped him in relations with the United States and Canada (Covarruvias, 1996).

In sharp contrast with his flamboyant predecessor, President Calderón wisely cultivated a style that highlighted traditional family values, thrift, and philanthropy (Camarena and Zepeda, 2007: 45). Nevertheless, his professional background as a party-man, and the absorption of many party members into his administration, made it difficult for him to act as an unbiased head of state. Being the underdog in different episodes of his political career engendered in his personality an attitude of pride and resilience that affected both his attitude towards power and his management style. As president, Calderón was inclined to exercise a centralized decision-making process, relying on allies in his political party and his inner-circle, rather than negotiating.

Constitutional Reforms and Bargaining with Congress

Until 1982, the Mexican Congress had a minor influence on decision-making, as every PRI president elected since the early twentieth century had enjoyed the support of more than two-thirds of the politicians in both chambers. In a presidential system, one of the most meaningful aspects in the relation between the executive and the legislative branch is related with legislatures' entitlement to support or reject the president's bills on public policies (Tsebelis, 1995). In this regard, as Casar (2008) suggests, presidents from the PRI were historically the biggest legislators, as they were able to introduce a considerable number of bills with almost 97% acceptance.

The result of the 1997 mid-term elections meant that, during the second half of Zedillo's administration, a PRI president was for the first time faced with a legislature in which other parties held a majority of seats in the lower house, although the PRI retained 59% of seats in the Senate. The new configuration of the legislative branch allowed these other parties to gain leverage in the bargaining process and promote their political agendas. At the same time, the potential for gridlock threatened Zedillo's ability to win timely approval for key proposals.

Across the six years of his mandate, 84% of the 92 bills sponsored by the president were approved and four were pending on resolution. Remarkably, a new tax policy and energy reform, two issues of strategic importance, were rejected. This is largely explained by the creation of a temporary coalition of four parties—PAN, the PRD, the Green Party, and the Labor Party—that teamed up to vote against the president's bills. This coalition also forced him to give up some posts in influential commissions of the Chamber of Deputies and the cabinet (Casar, 2013: 234).

It is worth mentioning that the formation of opposition coalitions was not a common practice in Mexico, and cooperation levels between Mexican presidents and opposition parties used to be reasonably high (Nacif, 2004). Even under circumstances of tension and political pressure, Zedillo had the margin to cooperate with his political adversaries. Arguably, for that reason, he did not once exercise his power of veto during his entire mandate (Weldon, 2004).

In contrast to Zedillo, Felipe Calderón experienced a strained relationship with the legislative branch. He is the only president who was unable to perform his inaugural speech in the Chamber of Deputies, due to the disruptive atmosphere generated by left-wing legislators who challenged him over the electoral results of 2006. Furthermore, during the six years of his mandate, he returned to that venue only to attend the official ceremony in which he transferred power to his successor. Arithmetically, Calderón faced a situation of divided government in which his party needed the votes of other parties to obtain a majority. In the first half of his administration, PAN legislators represented a plurality in both chambers of the XV legislature (2006–2009), with 41% of seats. However, during the XVI legislature (2009–2012), the party's presence in the Chamber of Deputies shrank dramatically, to 29% of seats, although it retained its 41% share in the Senate (Casar, 2013). In six years, Calderón sponsored 92 bills. Forty-nine were sent to the Senate and 43 were received by the Chamber of Deputies. In order to take advantage of the slight advantage of his party in Congress, 63% of these bills were released during the first half of his mandate. The president's bills had an approval rate of 64% (59 out of 92). Surprisingly, however, 24 bills experienced a sort of paralysis: the opposition parties deliberately stopped their discussion and, therefore, they were not voted on. Finally, seven bills were left pending on revision, and two were rejected (RRC, 2012).

In qualitative terms, Calderón was able to influence public policies through Congress in specific matters like the creation of new taxes, the promotion of a new pension law for civil servants, laws modernizing the police and the office of the Attorney General, and changes to the Mexican Constitution to address the shortcomings of the 2006 elections via electoral reform. Nevertheless, regarding other substantive issue such as the anti-monopoly law, energy reform, and the labor law, the president's bills became the object of deep amendments by the opposition parties, and their final contents were far from the original purposes envisioned by Calderón. A sensitive issue like the modernization of the telecommunication sector was not even presented for discussion in Congress, because the president's advisors judged that it would not be approved (Magar and Romero, 2008). It is also remarkable that Felipe Calderón used his veto power against congressional bills 16 times between 2010 and 2012 (Casar, 2013: 246). Some aspects rejected by the president were associated with new rules for fighting organized crime, and regulating the prosecution of criminal offenses— rules he deemed incompatible with his own strategy. The Senate fought back and presented six constitutional controversies to the Supreme Court of Justice in order to challenge some of the president's vetoes, notably Calderón's decision to close the state electricity company and delays in the enactment of a law protecting the human rights of victims of violent crime.

Judicial Reform

The process of strengthening the Mexican judiciary had begun in 1987 under President Miguel de la Madrid. He recognized that the judicial sector was far weaker than either the executive or the legislature, and it was necessary to address the prevailing lack of strength in the administration of law and order (Fix-Fierro, 2003). Looking at the most emblematic policies implemented by the last five administrations, it is remarkable that the most comprehensive reforms to the judicial sector were undertaken during Zedillo and Calderón's presidencies. Although the reforms were conceived and implemented under different political circumstances, they seem to respond to the same strategic imperative—ultimately to legitimize presidential rule in a context marked by political competition and a discredited Supreme Court (Inclán, 2009).

In his inaugural speech, Ernesto Zedillo forcefully expressed an interest in having a strong, independent, and efficient judiciary. In December 1994, he submitted to the Senate an initiative to change articles of the Mexican constitution related with the prosecution of crime and the administration of justice. The major change, however, involved a total restructuring of the membership of the Supreme Court. His reform prompted the resignation of 26 magistrates, who were replaced by 11 new ones. Moreover, in keeping with his idea to decentralize executive power, he proposed that members of the Supreme Court nominated by the president be approved by a qualified majority in the Senate. The reform also gave the court the capacity to rule on constitutional matters that allow the executive and legislative branches at the federal and local level, as well as political parties, to challenge the constitutionality of legislation or other government actions. Finally, in an attempt to make the judicial branch accountable, a new oversight mechanism was created, known as the Federal Judicial Council (Consejo de la Judicatura Federal). Its main goal was to monitor the actions and administrative activities of all tribunals at all levels, with the exception of the Supreme Court and the Electoral Tribunal (Ruíz and Rocha, 2012: 20–21). Zedillo's judicial reform was approved with minor changes and enacted in less than 30 days, just weeks after he took power. In Congress, PAN supported the president's action, but the PRD criticized the fast-track method by which the reform had been processed. In general terms, it was perceived that, although the reform was a brave assault on corruption and mismanagement, in the end the president contradicted his principle of non-intervention by using his fiat power to purge judges and personnel from the judicial branch at will (Ai Camp, 1996: 4).

Felipe Calderón also advocated for deep change in the Mexican judicial sector. His interest in a modern and efficient system of crime prosecution and administration of justice was an intrinsic part of the new framework of public security envisioned by his government (Chabat, 2010). His reform is regarded as a wide-ranging transformation of the Mexican judicial system, because it covers all the key actors and procedures embedded therein: the police, prosecutors, public defense lawyers, the courts, the penitentiary system, criminal procedures, access to justice, law enforcement and public security agencies in the administration of justice, and punishments against organized crime (Shirk, 2010: 205). In terms of the most salient topics of the 2008 reform, the introduction of 'oral trials' stands out as an innovation intended to increase the procedural efficiency of criminal courts and achieve restorative justice. Under the new model, prosecutors present their evidence in live oral hearings, and, if required, damages are paid. The controversial topic of the presumption of innocence was also addressed. In this regard, the reform strengthened the system of guarantees protecting the rights of the accused with specific measures like enhancing the quality of the legal defense, or banning torture. Notably, the reform also looked to integrate the police into the administration of justice, giving them the capacity to help prosecutors, judges, and defense attorneys. Furthermore, the acute concern of Felipe Calderón about the increasing power of organized crime syndicates and drug cartels was tackled with the introduction of new rules and procedures that involved tougher punishments against them. For example, in the case of serious crimes, the new legislation included provision for solitary confinement in special detention centers. Although the Mexican Congress and the 32 local legislatures of Mexico enacted the bill with the constitutional amendments on June 18, 2008, the federal and state governments were given a period of up to eight years to adopt the new legislation (Shirk, 2010).

Conclusions

Zedillo and Calderón were two political figures with a similar social upbringing but very different professional backgrounds and political careers, who coincided in the acute challenge of running a country immersed in a rapid and chaotic transition. Although both presidents faced the adversity of starting their mandates amid political turmoil and economic instability, each handled the crisis with a very distinctive style. Their psychological traits, the mutating sociopolitical context, and the rise of new rules and institutions combined to leave distinctive marks on various aspects of the Mexican political system.

Driven by the aspirational energy of their middle-class origins, Zedillo and Calderón both overcame the barriers of class and achieved social mobility, working on the professionalization of their respective careers. Zedillo embodied the generation of the pragmatic technocrat, educated to understand the complexity of the underlying principles of economics and their effects on public administration. Calderón laid his own path, accumulating practical experience in hardcore politics and refining his skills as a civil servant. Yet the distance that separates these personalities arises from differences between their core political foundations. Ernesto Zedillo enjoyed considerable political autonomy because he did not belong to the PRI's elite. Moreover, he had to look for external alliances that included exceptional negotiations with opposition parties in order to advance his political agenda. However, his unexpected nomination as a presidential candidate, and his lack of experience in party politics, deprived him of the chance to consolidate his control over the PRI's massive structure. Conversely, Felipe Calderón constructed his entire political career within PAN. His comprehensive knowledge of the internal functioning of that party, and his ascent through the ranks of local leaders and delegates in Mexico, provided him the bedrock for consolidating a successful and meteoric career. Notably, Calderón did not trust the volatile elite of his party; instead, he empowered his own group inside PAN to fight for control over influential posts. Ironically, the elections of both presidents were marked by exceptional and distressing conditions. In the case of Zedillo, the key concerns were the context of political and economic agitation generated by the assassinations of top politicians, the Zapatista uprising, and the financial crisis. For Calderón, the main challenge was to deal with one of the longest and most contentious post-electoral conflicts in the contemporary history of Mexico.

In terms of their leadership styles, it is noticeable that Zedillo overrode the ritualistic style of the former 'imperial' presidents. Once in executive power, he operated the state with the methodical orthodoxy of a bureaucratic mind. Yet, probably because of his distant personality, he was not a popular figure and his public image was evaluated with low scores at the end of his mandate. Interestingly, although Calderón also avoided ostentation, he deliberately invested in an expensive and intense strategy of mass media advertising to gain legitimacy for his public policies. He concentrated especially on the achievements of his government in the war on drugs. Both presidents seemed aware of the effect of public opinion on their governments' credibility and therefore maintained a close and cautious relationship with the biggest television broadcasters in Mexico, Televisa and TV Azteca.

Finally, Zedillo and Calderón shared the experience of dealing with a new system of checks and balances and political pluralism that radically transformed the relationship of the executive with the legislative and judicial branches. In an era of divided governments, both Mexican presidents were forced to negotiate key structural reforms with opposing parties. Whereas Zedillo was able to uphold a satisfactory interchange with Congress during his entire mandate, Calderón suffered a tense and belligerent relationship with the legislature in the second half of his administration. Some of the most important bills endorsed by his government were blocked or transformed during the legislative bargaining process. Likewise, Calderón used his veto power to stop certain opposition bills from making it into law. The Supreme Court had to intervene on more than one occasion to resolve constitutional disputes between the executive and legislative branches.

It is worth noting that both presidents were also interested in the modernization of the judicial branch. In their respective mandates they transformed the structure of the judiciary and enacted new laws to make the administration of justice more efficient. Nevertheless, the number of affairs related to rampant corruption in the private and public spheres, and the record of unsolved cases of human rights abuses accumulated in the last 20 years, reveal shortcomings in the Mexican political system that persist to this day.

References

Aguilar, R. and Castañeda, J. (2010). *El narco: la guerra fallida*. Mexico: Punto de lectura.
Ai Camp, R. (1995). The Zedillo Cabinet: Continuity, change, or revolution? *Series Electoral Studies in the Western Hemisphere*, CSIS Americas Program.
Ai Camp, R. (1996). The Zedillo legacy in Mexico. *Policy Papers on the Americas*, 7(6), CSIS Americas Program.
Ai Camp, R. (2011). *Mexico: What everyone needs to know*. Oxford: Oxford University Press.
Ai Camp, R. (2013). *Political recruitment across two centuries: Mexico, 1884–1991*. Texas: University of Texas Press.
Alcántara, M. (2006). *Políticos y política en América Latina*. Madrid: Siglo XXI
Babb, S. (2005). *Del nacionalismo al neoliberalismo: el ascenso de los nuevos Money Doctors en México. Políticas de economía, ambiente y sociedad en tiempos de globalización*. Caracas: Facultad de Ciencias Económicas y Sociales, Universidad Central de Venezuela, 155–172.
Becerra, R., Salazar, P., and Woldenberg, J. (2000). *La mecánica del cambio político en México. Elecciones, partidos y reformas*. Mexico: Cal y Arena.
Beltrán, U. (2009). El proceso electoral: Precampañas, campañas y resultado. *Política y Gobierno*, (1), 5–39.
Beltrán, U. and Cruz, A. (2012). *Encuesta Nacional de Vivienda*. BGC-Excelsior, November. Retrieved from: www.excelsior.com.mx/2012/11/12/nacional/869245.
Berman, S. (2006). Felipe Calderón, las tribulaciones de la fe. *Letras Libres*, 90, 29–38.
Bruhn, K. and Greene, K. (2007). Elite polarization meets mass moderation in Mexico's 2006 elections. *Political Science and Politics*, 40(1), 33–85.
Buen Día y Laredo (2012) *Encuesta Nacional*, November.
Calderón, F. (2006). *El hijo desobediente: notas en campaña*. Mexico: Aguilar.
Calderón, F. (2010). *Diálogos por la Seguridad hacia una Política de Estado*. Mexico: Presidencia de la República.
Calderón, F. and Cazés, D. (1996). *Las elecciones presidenciales de 1994 (Vol. 1)*. Mexico: UNAM.
Camarena, S. and Zepeda, J. (2007). *El Presidente electo*. Mexico: Planeta.
Campos, R. (2012). *México evaluación final del gobierno: Felipe Calderón 2006–2012*. Consulta Mitofsky, November.
Carpizo, J. (2002). *El presidencialismo mexicano*. Mexico: Siglo XXI.
Casar, M.A. (2008). Los gobiernos sin mayoría en México: 1997–2006. *Política y Gobierno*, 15(2), 221–270.
Casar, M.A. (2013). Quince años de gobiernos sin mayoría en el Congreso mexicano. *Política y Gobierno*, 20(2), 219–263.
Centeno, M. (1994). *Democracy within reason: Technocratic revolution in Mexico*. Penn State: Penn State University Press.
Chabat, J. (2010). Combatting drugs in Mexico under Calderón: The inevitable war. *Documentos de Trabajo*, 205, CIDE.

Covarruvias, A. (1996). *México: crisis y política exterior*. Mexico: Foro Internacional, 477–497.
Eisenstadt, T.A. (1999). Electoral federalism or abdication of presidential authority? Gubernatorial elections in Tabasco. In: Cornelius, W. et al. (eds), *Subnational politics and democratization in Mexico*. San Diego: Universidad de California, 269–293.
Espinoza, R (2004). *El PRI en 1995. El año del desencuentro*. Retrieved from: http://biblio.juridicas.unam.mx/libros/4/1762/25.pdf
Estrada, L. and Poiré, A. (2007). Learning to lose, taught to protest: Mexico's 2006 election. *Journal of Democracy*, 18(1), 73–87.
Fix-Fierro, H. (2003). La reforma judicial en México: ¿De dónde viene?¿Hacia dónde va? *Reforma Judicial: Revista Mexicana de Justicia*, 2, 251–324.
Fundar (2012). *Gasto del Gobierno en Publicidad*. Retreived from http://fundar.org.mx/mexico/pdf/presupuestofederal.pdf
Garrido, S. (2011) *Eroded unity and clientel migration: An alternative explanation of Mexico's democratic transition*. Paper presented at the annual meeting of the Midwest Political Science Association, April.
Inclán, S. (2009). Judicial reform in Mexico: Political insurance or the search for political legitimacy? *Political Research Quarterly*, 62(4), 753–766.
Krauze, E. (2000). El estilo personal de Ernesto Zedillo, *Reforma*, 3 November. Retrieved from: www.enriquekrauze.com.mx/joomla/index.php/biogr-retrato/90-biogra-critica-politica/360-estilo-personal-ernesto-zedillo.html.
Krueger, A. and Tornell, A. (1999). *The role of bank restructuring in recovering from crises: Mexico 1995–98, w7042*. National Bureau of Economic Research.
Lawson, C. and Moreno, A. (2007). El estudio panel México 2006: Midiendo el cambio de opiniones durante la campaña presidencial. *Política y Gobierno*, 14(2), 437–465.
Linz, J.J. (1978). *The breakdown of democratic regimes, Latin America*. Baltimore: Johns Hopkins University Press.
Linz, J.J. (1990). The perils of presidentialism. *Journal of Democracy*, 1(1), 51–69.
Loaeza, S. (1974). *El Partido Acción Nacional: la oposición leal en México*. Mexico: Foro Internacional, 352–374.
López-Portillo, J. (1988). *Mis tiempos, biografía y testimonio político*. Mexico: Fernández Editores.
Lustig, N. (1995). *The Mexican Peso crisis: The foreseeable and the surprise*. Washington: Brookings Institution.
Magar, E. and Romero, V. (2008). México: Reformas pese a un gobierno dividido. *Revista de Ciencia Política, Santiago*, 28(1), 265–285.
Manaut, R.B. (1996). *La ONU en México. Elecciones presidenciales de 1994*. Mexico: Foro Internacional, 533–565.
Nacif, B. (2004). Las relaciones entre los poderes ejecutivo y legislativo tras el fin del presidencialismo en México. *Política y Gobierno*, 11(1), 9–42.
Núñez, E. (2012). *Crónica de un sexenio fallido*. New York: Random House Mondadori.
Parametría (2012). *Evaluación del Presidente Calderón*. Encuesta Nacional de viviendas, Octubre y Noviembre.
Peraza, C. (1996). Letter to Felipe Calderón, published in *Etcetera*, 2009, July 22. Retrieved from: www.etcetera.com.mx/articulo.php?articulo=827
Pichardo, I. (2001). *Triunfos y traiciones en México*. Mexico: Océano.
Portillo, M. (2012). Campañas negativas y preferencias electorales: el caso de las elecciones presidenciales de México en 2006. *Razón y Palabra*, 17(79).

Presidencia de la República (1998). Cuarto Informe de Gobierno. Mexico.
Reveles, F. (2004). La coalición dominante en el Partido Acción Nacional: líderes, parlamentarios y gobernantes. In: Mirón, R and Espinoza, R. (eds), *Partidos políticos. Nuevos liderazgos y relaciones internas de autoridad*. Mexico: UAM-IIJ/UNAM/AMEP.
Reveles, F. (2007) El sistema de partidos y el Presidente de la República: Relaciones e interacciones. In: Peschard, J. (ed.), *Dos de Julio: Reflexiones y alternativas*. Mexico: FCPyS-UNAM.
Rodríguez, R.H. (2003). *Ernesto Zedillo. La presidencia contenida*. Mexico: Foro Internacional, 39–70.
Rodríguez, R.H. (2011). *¿Aprende a gobernar la oposición? Los gabinetes presidenciales del PAN, 2000–2010*. Mexico: Foro Internacional, 68–103.
Romero, V. (2012). *Impacto de la evaluación de políticas públicas en la aprobación presidencial*. Tesis de Maestría en Políticas Públicas. Instituto Tecnológico Autónomo de México.
RRC, Red por la Rendición de Cuentas (2012). *El paso de las iniciativas de Calderón por el Congreso*, December 6. Retrieved from: http://rendiciondecuentas.org.mx/el-paso-de-las-iniciativas-de-calderon-por-el-congreso/.
Ruíz, G. and Rocha, A. (2012). La reforma al Poder Judicial de 1994, ¿un golpe de Estado? *El Cotidiano*, Marzo-Abril, UAM.
Santaella, J. (1998). *Economic growth in Mexico: Searching for clues to its slowdown*. Document prepared for the Inter-American Development Bank, December.
Scherer, J. (2012). *Calderón de cuerpo entero*. New York: Random House Mondadori.
Shirk, D. (2010). Justice reform in Mexico: Change and challenges in the judicial sector. In: Olson, E., Shirk, D, and Selee, A. (eds.) *Shared responsibility: US-Mexico policy options for confronting organized crime*. Washington: Woodrow Wilson International Center for Scholars, Mexico Institute.
Sidaoui, J., Ramos-Francia, M., and Cuadra, G. (2010). The global financial crisis and policy response in Mexico. *BIS Papers No, 54*, 279–298.
Trejo, R. (1997). *Volver a los Medios: de la Crítica a la Ética*. Mexico: Cal y Arena.
Tsebelis, G. (1995). Decision making in political systems: Veto players in presidentialism, parliamentarism, multicameralism, and multipartyism. *British Journal of Political Science*, 25 (3).
Valentín, R. (2012). El proyecto político de Ernesto Zedillo y su relación con el PRI. *El Cotidiano*, 172, 52–59.
Vázquez, F.R. (2002). *Partido Acción Nacional, los signos de la institucionalización (Vol. 37)*. México: UNAM.
Villamil, J. (2012). Televisa y Ernesto Zedillo, la Era Azcárraga Jean. *El Cotidiano*, 172, 65–71.
Volpi, J. (2006). El año que vivimos en peligro. *Proceso*, April 23, 1538, 66–67.
Weldon, J. (1997). The political sources of presidencialismo in Mexico. In: Mainwaring, S. and Shugart, M. (eds), *Presidentialism and democracy in Latin America*. Cambridge: Cambridge University Press.
Weldon, J. (2004). Changing patterns of executive-legislative relations in Mexico. In: Middlebrook, K.J. (ed.), *Dilemmas of political change in Mexico*. London: Institute of Latin American Studies, University of London–Center for US–Mexican Studies, UCSD.
Zedillo, E. (1995). *Discurso en el LXVI Aniversario del Partido Revolucionario Institucional*. Retrieved from: http://zedillo.presidencia.gob.mx/pages/disc/mar95/04mar95.html.

6 Colombia: Political Leadership in a Turbulent Environment
César Gaviria and Álvaro Uribe Vélez

Javier Duque

New interest has been shown in the subject of leadership in the political process in recent decades. This area of study has acquired importance, transcending structuralist approaches and those that focus only on personality and overstate the role of political players. This field involves new analyses that consider leadership within its period and context, and thereby reveal the importance of the individual in politics and the attributes, perceptions, and personal abilities of political leaders.

From this perspective, the present chapter analyses the presidential leadership of César Gaviria and Álvaro Uribe in Colombia. To this end, the chapter adopts three analytical perspectives, discussing each president's origin and development; strategies and modes of action; and conceptions of society. Based on these analytical perspectives, we address the question of what both presidential leadership experiences exemplify and illustrate with respect to Colombian politics and society. The response to this question includes five dimensions:

(1) These approaches to leadership illustrate the transformation of Colombia's partisan politics over the last three decades. In particular, they show the transition from party structures characterized by a fragmented leadership (formed by a small circle of national leaders in Bogota, where most presidential candidates are based) to divided and more open structures and the emergence of new leaders from developing social sectors and other regions who manage to successfully enter national politics.
(2) The chapter describes forms of leadership that maintain a high level of personalism in politics within a presidential system characterized by weakly organized parties and functions, based on patronage within a context of conflict and the presence of illegal armed actors.
(3) Two successful leaders are compared based on certain action strategies and their relationships with other spheres of power in critical social and

economic circumstances. The rise of these two presidents entailed strategies that were similar in certain respects, but significantly different in others.
(4) The relationships of both leaders with other political and social actors are analyzed, as well as how those relationships affected their respective ascensions to power and governmental actions. In this regard, both leaders relied on regional political powers and powerful economic groups from which they received funding, as well as public demonstrations of support.
(5) The comparison between the two leaders further allows us to distinguish between their respective conceptions of society, their modes of governing, and their contrasting styles of political leadership.

The period encompassed by the beginnings of these presidents' political careers, their ascensions to the national level, and their access to national circles of political power corresponds to the post-National Front era (1974–1990) and the country's recent history (1990–2015). These were periods of social upheaval, significant violence, institutional changes, and the proliferation of narcotrafficking in a society characterized by a weak state partially overtaken by crime.

Traditional Politics, Clientelism, and Leadership

César Gaviria and Álvaro Uribe are two Colombian political contemporaries whose political paths have many elements in common but diverge upon their respective entries into Congress. Both men were provincial politicians who achieved national prominence; both began their careers in the Liberal Party; both were members of local factions and mentored by faction leaders; and they both eventually created their own factions in which clientelism prevailed. The political careers of these two leaders illustrate their social rise within traditional parties through politics and competition.

Until the beginning of the 1990s, Colombian bipartisanship existed at two levels. At the national level, there were fractions led by natural leaders who developed networks of political and economic support and exerted significant influence on the country's politics. These leaders held high social and economic status and aspired to be elected or re-elected as president. The fractions were named for their respective national leaders. In the Liberal Party, fractions were developed by Alfonso López Michelsen ('lopismo'), Julio César Turbay Ayala ('trubayismo'), and Carlos Lleras Restrepo ('llerismo'). In the 1980s, the 'llerismo' fraction spawned the New Liberalism movement, which was led by Luís Carlos Galán ('galanismo'). In the Conservative Party, the two dominant fractions were led by Álvaro Gómez Hurtado ('alvarismo') and Misael Pastrana Borrero ('pastranismo'). At the regional level, the factions were headed by chiefs ('caciques'), who were politicians with electoral capital who competed with each other and with factions of the rival party. Fractions had their own organizational structures and enjoyed access to power, bureaucracy, and the distribution of patronage resources from the state. The parties formed federations of political leaders characterized by weak national organization and leadership that were built on foundations of initiatives, personal qualities, and skills, often in the shadow of political godfathers.

The beginning of César Gaviria's political career occurred in the context of political parties, fractions, and factions. In 1970, he was elected municipal councilor of Pereira, a small town and the capital of the Risaralda department. Although he was from un upper middle-class family, Gaviria was not part of the country's social and political elite, nor was he the head of any of the main fractions of the Liberal Party, which was historically majoritarian and had won three of the four presidential elections after the political competition which was restored in 1974, following the National Front coalition (1958–1974).

Risaralda was created as a department in 1966, and local politics were initially dominated by the 'cacique' Camilo Mejía Duque. In the early 1970s, a new faction led by Óscar Vélez Marulanda emerged to challenge the chiefdom of *cacique* Mejía Duque. The new group, called the 'Civic Bloc,' won seats in the Senate and the House, and the leader of the group was elected senator until 1990. César Gaviria was a member of this faction and was elected as mayor (1975/1976) and substitute for the House of Representatives (1974) before winning a seat in the House for three consecutive periods (1978, 1982, and 1986/1990). In 1988, Gaviria separated from the Civic Bloc (due to a dispute over the nomination for mayor of Pereira) and created his own faction. Between 1970 and 1986, his political career was mainly regional in nature. Gaviria, a young politician who had graduated with a degree in economics from an elite university in Bogota (University of the Andes), came from a family of coffee entrepreneurs who partnered with *La Tarde*, a very influential regional newspaper in his department (Santamaría, 1998; *La Silla Vacia*, August 18, 1998; Dinero, March 2012). At the national level, Gaviria initially had ties with the 'llerismo' fraction and then joined the 'turbayismo' fraction, which wielded more political and bureaucratic power in the country and was the group to which most 'caciques,' or 'electoral barons,' belonged. This fraction has been identified as a clientelistic system of political leaders surrounding a national leader (Arango, 2015). During 1986, a key year in César Gaviria's political trajectory, he made his breakthrough into national politics by joining the support network of Virgilio Barco, the party-appointed presidential candidate, who named Gaviria as campaign manager and deputy director of the party. Barco won the election, and Gaviria was appointed Minister of Finance (1986–1987) and then Minister of Government (1987–1989), which were the two most important cabinet positions—particularly the latter, which put Gaviria in direct contact with all 'electoral barons,' the political class, and Congress, and which gave him a central role in negotiations among the parties and their various fractions and factions. During this regime, the expression 'Sanhedrin' was commonly used to refer to the president's inner circle, which comprised advisors and leaders who influenced the president's decisions and which included Gaviria and other political figures, particularly graduates and other people connected to the University of the Andes. This circle was a combination of technocrats and powerful regional politicians (*Semana*, October 29, 1986; *Semana*, November 17, 1986).

While César Gaviria ascended and advanced from local politics to national politics at the end of the 1980s, Álvaro Uribe was building his own trajectory in Antioquia, which would also lead to national politics. Narcotrafficking had become a political party characteristic in certain departments, including Antioquia, where a liberal faction had elected Pablo Escobar as a substitute in the House of Representatives for the period 1982–1986. Therefore, guerrilla groups were also expanding, especially the Revolutionary Armed Forces of Colombia (*Fuerzas Armadas Revolucionarias de Colombia*—FARC), the National Liberation Army (*Ejercito de Liberacion Nacional*—ELN), and the 19th of April Movement (*Movimiento 19 de Abril*—M-19). This is the context in which Álvaro Uribe began his political career within the Liberal Party at the end of the 1970s.

In the mid-1970s, when he was still a law student in the University of Antioquia, Álvaro Uribe was tied to the faction of Liberal Antioquia in March (*Antioquia Liberal en Marcha*). With the support of his political boss, he acceded to the state bureaucracy and was head of public companies of Medellin (1976), general secretary of the Ministry of Labor (1977–1978), director of Civil Aeronautics (1980–1982), and mayor of Medellin for four months (1982). In 1984, his faction merged with the Liberal Directory of Antioquia (*Directorio Liberal de Antioquia*), a faction directed by Bernardo Guerra Serna, a congressman since 1964 and then Senator of the Republic. Guerra Serna was the great 'cacique' and 'electoral baron' of the department. Through this alliance, Uribe headed the list for the Council of Medellin, and in 1984 he acceded to a popularly elected seat for the first time. Álvaro Uribe came from a middle-class family. His father, Alberto Uribe Sierra, owned several plantations. The main plantation, called 'Guacharacas,' was located in the northeast of Antioquia, which was a zone influenced by guerrillas and the country's first paramilitary groups. His father was killed in 1983, presumably by FARC. This was a significant event in Álvaro Uribe's life, not only given his later radical positions regarding guerrilla groups but also because the question arose on several occasions whether the helicopter that transported Uribe to where his father had been killed belonged to Pablo Escobar, who was then a substitute congressman and the head of narcotrafficking cartels. In later years, Escobar would put the country in jeopardy with his terroristic actions.

In 1985, Álvaro Uribe separated from his faction and created a new group called Liberal Directory of Antioquia, democratic sector (*Directorio Liberal de Antioquia, sector democrático*). The creation of a new faction by Álvaro Uribe was possible because double militancy was not prohibited in Colombia, and thus every local leader could have his own political group while continuing to belong to the party. Like their national counterparts, these political parties were very weak, and each local leader had total autonomy over his party. Local leaders positioned themselves as candidates, made alliances, self-financed the party, associated with other groups, and/or separated from their respective factions when they felt they had strengthened and consolidated their leadership.

In the elections of 1986, this new faction won a Senate seat for Álvaro Uribe and became one of the most influential factions in the department with ties to national politics. Álvaro Uribe maintained ties with national politics through his relations with the People's Power faction led by Ernesto Samper, whom Álvaro Uribe had supported in his campaign for the presidency in 1994, and who had been questioned about receiving financing from the Cali cartel. That same year, Álvaro Uribe decided to withdraw from the Senate and run for governor of Antioquia. In a very competitive election, he was elected governor with the support of his own organization and two factions of the Conservative Party. Because of mutual accusations between the candidates regarding the results, the National Court of Guarantees, the Regional Office, and the National Electoral Council were forced to intervene (*El Tiempo*, November 6, 1994). When his term as governor ended, Álvaro Uribe lived abroad for a time and took several courses at Harvard University. In 1998, he supported the presidential candidacy of Horacio Serpa Uribe. Although he was not very active, Álvaro Uribe maintained ties to the Liberal Party, in which he had been involved for more than three decades, and prepared for his return to Colombia with presidential aspirations.

Before they became presidents, César Gaviria and Álvaro Uribe built their careers upon traditional politics in parties that were divided at the national and regional levels, organized around their leaders, and lacking in consolidated organization. In Colombia, departmental political machines predominated over the national organization of parties, and leadership was developed through individual initiatives and driven by political godfathers who later became independent and created their own factions. Liberals and conservatives competed for power, and there was no third party with the power to remove them from their positions of prominence.

Presidents at Critical Junctures

The circumstances in which César Gaviria and Álvaro Uribe acceded to the presidency correspond to two critical junctures in Colombia's history. In both cases, the country was experiencing crises characterized by high levels of violence; the presence of various illegal armed groups that challenged the state, which did not have sufficient capacity to respond effectively and instead showed weakness and instability; internal party divisions; and impunity for and partial control of the state by criminals. Both political leaders accurately read the moment and established electoral strategies and alliances that enabled them to win the presidency.

In César Gaviria's political career, the years 1989–1990 were decisive. Colombia was going through one of its worst periods of violence and failure of social regulation by the state, which caused Colombia to be described as a 'failed state' or, at best, a 'partially collapsed state' or a 'state on the brink of institutional collapse' (Pizarro and Bejarano, 1994).

At this juncture, a combination of factors led Gaviria to the presidency of the Republic. On the one hand, there was violence. In all international reports,

Colombia was distinguished by the highest rates of homicides, kidnappings, massacres, and human rights violations. In 1989–1994, Colombia was a bloodied country experiencing the highest homicide rates in its history, and in the world. This situation was the result of actions by the drug cartels, especially actions taken by the Medellin cartel against the state, which had declared war on the cartels after the government of Belisario Betancur (1982–1986) due to the assassination of the Minister of Justice, Jaime Lara Bonilla (1984). The state was unable to effectively combat the cartels, which had allies both within the state itself and in the military. The state also demonstrated its inability to quash the terrorist actions of the two largest guerrilla groups, FARC and the ELN, as well as other small movements, including M-19, the Quintín Lame indigenous movement, the Socialist Renewal Current, and the People's Liberation Army. Thus, counterinsurgency paramilitary groups with ties to landowners and drug traffickers proliferated throughout the country, going far beyond common crime. Before the elections, three presidential candidates were assassinated. The state was impotent to maintain public order. It could not guarantee basic freedoms or coexistence, implement justice (due to high levels of impunity, bottlenecks, inadequate resources, coercion, and violence against judges), or regulate its own operations (due to inefficiency and corruption). Moreover, a segment of the political class was allied with the narcotraffickers and used this alliance to ascend to and enter Congress. Even Pablo Escobar was elected to a congressional seat in 1982.[1]

Meanwhile, the party system remained bipartisan, although with several important changes. First, the factionalism of parties evolved; large national factions led by 'natural leaders' were replaced by temporary nuclei that were connected to national leaders and bolstered by regional support but lacked the strong bonds of loyalty and permanence of the old fractions. After the early 1990s, 'gavirismo,' led by César Gaviria, and 'samperismo,' headed by Ernesto Samper, emerged in the Liberal Party, along with other minority sectors, such as 'santofimismo,' which was headed by Alberto Santofimio Botero. Factions multiplied at the regional level. In addition, the economy was floundering. The country experienced modest growth (3.5% of GDP) between 1988 and 1990. But between 1988 and 1991, Colombia experienced the highest rates of inflation in the country's history (28.1%, 25.9%, 29.1%, and 30.4%), and in 1989, the poverty index was at 57% (Orozco, 2012). Against this dramatic background of conflict, high levels of violence, economic insecurity, and transformation of the party system, César Gaviria became the presidential candidate for the Liberal Party thanks to several situations that he knew how to exploit.

Gaviria strengthened his image as a congressman, a participant in the presidential campaign of 1986, a member of the party leadership, and a veteran of two key cabinet ministries. As a result, he appealed to those who disputed the presidential candidacy due to liberalism, which was largely majoritarian. The presidential pre-candidate Luís Carlos Galán, the chief of the old New Liberalism fraction and a favorite in the polls, offered Gaviria a position as his campaign manager for internal consultation with the party, which Gaviria accepted. He preferred this option over other short-term options, which included running for a Senate seat in the 1990 elections, being appointed a new minister, or aspiring to the position of presidential designate (who replaces the President of the Republic in his absence). In the absence of other outstanding leaders in this political movement, Gaviria took the position of second in command, after Galán, within the political movement.

An internal change in the Liberal Party was also instrumental in Gaviria's rise. The party had adopted an internal referendum mechanism to choose its presidential candidate, whereas all previous candidates had been selected by very small and limited conventions. This new rule was one of the concessions made to *galanismo* to reinstate this faction in the party after a decade of dissent. Shortly after the internal referendum took place, which positioned Gaviria within the new organization, violence paradoxically favoured Gaviria's political career. Specifically, Gaviria had become the main support for Galán's candidacy, and when Galán was assassinated on August 18, 1989, Gaviria's name was brought to the forefront as a possible successor. Facing the risk that the movement would be diluted in the absence of its leader, Galán's family decided to propose that César Gaviria replace Galán, which quickly gave Gaviria a support network and provided an alternative to the other pre-candidates, allowing him to win the internal referendum by a significant margin.

Up to 1989, Gaviria's career had been on the rise, fuelled by growing ambition and political calculation. He had risen from councilman to alternate in the House of Representatives, linked to a network of regional clientele; from alternate to the 'cacique' to the formation of his own group with a seat in the House of Representatives from 1978 to 1986; and from congressman to director of the presidential campaign and Minister of State. He enjoyed a new political leadership that had changed the political fractions and was linked to the pre-candidate with the greatest chance of becoming president, which ultimately led Gaviria to the official nomination of his party and thus to the gates of the presidency during this critical juncture in Colombian history.

A great deal of work had been done by Galán, who was leading the polls and had begun to gain the support of regional politicians, including many political leaders whom he had previously criticized for patronage, but who were now recruited to help him win the presidency (*Semana*, June 26, 1989). Another advantage was the lack of a strong opponent: the Conservative Party was divided between the National Salvation Movement, led by Álvaro Gómez Hurtado, andthe official candidate, Rodrigo Lloreda Caicedo. The other candidate was the former M-19 guerrilla, Antonio Navarro Wolf, who had neither strong party organization nor an important bloc of congressmen. In the elections, it was expected that the votes from liberal regional political leaders, in addition to the support of the public opinion votes that had been mobilized by the flags of the new liberalism, would be sufficient for victory, and Gaviria won by a comfortable margin with 47.8% of the vote, defeating Álvaro Gómez Hurtado, who came in second with 23.1%.

An important factor in this election was the high rate of abstention: only 43% of Colombians voted, and thus Gaviria had been elected by only one-fifth of the potential voters. There was much disagreement in the country and widespread fear because of the increasing violence; three presidential candidates had been assassinated (Luís Carlos Galán in August 1989; Bernardo Jaramillo Ossa of the Patriotic Union in March 1990; and Carlos Pizarro of the M-19 Democratic Alliance in April 1990), and violence was at its peak.

Twelve years later, also at a critical juncture for Colombia, Álvaro Uribe won the presidency. Violence and the economic crisis had been exacerbated, and the traditional parties were gradually decaying and losing their historical dominance. Like Gaviria, Álvaro Uribe had learned how to take advantage of the prevailing circumstances. The conditions surrounding the 2002 presidential elections were critical. The economy had undergone a crisis, and GDP growth was very low, averaging only 0.5% during 1999–2001. The country had high rates of poverty (57%) and indigence (18.7%), unemployment had reached 15.7%, and the informal sector of the economy had grown to more than 61% (Ramírez and Guevara, 2006). Conflict and violence were at their zenith in terms of victims (with an average of 24,500 homicides per year from 1990–2002) (Acevedo, 2007), and Colombia had the highest number of homicides in its history in 2002. In light of the failure of successive peace processes (the most recent under President Andrés Pastrana, 1998–2002) and the increasing number of victims of the conflict generated by guerrillas and right-wing paramilitary groups, the perception that Colombia was a threatened society at risk of a general war, and that the state was unable to provide solutions, grew stronger.

In addition, there was great resistance to the parties and the political class due to prevailing political practices, clientelism, corruption, and scandals involving congressmen. Several events had affected the image of the parties and the political class during the late 1990s. In particular, the negative image of parties and politics was reinforced by the widespread practice of political patronage; the private appropriation of public goods; and the need to belong to political networks to gain access to goods, services, and public employment. The expectations regarding the transformation of 'old politics' that had been generated by the institutional change of 1991 had apparently been frustrated. Patronage continued, and numerous congressmen lost their seats due to conflicts of interest, violations of the regime governing incompatibilities and disqualifications of political officeholders, and improper allocation of public money, all of which contributed to the public's mistrust of political actors (Payne, Zovatto, and Mateo Diaz, 2003). The predominant notion was that politics and politicians had little support and did not contribute to improvements in the living conditions of the population, but rather harmed society, because politicians were dedicated exclusively to their personal enrichment and to the maintenance of their positions, social prestige, and power (González, 2006).

In this critical context, Álvaro Uribe presented himself as the saviour of a country that seemed to be on the brink of destruction. He portrayed himself as a messiah who would redeem Colombia of all its evils, and he built a strategy around six core components:

(1) He adopted a radical discourse against armed groups and proposed resolving the internal conflict through war and the subjugation of guerrillas. This position attracted public sectors that had been affected by decades of violence, entrepreneurs whose businesses were harmed by insecurity, and rural landowners who were often the victims of kidnapping.
(2) He withdrew from the Liberal Party, to which he had belonged throughout his political life. This decision was motivated by the balance of forces within the party, under which Uribe had no immediate opportunity because former congressman and Minister Horacio Serpa had more support among legislators and was more likely to become the official candidate (*El Tiempo*, September 19, 2001). Although the liberal directives and leaders invited Uribe to participate in the internal referendum of the party, he did not accept this invitation, stating that the rules and 'electoral mechanics' were not a priority for him and that it was more important to make proposals to the country than to be involved in partisan procedures (*El Tiempo*, February 16, 2001). At this time, he revealed qualities that would become central features of his political career: his willingness to ignore the rules and his prioritization of self-interest and voter support above organizations and laws.
(3) He spoke out against the parties and the political class despite having belonged to both and adhering to their norms and rules throughout his political career.
(4) Nevertheless, when he rose in the polls and was supported by many of the congressmen and regional politicians whom he had previously criticized, he did not reject their support and thereby added voters from diverse backgrounds, including many politicians who were later linked to paramilitary organizations. The Conservative Party, the National Conservative Movement, a significant portion of the Liberal Party, the Radical Change Party, Christian organizations, and former guerrillas from M-19 and the People's Liberation Army (*Ejército Popular de Liberación*—EPL) joined his campaign. All of these parties composed the coalition government for eight years, ensuring that all government projects and policies were approved by Congress, including an amendment to the constitution that allowed the president to remain in power and to run for another term. He also had the support of a large segment of opinion voters who were attracted to his discourse on harsher treatment for violent actors and political corruption.
(5) He conducted his campaign with many visits to towns and cities and frequent and direct contact with the population through community meetings, interviews with local stations and newspapers, and visits to private universities and religious congregations.
(6) He attracted the most powerful economic groups in the country with his proposal to boost investor confidence, subsidies, and tax exemptions and

his offer to eliminate the coercive presence of the state. His campaign received significantly more support from businesses compared with other campaigns.

Amid the financial crisis, increased violence, and negative perceptions about parties and politicians, Álvaro Uribe's strategies paid off and paved the way for his electoral victory. He won the election in the first round with 53% of the vote, defeating the official Liberal Party candidate Horacio Serpa, who garnered 31.8% of the vote. He was the first president in the history of the country who won an election without recourse to any official endorsement from the historic Liberal or Conservative parties, although his support came from both. He was able to build a coalition not by identifying with a party, but by gaining the support of a majority.

After Uribe's first term, he maintained a wide margin of support in the polls and was re-elected in 2006 in the first round (he won 62% of the vote, giving him a comfortable victory over the leftist candidate, Carlos Gaviria of the Alternative Democratic Pole, who won 22%, and the liberal Horacio Serpa, who received 11.8% of the vote). His electoral success resulted from a combination of his support network, which included most members of Congress, and his ability to persuade a large proportion of voters. In certain cases, he relied on lawful strategies and the support of the same parties and economic groups that had backed and financed him, respectively, in 2002. However, in other cases, he resorted to trading and patronage practices; in some areas of the country, he used pressure on voters because many of the regional politicians who supported his two electoral victories were allied with paramilitary groups. This strategy proved to be critical to his electoral victories.

The re-election of Uribe was preceded by a change in the constitution that he and the governing coalition had promoted and approved in Congress. Because the constitution prohibited presidential re-election, Uribe and the governing coalition had to submit a reform bill to Congress for approval (and the coalition had majorities in both houses), but the bill first had to get through an initial House committee in which the governing coalition did not initially have enough votes. To obtain a majority, the coalition pressurized members of the committee economically and through bureaucratic quotas and successfully persuaded two representatives to change their votes. This was a questionable process that ultimately led to the imprisonment of the two congressmen on grounds of bribery, and to legal proceedings against two former Ministers of State.[2]

In both campaigns, Álvaro Uribe faced public questioning about his past and that of his family. During his first candidacy, there were allegations that linked him, his father, and his family to the Ochoa family and the Medellin cartel and connected his brother to the paramilitary group 'The Twelve Apostles,' which his brother had indeed directed and financed. He was also accused of having supported paramilitary groups when he was the governor of Antioquia. The proximity of his campaign to people linked with drug trafficking and paramilitarism was also noted (*El Tiempo*, April 21, 2002; Contreras, 2002).

In 2002, during this critical period for Colombia, the proposals, styles, and strategies of Uribe and his campaign prevailed over accusations and questions. In 2006, his re-election was made possible by his broad support at the polls, his democratic security policy, the populist features of his leadership style, and the use of power resources to manage incentives for congressmen and regional politicians.

Two Opposing Leadership Styles

The leadership styles of César Gaviria and Álvaro Uribe have several elements in common: pragmatism, cunning, ability to rally political support for their campaigns and their governments, and use of patronage to conduct politics. There are also important differences between them; for example, César Gaviria was more moderate in his positions. He was also more tolerant of opponents, employed technocrats, delegated functions, and conducted politics without approaching the population. In contrast, Álvaro Uribe adopted radical positions, exercised politics in a more authoritarian, intemperate, and intolerant manner, and imbued politics with a neo-populist style in his speech and in relation to citizens and voters.

The words that appear most frequently in the various profiles prepared by both defenders and critics of César Gaviria are 'pragmatic' and 'strategic'. For his supporters, these qualities are virtues that made his political rise possible, helped him to meet critical situations, allowed him to gain the support of many 'electoral caciques,' facilitated his initial ascension within his faction, enabled his entry into national politics, and, once in government, helped him to successfully overcome certain major challenges (Vargas, 1993; *Semana*, September 9, 1998). For his critics, these qualities represented a generation of patronage politics without projects and were ultimately counterproductive for Gaviria, preventing him from becoming a politician with greater achievements and scope.

Gaviria's pragmatism came into play in four crucial incidents during his rule. First, in 1989, amid the wave of violence in the country, students at private universities in Bogota originated a proposal to convene a National Constituent Assembly (*Asamblea Nacional Constituyente*—ANC) to allow an institutional transformation of the country. This initiative gained momentum and attracted academics, intellectuals, social organizations, and leftist parties. During the 1990 elections, there were more than two million votes in favor of the initiative. After the Supreme Court endorsed the initiative, Gaviria also endorsed it, calling on all parties to agree on the terms of its operation and urging its popular passage by the constituents. Rather than opposing the initiative, he joined the consensus around it.

The second incident relates to the operation and decisions of the ANC. After asserting that the ANC was boundless in its powers, Gaviria emphasized the difference between what is institutionally desirable and what is feasible in the context of warring political forces and voter disputes. He stressed the need to consider standards in light of the country's reality. He tried to control the agenda and to diminish the scope of the reform, which, after receiving *carte blanche* from the Supreme Court that had established the ANC, had unlimited power to promote changes to the institutional form of the country (Vargas, 1993). A conciliatory dynamic prevailed, and the presence of political forces other than bipartisanship made it possible to establish rules that reduced presidential and congressional power and provided greater political pluralism and inclusion.

The third incident involved negotiations with the drug cartels. The country was plagued by the narcoterrorism of the Medellin cartel, which had caused the death of a Minister of Justice (Rodrigo Lara Bonilla in 1984), an attorney general (in 1988), the governor of Antioquia (in 1989), three presidential candidates, and hundreds of judges, police, and civilians in dozens of targeted terrorist attacks and kidnappings of Colombian political figures. Before the siege of terror, Gaviria had defended a policy of surrendering to the narcotraffickers and offering them broad benefits, which convinced many narcotraffickers to turn themselves in, including Pablo Escobar and his lieutenants in June 1991. Although this policy caused a substantial reduction in terrorism, the cost was impunity for narcotraffickers and the scandal that ensued when the kingpin escaped. When Escobar escaped, the president changed his policy and created the 'Search Block,' an elite prosecutorial body supported by the US.

The fourth incident was the appointment of a former M-19 guerrilla, Antonio Navarro Wolf, to Gaviria's cabinet, which effectively granted political participation to a rising political force and sent a message to other guerrilla groups about the benefits they would receive if they embraced demobilization and negotiation with the government. This strategy was partially successful; during Gaviria's government, a peace agreement was reached with the EPL, the Quintín Lame Movement, and the Socialist Renewal Current.

In addition to the strategic actions and practices adopted by Gaviria in search of results, several of his actions were characterized by a certain calculated boldness and manifested crucial decisions that would define the course of his political career. He had named his government 'the wipe-out' ('el revolcón'), a label that gave substance to certain decisions that distinguished Gaviria's administration from previous governments, such as his support and promotion of the ANC initiative; the staffing of his cabinet and advisory body with young people—a new generation in the top bureaucracy—without neglecting agreements with the parties and their respective political leaders; the controversial policy of negotiating with the drug cartels; economic liberalization; and the appointment of the first civilian defense minister in the country's history.

Gaviria's pragmatism and particular form of calculated boldness were complemented by the decisions he negotiated with political and electoral forces. After winning the election, he announced: 'I will consult with everyone' (*El Tiempo*, May 29, 1990), meaning anyone who had an important electorate and was vulnerable to pressure and blackmail. With his party, he consulted on the convocation and on decisions regarding the content of the new constitution, which Gaviria believed would prevent him from losing control of the process. He reached an agreement on the content of the convocation to the ANC with

Colombia: Gaviria and Uribe 129

the parties that had the most representation in the 1990 Congress. He negotiated his most controversial and important decisions with the largest blocs of the ANC (the Liberal Party, the M-19 Democratic Alliance, and the National Salvation Movement), and each of his cabinets was built based on the representation of fractions of political parties and the importance of the main political leaders in Colombia.[3] During his government, he shared power and consulted with various forces[4] due to four factors. First, he was not backed by a unified party, but by a federation of factions and interests led by several national leaders. There was no presidential party but rather a collection of interest groups. Second, he did not have party power because he was not a party leader and never had been, and there was no single leadership with which he could identify and agree. The Liberal Party had a weakly institutionalized structure. Third, as voter abstention was at its highest level in the country's history, his popular base and legitimacy was very weak. The vast majority of Colombians had not voted for him, which caused him to try to win more voter support through government representation. Fourth, the ANC had produced a rupture in the country's traditional two-party dominance and had opened the door to other political forces, which demanded to be included in decisions. These groups posed a challenge for the president, who had to seek agreements in a country affected by a severe crisis of legitimacy.

Gaviria was a pragmatic, calculating president who adhered to the traditional policy of allocating shares of power. Regarding his political behavior, after more than two decades of traditional patronage, he did not establish communication strategies, language, or actions that would allow him to have direct contact with voters during the presidential campaign. Therefore, during his presidency and subsequent tenure as leader of the Liberal Party, he did not vary from this mode of conduct and was not close to the people of Colombia, preferring instead to act through advisors and intermediaries.

In contrast, the leadership style of Álvaro Uribe was a manifestation of the attributes that characterize populist strategies: the presence of a leader who appeals to a heterogeneous mass of followers who feel isolated, abandoned, and adversely affected by societal conditions and who are willing to support alternatives to these conditions; an almost direct personal relationship between the leader and his followers, which diverts attention from established intermediary organizations, especially the parties; the use of a common language that creates a feeling of closeness to the leader; and the creation of a new party as the leader's personal vehicle (Weyland, 1999).

Throughout his political career, Álvaro Uribe established a direct relationship with the people. In the 2000–2002 presidential campaign, he replicated nationally what he had done during his political campaigns in Antioquia, using hundreds of 'democratic workshops' ('Talleres democráticos') where he met with people from towns and communities and presented his programs. After winning the presidency, he implemented the 'Community Councils of Government' ('Consejos Comunitarios de Gobierno'), which were meetings directed by himself and attended by ministers, deputy ministers, mayors, and governors, where he called for accountability and responded to questions from the audience. He made plans, proposed programs and solutions to address problems, and distributed state resources personally, which was a form of micromanagement that gave him greater popularity and acceptance (Duzán, 2003; De La Torre, 2005). The president was in contact with the people; he personally greeted all those who attended, he acted as a moderator, listened, had questions for officials and authorities, and proposed solutions—which in many cases were only promises. These practices of 'direct democracy' were complemented by wide dissemination, with live broadcasts for the entire country on a state channel and press releases that were reproduced in all national and regional media.

Álvaro Uribe was also constantly active and traveled to places where there were problems and demands from the population. The president's style was to be on the street and face to face with people. He declared that 'power is not a matter of vanity but concerns all institutions, the first of which is the citizen' (*Semana*, August 6, 2007). He was seen in the street talking to protesters, in a town talking to peasants, on the Plaza de Bolivar in Bogota intervening before a crowd demanding to see him, and, during a protest by indigenous people, speaking from a bridge with a megaphone in his hand to a crowd that rebuked and insulted him. All of this activity was complemented by intensive and strategic use of image. There was a clear pattern of action that systematically used media exposure. The president cultivated the image of himself as a redeemer of the people, a fighter against corruption and 'politicking,' and a defender of Colombians from terrorists. He is regarded with great sympathy by broad sectors of the population, addresses the people in familiar terms, criticizes those who govern 'from the capital and from the cocktails,' and uses television stations and newspapers in villages to communicate his thoughts, without forgetting the major media that frequently engage him in extensive interviews.

The populist strategies of Álvaro Uribe, which are characterized by a combination of direct contacts and appeals to the people and systematic and frequent media management, is complemented by the creation of a party as the vehicle for his aspirations. Although his two presidential candidacies were presented under the banner of Colombia First and he resorted to collecting signatures to legally validate his candidacies, he also created a new political party in 2005, the Social Party of National Unity, which was labeled the U Party. When President Juan Manuel Santos, who had been elected with Uribe's endorsement and with the support of the government coalition, began to make his own decisions, he appointed ministers who were disliked by Álvaro Uribe and initiated a peace process with the FARC. Uribe accused him of being a traitor and a scoundrel and declared himself in opposition. Driven by his view that leaders matter, rather than organizations, he created another new party called the Pure Democratic Centre, which was renamed a few months later as the Uribe Democratic Centre and then renamed again as the Democratic Centre. This party was created by and tailor-made for him, and it included former ministers, his former vice president, cattle ranchers, former military, and the support of powerful economic sectors.

Another characteristic of Álvaro Uribe's leadership was his authoritarian style and ideological intolerance. Although he attracts people with his speeches, interventions, and welfare-based actions, he rejects and dismisses those who think and act differently than he does. When referring to people who are active in the partisan left or who express opposing views, he uses an expression similar to that used by a paramilitary leader: 'plain-clothes terrorists,' a phrase he once used to refer to members of the leftist Alternative Democratic Pole. He has called non-governmental organizations and intellectuals who denounce acts of violence against members of civil society 'writers and politicians that serve terrorism and who cower behind the banner of human rights.' Candidates from other parties with different ideological tendencies were labeled as representatives of 'disguised communism.' He confronted other public authorities with the same tone when they questioned his actions, the acts of Congress, or the acts of his officials. It is more than an intemperate and intolerant style; it is his conception of democracy, which he associates with the electoral process, which confers legitimacy and cannot be resisted by other powers without the risk of violating the popular will. During his two terms, he was in permanent conflict with the Supreme Court. He questioned the Court's decisions and accused it of displaying an ideological bias in favor of terrorism, of pursuing congressmen and government officials, and even of wanting to overthrow him (Duque, 2012).

His attitude towards the opposition and the other branches of government went beyond words and eventually culminated in illegal acts of persecution and espionage. Through the Administrative Department of Security (*Departamento Administrativo de Seguridad*—DAS), which reported directly to the president, a series of illegal and improper actions were implemented against the judges of the Supreme Court, opposing politicians, and journalists who criticized the government. Hundreds of illegal wiretaps were implemented, private communications were monitored, and recording systems were installed to listen to Supreme Court sessions, all of which led the Attorney General's Office to begin an investigation and claim that there had been a plot against them (*Semana*, May 21, 2011). In 2011, Álvaro Uribe was required to appear before the Committee of Accusations of the House of Representatives to testify about this case. He stated that he did not order this conduct and defended his officials as correct and honourable.

Leadership and Popularity

These two distinct leadership styles produced different responses from the population. Whereas César Gaviria had a high percentage of acceptance in the polls only at the beginning and the end of his government, with a long period of doubt and loss of confidence in between, Álvaro Uribe is considered the most popular president in the country's recent history and has always enjoyed high levels of support.

Given his economic reforms, his political negotiations with and subsequent prosecution of the Medellin cartel, the approval of the new constitution in 1991, and the limited success in the demobilization of guerrilla groups, the popularity and image of César Gaviria can be divided into three distinct periods. Initially, Gaviria enjoyed high support in the polls during his first two years as president, which coincide with the work of the ANC, the promulgation of the new constitution, and the arrest of Pablo Escobar and other drug lords. Then, there was a dramatic drop in the polls in early 1992 due to Escobar's escape and the suspension of electricity service for most of one day as a consequence of an energy crisis, caused by a lack of government foresight, corruption that delayed new projects for power generation, and a prolonged period of drought that affected the country's hydroelectric plants.

Gaviria was not a very popular president. He was conciliatory and negotiated well with the political class and the parties but was not very close to the people, although he made extensive use of the media to boost his image. The critical moments of his presidency were related to the fight against drug trafficking and the 'blackout' caused by the energy crisis, both of which greatly affected his popular support. He eventually recovered in the polls after Pablo Escobar died and the power cuts ended (Figure 6.1).

In contrast, despite accusations about his past, his alleged ties to paramilitary groups, opposition from the Liberal and Alternative Democratic Pole parties, and questions from international organizations such as Amnesty International and Human Rights Watch, Álvaro Uribe maintained high levels of support at the polls during his eight years in government, averaging between 70% and 80% at the end of his regime (Figure 6.2). The 'popularity of populism' caused the media to speak of a 'teflon effect': whatever happened, the president's image was not substantially affected.

The popularity of Álvaro Uribe was influenced by various factors. First, his policy of combating the guerrillas and his emphasis on safety and order

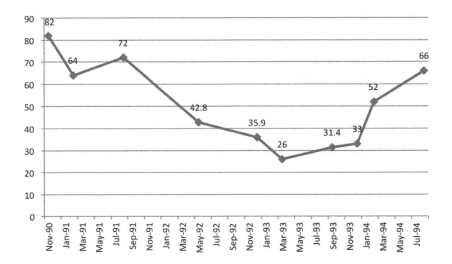

Figure 6.1 Evolution of César Gaviria's popularity, 1990–1994

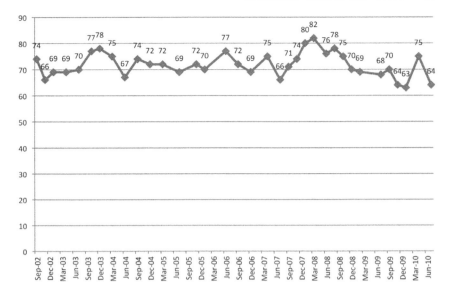

Figure 6.2 Favorable image of Álvaro Uribe Vélez, 2002–2010

generated the support of large sections of the middle class and landowners affected by kidnappings and extortion. He also had the support of unions, which favored his policies regarding exemptions and subsidies, and of the popular sectors, which benefited from his aid policies and appreciated that he conducted politics in direct contact with people and used simple language, which created the sense that he was allied with them. Moreover, Uribe made extensive use of the media to report on governmental acts and of speeches, interventions, and visits to areas affected by tragedies or disasters. Many media outlets supported the president, and when his two governments came to an end, former ministers and the vice president partnered with important television stations to direct programs in which they continued to defend his supposed achievements.

Two Conceptions of Society

Economically, both leaders defended neoliberal positions, and during their terms, they promoted policies of labor market flexibility, a reduced role for the state, privatization, defense of free trade, and the advance of free trade agreements. However, they differ significantly in other respects.

During his short presidential campaign, César Gaviria had championed several ideas that were not only embraced by himself and formed part of the pragmatism described above, but were also components of his vision of society. This vision combined his training as an economist and technocrat with his training as a liberal politician; he was an institutional reformer and neoliberal politician who established reforms aimed at reshaping the state and reinserting

Colombia into the international economy, advocated a negotiated solution to political conflict, and supported individual freedoms and political tolerance.

As an institutional reformer, he joined the calls for reforms proposed by social movements and civil society, supported the ANC initiative, and actively participated in the discussions. When he had to take a position on presidential re-election, he spoke in favor of a ban, notwithstanding that this ban would affect his own future aspirations. He also endorsed institutional changes aimed at greater political inclusion, pluralism, religious freedom, and secularization of politics.

Gaviria was a liberal with respect to freedom and a neoliberal with respect to the economy. During his government, he promoted an economic liberalization reform that included trade liberalization; the elimination of import restrictions; tariff reductions; international trade procedures; and the signing of international treaties. This policy also included labor flexibility in hiring, which was aimed at reducing the costs of manual labor, and the establishment of private pension funds. Additionally, the state was reoriented to reduce its economic presence and formerly public companies (including banks, power plants, industrial companies, and Pacific ports) were privatized. There was also a tax reform that raised the value added tax (VAT) from 10% to 12% and, after 1992, to 14%. However, large landowners continued to avoid paying taxes, no measures were advanced to enable redistribution through taxation, and dividends and large assets were not taxed.

Regarding his management of the armed conflict, Gaviria attempted during his government to engage in peace talks with the Simón Bolívar Coordinating Board (*Coordinadora Guerrillera Simón Bolívar*—CGSB), which brought together all of the guerrillas. Although he had ordered the bombing of FARC headquarters in 1990, there were initiatives for negotiations several months later, in 1991, at meetings in Caracas, Venezuela, and Tlaxcala, Mexico. In 1992, these efforts failed, and the government suspended negotiations after the murder of a former minister. Gaviria declared a policy to combat insurgency. During his rule, several small guerrilla groups (EPL, the Quintín Lame Indigenous Movement, the Revolutionary Workers' Party, *Partido Revolucionario del Trabajo*—PRT, and the M-19) were demobilized and obtained economic resources, special conditions to participate in politics, and even seats with a voice (but no vote) in the ANC. Gaviria also named former guerrilla Antonio Navarro Wolf as minister of health, and the M-19 Democratic Alliance was a part of his government.

Regarding other social issues, Gaviria took liberal positions in defense of democracy, tolerance, peaceful coexistence, and respect for individual rights. He defended reduction and modernization of the state, political democracy, peaceful resolution of conflict, and liberal principles of coexistence. However, there was no significant progress during his rule in other areas related to the development of social rights and the consolidation of the rule of law. At the end of his rule, economic indicators had not improved: poverty was at 55%, and the Gini index indicated that Colombia was one of the most unequal countries in the world in terms of wealth (0.569). In contrast to the situation of 1989–1991, when winds of change again blew in Colombia in 2002, a movement arose against some of the reforms and policies that had been implemented in the country. Whereas in Chile (Michele Bachelet), Brazil (Inacio Lula Da Silva), Ecuador (Rafael Correa), Bolivia (Evo Morales), and Venezuela (Hugo Chávez), the presidency was won by leaders who identified with various leftist tendencies, Colombia entered the new millennium as a 'conservative and right-wing enclave' in Latin America under the presidency of Álvaro Uribe Vélez.

Economically, Álvaro Uribe Vélez continued the neoliberal policies that had been originated by César Gaviria 12 years earlier. He proposed creating 'investor confidence' through large infusions of capital for domestic and foreign companies. The tariff on imports of capital goods was removed, and the value added to capital goods was exempted from the VAT for export companies. Additionally, several laws were passed to encourage business ventures at the expense of state revenues: the Law on Free Trade Zones (Law 1004 of 2005); the Law on Legal Stability for Investors (Act 963 of 2005) and its regulatory decrees; and the Law on the Flexibility of Labor Relations (Act 789 of 2002). Álvaro Uribe also continued the policy of privatizing large state enterprises (mainly with respect to Telecom, the Colombian telecommunications company).

Protected by the declaration of internal disturbance, he established the 'wealth tax' for assets above 3,000 million pesos (Decrees 1838 and 1839 of 2002). He also presented the tax reform of 2002 (Law 788 of 2002), which converted the estate tax into permanent legislation, reduced exemptions for labor income, increased the number of income reports for the middle class, and increased the tax on banking transactions. He tried to apply the VAT to products in the basic basket of goods, but this effort met with considerable resistance in Congress, even from his congressional allies (Vasco, 2004). In turn, he established assistance programs based on subsidies, such as 'Families in Action' ('Familias en Acción'—monetary support for mothers of families in poverty to assist with food and education expenses, which covered approximately 2.5 million people), 'Youth in Action' ('Jóvenes en Acción'—school support, which covered 100,000 people), partial unemployment benefits, and support for seniors (Villamizar and Díaz, 2010). He compensated subsidies to the poor by maintaining interests in capital.

Moreover, during his two terms, Álvaro Uribe emphasized security and the fundamental value of society above freedom. In one of his first speeches as president, Álvaro Uribe said that he had found Colombia at the brink, with 'a weak and foolish state that is continually losing real power in its jurisdiction.' He also reiterated the central proposal of his rule: the 'policy of democratic security,' aimed at strengthening the coercive capacity of the state to confront illegal armed actors, forming the largest army in Latin America, and redirecting the national budget. In addition, on the day after he took office, Álvaro Uribe declared a state of emergency, which he extended twice, as a legal tool to manage public order. Unlike all of his predecessors since 1982, who had attempted to advance peace processes, he implemented a political resolution of the conflict through military action against the guerrillas, while simultaneously initiating negotiations with paramilitary groups, which caused the demobilization of thousands of mercenaries and criminals with ties to drug trafficking. He granted these individuals the status of political offenders. In 2003, he presented a bill to Congress that became the Anti-Terrorist Statute, which gave powers to security forces to conduct raids and arrests, intercept communications without a warrant, and order registration of the population in designated areas. Problems with this law led the Constitutional Court to declare it unconstitutional.

The strategy of using a strengthened military apparatus to recover the internal sovereignty of the state produced results, and the number of terrorist acts declined, along with homicides and kidnappings. However, contemporaneously, thousands of people disappeared and there were hundreds of victims of illegal actions of the armed forces, known as 'false positives.' The country became first in the world in terms of displaced people, most of whom were peasants expropriated from their land by paramilitaries, landowners, and guerrillas. At the end of Álvaro Uribe's second term, the FARC and ELN guerrilla groups remained in force, although their ability to operate had been affected and there was a significant reduction in their terrorist acts. Hundreds of paramilitary groups, now called 'criminal gangs,' had resurfaced. Thus, although the state had regained some of its internal sovereignty in hundreds of municipalities where it previously had not been present, urban crime increased substantially due to the emergence of dozens of criminal gangs.

Another central feature of Álvaro Uribe's conception of society is his conception of democracy, which overvalues popular support (which he calls the 'state of opinion') and undervalues the rule of law. From his political perspective, the executive branch, due to its popular origin, has a legitimacy that cannot be disputed or limited by powers that do not have the same source (such as the judiciary and other powers of control). In the inaugural speech for his second term, he said as follows: 'According to public opinion, force is necessary for safety and to stop the virtue of the Republic from perishing. But legitimacy, the degree of confidence and popular acceptance that facilitates governance, comes essentially from the approval of public opinion' (*Semana*, August 7, 2006). Shortly after, in the course of a debate with the president of the Supreme Court, he made the following statement: 'The natural judge of the state is the law of public opinion' (*Semana*, October 9, 2007).

Uribe appeals to the people, approaches them, and speaks to them. He expresses himself in popular terms, promises redemption, and vows to solve all of their problems. He also appeals to the people to decide through referendums. A few days after he took office, the majority of Congress approved a call for a referendum containing numerous reform proposals that had politically polarized the country. The referendum was held in October 2003 and was not approved (*Semana*, October 9, 2007). Álvaro Uribe resorted to a referendum again in 2009, when he tried to amend the constitution to allow him to be elected to the presidency for the third time. This time, the Constitutional Court declared Congress's approval unconstitutional.

Álvaro Uribe was a conservative leader, and in various public speeches, he expressed an association between politics and religion. He made statements regarding his Catholic beliefs, attendance at mass, and prayer, as well as frequent references to God and religious ethics. To mark a national Catholic event, he defended denominational education: 'It is good to have this abundance of religious education in Colombia because it infuses morals, ethics, a sense of family, [and] a sense of community.'[5] Additionally, echoing the sentiments of members of the Catholic Church and conservative sectors of the country, Álvaro Uribe insisted on repealing the regulations that had decriminalized personal drug use and reinstated penalties for such behavior with the approval of the majority of Congress. He opposed the partial decriminalization of abortion, signaling that as a Christian, he was united with the Catholic Church in its efforts to strengthen respect for the right to life (*El Tiempo*, August 22, 2005).

The contrast between the two leaders is clear: although they were similar in their thinking about the economy (both neoliberal), they were very different in terms of their proposed resolutions of the armed conflict and their conceptions of society. In these areas, César Gaviria was a liberal whereas Álvaro Uribe was an exponent of neoconservative thought.

The Presidents and Their Relationships with Other Spheres of Power and Other Actors

There is a significant contrast between the presidents in terms of their relations with other actors and other spheres of power. Gaviria was moderate, who sought consensus, included nearly all political sectors in his government, maintained good relations with the media, and respected the separation of powers and the institutions responsible for inspection. In contrast, Uribe Vélez was radical and intemperate in his positions. He ruled and imposed majorities by sweeping out political minorities; he confronted, dismissed, and persecuted the media that criticized his government and that questioned his past and his family; and he challenged and advanced improper and illegal actions against the Supreme Court.

Notwithstanding the composition of his government and the guidance of his actions by pragmatism and logical consequences, Gaviria's government was not without opposition, although that opposition was very weak. For example, the Conservative Party was defeated in the presidential elections of 1986 and 1990 and had historically been a minority in competitive elections. The party was divided and although it participated bureaucratically in the government, it continued to proclaim its independence and occasionally expressed criticism of the government. Within Gaviria's own party, the strongest opposition came from the faction led by Ernesto Samper, who had been defeated in the internal referendum in 1990. Although Samper was a minister and ambassador during Gaviria's government, he always maintained a distance from the president and did not support the policy of liberalizing the country or other neoliberal reforms promoted by the government, which he considered 'savage capitalism.' However, Samper supported the ANC and the policy of bringing mafia bosses to justice (Garavito, 1993). In addition, the Communist Left, which was represented by the persecuted Patriotic Union, was in radical opposition to all governmental policies because of their neoliberal content. The Communist Left was the only political sector that was not included in Gaviria's government and exercised a deliberative opposition in Congress.

Gaviria's relations with the military were good, although he made an historic shift in the Defense Ministry by appointing the first minister of civil defense (Rafael Pardo), a title that was created in consultation with the generals, who did not oppose the change or the appointee (*Semana*, January 4, 2004). During his term, Gaviria had to address the narcoterrorism of the cartels, which he did by creating the 'Search Block' against the Medellin cartel. The Search Block was a task force that had technical and military support from the US and collaborated with illegal groups, such as the 'Pepes' and the Cali cartel, which served as informants. The armed forces and police had been permeated by narcotrafficking and had to confront many illegal armed groups simultaneously with few resources and little operational capacity. Therefore, Gaviria strengthened these entities by increasing their standing forces, salaries, and armaments.

As for inter-institutional relations, the main tension existed with respect to Colombia's attorney general, who proposed in 1993 that drugs should be legalized as a mechanism to combat drug trafficking. This proposal was vehemently criticized by President Gaviria. He also disagreed with the prosecutor on criminal policy. Specifically, the attorney general advocated a bill of surrender and negotiations with the Cali cartel, which the president opposed because he was trying to avoid repeating the mistakes made with respect to the Medellin cartel, and because he was under pressure from the US government. There were also tensions with the Constitutional Court because the president accused the judges of being an obstacle in the fight against crime (when the Court declared the anti-kidnapping Law 40 of 1993—which penalized people who paid ransoms and took measures to freeze the assets of kidnapped people to discourage this crime—to be unconstitutional). He contested the decision to decriminalize personal drug use in 1994 and accused the judges of wanting to co-legislate when, also in 1994, the Court declared unconstitutional an internal unrest decree which had been established to prevent dozens of criminals from being freed based on lack of proceedings by the Attorney General's Office. However, these tensions did not lead to clashes or institutional paralysis and were due in part to the transition between the old and new constitutions, which required that the relationships between the branches of government be adjusted.

In a turbulent and weak governmental environment, César Gaviria was guided by pragmatism in negotiations with electorally relevant political sectors and exhibited a certain calculated boldness. He was a new but very traditional leader and was able to establish convenient relationships with political parties and the powerful political class. He maintained a supportive relationship with Congress and, when needed, with the 'Pepes' paramilitary group and the Cali cartel, which he used as informers to fight the Medellin cartel and Pablo Escobar. Gaviria maintained an ambiguous position with regard to the guerrillas. He invited dialogue with FARC and included a former guerrilla in the cabinet but also fought against the state's limitations on resources and equipment. The government's attitude towards paramilitary groups that began to take hold in certain regions was passive, allowing these groups to grow rapidly and resulting in the multiplication of human rights violations, which in many cases stemmed from alliances between paramilitary groups and state agents.

Álvaro Uribe's relations with other spheres and actors in power were based on a 'friend or foe' logic, and many of these relationships were controversial and contested. His name has been linked to paramilitary groups, and there have been many complaints and inquiries in this respect, but he has yet to be convicted. As governor of Antioquia, he was a defender and promoter of security cooperatives—Coexist ('Convivir')—that later became paramilitary groups. In his 2002 and 2006 presidential campaigns, he was supported by many congressmen who were later condemned by the Supreme Court based on charges of conspiracy, coercion of voters, and, in some cases, homicide. In addition, the head of DAS and other members of this organization were sentenced because of their ties to paramilitaries. Many of Álvaro Uribe's relatives and inner circle have been convicted or involved in investigations. Among the closest of these relatives are his brother Santiago Uribe, who was investigated for organizing and funding a paramilitary group known as 'The Twelve Apostles'; Mario Uribe, his cousin and former political partner for three decades, who was convicted in 2010 for conspiracy and for ties to paramilitary groups; one of his former security chiefs in the presidency, who was extradited and convicted in the United States for cooperating with narco-paramilitary groups; and another former security chief who was arrested for alleged illicit enrichment and ties to narcotrafficking. The men responsible for the security of the president had links to the mafia, and former heads of DAS who were appointed directly by President Uribe have been convicted for their ties to paramilitary groups. Additionally, Álvaro Uribe's secretary general was arrested for unlawful interception of communications; the former minister of agriculture was arrested for corruption and mismanagement of a farm subsidy policy; and his former ministers of government and social protection are being investigated on charges of bribery related to congressional approval of a constitutional amendment to permit presidential re-election. The list is long and includes dozens of former officials and employees of his governments. One of his former advisors is also very controversial because he is a cousin of the late drug lord Pablo Escobar.

The ties of Álvaro Uribe's political associates, family members, relatives, and former government officials with paramilitary groups have generated much criticism and distrust among journalists, the media, and academic circles. Many former paramilitaries have testified against him, and there have been several proceedings and investigations are still underway. Negotiations with paramilitary groups have reinforced these criticisms.

Álvaro Uribe has been pragmatic with respect to his relations with political parties and has used these parties as vehicles for his personal aspirations as well as those of his relatives. He was active in the Liberal Party for more than two decades before presenting his dissenting candidacy and creating his own organization, 'Colombia First' ('Primero Colombia'). After his presidency, he promoted the creation of the Social Party of National Unity ('Partido Social de Unidad Nacional'), from which he later separated to create his own party, the Democratic Centre. This party was characterized by a personalized leadership style that placed greater importance on the organization's leader and concentrated a larger number of core functions and major decisions around Uribe. When required, he has forged party alliances to support his aspirations. During his two terms, he built large multi-party coalitions and maintained loyalties based on the selective distribution of state resources. In turn, he dismissed opposition from the Liberal Party and the leftist Alternative Democratic Pole. He broke the law by intercepting their communications and accused leaders of the left of terrorism.

Álvaro Uribe had a very close relation with the armed forces. He increased the size of the army and police and invested a large amount of state resources in strengthening the armed forces and improving their wages. The association of retired military personnel has supported his campaigns, and former military were included on the lists provided to Congress regarding his new party in 2014. He has also been an advocate of a special regime for members of the armed forces who commit crimes, and he has defended members of the armed forces accused of murdering civilians and then passing off their corpses as those of guerrillas. In addition to the armed forces, Álvaro Uribe was endorsed by unions, especially those with links to the country and to agribusiness companies.

Leaders with More Shadows than Lights

The trajectories of César Gaviria and Álvaro Uribe exhibit several similarities that arise from the context in which the two leaders emerged, transitioned from the local to the national stage, and acceded to the presidency and national political power. For four decades, the country has been plagued by constant violence and multiple illegal armed groups, which has created a complex structure and a turbulent environment.

Although in the late 1970s both leaders were members of the Liberal Party, and both have been councilmen, mayors, congressmen, and presidents, there are relevant differences in their trajectories and in the manners in which they acceded to the presidency. Whereas Gaviria became the official candidate of his party through an institutionalized process, Uribe employed a strategic dissent and aggregated votes from a heterogeneous coalition that, incidentally, contributed to the crisis in the party. As president, Gaviria championed institutional reform and led the campaign for a new constitution. Uribe subsequently urged changes to the new constitution, mainly to allow his re-election, which constituents had previously agreed to ban. This was not the only change implemented by Uribe. During his two terms, he prompted reforms that various social and political sectors have described as counter-reforms to the constitution.

These two men have coincided on the political scene for over three decades and have been key players in Colombian politics. They were never close to each other, and in the last decade, they have stood at opposite ends of the spectrum, with different styles and conceptions about society. César Gaviria was an institutional reformist, a pragmatist with a certain calculated audacity, and a facilitator of agreements with political actors. Álvaro Uribe was an authoritarian, a conservative in his conception of society, a pragmatist who was also intemperate and intolerant of differences, a driver of agreements with questionable political actors, and a defender of the political status of paramilitaries even as he labelled the guerrillas and political opposition 'terrorists'.

Like the seven other presidents who have come and gone since the end of the coalition regime in 1974, César Gavira and Álvaro Uribe left office without resolving the serious social and economic problems of Colombia. Colombia remains a society besieged by violent actors that adapt, resurface, and take on new forms; a democracy that is severely limited in terms of both procedures and results; a state partially dominated by criminal actors and organizations; a system teeming with impunity and corruption; and a country with high levels of poverty and social and economic inequality, and the largest number of forcibly displaced people on the planet. The actions of those who exercise political leadership do not seem to be very effective.

As noted at the beginning of this chapter, national leaders remain in the collective memory over time. However, given the persistence of problems in the society over which they presided, and their failure to contribute to solutions, their achievements are partially eclipsed. On balance, the government of César Gaviria is the more ambiguous in terms of achievements. Álvaro Uribe can be credited with strengthening the coercive capacity of the state and the presence of the state in large areas of Colombia that traditionally had no state presence. In addition, some of Álvaro Uribe's welfare policies have continued and contributed to limited improvements in the living conditions of certain social sectors. Despite these achievements, on balance, the governments of César Gaviria and Álvaro Uribe are characterized by many unresolved issues, dark areas, and improper and illegal actions.

Notes

1 Escobar was elected by the Alternative Liberal movement as a substitute for Jairo Ortega, and he even accompanied the Colombian delegation to the swearing in of Felipe Gonzalez in Spain in 1982. In 1983, in the face of scandal, he lost his position as congressman. For more information on the forms of cartel participation in politics, see Guerrero (1999).
2 This event is well documented and is known as the 'Yidispolitica,' a name derived from congressman Yiddis Medina, who changed his vote in exchange for incentives and then recounted what had happened during his trial, after which he was sentenced to 47 months in prison: see *Semana* (July 30, 2013); Duque (2012).
3 The first cabinet included two ministers of fractions of the Conservative Party, one member from the M-19 Democratic Alliance, and the three members to represent

the liberal factions with seats in Congress. In 1991, he replaced seven ministers and rearranged the representation of the same forces; he also included the son of former President Andrés Pastran to represent the New Democratic Force. The third cabinet was formed in July 1992 based on the same logic of sharing and representation of all factions and parties; this cabinet was mediated by a political agreement (see: *El Tiempo*, August 7, 1990; *El Tiempo*, November 9, 1991).

4   In the 1990 elections, the Liberal Party won 66 of the 114 contested seats in the Senate (57.95%) and 119 of the 199 seats in the House (59.8%). In the 1991 elections, after the revocation of the ANC mandate, the Liberal Party won 58 of the 102 seats in the Senate (56.8%) and 86 of the 161 seats in the House (53.4%) (*Registraduría Nacional del estado Civil, Estadísticas electorales años respectivos*).

5   Words of Álvaro Uribe Vélez at the IV Congreso Nacional de Educacion Catolica.

References

Acevedo, H. (2007). Violencia Homicida en Colombia. Liderazgo Político y Políticas Públicas. *Revista Criminalidad*, 49.

Arango Gaviria, J. (2015). Democracia y Clientelismo, una Visión Desde la Política Local 1970–1990. *Diario del Otún*, May 4.

Contreras, J. (2002). *El Señor de las Sombras, Biografía no Autorizada de Álvaro Uribe Vélez*. Bogota: Editorial La Oveja Negra.

De La Torre, C. (2005). *Álvaro Uribe Vélez o el Neopopulismo en Colombia*. Medellin: La Carreta Política.

Duque Daza, J. (2012). *El Presidente y las Cortes*. Cali: Editorial Oveja Negra y Programa Editorial Universidad del Valle.

Duzán, M.J. (2003). *Así Gobierna Uribe*. Bogota: Planeta.

Garavito, F. (1993). *Querido Ernesto*. Bogota: Editorial Lerner.

González, F. (2006). *El Fenómeno Político de Álvaro Uribe Vélez*. Retrieved from www.institut-gouvernance.org/en/analyse/fiche-analyse-245.html

Guerrero, J. (1999). La Sobre Politización del Narcotráfico en Colombia en los Años Ochenta y sus Interferencias en los Procesos de Paz. In: Peñaranda, R. and Guerreo, J. (eds), *De las Armas a la Política*. Bogota: Tercer Mundo editores, 219–296.

Orozco, C.A. (2012). *La Deuda Externa en Colombia y Su Efecto en el Producto Interno Bruto en el Periodo 1988–2008*. Colombia: Universidad Nacional de Colombia.

Payne, M., Zovatto, D.G., and Mateo Diaz, M.T. (2003). Banco Interamericano de Desarrollo e Instituto Internacional para la Democracia y la Asistencia Electoral. In: Payne, M. (ed.), *La Política Importa. Democracia y desarrollo en América Latina*. Washington, DC: Inter-American Development Bank.

Pizarro, E. and Bejarano, A.M. (1994). Colombia: Neoliberalismo Moderado Liberalismo Socialdemócrata. *Nueva Sociedad*, 133, 12–39.

Ramírez, M. and Guevara, D.A. (2006). Mercado de Trabajo, Subempleo, Informalidad y Precarización del Empleo: los Efectos de la Globalización. *Economía y Desarrollo*, 5(1), 96–131.

Santamaría, R. (1998). César Gaviria Trujillo. *Semana*, November 9.

Vargas, M. (1993). *Tristes Tigres*. Bogota: Planeta.

Vasco, R. (2004). *Reformas tributarias en los últimos 14 años*. Retrieved from http://actualicese.com/actualidad/2004/12/26/04124/

Villamizar, M.E. and Díaz, A.M. (2010). *Balance de las Políticas del Gobierno del Presidente Álvaro Uribe Vélez*. Retrieved from www.limpalcolombia.org/userfiles/balance.pdf

Weyland, K. (1999). Neoliberal Populism in Latin America and Eastern Europe. *Comparative Politics*, 31, 379–401.

News Sources

Dinero: www.dinero.com/
El Tiempo: www.eltiempo.com/
La Silla Vacia: http://lasillavacia.com/
Semana: www.semana.com/

7 The Singularity of Peruvian Politics and the Role of Presidential Leadership
The Cases of Alberto Fujimori and Alan García

Martín Tanaka and Jorge Morel

In this chapter,[1] we analyze the singularity of Peruvian politics in recent decades, a course which is clearly distinguishable from that of other countries in the region. We focus on the study of the governments of former presidents Alan García (1985–1990 and 2006–2011) and Alberto Fujimori (1990–1995 and 1995–2000). We point out the way in which specific and unexpected decisions they made set the country on an unforeseen course that would distance it from trends that marked the region as a whole. At the beginning of the 1990s, Peru saw an early collapse of its party system and the implementation of market-oriented reforms under an authoritarian regime. In the region as a whole, those reforms, although they marked a significant mutation in party systems and gave rise to 'delegative' ways of exercising power, were not accompanied by collapse or authoritarian forms of government. Those phenomena would occur in the following decade, as part of a re-emergence of populist and leftist ideas. Afterwards, in the first decade of the 2000s, the limitations of neoliberal policies caused a 'left turn' throughout the region, which also brought Alan García to power in 2006 (and, subsequently, Ollanta Humala in 2011). Unexpectedly, however, Peru continued to follow market-oriented policies, the left lost relevance and the political climate was characterized by a clearly conservative discourse.

We argue that the Peruvian singularity in the regional context is a consequence of unexpected decisions made and actions taken by Presidents Fujimori and García, for very particular reasons. We believe that analysis of their leadership and their decisions, the political 'agency,' is very important for Peru, where structuralist reasoning—which considers the course of politics to be 'predetermined' by the economic and social spheres—has excessive influence (see Tanaka, 2001). From that viewpoint, political leaders would have little participation and would be impotent witnesses or mere reflections of structural conditions that essentially predetermine the path taken by their governments. In the early 1990s, however, amid a serious economic and political crisis, the most likely outcome for Alberto Fujimori, a novice politician with an improvised party and a minority in Congress, would have been a weak government unable to implement significant reforms and hobbled by the opposition. Instead, Fujimori showed exceptional and disconcerting political will and ability to build an authoritarian, personalistic regime, implement neoliberal reforms, minimize the opposition and consolidate power so he could remain in office throughout the 1990s. Later, dissatisfaction with the distributive results of those reforms would return Alan García to power (and, subsequently, Ollanta Humala), which might have brought back a national-popular discourse, as it did in other countries. But García's desire to reinvent himself as a politician and not expose himself to the criticism leveled at his first government explains why his second administration took a markedly conservative turn, and why he did not implement large-scale redistributive social policies to take advantage of the country's economic boom, as occurred in neighboring countries that rode the wave of the political 'left turn.'

In more general theoretical terms, we believe that the Peruvian case is highly illustrative of the importance of studying political elites and leadership: in this case, they constitute a key independent variable for understanding political dynamics and events.

We will quickly review the prevalent method of viewing the evolution of Peruvian politics in recent decades, which emphasizes structural factors in which political leaders 'reproduce,' through their behaviors, certain 'balances of power' established in the economic and social spheres while appearing to lack initiative and impact. We will then analyze the first Alan García presidency (1985–1990), the decade of the two Alberto Fujimori administrations (1990–1995 and 1995–2000) and García's return to the presidency (2006–2011). We will examine the characteristics of these presidents' leadership, the circumstances in which they came to power and which surrounded their presidencies, and the institutional frameworks in which they governed, highlighting the specific role of leadership as a variable in defining the course of their governments. We will end with some general conclusions and implications that we believe can be drawn from this study.

Structure and Agency in Peruvian Politics

The study of Peruvian politics in general, and in the last few decades in particular, has tended to emphasize the economic and social structural conditions of the time and how they marked the specific course of political events. This is not surprising, considering the importance of an intellectual tradition strongly anchored in political sociology to explain political phenomena in Peru.[2]

In that view, the problems of Peruvian democracy in the 1980s are explained by the non-existence of a democratic tradition and an economy that was in crisis due to high vulnerability and dependence on the vagaries of the global economy. This weak, young democracy sat atop an extremely unequal society with high levels of poverty and discrimination, which led to the emergence of armed insurrections, reflected in the actions of the Partido Comunista del Perú—

Sendero Luminoso (SL) and the Movimiento Revolucionario Túpac Amaru (MRTA).[3] In the political sphere, parties inherited the tradition of a confrontational and polarized political culture, all of which augured serious problems for governance. Against this backdrop, the election in 1985 of the young President Alan García (who was 36 at the time), the candidate of the Partido Aprista Peruano, was seen as another step in a pattern of increasing polarization: it was thought that a center-left reformist effort would fail, unable to overcome the limits imposed by a context of crisis that would require more drastic measures, in either a leftist (social revolution) or right-wing (repressive military coup) style. García's political voluntarism thus seemed to offer practically no possibility of avoiding a fate of growing confrontation.[4] One of the first to warn of the risk of a coming catastrophe due to the exacerbation of problems and increasing polarization in the country in the late 1980s was Pásara (1987), who, in a famous work, warned of the risks of 'the Lebanonization of Peruvian democracy.' It should be noted that Pásara published that text in 1987, before the economic collapse of 1988–1990.

In fact, the García government ended with a country in serious economic crisis, plagued by recession and hyperinflation and devastated by an increase in subversive activity. This accentuated the political confrontation and polarization but also triggered a serious crisis of representation, which allowed the victory of an *outsider* with an anti-party discourse, Alberto Fujimori. Most analysts considered this to be the consequence of the seriousness of the crisis and the persistence of structural patterns not conducive to democracy, as well as changes that had occurred within Peru's social structure. For example, on the one hand, for Cotler (1993:14), 'the persistence of the deep divisions and social, regional, ethnic and racial prejudices' that 'reinforce political and governmental behaviors and values of a particularistic nature' would explain 'the failure of García's populism,' which 'precipitated the breakdown of the instrumental legitimacy of the parties and of the political regime.' On the other hand, for Grompone (1991: 62), Fujimori's election was the result of the fact that Peruvians were looking for 'new [political] connections' consistent with the emergence of the informal sector and with new forms of interpersonal relationship beyond the mass media and traditional representative relationships. Fujimori's victory was therefore proof of 'the existing imbalances, the depth of social gaps and the diversity of channels by which judgments are shaped and decisions are made.' Similarly, Degregori (1991) pointed out that 'fujimorismo's social base' consisted of popular sectors that aspired to a modernity 'different' from the 'occidentalized' modernity represented by Mario Vargas Llosa.

The years of 'fujimorismo' implied an enormous change in Peru, implanting a market-oriented economic model of 'neoliberal' reform; ending the threat of terrorism with the capture of the leaders of SL and the MRTA; and implementing an authoritarian form of government, reflected in both the 'self-coup' of April 1992 and the growing power and influence of the president's intelligence adviser, Vladimiro Montesinos, in government decisions. Following logic that appealed to 'long-range' factors unrelated to political agency, the authoritarian nature of 'fujimorismo' was also seen as a consequence of the characteristics of Peruvian political culture, its authoritarian history and the absence of democratic traditions. For example, Murakami (2007), in what is perhaps the most comprehensive work written about the period, emphasizes that 'fujimorismo' should not be considered a phenomenon separate from Peruvian political tradition. Rather, its essence should be viewed in light of the persistence of plebiscitarian traditions of political patronage in the relationship between the governing and the governed; patrimonial, authoritarian and 'caudillista' forms of exercising power; and relationships between political actors that are marked by confrontation and short-sightedness.[5]

Some authors have called attention to a 'structural' relationship between authoritarianism and neoliberal reforms. The latter may have benefited a small set of domestic and foreign business groups that would have gained enormous power and influence over state and government decisions, and imposed an exclusionary or authoritarian model of governance. The continuity of these interests would explain the 'failure' of the 'democratic transition' that occurred in 2000. With the fall of 'fujimorismo,' there was an expectation of significant change and substantive democratization of the political regime, in both the institutional realm and in terms of the economic model. Alejandro Toledo won the 2001 general election with the promise of democratic institutionalization, and Alan García and (even more so) Ollanta Humala won in 2006 and 2011, respectively, under the banner of a change away from neoliberal policies, reflected in their campaign slogans, 'The responsible change' and 'The great transformation' and following the 'left turn' that was occurring in the region as a whole.[6] The second Alan García government, however, proved to be markedly conservative, and Ollanta Humala, the 'anti-system' candidate, ended by breaking with allies on the left to follow a moderate path of continuity with the dominant economic model.

By the end of the first decade of the new century, at the dusk of the democratic transition, Peru demonstrated a great paradox: significant economic growth accompanied by a fully democratic political regime, but also great disenchantment with and lack of legitimacy of the institutions of the political system. For authors such as Adrianzén (2009), the explanation may lie in the 'truncated' nature of the democratic transition. While other countries in the Andean region (Venezuela, Bolivia and Ecuador) experienced profound changes, reflected in constituent assemblies that redefined the entire political system and sought new development models apart from neoliberal polities, Peru followed a path of continuity. The fact that there has been no great institutional reform or change in the economic model in Peru may explain the high levels of disenchantment with the democratic regime. For Adrianzén, the weight of 'de-facto powers' could be the key to maintaining the economic and political model inherited from 'fujimorismo.'

Along a similar line, Lynch (2009: 139) highlights the establishment of a 'crony-capitalism,' particularly during the second García administration, and a movement toward a 'patrimonial, neoliberal-style State,' where those who govern view national interests from the standpoint of the business elites.

This would explain various decisions made by the García government, such as its refusal to impose a tax on mining companies' 'windfall profits' or to review the free trade agreement with the United States—campaign promises that were later ignored during his administration. Lynch draws a parallel between the second Aprista government and the governments of the so-called 'second civilian period' at the beginning of the 20th century, when the government was headed by the bourgeois elite. Along the same line, for Durand (2012), governments in Peru since 1990 have been marked by a tendency toward a 'capture of the state' by business elites. The growing influence of the business sector was not necessarily accompanied by improvements in institutional capacity for control and regulation, so the private sector gained excessive influence over government decisions through mechanisms of direct access to power, such as the 'revolving door,' by which people move back and forth between jobs in the public and private sectors. For Durand, the second García presidency marks a 'return to the age of the oligarchy' (Durand, 2009).

What these interpretations have in common is that they deduce the behavior of the governments that followed the fall of 'fujimorismo' in 2000 from the continuity of the presence of economic power groups that have benefited from the neoliberal reforms. According to this view, Alan García distanced himself (as did Ollanta Humala) from more redistributive and leftist policies because of pressure from those interests. The course of politics appears to be determined by power stemming from position in the economic-social structure. In contrast, we argue here that the course of Peruvian politics could have been substantially different, that Peru had no reason to follow such a singular path in the regional context, and that the specific routes taken by its governments are largely explained by decisions made by its leaders, who took the country in unexpected directions.

As we will see, the great crisis at the end of the 1980s was not an inevitable outcome; rather, it was the result of unexpected decisions made by President García with a small group of advisers. These included critical decisions to nationalize banks in 1987 and to opt for an electoral management of the economy between 1988 and 1989; Peru's high inflation was not the result of a distributive battle between powerful unions and a weak government, but of political voluntarism exacerbated by García. Also, the most likely outcome during the first years of the Fujimori government would have been an extremely weak president who ended up dominated by the opposition and was unable to complete his term, allowing the political actors who predominated in the 1980s to return to power. Meanwhile, the market-oriented reforms that marked the 1990s could have occurred in a democratic context, as in other countries. But Fujimori's ambition and skill led to an unexpected outcome, which gave rise instead to the collapse of the system of political representation and the establishment of authoritarian order led by the president. Subsequently, it seemed most likely that the second Alan García administration would ride the wave of leftist governments that had appeared in the region in recent years, taking advantage of the economic boom to implement distributive social policies to build political legitimacy; instead, however, it was a relatively conservative government that suffered very low levels of public approval. As we will see, this can also be explained by García's personal decisions, mainly his desire to dissociate himself from his first administration.

This chapter is based on ideas presented in Tanaka (2013b), who indicates that, in theoretical terms, that the role of leaders should be considered a 'residual' independent variable, applicable once the relevance of structural and institutional factors is ruled out; and it should be to construct a credible counterfactual argument, showing that the leadership variable was crucial for following a path different from one which had been considered more likely. In Peru during the period under study, leaders are important, because if one thing characterizes Peruvian history in recent decades, it is structural change: first the exhaustion of the national-popular-statist model, and then the adoption of neoliberal policies which also failed to establish stable political legitimacy. This context of structural change can be considered as:

> an ambiguous and fluid period, a sort of critical juncture, a period of change and lack of definition, relatively limited in time, in which structural and institutional constraints are eased and there is more room for agency, so that what actors do or do not do, the institutional reforms they implement, will be decisive in shaping the region's future evolution.
>
> (Tanaka, 2013b: 39)

In such a context of crisis and change, with a weak party system and weak institutions, leaders take on particular importance. The specific characteristics of the leadership of García and Fujimori are crucial for explaining the course of their governments, which followed paths contrary to what would have been expected based on analysis of the overall political, economic and social context, as we will see in the next section.

Alan García 1985–1990: Excessive Voluntarism and Political Management of the Crisis

To understand the decisions made by Alan García during his first administration, it is necessary to pay attention to three factors: his origins as an active member of the Partido Aprista Peruano (PAP), the context in which he became president in 1985, and the large amount of maneuvering room he acquired for taking decisions alone, or with a very small circle of close friends and collaborators.

Alan García came from a middle-class family that had been active in politics since the middle of the twentieth century. His father, Carlos García, was an active member of the PAP and was imprisoned under the dictatorship of General Manuel Odría (1948–1956). His mother was founder of the Partido Aprista section in Camaná, a city in the department of Arequipa. Faithful to this tradition, in 1962 García joined the youth section of the PAP; after a short stint at the Pontifical Catholic University of Peru, García went on to study law at the National University of San Marcos. Along with other young leaders, García became very close to the founder of APRA, Víctor Raúl Haya de la Torre, who personally took charge of the most promising young party members; García stood out in that group, and in 1972, amid the proscription of political activity imposed by the military dictatorship of Juan Velasco (1968–1975), APRA sponsored his travel to Europe to continue his higher education. García studied in Spain and France, where he earned professional graduate degrees in law and sociology, respectively. With the transition to democracy in Peru in 1978, Haya recalled García to run for the Constituent Assembly, to which he was elected as a representative (see Rial, 2008).

After the death in 1979 of Haya, who had been the top leader of APRA for more than 50 years, the party's survival seemed questionable; the fight for succession led to bitter confrontations between the left and right wings of the party, and APRA was also perceived as an outmoded organization, headed by elderly leaders and disconnected from the new realities of the country. It was in that context that García emerged as a sort of 'savior' of the party. In 1977, he had been elected Secretary of Organization; in 1978, he was elected a member of the Constituent Assembly; and in 1980, he headed the party's Ideology and Doctrine Committee. In that year's elections, García was elected deputy, holding the first position on PAP's candidate list in the Lima jurisdiction. He later became leader of the party caucus in the Chamber of Deputies. In October 1982, García was elected secretary general of the party, the highest position. By then, he was already regarded as the leader of the opposition to the government of Fernando Belaunde. In 1984, García was nominated to be APRA's presidential candidate for the 1985 elections.

These accomplishments are surprising for someone so young (García was 33 when he became the party's secretary general). But García not only brought an image of youth to what was perceived as a party of old men; he also brought a new political discourse. He introduced ideas from renovated European socialism to the Peruvian scene, drawing on leaders such as Felipe González of Spain and François Mitterrand of France. The then-deputy also referred to the classics of European Marxism, such as Sartre, Marcuse and Althusser, social scientists such as François Bourricaud and Alain Touraine, and proponents of dependency theory (Barreda, 2012: 36 and 41).

Some early texts by the 'young García' shed light on the ambition of his plans for APRA. In an interview, García (1984: 13) spoke of the 'enormous responsibility' that would ensue if APRA won the presidency in 1985, for the first time in its history, which would 'oblige (the party) to continue and affirm the values of profound transformation represented by *aprismo*, updating its ideology in a changing and more unjust world.' As Barreda (2012: 55) notes, citing García's book *El futuro diferente* (1982), the author 'perceives the need for APRA to propose a model that breaks with the forms of dependency to which the national economy and national development had been subordinated; he also called for a break with the mindset of capitalism.' In updating the book *El futuro diferente*, García (1987) stated that after he was elected secretary general of APRA in 1982, there was a shift in his priorities and objectives, summarized as:

First, promoting the revolutionary objectives of the 'aprista' doctrine (. . .) Second, helping to catalyze the party in opposition to a regime that represented economic liberalism and the oligarchic concept of the State and society. But third, it had to perform these two tasks while building an image of a more rational and open party, which would allow 'aprismo' to overcome some forms of political behavior which, developed over long years of distance from power, had become, through inertia, constraints on its acceptance by new social groups in the country.

(García, 1987: 10–11)

The author later reaffirms that the 'aprista' government 'could not and cannot be an empirical government without a clear direction. We had to and must bring our efforts together around a system, a doctrine, an essential vision of transformation' (p. 11).

This shows that as early as 1982, García sought a substantial transformation of the country, which, in his view, was the least that could be demanded of a party that had spent 60 years struggling to come to power. García's proposal for renovation was attractive after the economic and political failure of the second Fernando Belaunde presidency (1980–1985). The country was suffering the effects of the external debt crisis and was experiencing high inflation and recession, and Sendero Luminoso was already perceived as a serious threat, especially in some departments in the Andes. APRA won the 1985 election with 53.1% of the vote and gained an absolute majority in both houses of Parliament, and the following year it won the mayoral races in Lima and in several of the country's largest provincial cities. García took the oath of office promising a 'democratic revolution' and a 'nationalist, democratic and popular' government. That same year, García became president of APRA, a position created especially for him.

From then on, García became firmly established as the indisputable (and, eventually, irreplaceable) leader of APRA; nevertheless, the relationship between García and APRA—beginning with the consolidation of his leadership in the 1980s—revealed a great paradox. Although the president was a man of the party, formed in its traditions and structures, and he shared with other active party members the ambition to create an 'aprista' government that would leave a profound imprint on the country's history. The particular way in which García's leadership was constructed gave him maneuvering room that went far beyond the party structure, creating a highly personalistic style leadership that tended to bypass the party as such. As president, García, made far-reaching decisions without consulting the party and, in some cases, against the party's wishes.

One example of that personalism in power, which had significant consequences for the government, was the July 1987 decision to nationalize the banking system. Although García's popularity was high during the first year and a half of his administration, and the country seemed to be on a good path, with an economic policy based on measures to stimulate demand, which reactivated the economy, reduced inflation and created a generalized sense of well-being,[7] in early 1987 there were signs that this strategy had run its course. Economic growth began to create problems for the balance of payments, and international reserves were rapidly exhausted; the government's revolutionary rhetoric did not sit well with the private sector, which led to capital flight and decreased investment; and policies to increase public spending began to cause inflation, which could not be stemmed with price-control policies. By the beginning of the administration's third year, perhaps the most reasonable and expected approach would have been for the president to opt for 'deceleration' of economic growth, with some adjustment measures and promotion of private investment. Instead, García deepened his 'revolutionary' plan, proposing the nationalization of banks and insurance companies, an initiative he announced in his July 28 speech before Congress. He took not only the country but his own party caucus by surprise, so much so that, although the nationalization law was approved by the 'aprista' majority in the lower house, it was not approved by the Senate, because it lacked the support of certain important APRA leaders such as Luis Alberto Sánchez.

The ultimately unsuccessful effort to nationalize the banking system was the beginning of what became a disastrous García administration. The distance between the government and the private sector became irremediable, as did the distrust between the president and his own party. Within APRA, the perception was that García governed with his own circle of friends and advisors, outside of the party.[8] Nevertheless, García's personalistic style of government decision-making continued to the end. In September 1988, with the situation spiraling out of control, a severe economic adjustment was inevitable. But García chose to manage the economy for political and electoral ends, ahead of the 1990 election, even though that meant high inflation and a virtual collapse of fiscal accounts. García sought to block a victory by Mario Vargas Llosa in those elections, a goal he finally achieved by supporting outsider Alberto Fujimori. If we compare Peru's experience of hyperinflation with that of Argentina during those years, or with that of Bolivia in the first half of the 1980s, we see more evidence of the importance of García's leadership in shaping the economic dynamics of his government. In those other two countries, one key element of the inflationary dynamic was a distributive battle between strong unions, which brought pressure for higher wages, and a state that felt cornered and was willing to make concessions, and whose tendency to spend caused inflation, thus exacerbating the unions' protests. In Peru, management of the economy for political ends, based on policies to stimulate demand, was due not so much to union pressure as to García's efforts to legitimize his leadership.[9]

What conclusions can be drawn from this review? We believe that García's singular method of leadership is absolutely crucial for understanding the course of his government. Without his leadership, an APRA government probably would have been less voluntaristic and more prudent, and would have turned in a relatively mediocre performance similar to that of its predecessor, without falling into the extremes of fiscal chaos and hyperinflation in which García's tenure ended. In short, excessive voluntarism and unbridled ambition led García to a highly ideologized management of his administration, which resulted in disaster. And that disaster had consequences: a serious crisis of political representation, which propelled outsider Alberto Fujimori into office.

Alberto Fujimori 1990–2000: Personal Ambition and Party Collapse

Alberto Fujimori's history is very different from that of Alan García. He was born in 1938 into a family of Japanese immigrants, spent his childhood in the Lima working-class district of La Victoria, and never showed a political bent. Despite economic difficulties, Fujimori graduated from La Molina National Agrarian University as an agronomy engineer. His good academic performance enabled him to do graduate studies in mathematics and physics at the University of Strasbourg in France and later at the University of Wisconsin in the United States.

Fujimori's first incursion into public affairs came in 1977, when he ran for the post of rector of his university, and although he won the first minority in the first round of balloting, he lost in the second (Bowen, 2000: 10). He ran again in 1984, and this time, he won. Bowen describes how, during that period, he began to exhibit the authoritarian tendencies that would characterize him as president of Peru: he worked with a hand-picked team of trusted people, never presented the mandatory annual reports of his administration, and made decisions without consulting the University Assembly (Bowen, 2000: 11). Nevertheless, he gained a certain legitimacy because of his serious and politically moderate style, at a time when political polarization was rampant in national universities, especially among groups on the extreme left. In 1987, during the García government, he was elected president of the National Assembly of Rectors (Asamblea Nacional de Rectores), a position he used to establish contacts with the political world. Those contacts helped him to broadcast a program, 'Concertando,' on public television. That venue—as Fujimori himself tells it[10]—allowed him to become known in the country's disparate regions, many of which received only the public television signal. His moderate image, according to Murakami (2007: 186), attracted even García's attention, and the president once unsuccessfully offered him the chance to head the Ministry of Agriculture.

Around 1988, Fujimori began to show an interest in entering politics. It is revealing that he approached both the APRA and groups on the left to find space as an independent candidate for the Senate. When they turned him down, he decided to create his own political organization. The plan was to run for president as a propaganda strategy to improve his chances of being elected senator, an office for which he would also run.[11] He sought the support of colleagues at the agrarian university and in evangelical communities, convincing them that 'Cambio 90,' the new party, would be a useful vehicle for them to win seats in Congress (Bowen, 2000: 18). Fujimori's political precariousness led him to choose his vice presidential candidates almost as an afterthought. Máximo San Román, a leader of small business associations and his first vice president, had met Fujimori barely two months before the deadline for candidate registration; and Fujimori chose Carlos García, his second vice president, from among evangelical leaders just hours before the deadline for registering as a presidential candidate. The participation of these people, according to Bowen, was due to Fujimori's interest in highlighting the multiethnic nature of his presidential ticket ('el chino, el cholo y el negro'), in an effort to gain the sympathy of the country's grassroots sectors.

The 1990 election campaign unexpectedly favored the unknown candidate Fujimori. García's main goal was to keep the liberal candidate, Mario Vargas Llosa, from winning the 1990 election, as his political identity was the antithesis of that of the outgoing president. As Bowen (2000), Schmidt (1996) and Daeschner (1993) note, the government mobilized the state-run media in an aggressive campaign against Vargas Llosa—partly orchestrated by the National Intelligence Service—and sought to promote an alternative candidate. With the weakness of Alfonso Barrantes' candidacy, amid the division of the left, and given García's antipathy toward APRA candidate Luis Alva Castro (whom he saw as a rival who could challenge him for control of the party), the president ended up supporting Fujimori's emerging candidacy.

Amid a campaign that was excessively ideologized by Mario Vargas Llosa, as well as the division of the left and the limitations of the APRA candidate running during a serious government crisis, Fujimori became the completely unexpected winner of the election; that surprise, in our view, casts serious doubts on post-facto explanations that attribute it to structural factors or variables. On the contrary, based on those analyses, the election would have been expected to reflect the growing political polarization and confrontation that characterized the country, and which would have been expressed in high vote counts for the candidates on the right (Vargas Llosa) and left (Barrantes). But given the peculiar characteristics of the 1990 election campaign, Fujimori ended up the winner. Once elected, his inexperience and the precariousness of his political movement foreshadowed a period of instability; because the president did not have a majority in Congress, the opposition parties could have been expected to have tied the hands of a weak president, as occurred during the first government of Fernando Belaunde (1963–1968). Considering that Fujimori came to power during a serious crisis of hyperinflation, virtual bankruptcy of government coffers, and a growing threat from terrorist groups, some analysts envisioned a scenario in which the president would be forced to resign and call new general elections (Kenney, 2004).

As Murakami (2007: 273–274) notes, however, from early in his presidency, Fujimori unexpectedly demonstrated 'strong leadership and a great ability to take the initiative.' Because he lacked a party, Fujimori depended increasingly on the support of the Armed Forces, committing himself to implementing their recommendations for an anti-subversive strategy, and the National Intelligence Service, used to implement political initiatives, in which adviser Vladimiro Montesinos became increasingly influential. In the economic sphere, Fujimori quickly changed his policy team and let himself be guided by pressure or recommendations from international financial bodies, and he called in independent technical advisers of a liberal bent. Between July 1990 and April 1992, Fujimori outlined a strategy in which criticism of the 'traditional parties' was a key part of his discourse and association with the Armed Forces and the intelligence services met his needs for political organization and operation. Once he gained legitimacy domestically and internationally for controlling hyperinflation, Fujimori opted for the path that would lead to the institutional coup of April 1992, which met with widespread public approval.

This outcome was surprising and contradicted the most likely scenarios envisioned by most political analysts, and the explanation can only be found in Alberto Fujimori's leadership and decisions. The only author who makes a sustained argument in retrospect about the 'foreseeability' of Fujimori's coup is Kenney (2004). He contends that Peru's historical tradition shows that it is too costly politically to govern with a minority in Parliament, so the coup should not have been surprising. Kenney's argument, however, applies to coups *against* the executive branch, not *by* the executive branch; this again leads us to consider the importance of Fujimori's leadership and his decision to confront the political class instead of building bridges with it. Moreover, in recent years, new literature about parliamentarized presidentialism notes that when a strong-president government exist, a chief executive without a majority in Congress is not necessarily condemned to paralysis and crisis, because he can build majorities through political negotiation. Fujimori could have tried to build a majority in Congress under strong presidential leadership, and he could have led a process of structural reforms around democracy despite 'delegative' tendencies, as occurred in countries such as Argentina or Bolivia during the same years. If that path had been taken, Peru would not have suffered the collapse of its entire system of political representation. Within the framework of the third democratizing wave, Peru is the only case of neoliberal reform implemented under an authoritarian regime, and the only country in which the party system collapsed during the implementation of those reforms.[12] As Tanaka (2005b) notes, contrary to the view of many authors who try to deduce the dynamics from structural factors, Peruvian politics during those years resulted not from a 'chronicle of a death foretold,' but from an enigmatic history of unexpected twists and surprising outcomes.[13]

Alan García 2006–2011: Personal Amends and Ideological Reconversion

The abrupt way in which the Fujimori government ended helps to explain the rebirth of APRA and Alan García in 2000. The last months of the Fujimori government were marked by massive protests against a second re-election for the president and complaints of growing authoritarianism and corruption in the government, which was meanwhile being seriously questioned over various cases of human rights violations that occurred during his first administration, and which were still awaiting investigation. Under those circumstances, APRA opted to join the other anti-'fujimorista' forces by raising the banner of democracy, which meant a 'complete about-face' for a party that had been specifically accused of human rights violations and corruption during its own first government.[14] When members of the Fujimori administration began to face legal charges toward the end of the first decade of the 2000s, Alan García managed to ensure that the statute of limitations had run out on the crimes for which he had been pursued during the 1990s. Without legal impediments, the former president returned in November of 2000, after a long absence from the country, and launched his candidacy for president in the 2001 elections. García's discourse was now more moderate, and he positioned himself as a center-left candidate who had matured and learned from mistakes made during his first administration. García, persecuted and exiled after 1992, appeared to be vindicated by the fall of 'fujimorismo' and was 'new' on the scene after an eight-year absence.

APRA's recovery and García's return also had much to do with the lack of other leftist or center-left options. With the fall of 'fujimorismo,' Perú Posible, led by Alejandro Toledo, became one of the main political groups, with a discourse focusing on the recovery of democratic institutions. Toward the right, the Partido Popular Cristiano, led by Lourdes Flores, reappeared as the main exponent. But the left practically disappeared from the political map; one more moderate strain ended up becoming part of Perú Posible, and another, more radical one tried unsuccessfully to reach the registration threshold that would allow it to participate in the election. García reappeared in this vacuum, positioning himself as a critic of the dominant economic model.[15]

APRA's performance in the 2001 elections was spectacular, compared to its poor showing in 1995 and 2000. In 1995, Fujimori had been re-elected with 64 percent of the vote, whereas the APRA candidate, Mercedes Cabanillas, won barely 4 percent, and the party list for the new unicameral Congress polled 7 percent. In 2000, presidential candidate Abel Salinas won just 1 percent of the vote, and the legislative list polled 6 percent. A year later, in 2001, García came second behind Alejandro Toledo, with the two of them winning 26 and 37 percent of the vote, respectively. In the 'ballotage,' Toledo won with 53 percent, compared to García's 47 percent. In Congress, APRA won 20 percent of the vote, which made it the main opposition force, increasing from six to 28 seats in the 120-member Congress. A year later, in the 2001 regional elections, APRA won twelve of the 25 regional governments. That impressive recovery gave APRA, and the country in general, the idea that without García the party was practically non-existent, and with him, a very competitive actor. This consolidated a highly personalistic leadership style that was contemptuous of the party apparatus.

During the Toledo government, García took a leftist opposition stance, speaking out against more flexible labor laws and precarious labor regimes and proposing the creation of a state-run bank for farmers—ideas that led business sectors to oppose and distrust him. García participated in several protest marches against the Toledo government, accompanying leaders of leftist unions such as the Central General de Trabajadores del Perú (CGTP) and the Sindicato Único de Trabajadores de la Educación Peruana (SUTEP). This alignment was to be expected amid the wave of criticism of the 'neoliberal' model sweeping Latin

America in those years, which translated into the so-called 'left turn.' The 2006 elections saw the unexpected rise in the polls of former Army officer Ollanta Humala, who was known for having led a small uprising against the government in October 2000, during the final weeks of the Fujimori administration, with a leftist and nationalist discourse. Humala won the backing of Venezuelan President Hugo Chávez, which situated him clearly to the left on the political spectrum, and he capitalized on discontent with the (thus-far-) limited distributive effects of neoliberal politics.

In the first round of balloting, Humala appeared to be the favorite candidate, although he failed to win 50 percent of the vote. The question, then, was who would confront him in the runoff. This pitted García against the candidate of the right, Lourdes Flores; García used a more leftist discourse in the first round to defeat Flores (accusing her of being 'the candidate of the rich'), although he won by a tight margin.[16] In the runoff, García moved toward the center-right, facing off against Humala with a discourse of 'responsible change,' which carried him to the presidency for a second time.

García in the presidency sparked distrust among conservative sectors, which feared that he would repeat his voluntaristic excesses and populist, 'caudillista' style of government, and that he would join the trends that marked the 'left turn' in the region, perhaps in the social democrat style of Presidents Lula in Brazil and Lagos and Bachelet in Chile. But what began as a strategy for winning a close presidential race with the help of a center-right coalition to confront the threat of Humala ended as a sort of ideological reconversion for the president, who put Peru on a path that ran counter to that of many other countries in the region, which were implementing ambitious social and redistributive policies that legitimized their governments. This distinctive turn was possible because of García's personalistic style of managing the governing party; it was driven by the president, not by his party.

Although there are other cases of populist or leftist presidents who moderated their views and moved to the political center, or even to the right, García made that shift precisely when the wave in the region was moving in the opposite direction. Moreover, the government's rhetoric became markedly conservative and its political orientation focused on creating a climate of confidence to promote large-scale private investment, especially in extractive industries. Significant redistributive policies were not implemented, either with an eye toward political patronage or for any other motive. This is remarkable, considering García's populist, nationalist and revolutionary rhetoric during the 1980s and even just a few years before winning his second term. Meanwhile, he developed a very conservative discourse, leading the charge on issues such as the death penalty for child rapists and Peru's withdrawal from the jurisdiction of the Inter-American Court of Human Rights, and criticizing the left and grassroots organizations for opposing large-scale investment projects that he proposed.

García set out his ideas in three controversial essays published in the conservative daily *El Comercio*: 'The dog in the manger syndrome' ('El síndrome del perro del hortelano') on October 28, 2007, 'Recipe for doing away with the dog in the manger' ('Receta para acabar con el perro del hortelano') on November 25, 2007, and 'The dog in the manger against the poor' ('El perro del hortelano contra el pobre') on March 2, 2008. In these essays, he identified large-scale investment as the driver of development, blocked by sectors characterized as pre-modern, which opposed development out of either ignorance or fear, or because they were defending special interests. Later, in his book, *La revolución constructiva del aprismo. Teoría y práctica de la modernidad* (2008), García justified the shift in his government's stance from a doctrinaire standpoint. In the book, García tries to establish continuity between the thinking of Haya de la Torre and the path taken during his second administration. For García, Haya de la Torre's thinking 'evolves over time,' and his old premises therefore cannot be applied literally to the current situation. The essence of Haya would be to seek 'concrete results in decentralized growth, in the creation of spaces for the employment, health and education of the majorities.' That would distance him from positions of the left: 'Haya de la Torre's fight against European communism and its creole followers does not allow "aprismo" to be confused with any form of red or pink extremism, or social democracy to be confused with irresponsible populism and statism' (p. 16).

How did García assess the nature of his first government, in hindsight? In a self-critical reflection, he noted that the model implemented during his first administration was not 'aprista,' but 'velasquista.' During the dictatorship of Juan Velasco (1968–1975), Peru had experienced its populist 'revolutionary nationalist' moment, with initiatives such as agrarian reform and nationalization of the largest oil and mining companies. According to García, the 'aprista' leadership, of which he was part,[17] took literally a populist mandate expressed in the 1979 Constitution (drafted under 'aprista' influence) and uncritically took stewardship of an economic model inherited from the revolutionary government of the Armed Forces (1968–1980). For García, that meant abandoning the doctrine of Haya de la Torre, who always advised applying 'aprista' ideas in accord with the times. The former president wrote that after the first two years of economic growth, between 1985 and 1987, the economic model should have been redefined to contain the looming inflationary cycle:

> After the reactivation, a policy should have been implemented to attract capital, privatizing some areas (. . .) to facilitate investment and employment under regulated and true free-market conditions, with the realistic sense that Haya called for, but did not apply. That would have compensated for the complete absence of global credit and the lack of investment (. . .)
> (García, 2008: 106–107)

García's conservative turn was unexpected and counterproductive, from the standpoint of his own political interests. That explains why García remained a president with low public approval in a context where approval levels had generally been high throughout the region, due to economic growth. In the Mitofsky poll of October 2010, García was the president with the lowest approval rating in Latin America, in the 51st month of his presidency, matching only Fernando Lugo in his 25th month. This result is even more disconcerting considering that the Peruvian economy is among those that have grown most in the region in recent years, making it possible for fiscal resources to increase substantially. The national government's revenues multiplied by 3.6 times between 2001 and 2012, and more than doubled between 2005 and 2012.

What caused this about-face? To a great extent, it was the result of his interest in leaving no doubt about whether his second administration would repeat the traumatic experience of the 1980s, and thus in reinventing himself as a political figure. Once again, García's leadership is decisive to the explanation of this outcome, distancing Peru's APRA government from what was being done in neighboring more countries characterized by redistributive policies, significant social-spending initiatives and anti-neoliberal rhetoric. The policies for stimulating investment in extractive industries unleashed a growing dynamic of sometimes-violent social conflicts, which marked the entire second administration. García avoided any initiative that would have served as even the most remote reminder of his first administration and opted for a conservative, pro-business rhetoric and governing term, distancing himself from the populist profile and leftist rhetoric of his past, and he paid the price in low approval ratings. Was this reversal imperative to avoid a boycott by the business sector? We don't believe so, because García appeared to be a defender of continuity of the economic model against the anti-system challenge posed by Ollanta Humala. This gave García plenty of room to emphasize redistributive social policies. From that point on, however, his discourse was dominated by a notoriously conservative mindset.

Conclusions

By examining the paths taken by Alan García and Alberto Fujimori, we have argued that politicians' leadership styles are key for understanding the distinct path taken by Peru in comparison to the region overall. Without these two leaders' intervention, Peru probably would have followed a course more similar to that of other Latin American countries. In nations such as Peru, marked by times of change, crisis and instability, structural and institutional determinants are less decisive, and there has been room for the agency of political actors who mark out directions that cannot be explained by those factors—routes that are unexpected and that are perceived, at the time, as unlikely. This is one aspect that justifies the study of elites and political leaders: they may sometimes be key independent variables for understanding important political phenomena (see Tanaka, 2015).

It might have been most 'reasonable' therefore to assume that the first García administration would be a mediocre government affected by the international crisis of the 1980s, as in the rest of the region, but without leading to a collapse of its system of representation; later, it would have been likely for the government of the outsider Fujimori to be weak and hobbled by its minority standing in Congress, which could have led to the emergence of a rightist coalition built around the implementation of neoliberal reforms. Later, the second García administration might have been expected to take a bolder redistributive course within a moderate macroeconomic model more in tune with the 'left turn' under way in the region. The role of leadership is therefore crucial to understanding the hyperinflation of the late 1980s (under García); the institutional coup of April 5, 1992, the consolidation of an authoritarian regime, and the collapse of the party system (under 'fujimorismo'); and later the markedly conservative nature of the second García administration, amid internal demands for social change and an international context more oriented toward progressive policies.

The leadership styles of García and Fujimori were key to these unforeseen outcomes, in which each left his mark because of his particular political formation and experience, personal interest, and the incentives he faced in each situation. Despite the great differences in their early development, one marked by strong party socialization and the other by political inexperience, they show striking similarities. In both cases, we see leaders with excessively personalistic styles who operated outside the boundaries of established groups and rules, placing priority on what they saw as their personal interests; that gave rise to the relatively unexpected paths they followed. It is fair to point out that the weight carried by the leader is certainly a consequence of the weakness of parties and political institutions; if they had had greater weight, the influence of the leader and the unforeseeable nature of their directions would have been more limited. Even in the case of APRA, the strongest party in the country, the weight of García's leadership was overwhelming; in the case of Fujimori, his leadership was a reflection of the collapse of the system of political representation as a whole.

For those reasons, the analysis presented in this chapter could be extended to other Peruvian political figures. For example, much of the dynamic of political violence in the 1980s and 1990s, which has been generally studied from an historical or structural standpoint, can be explained by the very peculiar leadership and the decisions made by Abimael Guzmán, the top leader of Sendero Luminoso, who styled himself as the 'beacon of the global revolution' and the 'fourth sword' of Marxism, after Marx, Lenin and Mao.[18] And other cases in which leadership became decisive to shaping trends that otherwise would never have occurred may also come to mind.

In recent years, Peru has advanced in its economic growth, as well as in the development of an economic institutional structure that partly explains its high growth rates. Nevertheless, it remains encumbered by a serious lack of political and institutional development. This continues to raise questions about the sustainability of democratic governance, which always appears to be 'hanging by a thread,' subject to the vagaries of circumstantial leadership.

Notes

1 A preliminary version of this chapter was discussed at the seminar 'The Study of Political Elites,' organized by FLACSO Spain and the University of Salamanca in June 2015. The authors thank Marcelo Camerlo for his comments on that occasion.

A first draft was presented at the Seventh Congress of the Latin American Political Science Association (ALACIP, for its Spanish initials) at the University of the Andes (Bogota) September 2013.
2 See Tanaka (2005a). A classic example of this approach can be found in Cotler (1978).
3 See Comisión de la Verdad y Reconciliación (2003).
4 According to Sinesio López (1985), 'APRA won, but IU obtained the right of opposition and succession, which shifted rapidly to the left. A vote for APRA is a vote-in-waiting for IU. Alan García and APRA are in the Government Palace, but Alfonso Barrantes and IU are on the threshold.'
5 See also Rochabrún (2007), who criticizes the tendency of various Peruvian social scientists to explain 'fujimorismo' appealing to the 'authoritarianism' of popular sectors.
6 See Castañeda and Morales (2008) and Morales (2008), who consider the second García government to be part of the 'left turn', although Tanaka (2008b), in the same book, characterizes his administration as conservative. What is true is that in the first round of presidential voting in 2006, García used a more leftist discourse to face against Lourdes Flores, accusing her of being 'the candidate of the rich.' In the runoff, when he faced Ollanta Humala, García began the conservative turn that would characterize his administration.
7 Assessing his first two years in office, García called for the government's main areas of action to be related to the fight against financial imperialism and external debt (the government set a limit for external debt payments equal to 10% of total exports), rejection of economic liberalism and his option for economic heterodoxy, the democratization of relations between the state and society, the quest for social justice, and the deeper rooting of what he called 'the ethic of the revolution,' which he shared particularly with the non-aligned international movement (García: 1987: 11–23).
8 In APRA's 16th National Congress in 1988, Luis Alva Castro, one of García's rivals, was elected the new secretary general and García lost the party presidency. During the opening of the event, while García was speaking to the Assembly, he was interrupted several times by shouts of 'Out with the friends!'
9 On the first García government, see Tanaka (1998); also Crabtree (2005), Reyna (2000), Iguíñiz et al. (1993), among others. On the dynamics of inflation and adjustment in Latin America, see Smith, Acuña and Gamarra (1994a, 1994b).
10 See 'Mi curriculum vitae,' cited in Murakami (2007).
11 Electoral legislation at the time allowed presidential candidates to run for Congress.
12 On coalition presidentialism, see Lanzaro (2001); on delegative democracy, see O'Donnell (1992).
13 On 'fujimorismo,' see also Tanaka (1998), López (1998), Pease (2003), Cotler and Grompone (2000).
14 Although it is fair to recognize that there also may have been a parallel strategy of rapprochement with the government. Agustín Mantilla, an important 'aprista' leader, was tried and imprisoned for receiving money from Vladimiro Montesinos in March 2000 to support Fujimori's re-election.
15 See Tanaka (2008a, 2008b).
16 In the first round of balloting, Humala won 30.6% of the vote, García 24.3% and Flores 23.8%.
17 Although all evidence indicates that the first 'aprista' government was basically directed by García and his group of close friends, the president—in this paper—constantly uses the expression, 'the *aprista* government,' leaving the impression that politics in 1985–1990 were guided by the party as a whole.

18 On Guzmán's leadership and his importance in Sendero Luminoso and in the dynamic of the internal armed conflict, see Degregori (2011), Portocarrero (2012), Tanaka (2013a).

References

Adrianzén, A. (2009). *La transición inconclusa: de la década autoritaria al nacimiento del pueblo*. Lima: Otra Mirada.
Barreda, J. (2012). *1987: Los límites de la voluntad política*. Lima: Mitin Editores.
Bowen, S. (2000). *El expediente Fujimori: el Perú y su presidente 1990–2000*. Lima: Perú Monitor S.A.
Castañeda, J. and Morales, M. (2008). The Current State of the Utopia. In: Castañeda, J. and Morales, M. (eds), *Leftovers. Tales of the Latin American Left*. New York: Rouledge.
Comisión de la Verdad y Reconciliación (2003). *Informe final*. Lima: CVR.
Cotler, J. (1978). A Structural-Historical Approach to the Breakdown of Democratic Institutions: Peru. In: Linz, J. and Stepan, A. (eds), *The Breakdown of Democratic Regimes. Latin America*. Baltimore: Johns Hopkins University Press, 178–206.
Cotler, J. (1993). Descomposición política y autoritarismo en el Perú. Documento de trabajo n°51. *Descomposición política y autoritarismo en el Perú N°7*. Lima: Instituto de Estudios Peruanos.
Cotler, J. and Grompone, R. (2000). *El fujimorismo. Ascenso y caída de un régimen autoritario*. Lima: Instituto de Estudios Peruanos.
Crabtree, J. (2005). *Alan García en el poder. Perú, 1985–1990*. Lima: Peisa.
Daeschner, J. (1993). *The War of the End of Democracy. Mario Vargas Llosa versus Alberto Fujimori*. Lima: Peru Reporting.
Degregori, C.I. (1991). El aprendiz de brujo y el curandero chino. Etnicidad, modernidad y ciudadanía. In: Degregori, C.I. and Grompone, R. (eds), *Elecciones 1990: Demonios y redentores en el nuevo Perú. Una tragedia en dos vueltas*. Lima: Instituto de Estudios Peruanos.
Degregori, C.I. (2011). *Qué difícil es ser dios. El Partido Comunista del Perú-Sendero Luminoso y el conflicto armado interno en el Perú: 1980–1999*. Lima: Instituto de Estudios Peruanos—Coordinadora Nacional de DDHH.
Durand, F. (2009). La gravitación del empresariado en la era neoliberal. In: Plaza, O. (ed.), *Cambios sociales en el Perú: 1968–2008*. Lima: CISEPA-PUCP, 269–286.
Durand, F. (2012). El debate sobre la captura del Estado peruano. In: Toche, E. (ed.), *Perú Hoy. La gran continuidad*. Lima: DESCO, 19–56.
García, A. (1982). *El futuro diferente. La tarea histórica del APRA*. Lima.
García, A. (1984). *El Perú es esperanza. Escritos de Alan García (con una entrevista de Julio Cabrera Moreno)*. Lima: Siglo XXI ediciones.
García, A. (1987). *El futuro diferente. La tarea histórica del APRA (cinco años después)*. Lima: E.M.I.
García, A. (2008). *La revolución constructiva del aprismo. Teoría y práctica de la modernidad*. Lima: Ed. DESA.
Grompone, R. (1991). Fujimori: razones y desconciertos. In: Degregori, C.I. and Grompone, R. (eds), *Elecciones 1990: Demonios y redentores en el nuevo Perú. Una tragedia en dos vueltas*. Lima: Instituto de Estudios Peruanos.

Iguíñiz, J., Basay, R. and Rubio, M. (1993). *Los ajustes. Perú 1975–1992*. Lima: Fundación Friedrich Ebert.

Kenney, C. (2004). *Fujimori's Coup and the Breakdown of Democracy in Latin America*. Notre Dame: University of Notre Dame Press.

Lanzaro, J. (2001). *Tipos de presidencialismo y coaliciones políticas en América Latina*. Buenos Aires: CLACSO.

López, S. (1985). Perú 1985: entre la moderación y la radicalidad. *El Zorro de Abajo*, 1, junio-julio.

López, S. (1998). Perú: Crisis de los partidos, nuevas mediaciones políticas, democracia e interés público en el Perú de los 90. In: Urzúa, R. and Agüero, F. (eds), *Fracturas en la gobernabilidad democrática*. Chile: CIEPLAN, Universidad de Chile.

Lynch, N. (2009). *El argumento democrático sobre América Latina: la excepcionalidad peruana en perspectiva comparada*. Lima: Fondo Editorial de la Facultad de Ciencias Sociales, UNMSM.

Morales, M. (2008). Have Latin Americans Turned Left? In: Castañeda, J. and Morales, M. (eds), *Leftovers. Tales of the Latin American Left*. New York: Rouledge.

Murakami, Y. (2007). *Perú en la era del Chino: la política no institucionalizada y el pueblo en busca de un salvador*. Lima: Instituto de Estudios Peruanos.

O'Donnell, G. (1992). Democracia delegativa. *Cuadernos del CLAEH*, 17(61), 9–19.

Pásara, L. (1987). La libanización en democracia. In: Pásara, L. and Parodi, D. (eds), *Democracia, sociedad y gobierno en el Perú*. Lima: CEDYS.

Pease, H. (2003). *La autocracia fujimorista. Del Estado intervencionista al* Estado mafioso. Mexico: PUCP-FCE.

Portocarrero, G. (2012). *Profetas del odio. Raíces culturales y líderes de Sendero Luminoso*. Lima, Fondo editorial PUCP.

Reyna, C. (2000). *La anunciación de Fujimori. Alan García 1985–1990*. Lima: DESCO.

Rial, J. (2008). Semblanza de Alan García. In: Adrianzén, A. J. and Roncagliolo, R. (eds), *Países Andinos. Los políticos*. Lima: IDEA Internacional.

Rochabrún, G. (2007). ¿Crisis de paradigmas o falta de rigor? *Batallas por la teoría. En torno a Marx y el Perú*. Lima: Instituto de Estudios Peruanos, 476–493.

Schmidt, G. (1996). Fujimori's 1990 Upset Victory in Peru: Electoral Rules, Contingencies, and Adaptive Strategies. *Comparative Politics*, 28(3).

Smith, W., Acuña, C. and Gamarra, E. (1994a). *Democracy, Markets, and Structural Reform in Latin America: Argentina, Bolivia, Brazil, Chile, and Mexico*. New Brunswick: Transaction Publishers.

Smith, W., Acuña, C. and Gamarra, E. (1994b). *Latin American Political Economy in the Age of Neoliberal Reform. Theoretical and Comparative Perspectives for the 1990s*. New Brunswick: Transaction Publishers.

Tanaka, M. (1998). *Los espejismos de la democracia. El colapso del sistema de partidos en el Perú, 1980–1995, en perspectiva comparada*. Lima: Instituto de Estudios Peruanos.

Tanaka, M. (2001). ¿Crónica de una muerte anunciada? Determinismo, voluntarismo, actores y poderes estructurales en el Perú, 1980–2000. In: Marcus, J. and Tanaka, M. (eds), *Lecciones del final del fujimorismo. La legitimidad presidencial y la acción política*. Lima: Instituto de Estudios Peruanos, 57–112.

Tanaka, M. (2005a). Los estudios políticos en Perú: ausencias, desconexión de la realidad y la necesidad de la ciencia política como disciplina. *Revista de Ciencia Política*,

25(1), Santiago, Instituto de Ciencia Política, Pontificia Universidad Católica de Chile, 222–231.
Tanaka, M. (2005b). Peru 1980–2000: Chronicle of a Death Foretold? Determinism, Political Decisions and Open Outcomes. In: Hagopian, F. and Mainwaring, S. (eds), *The Third Wave of Democratization in Latin America. Advances and Setbacks*. Cambridge: Cambridge University Press, 261–288.
Tanaka, M. (2008a). Del voluntarismo exacerbado al realismo sin ilusiones. El giro del APRA y de Alan García. *Nueva Sociedad*, 217, 172–184.
Tanaka, M. (2008b). The Left in Peru: Plenty of Wagons and No Locomotion. In: Castañeda, J. and Morales, M. (eds), *Leftovers. Tales of the Latin American Left*. New York: Rouledge, 193–212.
Tanaka, M. (2013a). Las ambigüedades del Informe Final de la Comisión de la Verdad y Reconciliación en la explicación de las causas y dinámica del conflicto armado interno. *Revista Argumentos*, 7(4), 20–33.
Tanaka, M. (2013b). Liderazgos y crisis de representación partidaria: ¿cuándo son una variable política relevante? Una aproximación desde los países andinos. In: Diamint, R. and Tedesco, L. (eds), *Democratizar a los políticos. Un estudio sobre líderes latinoamericanos*. Madrid: Los libros de la Catarata, 33–74.
Tanaka, M. (2015). Agencia y estructura, y el colapso de los sistemas de partidos en los países andinos. In: Torcal, M. (ed.), *Sistemas de partidos en América Latina. Causas y consecuencias de su equilibrio inestable*. Barcelona: Anthropos editorial, 161–182.

8 Presidential Leadership in a Robust Presidency
The Brazilian Case

Magna Inácio

Presidential systems are targets of recurrent criticism regarding the excessive risk of gridlock. Some of that criticism is associated with the strengthening of the president's unilateral authority vis-à-vis other political actors. That said, does presidential leadership result solely from the institutional and political centrality of the presidential actor? Conversely, is the likelihood of a president becoming a leader conditional on personal attributes and institutional characteristics?

It is argued here that the study of presidential leadership requires an understanding of how personal and institutional attributes combine, and define, the president's ability to shape policy decisions in interaction with other political and institutional actors, whether as catalysts or as facilitators of policy changes (Edwards and Wayne, 2010). Leadership effectiveness does not derive from a type of leadership but, instead, from the president's ability to anticipate, within a given conflict structure, rules and available resources, those actions that might promote certain changes. Therefore, presidential leadership is anchored in, and varies according to, the president's ability to make choices.

To understand how these choices take shape and acquire content, the following analysis utilizes three dimensions: the social background, the president's personal attributes and the institutional environment (Blondel and Thiébault, 2010). We seek to shed light on how presidential leadership emerges and varies based on the combination of these dimensions.

In this chapter, the exercise of presidential leadership in an institutionally robust presidency, that of Brazil, will be analyzed. The focus on Brazil allows for an exploration of how these dimensions are combined in a context in which political institutions can obscure the influence of the president's personal skills and prior history, given the abundance of the resources available to him or her. The study is centered on the four presidential terms of Fernando Henrique Cardoso (FHC) and of Luís Inácio Lula da Silva (Lula) in the period between 1994 and 2010.

The chapter is organized into three sections, in addition to this introduction. In the second section, the influence of the presidents' social background on their political careers, on the formation of their support networks, on their links with voters and on their memberships in the political elite will be addressed. In the third section, the personal attributes of the presidents and the influence of those attributes on the presidents' political careers, and on their performance in the government, will be analyzed. It is a goal of this section to map, albeit in an exploratory manner, the possible relationship between the presidents' personal skills and the style of presidential leadership. The fourth section addresses the influence of political institutions in the reconstruction of the conflict structure, the rules, and the institutional resources that partially shape presidential leadership. Accordingly, we seek to establish connections among the considered dimensions, through the analysis of presidential choices and presidents' actions as leaders throughout their administrations. Finally, tentative conclusions are presented.

The Analysis of the Influence of Sociological Factors on Presidential Leadership

The political careers of Fernando Henrique Cardoso and Lula converged in Brazil's recent democratic transition, during which both occupied leadership positions in opposition to the military regime. This political approximation, however, occurred via separate routes. Whereas FHC's political socialization was conducted in a family environment, Lula began a political career only in his adult life, through union militancy.

FHC, who hailed from a family with a military and political history, was immersed in national political life during the democratic interregnum of 1946–1964. The interest in politics and the involvement of his relatives in the democratic process were part of his political socialization. At university, FHC engaged in politics during one of the most critical moments of Brazil's democratic experience. However, the rise of the military in 1964, followed by the intense repression of student and leftist movements, interrupted his academic career in Brazil, and he self-exiled to Chile.

FHC's strong academic career allowed him to develop skills that guided the exercise of his presidential responsibilities, such as analytical capacity and systemic criticism. In the debates about Latin America's economic development, FHC constructed a solid and sophisticated view of the state and its role in this process. Without a doubt, this view cemented a presidential leadership style oriented toward the definition of strategic priorities, supported by a large organizational capacity and an integrated view of governance (Greenstein, 2000). According to FHC, a leader should invest in a game between symbolism and practical realities to construct his or her message.

In contrast, Lula's political engagement and leadership capacity were formed through his participation in the world of labor. Lula was from a humble background, and during his childhood, his family migrated from one of Brazil's least-developed regions to its industrial center, the state of São Paulo. At the age of 12, Lula integrated work and school, attending an institution designed to train the country's industrial workforce, and Lula joined the union movement in 1969, at the height of the military dictatorship. After seven years, his union leadership was unmistakable; he was elected president of the Metallurgist Union of São Bernardo do Campo and Diadema (*Sindicato de Metalúrgicos de São Bernardo do Campo e Diadema*) which, at the time, represented 100,000 workers.

Lula's political activity gained momentum under the 'new unionism,' which made him a national figure. The new unionism movement sought to break with the vertical union structure, supported by state corporatism, toward a horizontal and comprehensive model of worker organization. Under Lula's leadership, the union movement sparked intense mobilization in the ABC region that, after only 10 years, resulted in the resumption of strikes and work stoppages. Given this intense mobilization in the modern nucleus of the economy, the military regime re-intensified its repression of workers, with the imprisonment of leaders based on the National Security Law (*Lei de Segurança Nacional*). The imprisonment of Lula and of other union leaders led to the politicization and alignment of these movements with the military regime's opponents.

At the beginning of his union career, Lula's critical position with respect to parties and politicians favored the shaping—amply reinforced by the press—of himself as a leader distant from the traditional left. Nevertheless, he knew the risks of isolating workers in the context of political liberalization. Accordingly, he argued for the creation of a new political organization, capable of representing workers' interests in the emerging political arena through a new organizational model. In 1980, the Workers' Party (*Partido dos Trabalhadores*—PT) was organized under Lula's leadership, bringing together intellectuals, segments of the middle class and politicians split from the opposition and religious sectors, albeit strongly influenced by the union core. Gradually, the incorporation of the agenda of reclaiming social and political rights—the focus of popular movements—contributed to moderating the PT's class bias.

This organizational model—based on the party's social roots and the intense participation of the rank and file—left marks on Lula's conversion from union leader to party leader. Lula solidified his partisan leadership through the confluence of two organizational challenges experienced by the PT: on the one hand, investing in a partisan reputation through an alternative political project of the left and, on the other hand, aligning the party's internal decisions —under the strong influence of the partisan bases—toward that project. As a charismatic leader, Lula played a singular role in facing these challenges. Indeed, the PT's ability to forge considerable levels of party identification and cohesion, as a collective good, was the result not only of the internal makeup of the party but also of its main leader's political skills in managing the organization.

As president, Lula's skills as both a negotiator and a communicator were decisive in accommodating the diversity of positions and interests unified under the large coalition that supported his administration. On the one hand, those skills enabled him to confront the internal tensions arising within the PT from the resistance of internal groups to the government's programmatic moderation. On the other hand, Lula's skills were amply mobilized to strengthen his image as conciliator, reiterated not only in the handling of domestic agreements but also in the positioning of foreign affairs, for the political and economic elites. This identity was repeatedly reinforced by Lula, indicating the bases of his presidential leadership as follows:

> More than any other Brazilian, the President has to be available 24 hours a day to talk to anybody to make a political agreement and thank God, I bring from my union experience, which I am very proud of, the ability to negotiate. I like to listen, I like to reflect on what people have told me, and I like to make agreements.[1]

The renewal and flow of the elite through the power structure, triggered by democratization, created opportunities for the emergence of new political leaders (see Table 8.9, appendix). The two presidents were politically able to take advantage of this situation to construct their reputations and political leadership, albeit from different starting points. Nevertheless, personal factors left an indelible mark on the type of presidential leadership that they exercised in the highest position of the Brazilian executive branch.

The Influence of Personal Factors on Presidential Leadership

In the post-redemocratization period, the constitutional framework significantly expanded the powers of the Brazilian president. However, the first office-holders elected after the transition, Sarney and Collor, experienced extreme oscillations in the popularity and approval of their administrations. This instability greatly reflected those administrations' performances in the face of economic and political instability, exacerbated by the progressive loss of Sarney's and Collor's capacities for leadership.

A distinct framework emerged in the middle of the 1990s, breaking this initial cycle of political instability. This reversal is associated with the critical contexts that contributed to making FHC and Lula the most competitive candidates in the presidential contest. As two insiders in Brazilian politics, FHC and Lula built their reputations throughout their political careers; also, particularly significant was their personal ability to align their political platforms to specific situations, in order to both build victorious electoral coalitions and run their administrations with relative stability.

From Candidates to Presidents: Building the Reputation

The good fortune that paved FHC's road to the presidency began with his entrance into a caretaker cabinet, catalyzed by the economic and political instability that marked the government after the impeachment of Collor, who had been the first directly elected president after the military dictatorship. Without previous experience in the executive branch, FHC rapidly gained President Itamar's confidence, assuming responsibility for the economic portfolio after working in the area of foreign affairs. In this condition, the then-Minister of Finance coordinated a successful stabilization plan for Itamar's administration. FHC capitalized on the program's political visibility to solidify the candidacy of the Brazilian Social Democratic Party (*Partido da Social Democracia Brasileira*— PSDB) on its own, with FHC as the 'natural' candidate for the position.

In the context of hyperinflation and a series of failed economic plans, the success of the Plano Real ('Real' Plan) demonstrated, in the voters' view, that FHC's expertise and leadership were assets that were important for overcoming the country's chronic crisis. This differential was signaled by FHC's personal effort as minister to bring together a team of experts and to obtain domestic and international support for the new measures. This core, composed of experts with whom FHC maintained personal and academic connections, was responsible for the formulation and implementation of the economic stabilization and fiscal adjustment plan (Plano Real) in 1994.

The economic gains resulting from a stable currency translated the technical jargon and sophisticated architecture of the plan into a message easily absorbable by the majority of the electorate. FHC's rise in the opinion polls pointed to the robustness of the economic vote in defining the presidential contest. Having already been removed from his ministerial post, FHC surpassed the people's first choice in the opinion polls—Lula—as early as the beginning of the campaign.

FHC and his supporters conducted a presidential campaign that signaled continuity with the agenda of economic stabilization, but under a new party coalition. The plan's foundations of monetary policy and the reorganization of the state were clearly aligned with the electoral platform of the PSDB, focusing on the reform of the Brazilian state and a new model for state-market relations. Based on this project, the PSDB sought to link the candidate's image—and subsequently, that of the government—to the notions of competency and efficiency in public management. To forge this identification of the voters with the party, the party adopted this orientation to differentiate itself from both traditional politics—based on patronage and clientelism—and the political projects of the left.

Once in power, the implementation of FHC's agenda collided with the limits of the electoral cycle. By the middle of the first term, the intensification of conflicts with Congress in approving the presidential agenda signaled possible fractures related to the ongoing reforms. FHC's actions to overcome such threats had an impact on the institutional conditions of leadership. Together with political leaders, FHC participated actively in establishing a legislative supermajority to support the re-election of executive officers. In addition to signaling popular support for change and the importance of a new rule for coalition unity during the first term, the anticipation of the succession process contributed to engaging FHC in the issue of changing the constitution for presidential terms. In this sense, FHC's self-assessment about his role in the reform process influenced his activism as president:

Of course, I'm not naive. I began, yes, considering the possibility of re-election. I did not see who could unite the political forces necessary to carry forward the ongoing modernization. No leader arose with sufficient strength to exercise this role. Thus, in addition to my worries about my political strength for winning battles with Congress, the issue also emerged on the psychological horizon. I should admit, without a margin of a doubt, the temptation of re-election.

(FHC, 2006: 289)[2]

Again, the economic agenda and the emphasis on the government's managerial capacity were at the center of the 1998 contest for FHC's re-election. The instability created by the international financial crisis emphasized the negative consequences of the government's stabilization policies, particularly with respect to employment and wages. To neutralize the opposition's negative campaign, the incumbent's re-election discourse was based on an image of government competency and efficiency through the comparison of pre-Real Plan instability to the results of economic stabilization obtained in the first term. This image was used intensively to characterize FHC as the only candidate capable of leading Brazil through a period of economic instability. Seeking to minimize the loss of confidence in the government, the president engaged directly, through public appearances and official messages, in the dissemination of measures to address the effects of the crisis.

If FHC's ability was to use his previous experience in the executive branch as the key to his presidential candidacy, Lula's primary ability was to reconstruct his public image after four failed presidential contests. Lula was the sole presidential candidate for the PT in the elections between 1989 and 2006, facing candidates from the PSDB in four of the five elections.[3]

The difficulties of expanding the electoral base won since 1989 encouraged the introduction of changes to the party's internal organization, which strengthened the PT's national leaders. Centralized decision-making that began in 2001, carried out by the dominant coalition within the PT to which Lula was linked, proved decisive for the change to the party's alliance policy. The specter of three presidential defeats led Lula and his support group, holding the main positions in the national party leadership, to press for greater autonomy in running the party's campaign. Given that, over time, the party linked the partisan and the presidential projects, the actions of this coalition anticipated the effects of the election on the party's future, in the event of another defeat. The alliance with the center-right liberal party symbolically marked this shift to the center of the political spectrum, with the appointment of a businessman for the position of vice president on the ticket with Lula.

The consolidation of the PT as the main force on the left and the increased uncertainty about the presidential race in 2002 encouraged this shift in electoral strategies. Under presidential races marked by intense polarization between the PT and PSDB, the movement toward the center sought to expand the range of alliances, bringing together the political forces opposed to the PSDB

Brazil: Cardoso and Lula   173

from both the left and the right. The negative assessment of FHC's administration at the end of the second term and the difficulties of the PSDB in building a solid electoral alliance increased voter openness to other governmental alternatives.

Lula acted directly to expand the field of allies and to professionalize the campaign, involving a diverse group of experts and a large support apparatus throughout the country. The modernization of the 'Petista' (belonging to the PT) discourse was undertaken extensively throughout the campaign, presenting Lula as communicator, charismatic and conciliator. This image was disseminated through the centralization of campaign communication via the issuance of messages concentrated in the hands of the national staff. The emphasis on these attributes guided the entire campaign, which sought to maintain and expand Lula's position as an electoral favorite and to deconstruct the foci of his rejection by specific segments of the electorate.

In the face of the instability in the financial markets associated with the possibility of Lula being elected, which in May 2002 reached 43% in the opinion polls, the PT sent overt signals of political moderation. In June, Lula's campaign released a 'letter to Brazilians' signaling the candidate's commitment, once elected, to continue the stabilization policies to control inflation and to pursue fiscal balance, along with 'respect for the country's contracts and obligations.' After his victory, Lula reinforced that promise with the appointment of a financial market professional to a key position in the national monetary system, the presidency of the Central Bank, in addition to choosing the manager of his electoral campaign and governmental transition team for Minister of Finance, a move that was viewed positively by market agents.

Given that Lula's administration remained in line with the economic policies of his predecessor, the PT's differentiating factor was Lula's investment in the social agenda. The presidency was expanded to include specific agencies to formulate policies targeting political minorities whose demands were historically included in the party's platform, such as human rights, policies for women, and policies for blacks. The centrality of redistributive social policies sought to reconnect the PT's historical agenda to that of the government. To reinforce this link, Lula symbolically made constant references to his personal difficulties—such as childhood poverty and his lack of a university education—to highlight the redistributive and emancipatory components of actions and programs such as Zero Hunger (Fome Zero) and the University for Everyone Program (*Programa Universidade para Todos*—Prouni).[4]

If, on the one hand, Lula's first term allowed him to end resistance and negative expectations with respect to the performance of a leftist government, on the other hand, it introduced an issue heretofore distant from the PT's political reputation: corruption. In 2005, the Mensalão scandal[5] led Lula to leverage his personal credibility to circumvent the government's political instability and threats to re-election for the following year. Refocusing the role of institutions on determining responsibilities, Lula took on a more direct role in the political coordination of the government, which previously had been managed by party cadres in key cabinet positions such as the Political Council (*Conselho Político*), and a special secretariat for managing the relationship between the administration and Congress. With the removal of the main party leaders involved in the Mensalão scandal from both the administration and Congress, Lula reorganized his bases of internal coordination in the government, placing technocrat advisors into key positions to manage the priority projects of the presidency.

In 2006, Lula's personal credibility and the government's performance were again mobilized to mitigate the effects of two corruption scandals (targeted by the opposition) on Lula's candidacy for re-election. This process is considered by analysts as one of the ingredients of the personalization of the vote for Lula, called Lulism, and the increasing dislocation of his electoral base relative to the PT. In the absence of the main party leaders, who had been removed due to the Mensalão scandal, Lula took a more direct role in managing the government, ushering in the most stable period of his administration. With high popularity, the increased availability of revenue and greater cabinet stability, Lula adopted strategies to improve the party's future electoral chances at different levels through investment in new partisan cadres. By means of ministerial selection and the visibility conferred by his actions in the management of priority government projects, Lula placed himself at the center of decision-making as the primary articulator of future party candidacies.

Building a Reputation as President

Low presidential popularity and administrative instability marked the initial post-redemocratization phase in Brazil. Breaking with this initial cycle, the administrations of FHC and Lula operated under conditions of greater political stability and presidential popularity. This result is associated with factors such as the stabilization of the party system (Lima, 1997; Nicolau, 1996) and the strengthening of the institutional positions of the legislative and executive branches (Figueiredo and Limongi, 1999; Santos, 2003) since the 1990s. Nevertheless, little is discussed about whether, and in what direction, presidential attributes and style contributed to this result.

In the electoral arena, FHC obtained an electoral majority in the first round of the two presidential contests in which he ran, and he experienced minor fluctuations in voter preference throughout his campaigns, as shown in Table 8.1. With greater oscillation in his electoral base, Lula faced the second round in the two elections in which he emerged victorious, with his vote count increasing by 14.9% and 12.2% between rounds in the 2002 and 2006 elections, respectively.

This electoral performance contrasts with the ability to convert an electoral majority into governmental support. The approval ratings of governments beginning with FHC achieved higher and more stable levels over time compared to previous presidents. However, the two presidents differentiate themselves in terms of the electoral gains resulting from this retrospective vote, which becomes clear in the comparison of their performances during their second terms. FHC's

Table 8.1 Voter preference during electoral years for Brazilian presidents—1994, 1998, 2002 and 2006

Election month/year	Voter preference (%)			
	FHC1 (1994)	FHC2 (1998)	LULA1 (2002)	LULA2 (2006)
March	–	41	26	32
April	–	41	35	29
May	17	34	–	31
June	19	33	25	35
July	29	40	23	31
August	45	42	37	40
September	47	48	45	–
October (election month)	48	49	45	55
% of votes (1st round)	54.3	53.1	46.4	48.6
% of votes (2nd round)			61.3	60.8

Source: Authors. Data from the Instituto Data Folha (Datasheet Institute), Pesquisas 'Avaliação do Governo' ('Government Analysis' Research), various years.

and Lula's popularity—measured as the percentage of voters who evaluate the president's performance as either great or good—remained at similar levels during their first terms, oscillating between 30% and 45%.

However, the situation follows a divergent trend after re-election. Exhibiting a declining trend in 1998, his re-election year, FHC began his second term with an approval rate that corresponds to half of that achieved in 1994 (Figure 8.1). Although he had been elected with 53% of the valid votes in a single round, analysis of his performance in the second term remained at lower levels than in the first term, representing a 24% approval rating on average. Conversely, Lula's approval rate exhibited an upward trend at the end of his first term, reaching unprecedented approval levels among the presidents of the post-redemocratization period. In the last year of his administration, 2010, Lula's popularity reached its peak with an 80% approval rating among voters.

As demonstrated in the economic voting literature, the president's popularity is a factor influencing the voters' positive expectations of the government and its performance. Figure 8.2 shows a strong correlation (r=.81), from 2001 to 2010, between the president's popularity level and consumer confidence for the future. The timeframe corresponds to the last two years of FHC's administration and Lula's two terms. Once he was re-elected, Lula's presidential popularity grew more sharply than consumer confidence, which remained high but stable. It is interesting to note that the persistence of optimism, as well as the increase in presidential popularity, occurred in the context of the 2008 financial crisis. The president's activism, both internally and externally, contributed to maintaining this environment, aided by the relatively minor impact of the crisis on Brazil's economy compared to its impact on the European and US economies.

176　*Magna Inácio*

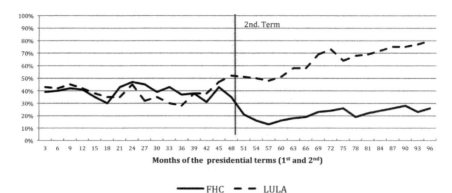

Figure 8.1 Approval rating of the administrations of FHC and Lula by term month (1st and 2nd terms)—Brazil, 1995–2010

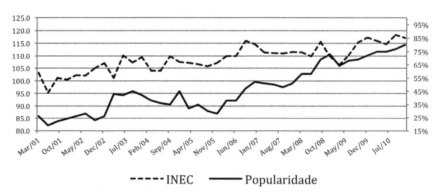

Figure 8.2 Evolution of the level of popularity and of the National Consumer Confidence Index (Indíce de Nacional de Expectativa do Consumidor —INEC)

An incumbent's level of popularity reflects various dimensions of his or her performance, including the strategies adopted to build their reputations and public images as leaders. To analyze the impact of these strategies, it is important to consider the communication resources that presidents have and use in the exercise of their duties, including resources used to offset messages conveyed by the media in general. The two presidencies, particularly that of the Lula administration, invested considerable resources in governmental communication. In addition to the Ministries of Communication and of Culture, both of which have responsibilities in this area, a Special Secretariat had been part of the structure of the presidency since the end of military rule. Having undergone no significant changes during FHC's tenure, this unit was expanded at the beginning of Lula's administration (2003–2005) and its actions were supplemented by those of other units, such as the Secretariat of Press and Communications and the Spokesperson for the President of the Republic. During Lula's second term, this structure was simplified and its functions were transferred to the Secretariat of Communication, which centralized all institutional policies in this area.

For direct communication with voters and opinion makers, presidents have used various media resources. They can make pronouncements, produced by the presidential communications team, on the national radio and television network (which are required to broadcast those statements). Used sparingly by presidents, there was considerable variation among the number of statements made to the nation by FHC (26) and Lula (21) during their terms. This resource was mobilized primarily to signal the government's positions in particular circumstances, as demonstrated by the increase in FHC's pronouncements during the last two years of his administration (2001–2002), which were marked by intense economic instability.

It is interesting to observe, in contrast to FHC, Lula's progressive use of this media resource, becoming more frequent in his second term. At the beginning of his administration, Lula suffered criticism because of the press's difficulty in gaining access to him. Due to his great skill as a communicator, Lula's exposure through the radio program assumed increasing importance over his two terms. This differed from the case of FHC, who mobilized this major resource in the early stages of his administration when he pursued a structural reform agenda. As shown in Table 8.2, Lula's exposure to national and international media increased considerably during his second presidential term.

The less-intensive use of these communication outlets by President Lula should be evaluated in light of other governmental strategies of institutional communication, focusing on civil society and economic agents. In 2007, the Brazilian Communication Company (*Empresa Brasileira de Comunicação*— EBC) was created. This company is responsible for overseeing the Public System of Communication (*Sistema Público de Comunicação*), linked directly to the presidency through the Secretariat of Communication, the new company's primary customer. In addition to the institutional strengthening of the federal government's communication policy, the executive began to rely on a comprehensive and diverse structure of advice and participatory mechanisms, such as public consultations and public policy conferences, with great potential for disseminating presidential messages and agendas.

Analysis of the Influence of Institutions on Presidential Leadership

Political institutions in Brazil confer considerable complexity upon the exercise of presidential leadership. Importantly, the presidential arrangement is influenced by rules that organize party and electoral competition and the relationship between the branches and other levels of government. These rules introduce considerable incentives to the formation of multiparty coalitions that modify the conditions of presidential leadership.

Table 8.2 Use of communication outlets by Brazilian presidents—1995–2010

President	Year	Media resource			
		Radio programs[1]	Pronouncements on national radio and television networks	National interviews	International interviews
		(N)	(N)	(N)	(N)
FHC	1995	32	4	NI[3]	NI
	1996	53	2	NI	NI
	1997	50	2	NI	NI
	1998	–	3	NI	NI
	1999	49	2	NI	NI
	2000	46	1	NI	NI
	2001	42	7	NI	NI
	2002	25	6	NI	NI
SUBTOTAL		297	27		
LULA	2003[2]	4	2	37	33
	2004	29	2	32	19
	2005	33	4	33	24
	2006	26	3	83	21
	2007	49	2	134	57
	2008	51	3	156	58
	2009	51	2	201	120
	2010	39	3	167	41
SUBTOTAL		282	21	843	373

Notes:
1 *Palavra do Presidente* (*President's Word*) (1995–2002) and *Café com o Presidente* (*Coffee with the President*) (2003–2007) radio programs.
2 The program *Café com o Presidente* (*Coffee with the President*) was aired starting in November 2003.
3 NI = no information.

Sources: Biblioteca da Presidência (Library of the Presidency) (2013); collection on the website of the Secretariat of the Press—2003/2010 (www.infoacervo.planalto.gov.br/index.htm).

Electoral Rules and Presidential Leadership

The first challenge is related to the competitiveness of the presidential candidacy and the candidates' abilities to make choices to establish alliances to extend their advantages in the majority electoral contest.[6] Multipartism, majority rule in two rounds of presidential elections, and proportional election for the legislative branch add to the uncertainty of the context and make alliances more complex. Several parties offer candidates that will increase voters' exposure to those parties and, consequently, elect more legislators. With larger congressional delegations, a party's bargaining ability grows with presidential candidates who are victorious in the first round. Thus, alliances are defined in different rounds: after the first round, informal agreements align the positions of the defeated candidate relative to the second-round challengers; once the president is known, new rounds of negotiations define the space of those allied with the government's cabinet. Additionally, the federal arrangement raises the costs of alliances because the electoral strength of the parties varies among states, requiring the combination of party and regional criteria in the electoral calculations for national contest.

In the election contests between FHC and Lula, the number of presidential candidates was significant, varying between 6 and 11. Even so, the dominant feature of the presidential races was the polarization of the PSDB and the PT. Since 1994, presidential competition has reflected a bipartisan logic, albeit based on the parties' converging agendas. Since then, this competition has been increasingly oriented toward voters positioned in the center of the ideological spectrum.

FHC sought electoral viability through alliances with nationally diffuse parties, which could increase the regionally concentrated electoral base of the PSDB. By excluding alliances for state elections, the party created conditions for the adhesion of allies and party leaders who have no clear presidential aspirations. PSDB's electoral alliance with the PFL[7] (the remnant of the ruling party during the military period) and the PTB, both situated to the right on the ideological spectrum, resulted from pragmatic calculations. Because the PT mobilized the leftist vote, the centrist PSDB sought the support of the electorate positioned at the center-right using solid partisan machines. With electoral support concentrated in the southeast of the country, the allied parties ensured an electoral presence throughout the territory, in addition to introducing political leaders and their brokers into regions where the PSDB had low electoral density. With the popularity of the Plano Real and the support of the above-mentioned coalition, FHC was victorious in the first round of the 1994 election with a significant margin (27.2%) over the second-place finisher. Additionally, FHC was victorious in almost all of the electoral districts in his two elections, indicating the backing of a coalition that was clearly national.

In 1998, because of the new rule for re-election, presidential participation in the contest curbed the establishment of alternative coalitions, and the electoral coalition essentially reproduced the administration's cabinet. Facing a deteriorating domestic economy, in the context of international financial crises, the voters' choice for governmental continuity prevailed. Support for the president in opinion polls reached 40% before the beginning of electoral propaganda and increased by 9% between August and October. FHC was again elected in the first round, but by a relatively smaller margin (21.9%) compared to the second-place finisher, due to the presence of a third candidate (Ciro Gomes-PPS) who obtained 10.9% of the vote.

The ideologically narrow alliance policy of the PT followed a distinct trend after the 1998 election. Until 1998, the coalition strategies had been oriented toward the formation of alliances that were ideologically more homogeneous and that reproduced national accords at the state level. After the party's third defeat, the presidential contest became the priority for its leaders and the electoral alliance became a sore subject within the partisan project. Thus, the barriers to other parties' entrance into alliances were relaxed, with state accords becoming more flexible, in return for support for the presidential candidacy.

In 2002, without an incumbent in the election, Lula obtained 46.4% of the votes in the first round but faced three challengers with significant vote totals: José Serra (PSDB) with 23.2%, Antony Garotinho (PSB) with 17.9% and Ciro Gomes (PPS) with 12%. This electoral fragmentation catalyzed a new round of presidential voting, which Lula won with 61.3% of the valid votes. Using the polarization with the PSDB, Lula reinforced to the voters his position as leader of a large alliance to renovate Brazilian politics, using symbolic and media resources to associate his candidacy with the spirit of change.

In the re-election attempt, the use of this image was obliterated by corruption scandals from the previous year that directly involved the PT leadership, its ministers and deputies, and its congressional base. Accordingly, the campaign strategy was centered on the government's social agenda, seeking to counter the opposition's negative campaign, which highlighted the corruption scandals and the expansion of public spending under PT administration. Despite the seriousness of the charges and their immediate effects on the government, Lula's popularity went relatively unscathed. With the recovery of the government's approval ratings, Lula remained the favorite for re-election with 32% of the votes at the beginning of the electoral year. Nevertheless, less than 20 days before the election, Lula's candidacy was again weakened by allegations of corruption involving the PT. As a result, the election was won in the second round with a margin of 7% of votes relative to the second-place finisher, Geraldo Alckimin of the PSDB. This was the lowest margin observed, in any direct presidential election, between 1989 and 2006.

With the intense mobilization of official electoral propaganda through the media, Lula recovered electoral support and was elected in the second round, with a margin of 21% relative to the challenger—similar to the 2002 result. This result provided support for arguments about a new phenomenon, Lulism,[8] understood as the personalization of the Lula vote (Samuels, 2009), or the realignment of the administration's electoral base, fostered by the redistributive impact of its policies, with the gradual adhesion of the poorest segments and the distancing of the middle sectors (Singer, 2009). Such a phenomenon would cause a gradual detachment between the image of the PT and of Lula, which guaranteed the restoration of the president's popularity after the 2005 scandals. The redistributive policies, conducted through monetary transfers to poor segments of the population, real growth in the minimum wage, and an increase of the credit supply, were at the foundation of the consumption-based growth model that the government implemented. This redistributive agenda was the focus of Lula's electoral campaign in 2006 to differentiate the PT administration from the previous one that, according to the administration, focused only on the problem of economic stabilization.

Table 8.3 Electoral results and performances of the presidents elected in 1994, 1998, 2002 and 2006

President (election year)	Parties in the electoral coalition	Candidates running (N)	Votes (T) 1st round	Votes (T) 2nd round	Valid votes (%) 1st round	Valid votes (%) 2nd round	Margin of vote relative to 2nd-place finisher (%) 1st round	Margin of vote relative to 2nd-place finisher (%) 2nd round	States in which the president finished in 1st place (N) 1st round	States in which the president finished in 1st place (N) 2nd round
FHC 1 (1994)	PSDB/PFL/PTB	7	31,253,166	NA	54.3	NA	27.2%	–	25	NA
FHC 2 (1998)	PSDB/PFL/PTB/PPB	11	35,936,916	NA	53.1	NA	21.9%	–	24	NA
LULA 1 (2002)	PT/PL/PC do B/PMN/PCB	5	39,455,233	52,793,364	46.4	61.27	23.2%	22.6%	24	26
LULA 2 (2006)	PT/PRB/PC do B	6	46,662,365	58,295,042	48.6	60.83	7%	21.6%	16	20

Source: Superior Electoral Court of Brazil (2013).

This result is interpreted in many studies as a result of the change in the geography of Lula's vote in 2006, with the growth of his electoral strength in smaller cities located in the poorest regions of the country, and a reversal in the relationship between the Human Development Index (HDI) and the vote for Lula (Hunter and Power, 2007; Zucco, 2008; Nicolau and Peixoto, 2007; Soares and Terron, 2008). Such analyses point to the effects of income-transfer policies, notably the Family Allowance Program (*Programa Bolsa Família*—PBF), which resulted in the displacement of Lula's electoral base in 2002 and 2006. This displacement was also responsible for the reduced impact of the corruption scandals, which were more prominent among the middle sectors and the more wealthy and educated segments. Indeed, Lula's electoral base became more diversified from the standpoint of social composition.

The complexity of the electoral rules, combined with the multiparty and federative electoral arrangement, place significant constraints on presidential candidacies. However, it should be noted that, on the one hand, the president's calculations considered these limits to the electoral alliance; and, on the other hand, those calculations included expectations about the resources at his disposal once elected. The broad powers provided to Brazilian presidents allow office-holders considerable leeway, including how to address the costs of managing electoral coalitions.

Institutional Bases of Presidential Leadership when Running the Government

The chief executive's institutional powers extend to different decision-making arenas. Provisions concentrating power in the hands of the president, introduced by the military governments, were maintained by the democratic constitution of 1988, with amendments. The powers of decree, of legislative initiative, of budget control, and of the appointment of an extensive number of positions in the executive branch allow presidents to control the legislative agenda and the various resources for implementing their governing agendas.

The use of these resources by the two presidents studied here varied, owing to the nature of each administration's agenda and priorities, in addition to those administrations' timing during the redemocratization period. The agenda of structural reforms—some of them defeated in the constitutional process—of FHC's governing program gave a strategic role to constitutional amendments and supplementary laws in the legislative agenda of the executive. FHC undertook the effort to amend the constitution, which required supermajorities (two-fifths of the members of each house). In the honeymoon period—the administration's first year—alone, the executive presented 16 of the 27 constitutional amendment proposals (*propostas de emenda constitucional*—PECs) put forward in the first term, a higher number than those proposed in the second term (11 PECs). Lula, anticipating possible desertions from his heterogeneous legislative supermajority and wishing to benefit from the changes made by the previous administration, virtually excluded constitutional amendments from his legislative agenda. Only 16 PECs were proposed during his two terms, showing the executive's retreat from constitutional reform.

The two presidents, separately, resorted to the power of decree to ensure that the executive branch would enjoy strategic advantages in the decision-making process and to accelerate the timing of the implementation of their policies. Provisional measures (*Medida Provisória*—MP),[9] which allow presidents to issue decrees with immediate legal force, proved their efficiency for the implementation of economic and financial matters and became routine instruments for the execution of administrative actions. In his first term, FHC issued an average of 39 MPs annually; during Lula's administration, the average rose to 60. The costs arising from the use of these instruments were relatively low until 2001, because presidents could reissue measures if Congress did not approve them within the prescribed period. This tacit non-decision by legislators was recurrent in FHC's government, which maintained the legal effectiveness of many of its measures without incurring the costs of a plenary decision. However, despite FHC's initial resistance, his party sponsored a change to this rule (Constitutional Amendment no. 32/2001), effectively vetoing the reissues of MPs and requiring congressional deliberation of each measure.

Contrary to expectations, the willingness of presidents to resort to MPs to approve their agendas persisted, but the dynamics of the negotiation of these initiatives in Congress changed considerably. Without the possibility of reissues, the paralysis of plenary voting (*trancamento da pauta*) with suspension of voting sessions became recurrent, generating gridlocks in the decision-making process. During Lula's first term, the legislative agency was paralyzed in 63.6% of the deliberative sessions of the Chamber of Deputies (Inácio, 2009). The strategic use of legislative paralysis was adopted by both the executive and the opposition, either to force the prior negotiation of issues or to enlarge concessions in exchange for removing voting obstructions.

In addition to these prerogatives, the president has exceptional resources available to shape the legislative agenda through an exclusive initiative in matters of taxation, budget, and organization of the executive branch, including the creation or dissolution of ministries or federal administrative agencies (CRFB, art. 61, section 1). Both the budgetary and appointment powers allow Brazilian presidents to accommodate the interests of the coalition parties both in Congress and within the executive branch.

Because budget law involves authorization, the executive has the final word on how much and on how to spend the considerable amount of public resources, including the implementation of budget amendments (Pereira, 1999; Pereira and Muller, 2003; Pereira and Renno, 2001). This prerogative is exercised by the ministries in the economic area, which operate as a coordinating core of the government that is capable, through budgetary decisions, of constraining the movements of the overcrowded parties in the ministries. The Ministry of Finance assumed a central role in the coordination of FHC's administration under the management of an expert trusted by the president; in

184 *Magna Inácio*

Table 8.4 Number of provisional measures issued per year by the presidents—Brazil, 1988–2007

Year	President	Constitutional amendment proposals	Ordinary bills	Provisional measures (PMs)		
				Original	Reissued	Total
1988	Sarney			15	9	24
1989				97	6	103
1990				20	–	20
1990	Collor			75	68	143
1991				9	2	11
1992				4	2	6
1992	Itamar			4	–	4
1993				48	48	96
1994				86	319	405
1995	FHC I	16	66	29	408	437
1996		5	62	34	615	649
1997		3	42	40	680	720
1998		3	43	53	750	803
1999	FHC II	4	34	47	1,040	1,087
2000		3	61	23	1,088	1,111
2001		4	68	33	478	511
2002		0	74	82	–	82
2003	Lula I	2	34	58	–	58
2004		4	57	73	–	73
2005		2	48	42	–	42
2006		0	36	67	–	67
2007	Lula II	5	34	63	–	63
2008		2	65	40	–	40
2009		1	73	27	–	27
2010		0	31	42	–	42

Source: Federal Senate of Brazil (2013).

Lula's administration, this function was increasingly compartmentalized, first through presidential agencies and gradually through the Ministry of Planning. This coordinating center was maintained under the control of the president's party.

The Brazilian president enjoys great autonomy in assembling the cabinet, with the power to nominate and to dismiss ministers (CRFB, art. 84, section I), without the requirement of congressional approval. Despite electoral and partisan incentives and constraints, the appointment power puts the chief executive in a unique position with respect to government coalition building. The centrality of a portfolio to the president and/or the congressional or regional weight of the appointed party drive the ministerial selection.

The influence of these formal rules and prerogatives on presidential leadership is not trivial. Under this arrangement, the transaction costs of negotiations with parties, the Congress, the bureaucracy, etc., can be mitigated to avoid putting the government's management at risk. Nevertheless, the crucial point is whether and how presidents address the opportunities offered by this system that places the chief executive at the center of the decision-making process.

Presidents and the Cabinet

Brazilian presidents, when elected with a legislative minority, rely on the robustness of the presidency to build majority coalitions. The president's constitutional powers allow him or her to change the payoffs of the electoral contest and to incentivize adherence to the administration (Figueiredo and Limongi, 1999, 2009; Amorim Neto, 2000; Santos, 2003). That notwithstanding, presidents differ in how they use institutional resources to form multiparty cabinets. Throughout their presidencies, FHC and Lula formed supermajority coalitions, which operated from 11 multiparty cabinets.

The cabinets formed between 1995 and 2010 varied with respect to important dimensions of the government's internal coordination (Table 8.5). FHC built coalitions that were more compact, with fewer parties and more ideological homogeneity; Lula's administration formed more fragmented coalitions, with the inclusion of ideologically distant and nonadjacent parties.[10] With respect to the delegation of power to the parties, the anticipation of coordination problems influenced the distribution of portfolios among the allied parties. The differences between FHC and Lula in this respect were not restricted to the proportion of ministries that each president put on the negotiating table with the coalition parties, but extended to partisan bias in the allocation of these resources.

The level of cabinet partisanship increased in both administrations, corresponding to more than 60% of the portfolios, through the distribution of ministerial portfolios to congressional parties. This trend was less intense in FHC's administration, affecting 61% of the ministries on average, due to the significant presence of non-partisan, technocrat ministers.[11] This situation changed in Lula's administration, with almost 80% of the portfolios controlled by political parties. However, this polarization was marked by the pro-party bias of the president, with the PT controlling a majority of the ministers, especially in the first term (Inácio, 2006). When the partisanship of the presidential office is considered, presidential strategies differed considerably (Inácio, 2012). Under FHC's administration, partisanship could be described as a strategy for the ministries, not for the presidency. This structure became more partisan only at the end of FHC's second term. Control of the presidential office under Lula assumed a distinctive dynamic, with more intense partisanship, which reached 80% of management posts. In addition to its high magnitude, this partisanship

Table 8.5 Coalitions in the Brazilian government, 1995–2010

Coalition	Party of the president	Start	End	Duration (months)	Member parties	No. of parties	Congressional support	Level of cabinet partisanship
FHC I 1	PSDB	01/01/95	04/25/96	15.8	PSDB-PTB-PMDB-PFL	4	56.34	66.7
FHC I 2	PSDB	04/26/96	12/31/98	32.2	PSDB-PTB-PMDB-PFL-PPB	5	77.00	65.2
FHC II 1	PSDB	01/01/99	03/05/02	38.1	PSDB-PMDB-PPB-PTB-PFL	5	73.88	69.0
FHC II 2	PSDB	03/06/02	12/32/02	9.8	PMDB-PSDB-PPB	3	45.42	46.2
Lula I 1	PT	01/01/03	01/22/04	12.7	PT-PL-PCdoB-PSB-PTB-PDT-PPS-PV	8	42.69	87.1
Lula I 2	PT	01/23/04	01/31/05	12.3	PT-PL-PCdoB-PSB-PTB-PPS-PV-PMDB	8	77.19	87.1
Lula I 3	PT	02/01/05	05/19/05	3.6	PT-PL-PCdoB-PSB-PTB-PV-PMDB	7	73.10	83.9
Lula I 4	PT	05/20/05	07/22/05	2.1	PT-PL-PCdoB-PSB-PTB-PMDB	6	73.10	83.9
Lula I 5	PT	07/23/05	12/31/06	17.3	PT-PL-PCdoB-PSB-PTB-PP-PMDB	7	69.40	80.0
Lula II 1	PT	01/01/07	04/01/07	3.0	PT-PCdoB-PSB-PTB-PP-PMDB	6	53.80	85.7
Lula II 2	PT	04/02/07	12/31/10	45.0	PT-PCdoB-PTB-PP-PMDB-PR-PDT-PV	8	68.62	81

Source: Amorim Neto (2000); Figueiredo and Limongi (2008); Inácio (2006); Inácio and Rezende (2015).

reached, at similar levels, the two structures—the ministries and the presidency—during Lula's two terms.

These variations point to differences in coalition management strategies. It is only recently that the problems of coalition management and their constraints on presidential leadership have attracted scholarly attention (Amorim et al., 2003; Inácio, 2006, 2012, 2013; Gaylor and Rennó, 2012; Batista, 2012). The president relies on a vast range of resources, in addition to the aforementioned prerogatives, not only to redesign and centralize decisions but also to politicize the presidential organization. Consisting of a set of agencies and councils directly subordinate to the president, the presidency is governed by the laws that regulate the organization of the executive branch. By virtue of these agencies and councils being subject to the exclusive initiative of the executive, the president can exercise strong control over the legislative agenda, and can place Congress in a reactive position, by using provisional measures to implement that agenda.

In addition to the powers of agenda/veto and the politicization of the executive, each president shaped his executive core differently (Inácio, 2012). During FHC's administration, this core was formed by the ministries of economic coordination and a relatively compact presidential office. The assembly of this core involved the return of functions that had been centralized in the presidency by the previous office-holder (Inácio, 2006) to the ministerial domain. The ministries assumed the responsibilities of executing the government's priority agendas related to policies of fiscal balance and reform of the Brazilian state. It is also worth noting that this allocation of responsibilities was combined with the strategy of distributing ministerial posts to ministries where the president's party controlled the implementation of these agendas.

Throughout FHC's administration, the decision-making style in the executive core can be characterized as hierarchical, given the roles of the ministries of economic coordination and a presidential organization directly managed by the president. The presidential office consisted of an average of 11 agencies essentially dedicated to managing the government and advising the president directly. The functions of policy formulation that remained centralized in the presidency were channeled to the Council of Government, which was created by President Collor and served as the initial agency of the presidential advisory system. This unit was organized on two levels: the first was oriented toward political control of the government with the participation of the state ministers; the second focused on the formulation of intersectoral activities managed by thematic technical chambers. Thus, there was no expansion of the policy units within the presidency.

Aware of the political pressures resulting from a multiparty government, FHC deliberately adopted—with varying degrees of success—initiatives to preserve the presidential organization in the face of political pressures, including those arising from his party. This clear vision of the president's role in coalition management translated into the valorization of the formal dimension of the presidency, combining a hierarchical logic with the formulation of concentric circles of presidential advisors. The ability to form support teams for the administration through the formation of technical cores and the allocation of strategic portfolios to members of FHC's party sought to preserve the president's role in governmental coordination. In justifying his criteria for defining who would participate in the 'President's inner circle,' FHC argued that:

> [This circle] adheres to the laws of variable geometry: for the administration, it is formed by certain people; for the political game in Congress, by others; for wider policy, by others still. If possible, they should be kept reasonably separate. The decision-making autonomy of the President depends on his or her ability to deal with the diversity of persons and with the information put at his or her disposal by each of the components of the various circles around him or her. Each has access to only part of the picture because the President shall have the largest amount of information, being at the best place to make the final decisions.
>
> (Cardoso, 2006)

Conversely, President Lula adopted an executive core based on the greater centralization of activities into the presidential office. The redesign of this structure by the government affected the entire nucleus of the presidential organization, making it more complex and functionally differentiated. The policies nucleus underwent strong expansion with the creation of new centralized structures, the special secretariats: Policies for Women (*Políticas para as Mulheres*); the Special Secretariat for Aquaculture and Fisheries (*Secretaria Especial de Aquicultura e Pesca*); the Special Secretariat for Human Rights (*Secretaria Especial dos Direitos Humanos*); and the Special Secretariat for Policies for the Promotion of Racial Equality (*Secretaria Especial de Políticas de Promoção da Igualdade Racial*). The presidential advisory system increased the informational resources of the presidency for the implementation of its agenda with the creation of two new agencies: the Council of Economic and Social Development (*Conselho de Desenvolvimento Econômico e Social*) and the National Council of Food and Nutritional Security (*Conselho Nacional de Segurança Alimentar e Nutricional*). In addition to focusing on specific issues, the expansion of this system focused on intersectoral issues with high potential for involvement by different ministries, thus expanding the information sources available to the president. The executive's intent to make this organization more open to the organized movements of civil society was also central to the process of expansion of presidential advisory services. In addition to electoral and partisan motivations and the PT's linkage to such movements, these new units increased the channels for the direct mobilization of social segments by the president and his assistants. Because of this organizational expansion, the presidential staff in Lula's administration grew gradually, expanding from 3,081 to 7,847 civil servants between 2003 and 2010.

Centralized decision-making manifested itself with respect to the executive core of Lula's government. The Office of the Chief of Staff became responsible for the political coordination and management of the government; it also incorporated the Secretariat of Management (*Secretaria de Gestão*) of the Ministry of Planning, Budgeting and Management (*Ministério do Planejamento, Orçamento e Gestão*) into its structure. Control of political appointments, which is a condition for politicization, was also centralized within this unit. The Chief of Staff assumed the power to appoint the government's senior management officers (DAS 5–6) and the heads of presidential agencies. Nonetheless, starting in 2005, the reaction to this hyper-centralization of decision-making led to the dispersion of powers among presidential units. The political management functions of this unit were transferred to the newly created Secretariat of Institutional Relations (*Secretaria de Relações Institucionais*) and to the Secretariat General (*Secretaria Geral*), and the government's involvement with social movements and subnational actors was strengthened.[12] At the end of the first term, the president created the Political Council (*Conselho Político*), a forum for discussion of the administration's agenda and its political support in Congress, consisting of party leaders and cabinet ministers. As an informal forum, the Council limited itself to discussion of controversial agendas without becoming a structure for managing the coalition. Thus, throughout Lula's administration, the decision-making style in the executive core changed from a highly centralized and hierarchical pattern under the control of the Office of the Chief of Staff to a more fragmented and competitive decision-making structure, which remained centralized in the presidency but included greater dispersion of powers among its agencies.

Presidents and Bureaucracies

With the executive's partisanship, resulting from the policy of coalition building, Brazilian presidents gradually adopted various mechanisms to contain ministerial discretion and strengthen control over bureaucracies.

One of the few changes in the constitutional powers of the Brazilian president explicitly refers to the president's control of the bureaucratic apparatus. Presidential discretion received a relative increase through a constitutional change (Constitutional Amendment, no. 32, 2001) that authorized the executive branch to issue decrees for the 'organization and functioning of the federal administration, when they do not involve the increase in expenditures or the creation or extinction of public agencies' (art. 84, VI, of the Constitution of 1988). As autonomous decrees, these normative acts are not subject to congressional deliberation. Thus, the redesign of the agencies of the executive branch and the distribution of functions and personnel became more flexible under such regulations.

This flexibility becomes relevant in a structure in which bureaucracies are coordinated on the basis of a chain of power delegation that begins with the president and devolves to ministers. Given the risks of ministerial discretion, both FHC and Lula introduced mechanisms to maintain the chain of command. An example was the strengthening of the role of the executive secretary in the ministries—a type of junior minister with skills in key areas for administering portfolios. Because this is a senior management position, the appointment of the executive secretary is the president's prerogative; the nominations to these positions by the ministers are subject to assessment by the Office of the Chief of Staff.

Given the possible biases of proposed laws originating from the ministries, FHC adopted various measures that regulated the flow of bureaucratic procedures from ministerial initiatives, thereby strengthening the president's control over the formulation of public policies by ministries. The legislature was subordinated to the legal advisory agencies of the presidency, with the Chief of Staff being responsible for the appointment of their heads. Later, the evaluation of alignment of the ministries' proposals with the administration's priorities became a duty of this unit of the executive branch.

As we have seen, the need to form governing coalitions alters the conditions of presidential leadership. However, presidents have mobilized their institutional power to reduce the constraints and risks associated with multiparty governance. In doing so, presidents have modified the environment in which they exercise leadership.

The Role of the Party (or Parties)

Cardoso's and Lula's paths to the presidency were largely aligned with the consolidation of their leadership within their parties. Although starting from different paths and at different times, these leaders' national projections occurred in parallel to their parties' differentiation efforts, vis-à-vis the alternative parties emerging in the partisan realignment processes of the 1990s. Therefore, the presidential vocations of PT and PSDB (Limongi and Cortez, 2010; Melo and Câmara, 2012) resulted from FHC's and Lula's conversion into competitive candidates in the primary arena of national competition.

FHC's ascension to party leadership positions should be understood in light of the congressional origin of the PSDB party structure. The constituent debate led to an intensification of internal divisions among PMDB legislators, which turned the PMDB into a catch-all party marked by the great internal heterogeneity of political groups. Such conflicts led to the departure of a group of legislators and politicians who subsequently created the Brazilian Social Democracy Party (*Partido da Social Democracia Brasileira*—PSDB), with FHC as an active leader.

In parallel to these ideological divisions, electoral calculations ascertained the initial positioning of the PSDB at the center-left. Created during the process of party realignment, with the increasing dispersion of political forces previously concentrated in the center-right,[13] the PSDB's founding group sought to occupy the center space in the ideological spectrum through an alternative organization. Indeed, Sarney's rise to the presidency, in place of Tancredo Neves, had shifted this group from the center of governmental influence, limiting it to the congressional arena. Sarney's loss of popular support at the end of his term, which increased the level of uncertainty regarding the presidential succession in 1989, strengthened the expectations of the PSDB's founders with respect to the political-electoral gains arising from the creation of a new party. The PSDB, which obtained the fourth-highest vote tally in the first direct election, became the opposition to the Collor administration, signaling its position as a center-left party by aligning with the PT in 65% of roll-call votes between 1990 and 1992 (Roma, 2002: 86).

The party's presidential vocation gained special momentum in 1992 with the formation of the pro-administration party front, in support of President Itamar, following Collor's impeachment. As a cabinet member, FHC increased his influence over the administration when he became the minister of the main economic portfolio after working in the area of foreign relations. As discussed above, success in managing the economic-stabilization plan paved the way for FHC's run for the presidency, supported by President Itamar Franco.

The PSDB's ascension to the presidency six years after its creation closely linked the party's dynamics to those of the government and, consequently, solidified FHC's position in the party's leadership. The opportunities to build this leadership resulted from the organizational structure prioritized by the party's founders. The fact that the PSDB was created as a 'party within the parliamentary system resulted in a weak and decentralized organizational structure, the absence of extra-electoral activities, little participation of members, and the lack of democratic institutions to veto the decisions of the party elite' (Roma, 2002: 72). Such characteristics created an ample margin of action by the party leaders, with respect both to electoral strategies and running the government. Formed by 40 deputies and seven senators, the PSDB's original congressional delegation comprised 8% of the members of the Chamber of Deputies, growing to 12% of the deputies when the party achieved the presidency. By the end of the presidential period, the party represented 19.3% of deputies, in addition to considerable territorial dispersal of its party machine, initially concentrated in the southeastern region of the country. This organizational expansion of the party, marked by flexibility with diffuse recruitment of members, including party migration,[14] revealed itself as unfavorable for the retention of new cadres (Inácio, 2013).

The PT's organizational model established very different conditions for Lula to rise to the position of main party leader. As highlighted above, the PT's structure grounded itself in the principle of partisan organization, based on internal democracy with highly mobilized militancy in the participatory processes of internal decision-making. Despite the union core's initial control over the party's creation, its organizational structure was shaped by internal pressures from the party's management bodies to accommodate different trends.

Historically, the PT maintained a restrictive policy related to the affiliation of new members, selecting its leaders from among its own cadres. Starting in the 1990s, the professionalization of these leaders gained momentum, with a growing number of members currently or formerly in public office occupying positions in the party's national directorate. As an extension of the PT's experiences in the legislative and executive branches, this segment exhibited considerable growth.

According to Ribeiro (2010), the trend toward control of the national directorate by the majority, to which Lula belonged, led to the centralization of decision-making within the PT and increasing decision-making autonomy by that group. Although this conjuncture was associated with a change in party financing rules, implemented beginning in 1996, these changes also revealed the impact of the presidential project on the intra-party dynamic. This process, whose landmark was the new statute in 2001, rested on changes in different dimensions of the PT's organizational model. The introduction of the process of direct election for the composition of different levels of party directorates simplified the intra-party process for the construction of majorities. This innovation, however, eliminated the role of meetings as discussion forums for the party's agenda and as the primary space for competition among internal groups to influence the party machine (Ribeiro, 2010). Changes in the internal flow of party resources, such as the centralization of financial contributions from members into the hands of the National Finance Secretariat, the obtaining of funds from major campaign donors, and the relaxing of both membership rules and alliance policy considerably widened the dominant coalition's control over Lula's 2002 campaign.

The Role of Congress

Starting in the mid-1990s, the relationship between Brazil's executive and legislative branches became more stable with the formation of party-coordinated governing coalitions. Although multiparty cabinets have recurred during Brazil's democratic periods, it is only since 1994 that these coalitions have gone on to act as stable legislative bases, providing greater clarity in the government-opposition divide. Even so, important variations in the relationship between the executive branch and the Congress can be seen among the various presidents, and even between the terms of particular presidents (Inácio, 2006).

Brazilian presidents prefer supermajority coalitions in Congress. FHC, who sponsored an extensive agenda of constitutional changes, formed coalitions that comprised more than 60% of the deputies. Lula grew his electoral coalition to a similar level, although constitutional changes were rare in his administration.

Frustrating many forecasts, the legislative parties in Brazil have shown high levels of party discipline in Congress since redemocratization. Generally, parties vote in accordance with the orientation of their leaders in 80% or more of roll-call votes. This party coordination benefited both presidents, supported by relatively predictable congressional coalitions.

Nonetheless, the differences in the internal composition of the coalitions—and the coordination problems resulting therefrom—have resulted in distinct patterns of congressional behavior, with variations among governments and throughout terms, as shown in Table 8.6. In FHC's case, not only his party (the PSDB) but also that of his vice president (then known as the PFL) acted in a highly disciplined manner (over 90% of the time). The remaining parties—the PMDB, the PDS/PP and the PTB—acted in a coordinated way throughout the entire period. Although the parties in Lula's coalition were disciplined, they were more fragmented and exhibited oscillations in the internal coordination of the congressional representation of each party. Once in power, the PT's discipline rate fluctuated, in addition to exhibiting a slight drop relative to its past performance as the opposition party. In 2005, marked by criticism and the excessive centralization of government by the PT, as well as allegations of corruption, every coalition party acted in a less disciplined way (Coalition Lula I3 and I4) indicating increased internal tensions within the administration.

In general, the two presidents had the joint support of their respective coalitions in the legislative arena.[15] The number of votes in which the coalition parties voted according to the administration's instructions was predominant, with voting divergences being less frequent among coalition members. However, when the coalition was divided, the decline of party discipline among other parties also occured, signaling individual- or faction-based divisions within the parties. Table 8.7 depicts the evolution of legislative support of the government coalition in the Chamber of Deputies from 1995 to 2010.

A comparison between the presidential terms makes it clear that Lula's coalition faced more frequent internal conflicts in the legislative arena. Lula's governing coalition cast a united vote in 81.9% and 71.1% of the voting sessions that occurred during his first and second terms, respectively. This is lower than the results obtained by FHC (at 88.2% and 91%), as shown in Table 8.8.

The control of positions of power in Congress is one of the assets that parties pursue to strengthen their bargaining power with the executive. Presidential interference in the process largely reflects the ability to address party pressures related to competition for such positions. To reward partners, FHC curbed the PSDB's ambition in the dispute over the presidencies of the Senate and of the Chamber of Deputies, alternatively occupied by the remaining coalition parties. This balance lasted until 2001 when, contrary to the president's position, segments of the PSDB competed for and assumed the presidency of the Chamber of Deputies, creating tensions within the coalition. Under Lula's administration, the PT, elected with the most votes, pressed for control of the position, electing one of its members as President of the Chamber of Deputies. The combination of that fact and the pro-PT bias in the distribution of ministerial portfolios were interpreted by the other coalition parties as signs of the threat of centralized power in the hands of the party. In the subsequent election for the position, an independent candidate linked to the 'baixo clero' (backbenchers) became president after defeating the candidate supported by the PT (following an intense intra-party fight for the position).

Table 8.6 Party discipline in the administrations of FHC and Lula by party—Chamber of Deputies, 1995–2010

Coalition[1]	Right											Left
	PFL/DEM	PDS/PP	PL/PR	PTB	PSDB	PMDB	PCB/PPS	PDT	PSB	PV	PT	PCdoB
FHC I 1	93.0	89.5	88.9	88.0	90.9	83.0	90.2	86.7	82.8	96.2	95.8	93.1
FHC I 2	94.0	80.2	71.0	87.0	92.3	80.5	86.3	91.7	90.4	97.4	97.0	98.1
FHC II 1	95.7	90.6	75.5	86.7	96.0	85.7	88.3	93.4	95.9	100.0	96.7	98.4
FHC II 2	93.9	89.0	75.1	83.7	94.6	88.1	69.3	91.6	93.8		93.8	98.3
Lula I 1	73.7	86.9	96.8	91.8	79.2	92.0	97.5	90.4	96.0	82.7	96.0	98.3
Lula I 2	85.2	83.8	94.2	91.7	85.1	81.3	92.9	85.7	95.3	82.6	94.4	98.0
Lula I 3	89.1	81.7	79.2	79.4	89.9	78.1	89.7	91.0	84.0	81.5	78.4	89.4
Lula I 4	83.6	83.4	84.4	85.8	81.7	77.0	72.0	75.9	94.3	72.9	97.6	100.0
Lula I 5	90.8	84.0	88.4	88.1	93.2	82.5	94.1	91.4	87.3	90.8	94.9	92.9
Lula II 1	87.9	91.5	92.9	90.7	88.6	90.5	72.9	95.9	97.1	94.5	88.9	98.5
Lula II 2	82.7	90.9	93.9	89.7	90.2	92.2	82.6	93.7	90.6	89.3	97.4	94.2
Lula II 3	84.1	87.8	87.4	88.5	92.5	83.7	90.2	84.9	92.4	85.3	88.6	93.2

1 The parties in FHC's governing coalition are listed in light gray and the parties in Lula's governing coalition are listed in dark gray.

Source: Figueiredo and Limongi (2013).

Table 8.7 Support of the government coalition for the executive's legislative agenda—Brazil, Chamber of Deputies, 1995–2010

Government coalition	United coalition[1] No. of roll calls	% of discipline[3]	Divided coalition[2] No. of roll calls	% of discipline[3]	Total No. of roll calls	% of discipline[3]
FHC I 1	83	90.35	13	60.82	96	86.35
FHC I 2	217	88.32	27	69.37	244	86.23
FHC II 1	188	93.55	19	69.69	207	91.36
FHC II 2	15	92.63	1	64.8	16	90.89
Lula I 1	78	95.03	7	78.86	85	93.7
Lula I 2	30	89.93	6	76.82	36	87.75
Lula I 3	10	76.50	2	44.83	12	71.22
Lula I 4	7	90.52	4	79.96	11	86.68
Lula I 5	24	88.64	14	67.24	38	80.76
Lula II 1	14	96.52	2	48.69	16	90.54
Lula II 2	143	95.70	55	73.86	198	89.63
Lula II 3	28	95.06	18	73.08	46	86.46
Total	911	92.32	216	66.8	1,127	85.64

Notes:
1 Party leaders in the government coalition vote according to the government leader's guidelines (includes cases in which at least one party leader liberates or abstains from the vote).
2 At least one party leader within the government coalition opposes the government leader's voting guidelines.
3 Percentage of votes by members of the parties in the government coalition.

Source: Figueiredo and Limongi (2013).

Table 8.8 Frequency of united and divided votes of governing coalitions per presidential term—Brazil, 1995–2010.

TERMS	United coalition (A) No. roll calls	Divided coalition (B) No. roll calls	Total No. roll calls	A/Total
FHC 1	300	40	340	88.24
FHC 2	203	20	223	91.03
LULA 1	149	33	182	81.87
LULA 2	185	75	260	71.15

Source: Figueiredo and Limongi (2013).

Even though the Chamber of Deputies is a strategic arena for presidents, the bicameral arrangement requires presidential strategies to build coordinated legislative support in both houses. The parties are more disciplined in the Chamber of Deputies than they are in the Senate, with the exception of leftist parties that exhibit greater bicameral coordination in their congressional delegations (Neiva, 2011). It is important to stress that the parties have a distinct composition in each house, especially from the regional perspective. These distinctions result from the adoption of different rules for the election of members—proportional for the Chamber of Deputies, and majoritarian for the Senate—and the format of the state party subsystems. Consequently, the negotiations between the president and Congress have a double bias—partisan and regional—that is reflected in the composition of the cabinet.

Often, the tensions and conflicts among the coalition parties lead to legislative clashes. The desertion of allies during votes considered strategic by the government—so-called 'friendly fire'—demonstrates the increasing costs of maintaining the fragmented and heterogeneous coalition formed by Lula's government.

Presidential Patronage?

Historically, the size of Brazil's state apparatus contributed to extensive patronage resources controlled by the federal executive. Despite the attention given to the budget amendments, as one of the primary bargaining chips between the administration and legislators, Limongi and Figueiredo (2005) argue that individual amendments are residual, and that both the collective amendments and those of the rapporteurs of budget projects are the primary methods of modifying government proposals. Thus, the centralization of budget decision-making indicates the deputies' delegation of powers to the party leaders in order to defend the government's agenda from attacks by the opposition. Furthermore, those authors assert that the interests of allied parties are accommodated in formulating the budget proposal, within ministries, and before the proposal's presentation to the Congress.

In the context of the centralization of the budget decision-making process, the capacity to negotiate constituents' demands with the federal administration has been valued by legislators. Coalition governments and access to the state apparatus have led to changes in the focus of legislators' action related to the casework (Inácio, 2011). On this point, FHC recognized that the creation of the Ministry of National Integration (*Ministério da Integração Nacional*), which was previously a secretariat, was an error. It had become a primary target both of parochial budget amendments and of legislators' various demands (Inácio, 2006: 277–278), with increasing tensions in the relationship between the parties and the administration.

Because coalition politics triggers the politicization of the ministerial portfolio, the president's challenge is to determine the optimal proportion of positions to be controlled by the parties as distinct from his own quota, whether for presidential patronage or for control of his or her agents. The number of ministries increased from 22 in FHC's first term to 36 in Lula's second term. It is interesting to see how, parallel to the expansion of their portfolios, presidents maintained control of political areas and offices to implement their own agendas. For example, during FHC's second term, secretariats with ministerial status, controlled by technocrats allied with the president, were created to strengthen the ability to oversee and manage governmental policies. In Lula's administration, the secretariats oriented themselves toward the priority policies of the PT's programs, supported by social and minority movements with historical links to the party.

To address the demands of parties and outside groups for positions of power in the executive branch, presidents can appoint numerous political positions, some of which can be occupied by freely recruited staff. In 2010, the executive relied on approximately 22,000 high-level management and advising positions (*Direção e Assessoramento Superior*—DAS). Because these positions cover different levels of advising and management, they ensure that the president has great flexibility in assembling political control of the government and its coordination. Through administrative reallocation by means of provisional measures and decrees, the president is capable of distributing and rearranging such positions without large administrative obstacles. As patronage resources, however, these positions are disputed by the parties in the cabinet, and some political appointments cater to partisan-political pressures. Given the centrality of partisanship in the executive branch as the glue of government coalitions, attempts to professionalize these positions have faced strong political resistance.

Conclusions

The question that has guided this discussion is whether robust presidencies favored these two performance of these two presidents as leaders. To develop this point, the proposed approach combined the analysis of three dimensions involved in presidential leadership: social background, personal attributes and institutional factors. By exploring the overlaps of these dimensions, we sought to identify the variants of leadership immersed in an institutional arrangement that places the chief executive at the center of the decision-making process. The analysis has focused on the experience of two presidents, FHC and Lula, for 16 years during the post-redemocratization period.

The leadership provided by these two presidents indelibly marked presidential performance and the dynamics of political competition in recent democratic history. Nevertheless, their impacts varied, based on the style and the guidelines that steered them in the exercise of their office.

Using a more formal and hierarchical style of governmental oversight, FHC reorganized the foundations of the relationships among the presidency, the member-parties of the cabinet coalition, and Congress, contributing to the emergence of a more stable pattern of interaction among the branches of government. Under his leadership, the construction of a clear and innovative political project, following the erratic administrations of the post-redemocratization period, had a significant impact on the structure of political conflict and on party competition. This was demonstrated by almost two decades of PSDB-PT polarization in presidential elections. The management of multiparty government demonstrated the Brazilian president's power of agenda control and the possibility of mobilizing institutional powers to build political majorities capable of reform, even at a high political cost. It is worth mentioning that FHC, in his politics of coalition management, knew how to use the opportunities offered by the legislative branch—such as the presidencies of the Chamber of Deputies and the Senate—to accommodate his allies' interests through a logic of balanced access to power. The results clearly reflected his ability to circulate among and negotiate with the political elite. However, this approach, which originated with the congressional logic that marked FHC's party, may have contributed to reducing the PSDB's ability to revamp its agendas and to claim credit with voters for the administration's actions, constraining the expansion of the electoral base of the coalition that carried FHC to the presidency.

Within a more stable scenario of democratic competition, Lula's leadership differentiated itself by its ability to construct institutional and political conditions to renovate public and political agendas, and to rebuild these bases in adverse scenarios. Although the timing of Lula's arrival to power after a cycle of structural and economic reforms created a favorable situation for this shift toward social and redistributive policies, the administration's leadership was decisive for the building of a political coalition on a societal base that sustained such innovations. The choices relating to the type of coalition and how to manage it resulted from non-trivial challenges to presidential leadership. Outbreaks of political instability demonstrated weaknesses in the administration's political support and increased the costs of managing its alliance, with a negative impact on the president's party. Important innovations, both institutional and in matters of presidential style, resulted from this phase of 'initial adjustment.' The reorganization of the presidency, which renovated the presidential advisory model, diversified the environment and altered the information flow underlying presidential decisions. In a way, these crises triggered alarms for the 'management' component of the governing project, and the president knew how to decipher these signs. Lula's choices, aimed at maintaining the stability of his administration, reinforced the voters' personal identification with the president. A charismatic and accomplished communicator, Lula offered efficient shortcuts for the voters to differentiate among contested political projects, which contributed to the personalization of the Lula vote. Nonetheless, the series of corruption scandals involving his administration required the use of this resource to its limit. The intensive use of these skills, previously employed in selective and economical ways, led to the overexposure of the PT's main leader in an environment of increasing rejection of the PT by considerable portions of the electorate. It should be noted, however, that, compared to other Latin American presidents, Lula knew how to mobilize such resources within the limits of political institutionalism.

Finally, the analysis has indicated how the robustness of the Brazilian presidency was fine-tuned by the institutional arrangement that places limits on and reshapes presidents' potential actions. The primary difference between the two presidents involved the ability to seize opportunities created by this arrangement, both before and during their presidential terms, to promote alternative agendas and to forge political majorities for their support. This is an equation that is not always easy to balance in Latin American democracies.

Notes

1 Transcription of the first press conference given by President Lula to the media on October 2, 2003. Available at Biblioteca da Presidência [Library of the Presidency]: www.biblioteca.presidencia.gov.br/ex-presidentes/luiz-inacio-lula-dasilva/entrevistas/1o-mandato/2003/20-10-2003-entrevista-coletiva-concedida-pelo-presidente-da-republica-luiz-inacio-lula-da-silva-a-emissoras-de-radio-que-cobrem-o-dia-a-dia-do-palacio-do-planalto/view
2 The amendment for re-election was approved with the support of 66% of the deputies and 80% of the senators in the respective houses. The change ignited a re-election scandal, stemming from allegations of corruption involving the 'buying' of votes in favor of re-election, which involved the minister Sérgio Mota, a spokesman for and personal friend of FHC. The allegations resulted in the resignation of two legislators who were accused of breaking parliamentary decorum.
3 FHC, in 1994 and 1998; José Serra in 2002 and Geraldo Alckimin in 2006.
4 The Zero Hunger (*Fome Zero*) strategy consisted of the coordination of various programs related to food security, income generation, support for family farming, and political-institutional articulation. The University for Everyone Program (*Programa Universidade para Todos—Prouni*) sought to increase the availability of openings in higher education through the granting of scholarships at private institutions, with priority for specific segments of the population, such as those from public schools.
5 The scandal known as the *Mensalão* scandal was sparked by allegations from the president of the PTB, a government coalition party, around corrupt practices involving members of both the administration and Congress; in particular, the 'buying of votes' of legislators. The allegations that ministers heading the secretaries of the presidential office were involved in the scandal brought to light the expansion of this structure during Lula's government and the PT's control over these newly created agencies. Throughout the first half of 2005, Congress's legislative activities were paralyzed due to the busy agenda of the congressional committees of inquiry and obstruction by governing coalition parties and the government.
6 The two-round presidential election was introduced by the Federal Constitution of 1988 (art. 77). Paragraph 3 of this article states, 'If no candidate obtains an absolute majority in the first round of voting, there will be a new election within twenty days of the proclamation of the result, contested between the two most-voted-for candidates, and whichever obtains the majority of valid votes is elected.'
7 Following internal differences, the PFL appointed vice-presidential candidate Marcos Maciel, who remained in the running in the re-election contest.
8 According to Singer, 'the disconnection between the bases of Lulism and those of the PT in 2006 can signify that a new force came into the picture, formed by

200 *Magna Inácio*

Lula leading a class segment that used to be subservient to the parties of order and that, more than indicating a general effect of de-ideologization and de-politicization, indicated the emergence of *another* ideological orientation which was not previously in play. It seems to us that Lulism, in executing the program of combating inequality within the order, concocted a new ideological view, uniting flags that seemed not to match.' (Singer, 2009: 96). Other authors, such as Renno and Cabello (2010), argue that the Lulist voter is not aligned, covering a portion of de-ideologized and de-politicized voters whose electoral choices are based on government performance.

9   The MP is regulated by article 62 of the Brazilian Constitution.
10 In FHC's administration, the coalitions included parties that were ideologically adjacent and situated on two ideological stances; that is, to the right and in the center of the ideological spectrum. Conversely, Lula's coalitions exhibited a larger number of parties and ideological heterogeneity and included parties of three different ideological stances (right/center/left) (Inácio, 2006).
11 In 2002, the coalition underwent a rupture following the departure of the vice president's party, the then-PFL, in the context of the selection of the candidate to succeed Cardoso.
12 This change represented the end of the centralized decision-making style in the context of the presidency, which was adopted at the beginning of Lula's government in 2004–2005. At that time, scandals involving the presidential staff, notably the Chief of Staff, occurred. The transfer of this unit's political management functions to the newly created Secretariat of Institutional Relations (*Secretaria de Relações Institucionais*) and the strengthening of the Secretariat General (*Secretaria Geral*), in its relationship with social movements and subnational actors were clearly actions related to this transition.
13 Until 1986, the PMDB and the PFL controlled 77.1% of the seats in the Chamber of Deputies. This party realignment gained momentum until 1992, particularly due to the permissiveness of the party organization and electoral legislation. Various studies highlight the effect of the rules on the increase in party fragmentation. These rules included permission for parties without definitive electoral registration to participate in the elections between 1985 and 1992; also, Constitutional Amendment no. 25 of 1985 permitted the reorganization of parties whose registrations had been annulled, rejected or canceled (e.g., Communist parties (the PCB and the PCdoB)), thus allowing micro-party formation.
14 The PSDB, which was formed by 40 dissident deputies and seven dissident senators, initially had a congressional delegation equivalent to 8% of the membership of the Chamber of Deputies. This congressional delegation grew to 12% of the deputies in 1994 and to 19.3% in 1998 during FHC's two presidential terms, promoting territorial dispersion of the party machine, which was initially concentrated in the southeastern region of the country (Inácio, 2013).
15 To coordinate his congressional base, the president can build a leadership structure in each legislative house through the appointment of legislators as spokespeople. Government leaders participate in the primary decision-making center of the Chambers, the College of Leaders (*Colégio de Líderes*) that, together with its presidents, defines the legislative agenda. Those leaders intervene directly in legislative work, expressing the administration's position in their vote on each bill.

References

Amorim Neto, O. (2000). Gabinetes presidenciais, ciclos eleitorais e disciplina legislativa no Brasil. *Dados*, 43(2), 479–519.

Amorim Neto, O., Cox, G.W. and Mccubbins, M.D. (2003). Agenda Power in Brazil's Câmara dos Deputados, 1989–98. *World Politics*, 55(4), 550–578.

Batista, M. (2012) *O Poder no Executivo: uma análise exploratória do papel dos ministérios no presidencialismo de coalizão brasileiro (1995–2010)*. 10o Encontro Anual da RedGob e I Conferência Internacional sobre Estudos Presidenciais Comparados e Presidencialismo. Brazil.

Biblioteca da Presidência, Brazil (2013) *Acervo da Secretaria de Imprensa—2003/2010*. Retrieved from www.infoacervo.planalto.gov.br/index.htm.

Blondel, J. and Thiébault, J.L. (2010). *Political Leadership, Parties and Citizens: The Personalisation of Leadership*. London: Routledge Research in Comparative Politics.

Cardoso, F.H. (2006). *A arte da política: a história que vivi*. Rio de Janeiro: Civilização Brasileira.

Edwards, G.C. and Wayne, S.J. (2010). *Presidential Leadership*. 8th edition. New York: Thomson/Wadsworth.

Figueiredo, A.C. and Limongi, F. (1999). *Executivo e legislativona nova ordem constitucional*. Rio de Janeiro: Editora FGV.

Figueiredo, A.C. and Limongi, F. (2008). *Política Orçamentária no Presidencialismo de Coalizão*. Rio de Janeiro: FGV/FAPESP.

Figueiredo, A.C. and Limongi, F. (2009). Poder de Agenda e Políticas Substantivas. In: Inácio, M. and Rennó, L. (eds), *Legislativo Brasileiro em perspectiva comparada*. Belo Horizonte: UFMG ED.

Figueiredo, A.C. and Limongi, F. (2013) *Cebrap—Banco de Dados Legislativos, 2013*.

Gaylor, S. and Rennó, L. (2012). *The Role of the Cabinet in Legislative Production in Brazil*. Paper presented at IPSA World Congress, Madrid.

Greenstein, F.I. (2000). *The Presidential Difference: Leadership Style from FDR to Clinton*. New York: Free Press.

Hunter, W. and Power, T.J. (2007). Rewarding Lula: Executive Power, Social Policy, and the Brazilian Elections of 2006. *Latin American Politics & Society*, 49(1), 1–30.

Inácio, M. (2006). *Presidencialismo de coalizão e sucessopresidencial no Brasil*. Tese de Doutorado em Ciências Humanas, Universidade Federal de Minas Gerais.

Inácio, M. (2009). Mudança procedimental, Oposições políticas e obstrucionismo na Câmara dos Deputados. In: Inácio, M. and Rennó, L. (eds), *Legislativo Brasileiro em Perspectiva Comparada*. Belo Horizonte: UFMG ED.

Inácio, M. (2011). Engajamento Parlamentar no Brasil. In: Power, T. and Zucco, C. (eds), *O Congresso por Ele Mesmo*. Belo Horizonte: UFMG ED.

Inácio, M. (2012). *Coalition Governments and the Institutional Development of the Presidency in Brazil*. Paper presented at Special Seminars, University of Oxford, Latin American Centre.

Inácio, M. (2013) Escogiendo ministros y formando políticos: los partidos en gabinetes multipartidistas. *América Latina Hoy*, 64, 41–66.

Inácio, M. and Rezende D. (2015). Partidos Legislativos e governos de coalizão: controle horizontal das políticas públicas. *Opinião Pública*, 21, 296–335.

Instituto Datafolha (2013). *Pesquisa 'Avaliação do Governo,' 1994–2010*.

Lima Jr, O.B. (1997). *O Sistema Partidário Brasileiro. Diversidade e Tendências, 1982–1994*. Rio de Janeiro: Fundação Getulio Vargas Editora.

Limongi, F. and Cortez, R. (2010). As Eleições de 2010 e o Quadro Partidário. *Novos Estudos*, 88, 21–37.

Limongi, F. and Figueiredo, A. (2005). Processo orçamentário e comportamento Legislativo: emendas individuais, apoio ao Executivo e programas de governo. *Dados*, 48(4).

Melo, C.R. and Câmara, R. (2012). Estrutura da competição pela Presidência e consolidação do Sistema partidário no Brasil. *Dados*, 55(1), 71–117.

Neiva, P. (2011). Coesão e disciplina partidária no Senado federal. *Dados: Revista de Ciências Sociais*, 54(1), 289–318.

Nicolau, J. (1996). *Multipartidarismo e Democracia: Um Estudo sobre o Sistema Partidário Brasileiro (1985–94)*. Rio de Janeiro: Fundação Getulio Vargas Editora.

Nicolau, J. and Peixoto, V. (2007). Uma disputa em três tempos: uma análise das bases municipais nas eleições presidenciais de 2006. In: *Anais XXI Encontro Anual da Anpocs*, 20 set.

Pereira, C. (1999). *What Are the Conditions for Presidential Success in the Legislative Arena? The Brazilian Electoral Connection*. PhD Dissertation. New York: The New School University.

Pereira, C. and Muller, B. (2003). Partidos Fracos na Arena Eleitoral e Partida Forte na Arena Legislativa: A Conexão Eleitoral no Brasil. *Dados*, 46(4), 735–772.

Pereira, C. and Renno, L. (2001). O que é que o Reeleito Tem? Dinâmicas Político-Institucionais Locais e Nacionais nas Eleições de 1998 para a Câmara dos Deputados. *Dados*, 44(2), 323–362.

Renno, L. and Cabello, A. (2010). As bases do Lulismo: a volta do personalismo, realinhamento ideológico ou não alinhamento? *Revista Brasileira de Ciências Sociais*, 25(74), 39–60.

Ribeiro, P.F. (2010). *Dos sindicatos ao governo: a organização nacional do PT de 1980 a 2005*. São Carlos: EdUFSCar/FAPESP.

Roma, C. (2002). A Institucionalização do PSDB entre 1988 e 1998. *Revista Brasileira de Ciências Sociais*, 17(49), 71–92.

Samuels, D. (2009). Raízes sociais e ideológicas do lulismo. *Novos Estudos Cebrap*, 95, 83–103.

Santos, F. (2003). *O Poder Legislativo no Presidencialismo de Coalizão*. Belo Horizonte: UFMG ED.

Singer, A. (2009). Raízes Sociais e Ideológicas do Lulismo. *Novos Estudos*, 85.

Soares, G.A.D. and Terron, S.L. (2008). Dois Lulas: a geografia eleitoral da reeleição (explorando conceitos, métodos e técnicas de análise geoespacial). *Opinião Pública*, 14(2), 269–301.

Superior Electoral Court (Superior Tribunal Eleitoral—STE), Brazil (2013). Retrieved from www.tse.jus.br/eleicoes/eleicoes-anteriores/eleicoes-anteriores

Zucco, C. (2008). The President's 'New' Constituency: Lula and the Pragmatic Vote in Brazil's 2006 Presidential Election. *Journal of Latin American Studies*, 40, 29–49.

Appendix

Table 8.9 FHC's and Lula's party activity prior to their presidencies

Party activity	FHC	LULA
Party affiliation	PMDB (1980–1988) PSDB (1988–)	PT (1980–)
National presidency	Honorary President of the PSDB (2003–)	PT President (1980–1988)
State presidency	PMDB-SP President (1983)	Honorary President of the PT
Member of the party executive committee	PMD-SP Vice President (1979)	
Party leader in the legislature	PSDB Leader in the Senate (1988–1992) PMDB Leader in the Senate and the Constituent Assembly (1985–1988) Leader of the Government in Congress (1985–1986)	PT Leader in the Chamber of Deputies and the Constituent Assembly (1987–1988)

Source: Author's data.

9 Menem and Kirchner
The Two Faces of Peronism?

Mario D. Serrafero

After Argentina's return to democracy in 1983, the country's politics were dominated by two Peronist[1] presidents, Carlos Saúl Menem and Néstor Carlos Kirchner, both from remote provinces far from Buenos Aires. Although ideologically different, both men governed within the framework of Peronism and enjoyed remarkable popular support. Both promoted significant changes in the social, political and economic structures of the country and provided clear political and social leadership: Menem implemented a 'neoliberal' program in the 1990s, whereas Kirchner led the country through a period of economic recovery after the devastating economic crisis of December 2001.

As is usual in the literature on politics, these men gave their names to the political variants of Peronism they developed: Menemism and Kirchnerism. These terms refer to their style of leadership as well as their social and economic policies. Previous work has been based on theoretical and methodological perspectives that distinguish the 'personal presidency' from the 'institutional presidency' and also combine them (Serrafero, 2011a). The literature has also dealt with institutions, parties and political leadership and their influences on the Menem and Kirchner administrations (Alcántara, 2004; Alcántara, 2006).

This chapter examines the different factors that shaped Menem's and Kirchner's presidencies, including their personal characteristics and social backgrounds, their previous political and institutional careers, their ability to communicate as presidents and their relationship with the media, their links with social organizations which provided political and social support, and their relationship with the party and with the institutional actors of the political regimes they created.

Beyond the obvious differences between the two administrations (which reflected two different models of Peronism), remarkable similarities are also evident in the way each president constructed and consolidated his power base.

Two Presidencies, Two Peronisms

Both presidents came to power in the wake of a crisis, although Menem's mandate was initially stronger than Kirchner's. President Menem took office on July 8, 1989 in the midst of an economic and political crisis that had caused

Raúl Alfonsín to resign five months before the end of his term. In the elections held on May 14, 1989, the Peronist presidential ticket of Carlos Menem and Eduardo Duhalde won with 47% of the vote against the Union Cívica Radical's Angeloz–Casella ticket, which received 32.5%. Menem was re-elected in 1995. That time, the Carlos Menem–Carlos Ruckauf ticket won with 49.8% of the votes against José O. Bordon and Carlos Alvarez, of the FREPASO, who obtained 29.50%. Menem served until December 1999, when he was succeeded by President Fernando de la Rúa.

In contrast, in the elections of April 27, 2003, Kirchner and his Frente para la Victoria party or FPV (Front for Victory) gained only 22% of votes against Menem's 24%. However, the ex-president decided not to compete in the second round, to avoid a likely crushing defeat, and Kirchner was thus sworn in as president. Néstor Carlos Kirchner governed for four years and then handed over the presidency to his wife, Cristina Fernández de Kirchner.

Each president had a very different vision of the role of the state. Menem's economic plan involved profound structural reforms, including privatization of public companies, economic deregulation and the opening up of the economy to foreign trade and investment. The government obtained congressional sanction for the laws of State Reform and Economic Emergency, allowing it to suspend state subsidies to industry, sell off public enterprises, and fire state employees by presidential decree. When Domingo Cavallo became Economy Minister, he introduced the Convertibility Plan, which pegged the Argentine peso to the US dollar at a 1:1 exchange rate in April 1991. The plan created the conditions for monetary stability and remained in force after Menem left office in 1999 and until the crisis of December 2001. However, policies of the Menem era led to a deepening of social inequality. Unemployment rose from 7.1% in October 1989 to 14.5% in October 1999, and although the poverty rate initially fell from 40% in 1990 to 22% in 1994, it rose again to 36% by 1998, affecting 4.1 million people. The privatizations under Menem were also questioned because of flaws and irregularities, and they were tainted with suspicions of corruption.

During his first two years as president, Kirchner likewise managed to pull the country out of a deep economic and social crisis. He renegotiated the external debt on much more favorable terms and the economy grew steadily. GDP increased by around 9% annually, thanks to the favorable international context. During Kirchner's government, social policies were implemented to mitigate the effects of the 2001 crisis and to transfer income toward more vulnerable sectors of society. However, it is worth mentioning that the Instituto Nacional de Estadísticas y Censos or INDEC (National Statistics Bureau) intervened in January 2007 so that the government could manipulate the official price indexes and pay lower interest on inflation-linked bonds. Néstor Kirchner fired Graciela Bevacqua, the Director of the Statistics Bureau, together with those unwilling to accept the government's new methodologies to measure national statistics. Towards the end of Néstor Kirchner's presidency, allegations of corruption began to surface. Cases included a mysterious bag of cash found in the Economy

Minister's bathroom, a suitcase filled with $800,000 from Caracas destined for Kirchner's wife's election campaign, and bribes allegedly paid by Swedish firm Skanska to government officials. The corruption allegations increased during Cristina Fernández de Kirchner's second term.

At the beginning of the 1990s, the army still cast a long shadow over Argentine politics. On December 3, 1990, Menem suffered the fourth armed uprising staged by right-wing officers in less than four years. A year earlier, Menem had released 220 military officers who led the military juntas that ruled Argentina from 1976 to 1983, along with 64 left-wing guerrillas. On December 29, 1990, he pardoned a new group of officers, together with Mario Firmenich, the former Montonero guerrilla leader. Kirchner, in his turn, adopted a different policy, and human rights became an emblem of his government. Kirchner cancelled the amnesty laws and activated trials against the military (but not the guerrillas) who had committed human rights violations in the so-called Dirty War.

Regarding foreign policy, Menem adopted the so-called Washington Consensus by opening up Argentina's economy, thus beginning a period of close ties or 'carnal relations' with the United States. The Kirchner government, on the other hand, distanced itself from the United States and was critical of international organizations such as the IMF. Argentina drew closer to other left-leaning Latin American countries, especially Hugo Chávez's Venezuela and its Bolivarian Revolution. These bonds would become even stronger during Cristina Kirchner's government.

These differences in economic, military and international policies are only a few examples of two very different presidencies in terms of public policies. However, both presidents reinforced presidential power, placing the president at the center of the political system and providing effective leadership for transformations to take place during their periods.

Sociological Background and Presidential Leadership

Menem was born on July 2, 1930, in Anillaco, in the province of La Rioja. His parents, Saúl Menem and Mohíbe Akil, of Syrian origin, ran a general store. Menem had four brothers; the youngest, Eduardo, was to become a close political ally. As a young man, Menem moved to Córdoba where he graduated as a lawyer. In 1955, he returned to La Rioja where he practiced law, defending political prisoners imprisoned by the new military government. In 1956 he himself was imprisoned for several months for supporting a strike against the military government of Pedro E. Aramburu, The following year he founded the Peronist Youth Party of La Rioja, meanwhile serving as legal advisor to the Confederación General del Trabajo or CGT (General Labor Confederation) and other labor unions in the province.

In 1961, Menem joined the Partido Unión Popular or PUP (Popular Union Party). This was Peronism under another name, because the Peronist Party had been outlawed by the provisional government. In 1962, he was elected provincial deputy but was not able to take his seat because of the military coup that deposed President Arturo Frondizi that same year. The following year, he withdrew his candidacy when Peron called on Peronists to cast blank ballots in the 1963 elections. In 1964, Menem paid a visit to Juan Domingo Peron in Madrid. In 1972, he had the distinction of accompanying Peron on his flight back to Argentina after long years in exile.

Kirchner was born on February 25, 1950, in the city of Rio Gallegos, Province of Santa Cruz. He died on October 27, 2010, in the town of Calafate in the same province. His father, Néstor Kirchner, was a descendant of Swiss immigrants and his mother, María Juana Ostoic, was a Chilean of Croatian origin. They had three children, and Kirchner's sister, Alicia, gave him invaluable support during his presidency. At the end of the 1960s, Kirchner moved to the city of La Plata. At the University of La Plata, he was a militant member of the Federación Universitaria por la Revolución Nacional or FURN (University Federation for National Revolution), which merged in 1973 with Frente de Agrupaciones Eva Peron or FAEP (Eva Peron Groups Front), later known as Juventud Universitaria Peronista or JUP (Peronist University Youth). In 1976, he graduated as a lawyer and returned to Rio Gallegos with his wife Cristina Fernández, also a law student at La Plata University.

During the military dictatorship, the Kirchners ran a successful law firm. However, there is no record of their defending political prisoners or advocating for human rights—themes that were to become hallmarks of Néstor Kirchner's presidency.

Political Careers of the Presidents

Both Menem and Kirchner were provincial leaders of the Peronist Party and occupied executive offices including that of provincial governor before becoming president. In 1973, Menem was elected governor of the Province of La Rioja with 67% of the votes, and he remained in power until the military coup of 1976. After democracy was restored in 1983, he was again elected governor of La Rioja. In 1986, the provincial constitution was reformed and he was re-elected in 1987.

Kirchner began his political career in 1987, winning election as mayor of Rio Gallegos, capital of the province of Santa Cruz. He remained in office until 1991, when he became governor of the province with 61% of the votes. Like Menem, he promoted a constitutional reform in 1994 enabling him to run for governor for one more term. In 1995 he was re-elected, this time with more than 66% of the votes. In 1998, a new constitutional reform introducing indefinite re-election allowed him to win a third term as governor in 1999.

Both presidents had enormous power in their provinces, which practically became their fiefdoms. Menem's governorship lasted for a total of more than eight years and, although it was interrupted by a military coup, his influence in La Rioja was constant. Kirchner remained in power in Santa Cruz much longer, first as mayor of the provincial capital for four years, and then as governor for a further 12 years until the presidential elections of 2003.

As mentioned earlier, both presidents were elected provincial governors with resounding majorities. Their electoral successes provided them with important credentials within the Justicialist Party because Peronism has always considered local winners as possible candidates for national leadership. In the case of Kirchner, it has been said that he ruled the country as he had ruled the province. His control extended to every political sphere: the party, Congress, the Senate, the Judiciary, businesses and the press. And of course both presidents would draw their cabinets from among friends and campaign workers in their respective provinces. Alberto Kohan and Eduardo Bauzá were part of Menem's inner circle in La Rioja, together with Menem's brother Eduardo. When Kirchner became president, those close to him—Carlos Zannini, Julio De Vido and Héctor Icazuriaga, among others—were known as 'the penguins' because they all hailed from the cold, southern province of Santa Cruz.

In theory, accumulated experience is important in allowing the president to manage relatively efficiently the fundamental areas of the state—government, administration, and the relationship between government and citizens. Substantial executive experience may be important, especially in times of crisis. Political career and institutional trajectory are directly linked with the professionalization of politics and the quality of representation (Alcántara, 2006).

During the nineteenth and early twentieth centuries, most of Argentina's presidents had both executive and legislative experience (Serrafero, 1997). In those times it was common for Argentine presidents to acquire their executive experience in the provinces. Urquiza, Mitre, Sarmiento, Juárez Celman, Figueroa Alcorta were all governors before becoming presidents, and Urquiza and Mitre went straight from the office of governor to the presidency, as did Menem and Kirchner.

However, from the mid-twentieth century onwards, presidents had legislative experience but not much executive experience. For example, Radical Party Presidents Alfonsín (December 1983–July 1989) and De la Rúa (December 1999–December 2001) came from a mostly legislative background. Interestingly, Peronist Presidents Menem and Kirchner had only executive experience and occupied no legislative posts during their political careers.

Personal Characteristics of the Presidents

Eccentric and sociable, Menem was a transgressive figure compared to the rest of the political spectrum. Ambitious and competitive, he combined politics with sports and an interest in show-business. Before reaching power, his personal appearance was extravagant, an attempt to emulate the historical Riojan *caudillo* Facundo Quiroga. He had an intuitive intelligence, with no substantial academic education apart from his law degree. Being sociable and outgoing helped him amass popularity, and he loved appearing in the media to communicate his ideas. He gave impromptu speeches in a colloquial language that was understood by every segment of society and won him the support of not only the poor and working classes—the traditional supporters of Peronism

—but other social classes as well. On several occasions during official government events, he laughed publicly at his own mistakes in protocol before correcting them.

Menem's personality played an important role in both his electoral successes and the way he governed. His informal approach made him a unique president, far removed from the seriousness and formality expected of a Head of State, and he was only eclipsed when his economic model became completely exhausted and accusations of corruption began to grow in number and importance in the media.

The personality of Kirchner was less clearly observed, in part because of his early and sudden death in 2010. Kirchner had the sort of Type A personality that made him prone to heart disease. Features of his behavior included impatience, hyperactivity, hostility, irritability and anger. Kirchner was an energetic person, extremely competitive and ambitious, whose life revolved around politics. His personal life, too, was infused with politics. Both he and his wife, Cristina Fernández, always said they were partners in their political careers and in life.

Another feature of Kirchner's personality was his obsessiveness, which translated to tenacity in political matters. His ambition, competitiveness and stubbornness were, without a doubt, what drove him to cling to power in his home province and then run as a Peronist Party presidential candidate after the 2001 economic meltdown, when it seemed that nobody was willing to take control of the country.

Kirchner seemed to have no physical limits. Even after his first stroke he made no attempt to reduce his hyperactive schedule. Confrontational behavior was another of his political hallmarks. He became engaged in disputes with the Catholic Church, businessmen, farmers and the media. He also crossed words with other heads of state in the region, for example President Tabaré Vázquez of Uruguay. The then-president of Mexico, Vicente Fox, famously noted the Argentine president's impoliteness.

Kirchner's relationship with money is also noteworthy—in particular, the wealth he accumulated as a lawyer in the province of Santa Cruz, his personal handling of the province's accounts, and his exclusive control of fiscal accounts while president. Distrust was also a prominent feature of his personality, and decision-making was shared only with a close circle of friends.

Image and Style of the Head of State

The personality of the Head of State will affect political management style. During election campaigns, Menem used language typical of the Peronist plebeian tradition; he presented himself as a kind of 'saviour,' or preacher appealing to God, and he invariably ended his speeches by saying 'follow me' (Nun, 1995: 85). He toured the country in his 'Menem-mobile' followed by long caravans of vehicles, in contrast to the more serious and formal image of Alfonsín or the Peronists, in an attempt to leave behind the Peronist folklore. In Nun's (1995) words, 'he embodied the *caudillo* who came from a poor province to speak to all the excluded and disenchanted in their own language. He showed himself as a successful governor, his popularity kept growing thanks to his constant public appearances in news magazines.'

Pragmatism and improvisation, negotiation and plain speaking—all these lay at the heart of Menem's presidential style. Because he was pragmatic, he was considered a true Peronist (Palermo, 1993). He was able to argue a position and then backpedal on it without embarrassment. He also knew how to remain ambiguous and non-committal in the face of questions. In institutional terms, he saw the president's office as a place of personal power and the president as the main player in the political regime, with a negative view of Congress and the Judiciary. Menem's leadership style has been labeled delegative, neopopulist or decisionist due to his continuous use of unilateral measures and emergency legislation in the form of Necessity and Urgency Decrees (*Decretos de necesidad y urgencia*, also known as DNUs) (Palermo, 1993; Palermo and Novaro, 1996; O'Donnell, 2009; Leiras, 2009).

Kirchner was an unexpected candidate as he did not occupy a central place in the party and was practically unknown outside his province. Adopting a firm stance, he went back to classic Peronist thinking to explain how the poorer and the weaker sections of society had been harmed by the Menemist and Alliance governments. The Alliance was a political coalition composed of two parties: the Radicals and the Front for a Country in Solidarity (Frente por un País Solidario or FREPASO). After Menem's second presidency, this Alliance defeated the Peronist Party in the presidential elections of 1999 and Fernando de la Rúa became president. Kirchner's policy of state intervention and protectionism was the exact opposite to Menem's neoliberalism, even though both men ran as Peronist candidates in the 2003 election.

Kirchner's presidential style was also quite different in the way he related to different political and social actors. This could be seen in his confrontational personality, his way of assigning responsibilities and apportioning blame according to the binary logic Friend/Enemy, and his determination to bend those he considered his opponents. As for his cognitive and perceptual style, his ability to simplify reality—mainly into binary oppositions—was remarkable. This decisiveness and lack of ambiguity were seen in many sectors of politics and society as a sign of strength. Many of Kirchner's institutional ideas can be inferred from his praxis, including the notion of the presidency as a place for moral leadership; the presidency as the driving force in the institutional system; the privileged relationship between president and people without any mediation; and the presidency as a key representative of popular sovereignty. Apart from these specific features, the general picture emerged of a president who was pragmatic in governance, and dogmatic in speech.

Menem's negotiating style suggested that any pact was possible. His flexibility allowed him to exploit opportunities and accumulate power. Kirchner's style was confrontational and tried to silence opponents by dividing the political field into friends and enemies. Both men had a strong inclination towards the idea of a hegemonic institutional regime centered on the presidency, and they belittled the importance of checks and balances and the separation of powers. However, this is less remarkable than it may seem. Peronism has a tradition of designing these types of institutional architectures, and it is worth recalling that Argentina's 1949 Constitution created a hegemonic presidential system (Serrafero, 2005b).

The Presidency, Communication and Media

Menem eschewed political rallies and mass mobilizations in the Plaza de Mayo, which were part of the traditional Peronist liturgy. Instead, he preferred to communicate with all kinds of people through the media. He felt comfortable in front of television cameras and his answers could be serious or amusing, depending on the situation. He was a regular guest on primetime programs. He never abandoned his colloquial style and even his formal speeches at the National Congress had emotional appeal (Bercholc and Bercholc, 2012).

Menem held press conferences regularly and had no problem answering questions from journalists (Schmidt-Liermann and Lavalle Cobo, 2009). During the 1990s, journalism played an active role in revealing the internal workings of government and promoting transparency in politics. President Menem tried to seduce the media industry by including it in his policies of privatization. Some groups were favored over others, strengthening their influence, and the media sector that emerged from these privatizations aligned itself with the new concentration of economic and political power. The media supported the government's economic policies until corruption scandals made them untenable and the media grew increasingly reluctant to carry the standard. Menem even went so far as to denounce a 'press dictatorship,' and when he won his re-election, he claimed: 'I defeated the opposition and the press' (Ulanovsky, 2005). Criticisms in the press kept growing, especially toward the end of his second term.

In both his administrations, critical journalism would arguably become one of Menem's toughest opponents, and he regularly accused journalists of attempting to destabilize the government and plotting a coup d'état. One of Menem's strategies was to sue journalists who criticized his government. Horacio Verbistky, for example, was one of Menem's most ferocious critics. The contempt of authority law had been eliminated in 1993 due to Verbitsky's international activism, but Menem sued Verbitsky for slander in 1994 on account of an article published in the newspaper *Página 12*. Verbitsky was found not guilty and the verdict protected the right of journalists to inform the public and practice their profession.

Kirchnerism considered the media to be an important actor in the public arena. Still, the Kirchner era was marked by conflicts and confrontations between the government and the media. Distortions of reality and opposition were conspicuous in the media, as they were among the political players pursuing their own agendas and economic interests.

As a communicator, Kirchner established 'direct and one-way' communication (Schmidt-Liermann and Lavalle Cobo, 2009). He neither debated publicly in electoral campaigns nor offered press conferences, and he did not hold cabinet meetings. This also restricted the knowledge each ministry had about the rest of the government and its decisions. Accordingly, officials were threatened with punishment if they spoke to the media. Contact with the media was only possible through a trusted official like the Cabinet Chief. Kirchner refused interviews and press conferences. His method of communicating was through his presidential speeches, which began and concluded with the president's word (Kitzberger, 2011).

Kirchner believed that press headlines determined people's perceptions and from his first days as president, his strategy toward the media was 'to control the agenda.' The first year he had favorable press coverage, but as media investigations against him increased, he resorted to the strategy of 'an announcement a day' as a way of recovering political initiative. Kirchner—unlike Menem—avoided television and did not appear on any programs while he was in power. In general, Kirchner maintained a relationship of 'live and let live' with the media, but he used official advertising—paid government announcements—as a mechanism for rewarding friends and punishing critics. The newspaper *La Nación* was viewed as an ideological opponent, whereas relations with the *Clarín* newspaper and media group were intimate, until the government's conflict with the agricultural sector in 2008 during Cristina Kirchner's government. Early into his term, Kirchner enacted a 'cultural goods' bill forbidding the 'cram down' mechanism that would have allowed foreign investors to purchase the heavily indebted media conglomerate. Only a few days before the assumption of the presidency by his wife, he approved the merger of two cable television companies, Cablevisión and Multicanal, which gave the Clarín group a dominant and privileged position in the market.

President Kirchner thought that the media companies had their own political agendas and would try to manipulate the economy and political candidates in their own interests. Other Latin American presidents, such as Chávez, Morales and Correa, shared the same idea. According to Kirchner, the hegemonic media represented corporate interests which ran contrary to the interests of ordinary people. Even opposition political parties were defined as mere representatives of the corporate media.

Electoral Results, Popularity and Opposition

Menem obtained notable electoral successes in 1991, 1993 and 1995. In the congressional elections for national deputies in 1991 he won 40.4% of the votes against the Radicals' 29%. In 1993, he obtained 43.4% of the votes against the Radicals' 30%. In 1995, he won 43% of the votes, against 21.7% for the Radicals and 21.1% for FREPASO. Why did low-income sectors vote for Menem in spite of his policies? One possible reason was the fear of returning to hyperinflation (Palermo and Novaro, 1996) as well as society's perception of Peronism as a by-word for popular representation despite the weakening of Peronist identity in the 1990s (Sidicaro, 1995). During Menem's first term, the opposition was led by the Radicals, who had left government after the 1989 hyperinflationary crisis. The Radicals tried to maintain a high profile as the main opposition party; but in 1993, Alfonsín and Menem negotiated the 'Olivos Pact' allowing Menem to revise the constitution of 1853 to permit his re-election as president in 1995. This damaged the Radical Party's image and it was only with the founding of the Alianza—the coalition of Radicals and FREPASO—that a viable opposition party was formed: one which went on to win the 1997 legislative elections and defeat Peronism in the 1999 presidential elections.

After his re-election in 1995, Menem's Presidential Approval Index was at 40%. Thereafter, it sank steadily, to 14% in the last quarter of 1996. After recovering slightly in the first term of 1997, his popularity remained at 18% until he ended his second term in 1999. These figures ran parallel with the macroeconomic indicators. However, corruption scandals also sapped the image of Menem's presidency and government, as did the expected lame duck effect. Finally, being in power for more than a decade almost inevitably affected his leadership (Blondel, 1987).

In the presidential elections, Kirchner obtained only 22.4% of votes and he had no opportunity to increase that figure, because Menem withdrew from the second round. In 2005, during the legislative elections, he obtained a resounding victory in nearly every part of the country (Calvo, 2005). FPV obtained 38% and Radicals 12% of the votes. In the province of Buenos Aires, the president's wife Cristina Fernández won her seat in the Senate with 46% of the votes against 19% obtained by Hilda 'Chiche' Duhalde, Eduardo Duhalde's wife. In the province of La Rioja, Carlos Menem was defeated by FPV in the elections for the Senate. By December 2003, Kirchner's positive image had climbed to 77% and in March 2004 it stood at 66%. However, in July of the same year it dropped to 35%, climbing to 44% in November and to 46% in early 2005 before sinking back to 35% in June 2005. Nevertheless, towards the end of his mandate his popularity rating was 44.5%, and he was able to transfer this to his wife Cristina Fernández during her campaign in 2007.

During Néstor Kirchner's term, the opposition parties remained separate, incapable of acting together or agreeing on common goals. This opposition was composed of a weakened Radicalism, Afirmación para una República Igualitaria or ARI (Affirmation for an Egalitarian Republic), Propuesta Republicana or PRO (Republican Proposal), and leftist and provincial parties. Peronism had also fragmented, and a great part of Kirchner's term was focused on solving the challenge of Peronist leadership.

The Presidencies: Support and Social Coalition

In 1989, Menem's main support came from the poor and the working classes that had traditionally been loyal to Peronism. Menem continued to enjoy popular support in spite of his neoliberal discourse, which was very different from traditional Peronist doctrines, and despite the fact that several Peronist leaders had deserted him. Nevertheless, sectors on the liberal right of the Peronist Party supported the neoliberal creed of Menemism, as did most of the entrepreneurial and business community.

The opening of the economy favored specific sectors whereas others were damaged. When Menem competed for re-election in 1995, he was elected by an even bigger majority in spite of the neoliberal policies he had implemented. He retained most of the loyal Peronist support and also gained support from the middle and upper classes. In 1995, Peronism was thus significantly more multi-classist and capitalist (Gervasoni, 1998) than before. Menem enjoyed the support of a large part of the workers' movement. Nevertheless, dissent appeared within the CGT soon after Menem assumed office in 1989, among sectors opposed to his neoliberal politics, and this deepened during his second term.

Kirchner's ideology was at the opposite end of the spectrum to Menem's. Kirchner railed against neoliberalism, which had deindustrialized the country and forced the low-income workers into poverty. Another important point of disagreement was human rights policies: Menem had pardoned the military juntas and the left-wing guerrilla movements for human rights violations committed between 1976 and 1983. Kirchner saw himself as part of the 1970s generation that had fought for its political ideas, claiming that he 'had not reached the government house leaving [those] ideals at the door.' Kirchner placed the blame for terrorism solely upon the state, holding the Peronist youth of the 1970s blameless.

Kirchner was supported by a heterogeneous coalition which consisted of historic Peronist leaders and also new sectors that identified with his ideological positions. His coalition was thus composed of the provincial Peronist parties (with the exception of San Luis, which was led by the Rodriguez Saá brothers, both former governors), the CGT led by Hugo Moyano, a variety of human rights organizations, part of the 'piqueteros' (unemployed workers and political groups whose primary form of protest is to block roads with 'pickets'), progressive organizations, and business sectors favored by the government. Kirchner soon realized that young people, as a demographic group, could be made to play an important role in his political project.

The human rights organizations gave the government a high-profile platform, both nationally and internationally, and seemed to guarantee the progressive values the government claimed to espouse. Indeed, they provided Kirchnerism with 'moral support.' Before Kirchner, human rights organizations had distanced themselves from political parties and governments: now large numbers flocked to the Kirchnerist social coalition, the most visible organizations being Madres de Plaza de Mayo (Mothers of Plaza de Mayo) led by Hebe de Bonafini, Abuelas de Plaza de Mayo (Grandmothers of Plaza de Mayo) and the HIJOS (Children of the Disappeared). The government granted them a special symbolic status and economic resources to continue their activities and undertake new ones.

The *piqueteros* were a major problem because they practiced 'street politics' which had already made Duhalde their first victim. Kirchner tried to either co-opt or neutralize them in order to prevent demonstrations and conflicts in the streets. He successfully enlisted the support of organizations such as Federación de Trabajadores de la Tierra, Vivienda y Hábitat or FTV (the Federation for Land, Housing and Habitat), Frente Transversal Nacional y Popular (National and Popular Multisectorial Front), Barrios de Pie (Neighborhoods Arise) and Movimiento Evita (Evita Movement). Practically half of the *piquetero* movement supported Kirchner. Through the Ministry of Labor, the government distributed welfare payments to the *piquetero* organizations. This policy of co-option was consistent with the government's policy not to criminalize social protests. In the following years, *piquetero* activity became less intense. When Kirchner assumed office, the number of regular street protests was 1,278; by 2007 that had descended to 608 (Ichaso, 2009b).

Peron considered the labor unions to be the backbone of the Peronist movement. After its defeat in the 1983 elections, however, the party rejected trade unionism in favour of a more modern image. President Menem continued this 'Justicialist Renewal' by reducing the number of union leaders in his government and neutralizing the labor unions' response (Acuña, 1995). Given its priorities of global finance, 'opening' the economy, stability and convertibility, traditional collective negotiations with trade unions were limited. There were more negotiations within companies than collective negotiations with labor unions. Collective bargaining legitimated the labor flexibility being pursued at the time and also allowed the unions to maintain their presence and receive financing through the administration of social welfare schemes (Mayer, 2012).

At the beginning of Menem's presidency, the Confederación General del Trabajo or CGT (General Labor Confederation) had been a unified organization. Soon, however, it split into CGT San Martín, headed by leader of the Mercantile Union Guerino Andreoni and the CGT Azopardo, led by Saúl Ubaldini and supported by historic leaders such as Lorenzo Miguel. In 1992 a number of trade unions belonging to the CGT broke away to form the Central de Trabajadores de la Argentina or CTA (Argentine Workers Central Union) and in 1994, the Movimiento de Trabajadores Argentinos or MTA (Movement of Argentine Workers), which opposed the president's policies, was founded.

The Menem era, marked by deregulation, deindustrialization and a loss of trade union membership, brought a corresponding decline in the political power of the unions. However, this situation changed radically under Kirchner, whose main allies were the CGT and its leader, Hugo Moyano. It was a strategic alliance, intended to ensure social-economic governance. Thus trade union power returned with all its benefits and its old vices (Etchemendy, 2011). Economic recovery gave the unions renewed influence through the collective negotiation of salaries while they continued to manage social welfare programs. Palomino and Trajtemberg (2006) note that collective bargaining increased significantly under the Kirchner administration. Indeed, although 380 and 348 agreements and contracts were signed in 2003 and 2004, respectively, this number rose to 568 in 2005 and to 930 in 2006. These figures were much higher than the average of 187 annual negotiations held during the Menem era.

Presidencies and Institutional Reforms

Both Menem and Kirchner carried out institutional reforms in order to increase the formal powers of the presidency. Nonetheless, it should be noted that the presidential system in Argentina has developed over time in the context of different institutional designs (Serrafero, 1997; Serrafero, 2005b): the Constitution of 1853/60, the Constitution of 1949, and the current one validated following the 1994 reform. The Constitution of 1853/60 created a 'strong' presidentialist regime with the president playing a predominant role in the political system. The Constitution was conceived as a blueprint for political order and economic progress; and only a strong president was capable of guaranteeing these objectives. The Constitution of 1949, introduced during Peron's first government, gave the president even greater power, mostly at the expense of Congress, and allowed the president to be re-elected indefinitely. The state—with the president at its center—also acquired a more important role. This could be called 'hegemonic' presidentialism. However, when Peron was ousted by a military coup in 1955, the Constitution of 1853/60 was reinstated, remaining in force during Raúl Alfonsín's presidency and Carlos Menem's first administration until it was reformed in 1994.

The 1853/60 Constitution granted the president the role of Supreme Chief of the Nation, as he was the Head of State and Head of the Government, Chief of the Nation's Capital City, and Commander in Chief of the Armed Forces. The Executive Branch was essentially a single person. The president could appoint and dismiss ministers on his own. He also held the initiative as regarded legislation; he enacted the laws approved by Congress and was able to veto them. Congress could only insist if it had the two-thirds vote required to overrule. The Senate had the right to approve the appointment of judges in the Supreme Court and the Federal Courts, and the appointment and removal of high-ranking diplomats and military officers. The presidential term lasted six years and immediate re-election was forbidden. The president could only run for office again after a period out of office. This was the most important limitation of the presidency under the 1853/60 Constitution.

Menem succeeded in amending the constitution to allow for immediate presidential re-election. The results of the legislative elections of 1991 and 1993 essentially meant a popular mandate for economic reform and the transformation of the state. When the opposition UCR party (the Radicals) rejected the reform, Menem resorted to different strategies to achieve his goals. He had even announced a nonbinding plebiscite on the question of presidential re-election. The Radicals, however, remained adamant that Menem should not reform the constitution for his personal benefit, and this remained a stalemate until a preliminary agreement between President Menem and Radical leader Raúl Alfonsín was announced. The reform was carried out following the broad outlines of the 'Olivos Pact.' At the heart of the negotiations and the final agreement was Menem's prime and ultimate goal of re-election, on the one hand, and Alfonsín's goal to give Argentina a more parliamentarian style of politics, on the other.

In 1994 the constitution was amended and the presidential system was reinforced, even though one of the principal aims of amendment had been to weaken it (Serrafero, 1997; Serrafero 2005a). The president retained his leadership except in the capital city of Buenos Aires. The Executive Branch remained uni-personal, and the power to appoint and dismiss ministers was left to the president. After the reform, the president gained significant legislative powers via NUDs (Necessity and Urgency Decrees), delegated legislation, and partial veto. A subordinate figure was created: the Chief of Cabinet, whose task is to organize the work of the other ministers and act as intermediary between the Executive Power and Congress at the service of the presidency (Serrafero, 2005a). The president can appoint and dismiss the Chief of Cabinet at will. The reform introduced one-term presidential re-election and shortened presidential terms from six to four years. The period of regular sessions for the Legislative Branch was increased and—within the Judiciary—a Council of Magistrates was created, composed of judges, lawyers, members of the Legislature, the Executive Branch and academics. There is no doubt, however, that the reform increased presidential power, especially by allowing immediate re-election and increasing the president's legislative powers to the detriment of Congress.

Kirchner governed with the amended constitution that had reinforced the strong presidentialism of the 1853/60 Constitution and, when he obtained legislative victory in 2005, he promoted three major institutional reforms (Serrafero, 2013): the Council of Magistrates, the regulation of NUDs and the so-called 'superpowers' law. Law 24.937 of the Council of the Magistracy (*Consejo de la Magistratura*), enacted by Menem in 1997 in accordance with the 1994 Constitution, established the *modus operandi* of the Council and allowed it to bring judges before an impeachment jury. However, the new law passed in 2006 gave the ruling party the possibility of vetoing the Council's decisions. It also gave the president a greater role in the appointing and removing judges.

According to the constitution, NUDs cannot be used in the case of criminal law, taxation, electoral matters, or the system of political parties. President Menem's inclination (and that of his successors) to rule by decree had been strongly criticized. But the reform did not limit their use, and NUDs issued by the president could only be annulled if both chambers voted against them, which meant that if the Executive had the backing of one chamber, the decree remained in force.

Finally, an amendment to the Financial Administration law (called the 'superpowers' law) allowed the Chief of Cabinet to reassign resources in budgets already passed by the National Congress.

In short, the reform of the Council of the Magistracy gave the government more say in the appointment and removal of judges, whereas the proposed limitation of NUDs and the use of 'superpowers' led to a reduction of the powers of Congress. However, it should be stressed that it was Congress itself which consciously and irresponsibly ceded its faculties to the Executive Branch. Menem and Kirchner introduced reforms to remove limits to presidential power and to expand it. Through negotiations with the main opposition party, Menem managed to reform the historic constitution of 1853/60 to enable his immediate re-election. By confronting the opposition, Kirchner initiated important laws giving him advantages over other state powers.

The Presidency, Bureaucracy and Cabinet

Argentina had no specialized or autonomous bureaucracy capable of significantly influencing the course of the presidency. It is presidents not other actors, who bring about changes in the bureaucracy through political appointments and reforms to the structure and organization of the state. Like most presidents (Moe and Caldwell, 1994; Moe and Wilson, 1994; Moe and Howell, 1999), Menem and Kirchner sought to exercise substantial autonomy and did so through strategies of politicization (that is, filling administrative posts with ideological supporters) and centralization (moving key policy decision-making into the Executive Office of the President). The 'institutional presidency' was composed of loyal staff from the president's inner circle, as well as some party members. Despite the reform of the state, centralization was a noticeable feature of the Menem era (Coutinho, 2007/2008) thanks to the creation of ministerial secretariats which allowed for greater presidential control. Kirchner, on the other hand, tried to personally guide the progress of the entire administration.

The way a cabinet is organized and operates is indicative of a president's approach and style. Menem had plenary cabinet meetings, joined by other officials and guests, who could number up to several dozen at a time. Meetings were held every week, usually on Thursdays, but these were not decision-making events, they were simply informative. In October 1996, Menem suspended these weekly meetings on the grounds that 'it is not possible to leak private comments and become journalists' gossip' (*La Nación*, October 26, 1996). After that, the number of guests was reduced to avoid press leaks and rumors.

Kirchner embodied the greatest concentration of executive powers since the return of democracy. He personally supervised each area of the administration; he had a radial relationship with members of the cabinet, meaning that he interacted with each minister separately; and he did not hold plenary cabinet meetings. Ministers occupied a secondary and opaque role. They were subjected to strict discipline and forbidden to discuss government actions with the press. The president's behavior and acts of government were guided by secrecy and surprise (De Luca, 2011). Decisions were concentrated in the presidential couple (Néstor and Cristina), and sometimes developed at a 'small table' composed of the Legal and Technical Secretary of the Presidency, Carlos Zannini, and the Cabinet Chief, Alberto Fernández.

Both presidents made their decisions at these 'small tables'; therefore, power was never spread among the ministers. In both cases, the Economy Minister was the most important—Cavallo in Menem's government and Lavagna in Kirchner's. On the other hand, the Cabinet Chief was not a counterweight to the president but rather a pawn at his disposal (Serrafero, 2005a).

Table 9.1 Ministers and ministries

President	No. of ministries (A)	No. of ministers (B)	Ratio of ministers/ministries (B)/(A)
Menem (1)	8	36	4.5
Menem (2)	9	18	2
Kirchner	11	19	1.72

Table 9.2 Reasons behind ministers' departures

Cause	1 Menem	2 Menem	Kirchner
Conflicts with Congress	–	–	–
Deficient performance	8 (33.33%)	–	–
Scandals	7 (29.17%)	4 (50%)	1 (12.5%)
Elections	–	–	3 (37.5%)
Internal conflicts	3 (12.5%)	3 (37.5%)	3 (37.5%)
Others	6 (25%)	1 (12.5%)	1 (12.5%)
Total	24 (100%)	8 (100%)	8 (100%)

Source: Camerlo (2013).

In terms of the turnover of ministers, Menem's first presidency was conspicuously unstable until Menem settled on a consistent course of government (Table 9.1). In contrast, Menem's second presidency and the presidency of Kirchner were significantly more stable. Menem rotated several ministers, whereas Kirchner appointed new ministers.

The changes within the cabinet were due to resignations and dismissals, cabinet reorganizations and competition for elected posts (Table 9.2). In the case of Menem, cabinet changes occurred in response to crises or changes in government policies. In Kirchner's government the changes were not linked to policy changes. Interestingly, both presidents had very tense relationships with their vice presidents and did not allow them a significant role in government (Serrafero, 1999; Serrafero, 2011b).

Party Control and Institutional Machinery

The Peronist Party has lost none of its importance since it was founded in 1946, despite persecutions, proscriptions and electoral defeats. It was founded by charismatic leader Juan Peron during his first presidency to replace the Labor Party which brought him to power a year earlier. In accordance with the times, its organizational structure was rather informal and so extremely adaptable. The idea that Peronism is a movement, and that the party is just an electoral tool, has also helped it survive over the years. Peron's leadership lasted until his death in 1974, giving birth to the 'Peronist Myth.' Menem was the first popularly elected Peronist president. Kirchner was the second. Peronism is a predominant party within a federal and strong presidential system (reinforced after the 1994 reform). With every new president, there is, sooner or later, a major realignment within the party around the executive's manner of governing—and this is what happened with both Menem and Kirchner.

Menem was an outstanding figure within Peronism even before he was elected president. He belonged to the 'Renewal Group' when Peronism was defeated by the UCR in the 1983 presidential elections. In 1988, control of the party apparatus passed to the hands of the governor of the province of Buenos Aires, the 'restorer' Antonio Cafiero. Cafiero had been a minister with Juan Peron and portrayed himself as a moderate social democrat. The ambitious and charismatic Menem was one of the few who dared to compete against him. The orthodox sectors of Peronism supported Menem, as did the labor unions that had been excluded from party leadership by Cafiero.

In contrast, Kirchner was governor of a Patagonian province far from Buenos Aires, and his weight within the party was small. Caretaker President Duhalde had wanted the then-governor of Santa Fe province, Carlos Reutemann, to be his successor, but Reutemann refused. The other chosen candidate had been José de la Sota, but he withdrew after poor showings in the polls. Kirchner reached the presidency not because of his influence within the party but due to the lack of any alternative candidate.

When Menem took office, many party members were against his emerging neoliberal policies, and this triggered changes within the party. In August 1990, the governor of the province of Buenos Aires and party president Antonio Cafiero summoned a plebiscite to reform the provincial constitution so he could apply for re-election. He failed, and he resigned from office almost immediately —thus Menem obtained the national presidency of the Justicialist Party. On several occasions, it was necessary for Menem to take control of the party in certain provinces. In the years that followed, his power within the party was almost absolute. Some high-profile members left the party because of Menem's neoliberal ideology, or because of government measures they disagreed with. Thus, for example, a group of deputies called the Group of Eight abandoned the Peronist bloc in the Chamber of Deputies, because they were against the pardon granted by Menem to members of the Armed Forces and former guerrillas.

It is a matter of debate how Menem managed to get the Justicialist Party to sign up to neoliberal reform, which was alien to the Peronist tradition. The answer is unclear. For some analysts the social climate had already changed from acceptance of an inefficient state to the desire for a more privatist and less statist society (Mora and Araujo, 1995; Zorrilla, 1994). The fear of hyperinflation also made Menem's proposals seem almost inescapable, even if they meant a 'flight forward' (Palermo and Novaro, 1996). This fear combined with Menem's popular leadership could explain why many people accepted this ideological turnaround (Gerchunoff and Torre, 1996), and Menem's leadership was, without a doubt, an important factor. Nevertheless, certain features of the Peronist Party also influenced this development. For instance, as Levitsky (2005) has pointed out, the absence of a stable bureaucracy lured leaders of different currents straight into Menemism to protect and further their political careers. Levitsky also argues that Menem paid little attention to developments within the Peronist Party because of the party's weak authority structures. The leaders were not convinced of his neoliberal strategy and accompanied him out of mere pragmatism in the face of an economic crisis that did not seem to offer many alternatives (Palermo, 1993; Levitsky, 2005).

The Renewal Group had the support of the party leadership and the party bloc in Congress, but it virtually disintegrated shortly after Menem took office. When Cafiero was president of the party, he frequently met with Menem, but Menem continued with his own policies regardless of the Party National Council. Menem established direct contacts between both sectors of Peronism, the light blue group made up of former renewers—who had gone along with Menemism despite their center-left ideas—and the scarlet red group, orthodox members who had been with Menem from the very beginning. Thus, the president established a balance between the different forces within Peronism (Levitsky, 2005).

The different Peronist districts remained Peronist, but they did not entirely accept Menem's neoliberal ideology. Provincial Peronist leaders supported the president at the national level, but he was unable to impose provincial congressional candidates within their territories. On the other hand, it was impossible to organize internal opposition to the president. Senator José O. Bordon obtained some support from the ex-renewers, but Menem soon regained their support. Bordon finally abandoned Peronism in September 1994 and founded the FREPASO, together with Carlos Alvarez (leader of former Group of Eight). It was only in Menem's second term that opposition emerged within the party, especially when he attempted to secure re-election for a third term. The governor of the province of Buenos Aires, Eduardo Duhalde, even headed a front to resist Menem's re-re-electionist intentions.

President Menem used the allocation of resources as a way of imposing discipline and obedience on different districts. He did this through the so-called National Treasury Contributions (Aportes del Tesoro Nacional or ATN). As Oszlak (2003: 540) explains, the ability to control the allocation of resources became a precious political bargaining chip that allowed the national government to tie public finances to discretionary funds for political favors, alliances, and acceptance of commitments. This style of politics was complemented by Menem's lack of transparency in governance, as well as his control of the institutional machinery and the unilateral government he intended for the presidency.

The state reform policy implied the dismissal of thousands of employees and the suppression of departments, offices and state enterprises. This rationalization eventually increased political and administrative centralization. Moreover, this redesign ended the patronage networks that were discretely managed by those who controlled various state departments. Patronage networks were replaced by lines leading directly from the Executive to different segments of society (Palermo and Novaro, 1996).

Kirchner's presidency developed in a context where Peronism was much more fragmented than in the Menem era. Before his election, Kirchner had defined Peronism as 'a vast confederation of provincial parties with clearly defined territorial leaders' (Kirchner and Di Tella, 2003). When Kirchner became president, he did not have complete power within the Justicialist Party. Due to the 2001 crisis, Justicialism had become a group of provincial parties without a national focus (Sidicaro, 2011). Duhalde was an important figure, especially in the province of Buenos Aires, and Kirchner was to partially inherit Duhalde's cabinet. Kirchner shared Duhalde's opposition to Menem's neoliberal vision and its focus on productivity. Soon, however, differences between the two men became noticeable—especially Kirchner's championing of human rights and the leftist Peronist youth of the 1970s. Kirchner pragmatically overturned Menem's pardons of 'Dirty War' crimes and turned his back on Duhalde and Duhalde's supporters who had enabled him to run for president. Consequently, Peronism became centered on social inclusion, human rights and a more central role for the state.

During Kirchner's first two years in office, the differences between Kirchner and Duhalde led to open confrontation. It should be noted that Kirchner tried not to depend on the Peronist Party. His efforts to build a 'transversal' or broad-based movement attempted to cull support from both the Peronist and non-Peronist left (Torre, 2004). Kirchner had to deal with Duhalde's supporters in the province of Buenos Aires, and he competed against them in the legislative elections in 2005. In short, Kirchner was forced to win the Peronist chiefs' support via the ballot box by facing and defeating Menem and Rodriguez Saá in 2003, and Duhalde in 2005. In 2006, he launched Concertación Plural (Plural Consensus), an electoral alliance for the 2007 presidential elections that included a group of Radical governors, among others.

In the Kirchner years, the Peronist Party had no influence as an organization. In order to rule without the control of a fragmented party and to keep the provincial governors in line, Kirchner used the resources of the national administration to establish direct contact with the mayors, especially those from the Greater Buenos Aires area. Kirchnerism used different tools to align and discipline governors and mayors (Lodola, 2011). Through changes in fiscal institutions, he reinforced his authority over the provinces and municipalities. Unevenly distributed taxes and duties were centralized. Discretional funding was used to build relations with mayors, public jobs being a favorite mechanism to reward political support. Although Menem had managed resources in a similar way, Kirchner continued and consolidated the process.

Congress and the Judiciary

The Senate, of which one third is renewed every three years, has remained Peronist territory over several decades. Both Menem and Kirchner had a majority in the Senate. Control of the Lower Chamber, however, is more difficult to achieve.

Menem counted on a significant number of legislators from the very beginning of his first term. In the Lower Chamber elections he obtained strong electoral results and had support from center-right allies, especially the Unión de Centro Democrático (UcD) and the provincial parties. In the 1995 re-election, his party was in the majority, and he obtained his best electoral results. Despite the majority that supported him as president, there were disagreements with his party in Congress, especially within the Chamber of Deputies, leading to divisions in the parliamentary bloc and modifications being introduced into bills sent by the Executive (Tommasi and Spiller, 2000).

Menem's leadership in Congress was noticeable at three different stages during the passing of his privatization bills (Llanos, 1998). During the delegative phase at the beginning of his term, he obtained approval of his bills thanks to the State Reform law. This law had the support of both Radicals and Peronists owing to the agreements they had reached immediately after Alfonsín's resignation. During the cooperative phase, he sent bills which were modified or amended by the Lower House. And during the conflict phase, after winning his re-election and being unable to pass his privatization bills, he had to resort to the use of NUDs.

Kirchner took office in a fragmented context (Zelaznik, 2011): the Justicialists had 122 legislators (48% of the Chamber), of whom 95 were loyal to Duhalde, 19 to Menem and eight to Rodriguez Saá. Two weeks after Kirchner took office, the Menemist legislators joined the Duhaldist bloc supporting Kirchner. Left or progressive legislators were added to these 114 Peronist deputies under the 'transversal' strategy. Later, the legislative elections of 2003 gave the government its own majority of 129 Peronist legislators. The break between Kirchner and Duhalde encouraged Kirchner to try to create his own following within the ranks of Peronism. In 2005 Kirchner had difficulties in getting his policies approved by Congress, but after the elections held the same year, the situation changed. The government added legislators from different political views to obtain a majority: the progressive parties, and legislators from other groups and from single blocs. Within months of the new Congress opening, 19 Duhaldist deputies left the dissident Peronist bloc and joined the ranks of Kirchnerism, giving the government 131 (51.4%) legislators with a Peronist background.

Regarding the legislative success of the two presidents (Jones and Micozzi, 2011), Alfonsín achieved the sanctioning of 52% of his initiatives, Menem 41%, Duhalde 46% and Kirchner 56%. Thus, Menem had the lowest number of legislative initiatives approved, whereas Kirchner had the highest.

Both presidents made excessive use of NUDs (Necessity and Urgency Decrees) (Serrafero, 2005b). Menem issued over 545 NUDs in 125 months, or an average of 4.4 decrees per month. Kirchner issued 270 NUDs in 54 months—an average of five decrees per month (Ichaso, 2009a). Most of the decrees—at least during Menem's presidency—were issued while Congress was in session, and only a small number were ratified by the Lower House. In some cases where his decrees were repealed, Menem used his total or partial veto to block laws that contradicted his decrees (Ferreira Rubio and Goretti, 1996).

Peronism's attempts to control the Judiciary have been part of its essence and history: a clear example would be the impeachment and removal of four members of the Supreme Court in 1947, during the first government of Juan Peron. Law 23,744 allowed Menem to expand the National Supreme Court of Justice from five to nine judges. Accordingly, he appointed four new members. The Supreme Court in Menem's period was criticized strongly for its alleged alignment with the president, to the extent that Menem was said to have an 'automatic majority.' The truth is that this majority did not always exist, but it supported the president in some key policies. Similarly, the government tried to control the Federal Judiciary, which acts in issues related to public administration and the state.

One of Kirchner's first major social and institutional measures was the renewal of the Supreme Court by removing the judges of the so-called 'automatic majority.' Faced with impeachment, Judges Julio Nazareno, Adolfo Vásquez and Guillermo López resigned in 2003, whereas Eduardo Moliné O'Connor was removed from office at the end of the year. The vacancies were filled with judges who guaranteed greater independence for the Supreme Court. Eugenio R. Zaffaroni was appointed in 2003, and Elena Highton de Nolasco and Carmen Argibay joined the Court the following year. In 2005, Antonio Boggiano was removed and Augusto Belluscio resigned. Since the government did not appoint any new candidates after this, the Court found it hard to reach a majority in most cases. Faced with pressure from various sides to fill the vacancies, the government passed a law returning the Court to its previous composition of five members and kept the current justices in their positions without filling the vacancies.

As previously noted, Kirchner tried to control the Judiciary by modifying the membership of the Council of Magistrates. Just like Menem, he also tried to control the Federal Judiciary.

Conclusions

Menem and Kirchner exhibited differences and similarities, both in the way they came to power and in their political behavior. Both presidents were the boldest Peronist leaders of their time, taking advantage of the opportunity that came their way while other politicians failed to act. The different psychological characteristics of the two men were striking, as were their manners and style of governance. Another difference between them was their ideological profiles, each the result of very different national and regional contexts.

Both presidents took office at moments of severe economic and social crisis, in each case following the debacle of a Radical president. Both belonged to the Peronist Party, which was generally thought to be able to govern despite tough times. Menem became the candidate for the presidency through internal party elections; Kirchner was nominated almost by default in the midst of the fall-out from the December 2001 crisis. Both presidents came from far-flung provinces, a long way from Buenos Aires. Both had thoroughgoing political experience in their provinces that shaped them politically. These provinces were their bastions, and were to shape their careers in national politics.

Both Menem and Kirchner's closest coworkers had been attracted by their leaders' effectiveness in governing their respective provinces. Once the two men reached the presidency, the Peronist Party mostly lined up behind them despite resistance from some sectors. Menem met with higher internal opposition as his second term ended because of the expected lame duck phenomenon. Kirchner, on the other hand, spent his first two years struggling against Duhalde for control of the Peronist Party and was more popular at the end of his term than at the beginning. However, instead of opting for re-election, he allowed his wife, Cristina Fernández, to succeed him.

True to Argentina's political tradition, both Menem and Kirchner believed in strong government and the personalization of politics. Beyond their differences of style, they both became central figures in Peronism and the political system. Unlike Menem, however, Kirchner had a notorious obsession with controlling everything and everybody. Both presidents used central government funds—the policy of *la caja* ('the money box')—to alleviate the delicate financial situation of the provinces, to obtain support, and to discipline governors and mayors. But in Kirchner's case, this way of controlling the institutional machinery was more marked. Under Kirchner poorer districts could only satisfy their financial and economic needs by aligning themselves with central government, in a scheme of rewards and penalties.

Menem maintained an easy relationship with the media and gave regular press conferences. When he perceived that criticism was becoming too intense, he treated the media as opposition. Kirchner went much further. From the very start, he considered the media to have their own economic and political agenda, and he saw them as opponents or even enemies. He never held press conferences and rarely gave interviews to journalists who were not within his circle of trust.

Neither president showed clear respect for institutional functioning and the republican separation of powers. Both exploited the unilateral powers of the presidency, abused NUDs, and placed Congress on the back burner. They also tried to control the Judiciary. In short, both men gradually reinforced their leadership, despite the problems that Menem faced in his initial stages and notwithstanding Kirchner's conflict with Duhalde.

During times of institutional crisis, the power of the president inevitably increases; and when a president takes measures to establish greater stability and control over the different variables, his or her electoral support increases as well. This was seen in the legislative victories of 1991, 1993, 1995 and 2005, which cemented the party together—or at least the forces that supported it. They also led to institutional reforms to increase presidential power. Both presidents intended to remain in office or to return to government at a later date. Both presidencies went through very similar stages: a) a situation of instability resulting from a severe institutional, economic and social crisis; b) the political support of a new social coalition resulting in a greater margin of action; c) relative control of, or an improvement in, the emergency situation; d) electoral victories in the subsequent elections; e) institutional reforms to increase presidential influence;

and f) attempts to remain in office. The two leaders reinforced the idea that Peronism is able to overcome difficult situations. But at the same time they created new problems for the consolidation of a democratic and republican political order. In Argentina, institutions seem to be constantly threatened by the temptations of the country's leaders, whether populist, delegative or decisionist.

Each of the two presidents' terms ended differently as a result of their time in office and political and economic changes, both domestic and foreign. After ten years in power, Menem left office an unpopular figure, for having taken measures that had, at the time, enjoyed widespread support, and for alleged corruption. In 2005, he was elected Senator for the province of La Rioja and was re-elected in 2011. Kirchner ended his period without standing for re-election and with a series of achievements that were acknowledged by the population, as he put the country back on track after the 2001 crisis. In 2009, Kirchner was elected deputy for the province of Buenos Aires. He died in 2010 while preparing to run for the presidency in 2011. Carlos Menem was sentenced to seven years in prison by the Criminal Court of Appeal in 2013 for illegal weapons sales to Croatia and Ecuador. The National Supreme Court of Justice will have the last word on this matter. As of now, he is the first Argentine president to be sentenced for corruption by the Judiciary.

Note

1 The terms Peronist/Justicialist, Peronist Party/Justicialist Party, Peronism/Justicialism are used interchangeably.

References

Acuña, C. (1995). *La nueva matriz política argentina*. Buenos Aires: Nueva Visión.
Alcántara, M. (2004). *¿Instituciones o máquinas ideológicas? Origen programa y organización de los partidos latinoamericanos*. Barcelona: ICPS.
Alcántara, M. (2006). *Políticos y política en América Latina*. Madrid: Fundación Carolina.
Bercholc, J. and Bercholc, D. (2012). *Los discursos presidenciales en la Argentina democrática 1983/2011*. Buenos Aires: Lajouane.
Blondel, J. (1987). *Political Leadership. Towards a General Analysis*. Bristol: SAGE.
Calvo, E. (2005). Argentina, elecciones legislativas 2005: Consolidación institucional del Kirchnerismo y territorialización del voto. *Revista de Ciencia Política, Santiago*, 25(2), 153–160.
Camerlo, M. (2013). Gabinetes de partido único y democracias presidenciales. Indagaciones a partir del caso argentino. *América Latina Hoy*, 64, 119–142.
Coutinho, M.E. (2007/2008). Un análisis institucional de la organización de la presidencia en Argentina. *Colección*, 18/19, 17–47.
De Luca, M. (2011). Del príncipe y sus secretarios. Cinco apuntes sobre gobiernos presidenciales en la Argentina reciente. In: Malamud, A. and De Luca, M. (eds), *La política en tiempos de los Kirchner*. Buenos Aires: Eudeba, 37–48.
Etchemendy, S. (2011). El sindicalismo argentino en la era pos-liberal. In: Malamud, A. and De Luca, M. (eds), *La política en tiempos de los Kirchner*. Buenos Aires: Eudeba 155–163.

Gerchunoff, P. and Torre, J.C. (1996). La política de liberalización económica en la administración de Menem. *Desarrollo Económico*, 36 (143), 733–768.
Gervasoni, C. (1998). Del distribucionismo al neoliberalismo: los cambios en la coalición electoral peronista durante el gobierno de Menem. Paper presented at XXI Congreso Internacional de la Latin American Studies Association, Chicago, September.
Ferreira Rubio, D. and Goretti, M. (1996). Cuando el Presidente gobierna solo. Menem y los decretos de necesidad y urgencia hasta la reforma constitucional (julio 1989–agosto 1994). *Desarrollo Económico*, 36(141), 443–474.
Ichaso, J. (2009a). En 15 meses de gobierno, Cristina Kirchner firmó 5 decretos de necesidad y urgencia. *Centro de Estudios Nueva Mayoría*, March 20.
Ichaso, J. (2009b). Desde 1997 se han registrado casi 17.500 cortes de rutas y vías públicas. *Centro de Estudios Nueva Mayoría*, Sep. 30.
Jones, M. and Micozzi, J.P. (2011). Control, concertación, crisis y cambio: cuatro C para dos K en el Congreso nacional. In: Malamud, A. and De Luca, M. (eds), *La política en tiempos de los Kirchner*. Buenos Aires: Eudeba, 49–61.
Kirchner, N. and Di Tella, T.S. (2003). *Después del derrumbe. Teoría y práctica política en la Argentina que viene*. Buenos Aires: Galerna.
Kitzberger, P. (2011). La madre de todas las batallas: el Kirchnerismo y los medios de comunicación. In: Malamud, A. and De Luca, M. (eds), *La política en tiempos de los Kirchner*. Buenos Aires: Eudeba.
Leiras, S.C. (2009). *El cono sur y sus líderes durante los años '90*. Buenos Aires: Lajoune.
Levitsky, S. (2005). *La transformación del justicialismo. Del partido sindical al partido clientelista, 1983–1999*. Buenos Aires: Siglo XXI.
Llanos, M. (1998). El Presidente, el Congreso y la política de privatizaciones en la Argentina (1989–1997). *Desarrollo Económico*, 38(151), 743–770.
Lodola, G. (2011). Gobierno nacional, gobernadores e intendentes en el período Kirchnerista. In: Malamud, A. and De Luca, M. (eds), *La política en tiempos de los Kirchner*. Buenos Aires: Eudeba, 217–227.
Mayer, J. (2012). *Argentina en crisis. Política e instituciones 1983–2003*. Buenos Aires: Eudeba.
Moe, T.M. and Caldwell, M. (1994). The Institutional Foundations of Democratic Government: A Comparison of Presidential and Parliamentary Systems. *Journal of Institutional and Theoretical Economics*, 150(1), 171–195.
Moe, T.M. and Howell, W.G. (1999). Unilateral Action and Presidential Power: A Theory. *Presidential Studies Quarterly*, 29(23), 850–873.
Moe, T.M. and Wilson, S.A. (1994). Presidents and the Politics of Structure. *Law and Contemporary Problems*, 57(1–2), 1–44.
Mora and Araujo, M. (1995). De Perón a Menem. Una historia del Peronismo. In: Borón, A., Mora and Araujo, M., Nun, J., Portantiero, J.C. and Sidicaro, R. (eds), *Peronismo y Menemismo*. Buenos Aires: El Cielo por Asalto, 47–66.
Nun, J. (1995). Populismo, representación y Menemismo. In: Borón, A., Mora and Araujo, M., Nun, J., Portantiero, J.C. and Sidicaro, R. (eds), *Peronismo y Menemismo*. Buenos Aires: El Cielo por Asalto, 67–100.
O'Donnell, G. (2009), La democracia delegativa, *La Nación*, May 28.
Oszlak, O. (2003). El mito del estado mínimo: una década de reforma estatal en la Argentina. *Desarrollo Económico*, 42(168), 519–543.
Palermo, V. (1993). El Menemismo, ¿perdurará? In: Iturrieta, A. (ed.), *El pensamiento político argentino contemporáneo*. Buenos Aires: Grupo Editor Latinoamericano.

Palermo, V. and Novaro, M. (1996). *Política y poder en el gobierno de Menem.* Buenos Aires: Flacso-Norma.

Palomino, H. and Trajtemberg, D. (2006). Una nueva dinámica de las relaciones labourales y la negociación colectiva en la Argentina. *Revista de Trabajo*, 3.

Schmidt-Liermann, C. and Lavalle Cobo, D. (2009). *Las conferencias de prensa en la Argentina: situación actual y herramientas alternativas para el diálogo entre periodistas y políticos.* Buenos Aires: Konrad-Adenauer-Stiftung.

Serrafero, M.D. (1997). *Reelección y sucesión presidencial. Poder y continuidad: Argentina, América Latina y EE.UU.* Buenos Aires: Editorial de Belgrano.

Serrafero, M.D. (1999). *El poder y su sombra. Los vicepresidentes.* Buenos Aires: Editorial de Belgrano.

Serrafero, M.D. (2005a). La Jefatura de Gabinete y los diez años de reforma. *Jurisprudencia Argentina-Suplemento Derecho Administrativo, LexisNexis*, 21–27.

Serrafero, M.D. (2005b). *Exceptocracia.¿Confín de la democracia? Intervención federal, estado de sitio y decretos de necesidad y urgencia.* Buenos Aires: Lumiere.

Serrafero, M. D. (2011a). *El área de estudios presidenciales.* Buenos Aires: Academia Nacional de Ciencias Morales y Políticas.

Serrafero, M.D. (2011b). Presidencia y vicepresidencia: otra difícil combinación. In: Malamud, A. and De Luca, M. (eds), *La política en tiempos de los Kirchner*, Buenos Aires: Eudeba, 23–35.

Serrafero, M.D. (2013), Argentina: tres reformas del Kirchnerismo, Revista Aragonesa de Administración Pública, n 41, 455–475.

Sidicaro, R. (1995). Poder político, liberalismo económico y sectores populares. In: Borón, A., Mora and Araujo, M., Nun, J., Portantiero, J.C. and Sidicaro, R. (eds), *Peronismo y Menemismo*, Buenos Aires: El Cielo por Asalto, 119–156.

Sidicaro, R. (2011). El partido peronista y los gobiernos Kirchneristas. *Nueva Sociedad*, 234.

Tommasi, M. and Spiller P.T. (2000). *Las fuentes institucionales del desarrollo argentino. Hacia una Agenda Institucional.* Buenos Aires: Eudeba-PNUD.

Torre, J.C. (2004). *La operación politica de la transversalidad. El Presidente kirchner y el partido Justicialista.* Buenos Aires: Universidad Torcuato Di Tella.

Ulanovsky, C. (2005). *Paren las rotativas. Diarios, revistas y periodistas (1970–2000).* Buenos Aires: Emecé.

Zelaznik, J. (2011). Las coaliciones Kirchneristas. In: Malamud, A. and De Luca, M. (eds), *La política en tiempos de los Kirchner,* Buenos Aires: Eudeba, 95–104.

Zorrilla, R. (1994). *El fenómeno Menem.* Buenos Aires: GEL.

10 Chile: Continuity and Change in Presidential Government

Patricio Aylwin and Ricardo Lagos

Carlos Huneeus

In this chapter I examine presidential government in Chile. First, I will outline the tendencies of continuity; then I will consider the peculiarities of the presidency as an institution; coordination within the government and its complexities; the important role played by the Senate, which limits the decision-making autonomy of the president; and relations with the parties. The chapter is based on an analysis of the first four post-dictatorship administrations of the Concertación of Parties for Democracy (a coalition of center-left parties). It focuses on Patricio Aylwin (1990–1994), a Christian Democrat and the first president after the dictatorship, and Ricardo Lagos (2000–2006), a socialist and the first left-wing president since Salvador Allende's overthrow by the military in 1973.

Chile's return to a democratic presidential system after General Augusto Pinochet's long and repressive authoritarian regime (1973–1990) was not easy. The regime had been responsible for 3,000 deaths, including the assassination by the secret police, the DINA, of a former minister, Orlando Letelier, in Washington DC. The truth about what happened during those years had to be faced and justice sought for the crimes committed. Aylwin created the Truth and Reconciliation Commission (known as the Rettig Commission) to clarify acts of repression that resulted in deaths. Later, Lagos created the National Commission on Political Imprisonment and Torture (known as the Valech Commission), which received the testimonies of victims who survived. For eight years, Pinochet remained in his position as commander-in-chief of the army and was determined to defend his personal interests and those of his institution, intervening in the political arena and staging acts of provocation against the civil authorities that in 1990 and in 1993 almost amounted to a military coup (the so-called 'boinazo').

Historical Background of Chilean Presidentialism

Chile's long democratic tradition has preserved institutional features and leadership styles that have defined the presidency as an institution, and influenced the leadership style of presidents. After the United States, Chile has the longest history of presidential government, with administrations alternating at the end of constitutionally established terms and led by presidents elected in competitive contests without re-election (since 1865). This tradition was accompanied by the establishment of the rule of law, with an autonomous legislature and independent courts that set limits to the power of presidents and lawmakers.

This tradition of presidential government was characterized also by the presence of a congress that historically has held considerable power since the 19th century, when it began to counterbalance the power of the president. This was not an easy relationship, leading as it did to the civil war of 1891 in which the congress prevailed, accentuating its power over the presidency. No president had a majority in both chambers due to an inability to secure a majority in the Senate, whose members had an eight-year mandate and were partially renewed every four years, thus exceeding the mandate of the president (lasting six years from 1932 to 1973, and increasing from four to six years after 1990). Therefore Chile has always had divided governments, and coalition governments have been the rule. The exceptions were the first three years of the presidency of Jorge Alessandri (1958–1964)—whose cabinet did not include the parties that got him elected, but independent ministers—and the government of Eduardo Frei Montalva (PDC) (1964–1970), which was elected by 56% of the voters and obtained a majority in the Chamber of Deputies in the 1965 elections.

Presidentialism has also been characterized by the active role of parties in the political process, with parties demanding cabinet appointments and power positions at other levels of the executive branch. The expectations of parliamentarians that the government would deliver benefits to satisfy clientelistic campaign promises made in their districts has often led to a difficult relationship between the president and his/her party.

Chile's long tradition of presidentialism was used by its two 20th century dictators (Gen. Carlos Ibañez (1926–1931) and Gen. Augusto Pinochet), both of whom presented themselves as presidents and held non-competitive elections to legitimate their power. Pinochet went a good deal further; his was a highly personalized dictatorship in which he played a triple role as president, head of government and commander-in-chief of the army, positions which he held for 17 long years. Pinochet was an exception among the Latin American dictatorships that took power in South America beginning in the 1960s (Huneeus, 2007). His style of government was highly centralized; he concentrated in his office all the major public policy decisions and was extremely belligerent toward the opposition, as reflected in his statement 'we are at war, gentlemen.' Moreover, he established ample presidential power in the 1980 Constitution, giving himself a mandate of eight years (it was six years under the 1925 Constitution); he controlled the Senate by means of appointed senators and held enormous power over the Chamber of Deputies by giving himself powers to dissolve it—thus holding a sword of Damocles over its members if they voted against him. Pinochet weakened congress further by moving its seat from Santiago to Valparaíso. This decision to remove it from the city that had always been home to both branches of government was without historical precedent; it was intended to increase the government's autonomy from congress and to hinder the latter's watchdog role, as traditionally exercised by the Chamber of Deputies.

When democracy was re-established in 1990 the Aylwin government found itself confronted by a difficult past: Pinochet's authoritarian presidentialism, which had to be broken with, and a long tradition of democratic presidentialism clouded by the traumatic experience of the crisis and collapse of democracy in 1973. The political polarization and confrontation since the late 1960s haunted the Coalition with the fear that crisis could return. Party leaders took an initial decision to engender a strong president: they gave Aylwin freedom to appoint his ministers and to define the programs and policies of his government (indeed, Aylwin suspended his membership in the Partido Democrata Cristiano (PDC) to symbolize that his was a coalition presidency, and that he would govern for all Chileans). But in practice, Aylwin took the parties into account when he named his ministers and defined his programs. The parties were considered in the composition of the cabinet and changes of ministers, preserving a certain criterion of proportionality to the size of their vote, whereas the president named appointees from the ranks of his party in the two most important ministries, the interior and the treasury.

These historical antecedents led the presidents to change the style of the presidency, rejecting an authoritarian profile and using a leadership style that distanced itself from Pinochet's. Aylwin was careful to adopt both changes.

Such institutional changes began following Pinochet's defeat in the plebiscite of October 5, 1988, triggering the transition to democracy. The regime negotiated with the opposition a constitutional reform that mitigated some of the excesses imposed by Pinochet in the 1980 Constitution, in particular the excessive powers it gave the president. The presidential mandate was reduced from eight to four years; the president's power to dissolve the Chamber of Deputies was abolished; the power of the nine appointed senators (who now supported the opposition) was weakened to some degree by increasing the number of elected senators from 24 to 38; and the power of the National Security Council, established as a control over civilian government, was reduced. However, the new rulers appreciated that the seat of the congress was now in Valparaíso, as established by the dictatorship, because this enabled them to retain some autonomy from the legislators who were in another city, and they kept it in that city.

A democracy following a personal dictatorship also favored the strengthening of horizontal accountability. Institutions like the Constitutional Court, the Comptroller General of the Republic and the Attorney General's Office gained increased power—the latter created during the second democratic administration of Eduardo Frei Ruiz-Tagle (1994–2000)—thereby setting limits to the power of the president.

This tradition has equally been defined by a certain presidential leadership style that emphasizes the function of head of state around that of head of government, even though in the past there was little clarity around who was actually leading the government (in some cases it being the minister of the interior). There has been a return to the tradition of former presidents seeking re-election at the end of one mandate. Arturo Alessandri secured re-election in 1932; his son, Jorge Alessandri Rodríguez (1958–1964), attempted it in 1970; and former dictator Gen. Ibañez achieved it by being elected president (1952–1958) after two failed bids in 1938 and 1942. With the exception of Aylwin, the other Coalition presidents have also sought re-election.[1] Only Michelle Bachelet achieved this, in 2013, following the administration of Sebastián Piñera (2010–2014), who was the first right-wing president elected since 1958.

The trajectory of Chilean presidential rule has also been marked by the economic difficulties Chile has experienced as an underdeveloped country, difficulties that have been a factor in social discontent and have led successive governments to promote policies to overcome poverty and improve the living standards of the immense majority of the population. Since the 1930s presidents of different political colors have pursued development policies characterized by the active participation of the state, creating public companies in strategic areas of the economy. These policies gave the president enormous powers of patronage due to the jobs he could distribute in return for favors, although without promoting the modernization of agriculture, which proved to have an economic and social cost for the country. The turnover of ministers and changes of president did not favor the continuity of pro-development policies. Efforts to overcome underdevelopment in a democratic context ultimately failed. These included the 'Revolution in Liberty' ('Revolución en libertad') promoted by the government of President Eduardo Frei Montalva (1964–1970), and the socialist revolution of the Popular Unity administration of President Salvador Allende (1970–1973), which had the support of only a minority of the electorate and neglected economic policymaking. The resulting economic crisis fueled a political crisis that led to the 1973 military coup (Valenzuela, 1978; Huneeus, 1981).

The turning-point with respect to the weight of economic backwardness on political development came with the neoliberal transformation driven by the Pinochet dictatorship, which overcame the economic crisis existing in 1973, privatized almost all public enterprises, and dismantled the welfare state. The dictatorship pursued policies which resulted in an economy that was growing and generating employment when democracy was finally re-established, albeit with profound inequalities (Ffrench-Davis, 2002). The changes imposed by the dictatorship had consequences for the organization of government, because the key cabinet member ceased to be the economics minister, who in the past had held responsibility for the dozens of public enterprises, but rather the treasury minister. In practice, the treasury minister takes crucial decisions over matters that would ostensibly fall under the control other ministries, unrelated to functions of the treasury (such as education and health), thus influencing the definition of crucial policies (Pribble, 2013). Treasury's key role in preparing the budget and controlling expenditure has further given it control over policies such as public works and transport, sometimes generating disputes with those respective ministers over policy priorities and content.

This democratic tradition, with its deep political and social conflicts from the 1960s onwards, an economic context of underdevelopment and a late economic take-off during the dictatorship, led the Concertación to opt for continuity rather than reform of the economic system left by the military regime, and to follow a politics of consensus with the right. The consensus climate was also favored by the presence of the authoritarian enclaves established in the 1980 Constitution (Garreton, 1995) such as appointed senators (who voted for the opposition) and supermajorities being required to pass laws (Huneeus, 2014). A preference for stability, moreover, meant that institutional obstacles that persisted throughout the transition were not addressed. Chief among these was the continued presence of General Pinochet for eight years as commander-in-chief of the army. The former dictator acted in the political arena to keep pressure on the government, even provoking a near coup in the incident in May 1993 known as the 'Boinazo' while the president was on a visit to Europe. This was resolved by significant concessions made by the vice-president, Enrique Krauss (PDC), and the minister of the general secretariat of government, Enrique Correa (PS).[2] These concessions damaged the government's image in public opinion and the latter's support for democracy (Huneeus and Maldonado, 2003).

Strong Presidents? The Weakening of the Presidency, and Mechanisms of Coordination in the Executive Power

The dominant view in studies of presidentialism emphasizes the great power that presidents wield (Shugart and Carey, 1992; Mainwaring and Shugart, 1997; Lanzaro, 2003; Siavelis, 2000). Chile's constitutional tradition until 1973 confirms this, as it reflects the ever-growing power of the president vis-à-vis the congress, particularly after the 1970 constitutional reform, which Pinochet took to extremes in the 1980 Constitution. I believe that this interpretation needs to be nuanced. In what follows, we shall describe a certain weakening of the presidency as an institution, with the balance of power shifting toward other institutions and making the president's personal job more difficult.[3] Paradoxically, this change can be traced back to Pinochet's own constitution, which established limits to the power of the president. The president lost control over monetary policy, which passed to the autonomous Central Bank, the first in Latin America, and which has since exercised its autonomy (Boylan, 2001).[4] It also set up a very strong Constitutional Court, one of the most powerful in the world, with the power to block important legislative bills approved by congress, and even to halt government policies (Couso, 2003). As we have seen, the constitutional reform of 1989 reduced the president's power even more. It is a pity that Shugart and Carey (1992) did not consider this reform, which would have led them to qualify their generalizations about Chilean presidentialism.

Moreover, the president saw his power to designate the top officials of numerous executive branch institutions eroded, including the posts in Civil Register, the National Economic Attorney General's office, and the Consumer Protection Service (Sernac), among others. A legal reform that created the Civil Service in 2003 established that there should be a widely advertised, public and competitive appointment process with an anonymous review of applications resulting in a shortlist of three candidates to be given to the president, which he may reject. This is directed by the Council of Senior Public Administration (CADP), chaired by a person of the president's confidence and composed additionally by four councilors appointed with the agreement of the Senate, requiring the assent of the opposition. As no modern president has enjoyed a majority in the Senate, each of these appointments has had to be negotiated with the opposition, allowing the latter to place councilors on these councils, from the Central Bank to the CADP. As we shall see below, it is the Senate that has gained in power.

Compared with the United States, where the presidency was strengthened after Franklin D. Roosevelt (with a steady increase in the number of officials who supporting the president, including the treasury and the press office, while relations with congress are coordinated by a chief of staff with enormous influence on presidential decision making), Chile's executive institution is small. The staff that provide support to the president in carrying out his or her functions as head of state and government are few in number. Three functions that are the responsibility of specialized White House agencies in the United States are implemented through three ministries in Chile: the treasury (Hacienda) directs the budget; the press office is based in the ministry of the general secretariat of government; and relations with congress have been primarily concentrated in the ministry of the general secretariat of the presidency, although in practice responsibility for this function has varied, as indicated below. These last two ministries have their offices in the governmental palace of La Moneda.

This view of the presidency as an institution of limited strength is reflected in a long tradition whereby the president prefers to work with and through his or her ministers, a tradition facilitated by the presence in La Moneda of three ministries, notably (for historical reasons) the ministry of the interior. This minister, the president's closest collaborator, is considered to be the 'head of the cabinet,' because he coordinates the work of the other ministers and stands in as vice-president when the president is out of the country. The most important ministries are located in buildings situated alongside the La Moneda palace, accentuating this vision of the presidency. Thus, the Chilean presidency tends toward a more collegial style of decision-making rather than individual exercise of power by the president, as is the case in other presidential systems, like that of Argentina since 1983.

The weakening of the presidency can also be appreciated in the four-year mandate without re-election established in the constitutional reform of 2005, which reduced to four years the six-year term that had been served by presidents Eduardo Frei Ruiz-Tagle (1994–2000) and Ricardo Lagos (2000–2006). The four-year period is too short, as it encourages the parties to busy themselves with the next presidential election (which coincides with the next parliamentary election). Indeed, candidates for La Moneda are launched (especially from the Senate), and legislators are already preparing their re-election campaigns when the government has only recently gained strength. This short-term of office favors a government agenda that focuses on short term issues, without addressing more complex problems that require medium- and long-term policy goals.

This weakening of the presidency as an institution does not necessarily denote weakness in person, as the president has powerful institutional and informal resources and runs the government in close collaboration with the three ministers of La Moneda. These three ministers, who form what is known as the 'political committee,' meet at the start of each week and in this 'political committee' meeting, the weekly government agenda is defined, priorities are distributed between ministries, and the legislative agenda agreed on. This is the top coordinating body in the government; it was established by Aylwin and has continued to the present day, although presidents have different abilities to direct a government, as we shall see below (Huneeus, 2005). The functions of the political committee have reduced the importance of the cabinet (*consejo de gabinete*) in ministerial coordination: that body—with the exception of the government of Aylwin, who convened it every two weeks—has not been periodically convened by presidents. Coordination of government has been carried out under the watchful eye of the ministry of the general secretariat of the presidency (Aylwin), the interior ministry (Frei and Lagos), or in practice the Treasury, as occurred during the first government of Michelle Bachelet (2006–2010). After the political committee meeting, the minister of the interior meets with the presidents of the coalition parties and the head of the parliamentary benches to inform them of the committee's agreements and to gain assurances of party support for the agreements, especially the support of party benches to steer legislative bills through congress.

Intra-government coordination is also carried out by the ministry of the treasury, which has held enormous power since 1990. Every president has given wide autonomy to this minister, except for Piñera, an economist with a PhD from Harvard whose presidential style was to personally direct the most important spheres of government, including this ministry.

The president has a small number of collaborators who provide support in drafting presidential speeches and organizing the agenda of meetings, as well as presidential activities outside La Moneda in which the president makes speeches or gives statements to the press intended to influence public opinion. The prominent role of the ministers explains the importance of the president's skill in appointing personalities with the ability to help him or her conduct the government efficiently (Greenstein, 2000).

There is a tendency to adopt a leadership style of looking for public approval, on the understanding that popularity strengthens the execution of policies and gains support in the legislative process. This style of personalizing the presidency involves a close relationship with the media, which is monitored by the general secretary of the government. This office achieved ministerial rank during the Pinochet regime; it was formerly a department under the ministry of the interior and supported the president with a small staff and limited functions, essentially acting as the president's personal secretariat. The military saw a need to gain support among the population through the media, in order to reduce the need for repression as a mechanism for neutralizing the opposition, while always retaining it in the background. Moreover, this ministry was given other functions such as the mobilization of youth and workers, and allotted financial resources and political functions gave it an important role has continued under the democracy.

The institutional weakening of the presidency has been accompanied by changes in the number of ministries that work with the president. This would appear to be an opposite dynamic tending to increase centralization of decision-making in the presidency, but this has not been the case. There is now a greater differentiation of presidential functions, but this does not confirm the strength of the presidency as an institution. There is a new ministry to directly help the president, the ministry of the general secretary of the presidency, created in 1990; it had its origins in an organization introduced by the Pinochet regime when the dictator saw a need for political advisors, so he could conduct the presidency without neglecting his role as commander-in-chief of the army, and without politicizing the army. For this purpose, he resorted to the tradition of advisory services to the commander-in-chief based on the Prussian model of staff officers, by creating a 'Presidential General Staff' composed of military officers who assisted him in his presidential role. Its functions were to help him select his ministers and top officials, to take care of his relations with supportive civilian groups and executive branch personalities, and to identify courses of action when faced by difficulties or economic crises, providing Pinochet with much assistance in running his government.

In the early 1980s, the functions and number of the presidential general staff were enlarged, incorporating civilians, and converted into the 'general secretariat of the presidency,' which was directed by a general (Huneeus, 2007). Edgardo Boeninger, who was in charge of drafting the Coalition government's program and who helped Aylwin form his government, valued this organization and was influential in securing its continuity. Boeninger saw its advantages in allowing coordination of the ministries' activities and ensuring a coherent government strategy. He also saw that it helped maintain relations with congress, so that the government's legislative program could be implemented efficiently and the president could be freed from the need to monitor the action of the ministries in order to concentrate on strategic questions. Boeninger was careful to press for rapid approval of the bill creating the ministry of the general secretariat of the presidency (popularly known as the 'Segpres').[5] The considerable power of the Segpres during Aylwin's presidency, however, was due to Boeninger's exceptional political skills and organizational capacity. Having been an official of the budget office, a subdirector under Alessandri and director under Frei, Boeninger had long experience in government. The Segpres has never had so broad a function under any other president.

Patricio Aylwin and Ricardo Lagos

In the pages that follow, I shall focus on presidents as leaders and discuss Presidents Patricio Aylwin, a Christian Democrat, and Ricardo Lagos, a Socialist. I pay particular attention to the influence of sociological and personal factors on presidential leadership.

Aylwin had to deal with the transition's most difficult moment. His main tasks were to initiate government by a coalition whose main partners had been bitter opponents prior to 1973; to pursue a policy of truth and justice for human rights violations committed by the Pinochet dictatorship, even though the dictator still commanded the army; and to address the dictatorship's economic legacy, with 40% of Chileans living in poverty. It is in difficult contexts like these that presidents can show their leadership capacities and take decisions that leave a mark on a country's history. Aylwin led a center-left coalition government and gave his ministers wide autonomy, limiting his own power and leaving his ministers to make important decisions themselves. His was a style of collective leadership and cooperation with ministers, more commonly found in a parliamentary than a presidential system. Strategic economic policy decisions were successful, achieving a 7% average annual growth rate until 1998, when the Asian crisis hit the national economy, and effective and opportune coordination between the treasury ministry and the Central Bank proved to be lacking.

Lagos, for his part, not only had to continue and deepen the reforms of the two preceding governments, but also to demonstrate that the left was capable of running the presidency responsibly, in order to win back the confidence of the business sector and dispel the shadow of doubt that had hung over the left's leadership capabilities since the Allende government. On both dimensions he was successful. Lagos introduced far-reaching reforms in health policy (known as the Plan Auge) that ensured free treatment for numerous pathologies, rebuilding the public health institutions that the dictatorship had dismantled. His presidential style differed from Aylwin's: it was more centralized and less collegial, and he directed important reforms personally, with the aid of a group of advisors and leaving out the Segpres ministry. These contrasting presidential styles can be explained in large part by biographical differences.

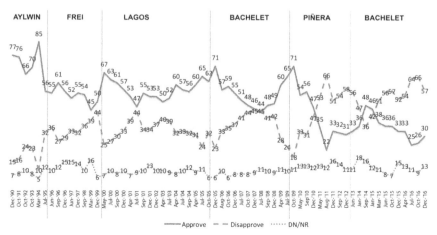

Figure 10.1 Presidential approval in Chile, 1990–2016

Source: Barómetro de la Política Cerc Mori

Similarities and Differences

The two presidents were of different generations: Aylwin was born in 1918, Lagos in 1938, but both were haunted by the crisis and breakdown of democracy in 1973. In terms of similarities: both were of middle-class origin, and both studied at state schools. Moreover, both later studied law at the Universidad de Chile, although Aylwin went on to practice law, whereas Lagos switched to economics, receiving a doctorate from Duke University in the US. This experience allowed Lagos to get to know the US political system and to become familiar with the style of its presidency, something that I believe he kept in mind when he put together his own staff on becoming president. He surrounded himself with a team of direct presidential advisors, who related directly with his ministers, thus allowing Lagos to run a centralized presidency without considering the Segpres, and Lagos himself took on the role of central coordination. Once in office, Lagos also closely followed the prime ministerial leadership style of Tony Blair, and the two teams of advisors built up close contacts.[6] In contrast, Aylwin's vision of the presidency was closer to that of previous Chilean experiences.

Both presidents had been active in politics in the democratic period before the military coup, and neither became as radicalized as many of their centrist and left-wing counterparts during the same period. Their trajectories were nonetheless quite different. Aylwin had a long-running political career, in the course of which he was made leader of the Christian Democrat Party on various occasions—one of which was at the moment of the 1973 coup—and he was elected senator in 1965. Lagos, on the other hand, served as head of an academic department and then as General Secretary of the Universidad de Chile. These posts required considerable political skill as the university, and the country in general, became intensely polarized around the reforms of the Eduardo Frei Montalva government. These included university sector reform, after 1965, which introduced direct election of university authorities by faculty, staff and students. Political parties were influential in the outcomes of these elections, which were significant in national life given the status of the Universidad de Chile as the country's principal university.

Aylwin and Lagos were not the political personalities with highest public visibility around the time of the 1988 plebiscite. A poll conducted by CERC in December that year, under my direction, placed Eduardo Frei Ruiz-Tagle, son of ex-president Eduardo Frei Montalva, as the presidential candidate with highest levels of public support. He gained the highest percentage of mentions as respondents' preferred next president, at 20% in open questioning and 30% in closed questioning. Aylwin was the second favorite, scoring 11.3% and 14.1% in the same categories. Lagos came only fourth on the list in replies to the open question, with a low score of only 5.5% of preferences. He did not even feature in the relevant closed question, having never previously been selected as candidate for the presidential nomination by either of the two parties to which he belonged (the PPD, his own party; and the PS, of which he was also a member).

Both Aylwin and Lagos were intelligent and strong-minded politicians, and each approached their presidencies with a sense of mission strongly influenced by their respective biographies. Aylwin's main goal was to consolidate democracy, a task in which he excelled, and he overcome the sharp divisions that had arisen between the Christian Democrats and the left since 1964—a rivalry that contributed to the kinds of polarization and party confrontation that ultimately produced the democratic breakdown of 1973. Lagos, on the other hand, set out to restore the faith of Chileans in general—and of the business sector in particular—in the left as a credible and responsible political force capable of running the country. This faith was at a low ebb after the mistrust caused by the failings of the Popular Unity government of Salvador Allende.

Patricio Aylwin: Personal History

Aylwin was born in Santiago, the eldest of five children. His father, a judge, went on to become Supreme Court president. Because his father was not Catholic, the children all studied in lay state schools and the four sons of the family all studied law at the state-run Universidad de Chile. This already set Aylwin apart in important ways from the shared experience of many other prominent Christian Democrat leaders of the day, including Eduardo Frei Montalva, Bernardo Leighton and Gabriel Valdés. All of the latter took a more traditional route, educated in Catholic schools and then enrolling at the Catholic University of Santiago. The fact that Aylwin's father had been a judge is important in understanding his own vocation for the law. It helps explain why, as president, he later placed so much emphasis on the need to discover the truth about dictatorship-era crimes, and why he criticized judges who had failed to protect the lives of detained regime opponents.

The Aylwin family lived in different parts of the country, moving around in accordance with their father's judicial career. When Miguel Aylwin was eventually named to the Supreme Court, the family settled in the San Bernardo suburb of Santiago. Their mother was a Catholic, a strong-minded woman who ensured that despite their non-confessional schooling the children were brought up Catholic.

Patricio Aylwin: Professional Background

Like the vast majority of politicians of the pre-1973 generation, Aylwin was a lawyer by profession. He had been an outstanding student of the Law Faculty of the University of Chile and began an academic career at the same institution, going on to become a professor of administrative law. His undergraduate dissertation for the degree of social and juridical sciences became a classic text in its field of arbitration law. It is still regularly reprinted and cited (Aylwin, 1943).

Aylwin developed a thriving legal practice alongside his teaching career, litigating before the courts and providing arbitration services, a field in which he soon acquired wide prestige. In a sign of this growing recognition he was elected to the Council of the Bar Association in 1951, and re-elected in 1955, this time as the candidate with the second-highest level of support. At the time, membership of the Council was generally the preserve of the country's most distinguished jurists.

Aylwin's legal training was one of the qualities that allowed him to clearly perceive the real strategic importance of human rights policy as a basis for the legitimacy of the new democracy upon its restoration in 1990. At the time this was a risky strategy: the issue of human rights was strongly resisted or rejected by the military, who claimed any so-called 'excesses' had been justified by the existence of a 'civil war,' begun, they claimed, by Allende. Moreover the Chilean military, unlike their Greek or Argentine counterparts, had not been defeated in war and disgraced before society. Instead they had handed over power after being defeated in a non-competitive election (the 1988 plebiscite).

No other transitional president of the time initiated policies seeking truth and a measure of justice on taking over a 'new' or newly re-established democracy: all were nervous at the implications of confrontation with the military. Of the others, only Raúl Alfonsín, of Argentina (1983–1989), came close, but in his case the military establishment had already been seriously weakened by the loss of the Malvinas war.

Aylwin's legal training also allowed him to perceive the importance of seeking a path from dictatorship to democracy that would be legitimated by the preservation of legality. He was the first opposition politician to come out in favor of seeking transition through the procedures laid down in the 1980 Constitution, rather than by rupture, something that would have required seeking Pinochet's resignation as president and as army commander-in-chief.[7] He maintained that attitude once he became president, tolerating Pinochet at the head of the army as the Constitution demanded, and cultivating a cordial but firm relationship with him, not allowing himself to be intimidated.

Patricio Aylwin: Political Biography

Aylwin joined the Christian Democrat Party once he was already established as a lawyer and law professor. This was another unusual feature, as most other presidents, and indeed most of the Chilean political class, began their political careers earlier, becoming active in party politics while at university. In his youth, Aylwin had also been more sympathetic to socialism, becoming friendly with other young men who would go on to hold high office in the Socialist Party, such as Clodomiro Almeyda (Allende's Foreign Minister, and leader of the Socialist Party's left-wing faction during the dictatorship). These early friendships later stood him in good stead, as we will see below.

On his arrival at La Moneda in 1990, Aylwin was the most distinguished opposition figure, with long political experience, and at 71 (the age of Adenauer when he became federal chancellor) he was older than all his ministers and almost all members of congress. He was certainly the person with the best claim to represent the country's chequered recent institutional past. He had been a frontline protagonist in the Christian Democrats since the late 1940s, with only a few brief interruptions over the course of the 1950s, which shaped his vision for his presidency and his beliefs about the conditions that were needed for a stable democracy. He was vice-president of the National Falange ('Falange Nacional'), as the Christian Democrat Party was then called, between 1947 and 1948, and he was its president in 1951–1952. He then presided over the Christian Democrat Party proper in 1958, product of an invitation by the then-Senator Eduardo Frei Montalva, who considered him the politician most suited to lead the party at that time. Frei, for his part, had made a very strong showing in the 1958 presidential election. This left him extremely well placed for the 1964 presidential contest, and he believed that Aylwin's leadership would enable the Christian Democrats to capitalize and build on the high levels of support obtained in 1958.

Elected senator in 1965, Aylwin returned as party president again between 1965 and 1967, coinciding with the early years of Frei's 1964–1970 presidential administration. Frei's government introduced a program known as the 'revolution in liberty,' *revolución en libertad*, which included, among other structural reforms, substantial agrarian reform and unionization of agricultural workers.

These were difficult times in which to be party president. The Frei government faced opposition from the left and the right, but also from within its own ranks. Some parliamentarians, and the party's youth league, were critical of the direction the government was taking. This internal criticism fell into one of two camps: the 'rebeldes' (rebels), who wanted faster and deeper reform, and the 'terceristas,' advocating a 'middle way' involving greater moderation.

Aylwin could not even count on majority support from the party's national committee, its executive decision-making body. He was forced into difficult negotiations around repeated attempts by dissidents to propose and pass strong criticisms of the actions of their own government. Frei was not a source of much support: he kept his distance from internal wrangling and did not exercise the strong leadership that might have counteracted the power of the dissidents. He failed to act until this bloc had taken over the party executive in 1967, in what the party and the public perceived as a direct challenge to his leadership. A few months later, Frei was finally moved to act, intervening to reassert his authority over the party and to ensure its backing for the government of the day. He was able to have the troublesome executive replaced. In 1969, the dissident faction ('rebeldes') resigned from the party altogether to form the breakaway MAPU Party, which became part of the Popular Unity coalition. Throughout the Frei administration, Aylwin was the best-known figure of the 'oficialista' sector of the Christian Democrats, so-called for its defense of the government of the day from attacks from external and intra-party opposition.

This period of conflict in the DC made its mark, and the memory of it clearly weighed on Aylwin when, as president, he was careful to maintain his own internal position in the party, at the same time cultivating relationships with the left-wing parties that made up the remainder of his governing coalition, the Concertación de Partidos por la Democracia (Coalition of Parties for Democracy)—'la Concertación'.

Aylwin was once again elected president of the DC in May 1973, by a narrow majority, in the aftermath of the parliamentary elections that had been held in March of the same year. These had deepened political conflict between the opposition and the Allende administration, and there were disagreements within the DC as to how to conduct political opposition while avoiding creating the conditions for a military coup—a possibility that was already foreseeable.

Aylwin accentuated the party's internal differences when he chose to campaign for the party presidency with the slogan 'no dejar pasar ni una' ('let nothing get by you' in English), aimed at the Allende government. It was a call to maintain inflexible opposition at a moment of extreme political polarization in the country. Aylwin was therefore DC president at the time of the coup and remained so until late 1976, when he resigned.

A man of decision, conviction and firm temperament, Aylwin did not shy away from conflict and always defended his corner. A skilled orator, he was often able to win over the party leadership or its senatorial group, as he had managed to do in 1966 faced with a majority critical of the government. Notwithstanding, this course brought intense personal frustration, as the party split in 1969, and again in 1971—when a faction of the 'terceristas' left—and the country fell under dictatorship when he sought the presidency of the PDC in 1973. Aylwin let this frustration show through in a press interview, in April 1987, in the course of which he declared that he belonged to a 'failed generation' that had not only failed to put an end to underdevelopment, but had also seen the loss of democracy.

Just a few months after this interview, however, everything changed. He was elected DC president when the dictatorship was on the brink of calling for the plebiscite on presidential succession. This provided an opening to move towards democracy, and Aylwin knew how to draw on his previous political experience to make his party presidency into a springboard for restarting his political career. One milestone was the achievement of a pact with the left-wing faction of the Socialist Party, known as the 'Almeyda socialists.' The agreement, which Gabriel Valdés, his immediate predecessor in the party presidency, had attempted but not been able to achieve, paved the way for the formation of the Concertación. Aylwin's longstanding friendship with Clodomiro Almeyda was directly instrumental in facilitating the deal, something which Aylwin himself underlined when his first act as newly chosen party president was to visit Almeyda in prison, initiating the discussions that would later allow the two parties to forge an agreement that in turn made the Concertación possible.

Despite his long political trajectory, Aylwin had never actively sought to become president of the nation. That alternative presented itself only after the plebiscite of October 5, 1988, during which he had acted as spokesman for the No campaign and the visible face of the finally victorious opposition. Aylwin was pressed to stand by those within the DC who opposed the candidacy of Gabriel Valdés. Valdés, DC president between 1982 and 1987, had decided after the 1982 death of Frei Montalva that he wished to become President of the Republic. Although Aylwin finally succeeded in being chosen as DC presidential candidate, his victory in the relevant ballot was impugned by Valdés, alleging supposed irregularities that were the responsibility of the party hierarchy—a hierarchy that was of course still Aylwin's responsibility to oversee. The resulting scandal was christened 'Carmengate.'

Aylwin's last-minute decision to seek the presidential nomination had repercussions for his subsequent exercise of the office: he was not particularly familiar with the functions of executive office and had not prepared a manifesto or presidential plan to act as a blueprint for his term. Neither was he surrounded by a team of politically and professionally respected collaborators or advisors. His cabinet of ministers was accordingly given almost free rein. Four ministers had particular autonomy: the minister of interior, the minister in charge of the president's office, the minister general secretary of the government, (who is the government spokesperson), and the treasury minister. All of them went on to take decisions that had negative repercussions for the administration and/or for the democratization process as a whole.[8]

The conflicts between the parties and inside the DC in the 1960s and early 1970s led Aylwin to prioritize the search for agreement between the coalition parties. He pursued a politics of consensus and avoided confrontation with the opposition; his government put greater emphasis on continuity than reform of the neoliberal economic system imposed by the dictatorship, whose underlying political orientations and implications were overlooked by Aylwin and his economic team. The preference for consensus was, however, shared by the left and by Lagos.

Aylwin stood up decisively and courageously to Pinochet, who constituted the main threat to democracy given his continued presence on the political scene and the fact that he continued to enjoy the confidence of right-wing parliamentarians and business organizations. Unlike his successors, Frei Ruiz-Tagle and Lagos, Aylwin's nomination as the Concertación's presidential candidate came about by negotiation among the coalition's constituent parties. No primaries were held, as they were in the two subsequent cases.[9]

Ricardo Lagos: Personal History

Lagos, like Aylwin, came from a middle-class family, though, he was an only child. Brought up by his mother after his father died when Lagos was still a child, he was an outstanding student at the Instituto Nacional, a prestigious state high school, and, later, at the Law School of the Universidad de Chile. His undergraduate thesis on the concentration of economic power drew on a wide range of data to analyse the wealth of large economic groups. When finally published it became a success (Lagos, 1962), widely read in political circles and among the elite and running to various editions. Lagos turned from law to economics, receiving a doctorate in the latter from Duke University in 1965. Intelligent, with excellent powers of recall and a strong personality, Lagos emerged towards the end of the Pinochet regime as the left's principal political figure.

Ricardo Lagos: Professional Background

Prior to the 1973 coup Lagos, unlike Aylwin, was mainly dedicated to academia. He was professor of political economy, director of the School of Political and Administrative Sciences, and general secretary[10] of the Universidad de Chile. He was elected to the latter post in 1969 and held it until 1971, when he lost out to a rival candidate in the next cycle of elections of university authorities. He was made general secretary of Flacso, the Latin American Social Science Faculty ('Facultad Latinoamericana de Ciencias Sociales'), a regional academic organization headquartered in Santiago; this was a post he still held at the time of the coup. Lagos left the country, though not as a forced exile: he was invited for a stint as visiting professor at the University of North Carolina, then went to work for the UN in Buenos Aires, Argentina. He returned to Chile in 1978 as a consultant to the UN Development Program me, UNDP.

During the next years of the Pinochet dictatorship, Lagos worked principally as a consultant for international organizations and collaborated with private research centers created by opposition academics and politicians that had important political functions during those years (Huneeus, Cuevas and Hernández, 2014).

Ricardo Lagos: Political Biography

Lagos was active in the Radical Party as a young man, but he left in 1961 when this party joined the cabinet of right-wing president Jorge Alessandri Rodríguez (1958–1964). He supported Salvador Allende in the presidential elections of 1964 and subsequently operated as a left-wing independent until his return to Chile in 1978, when he joined the Socialist Party. A supporter rather than a particularly active member, his activity consisted mainly of joint work with left-wing academics working in the private research centers that had been created with overseas funding after the coup.

Lagos did not identify with either of the two principal socialist parties that existed—both unofficially—at that time, namely the 'PS-Altamirano,' after the individual who had been party leader at the time of the coup, and the 'PS-Almeyda,' more radical in its anti-dictatorship stance, led by Allende's former foreign minister.[11] However, he quickly became a leading opposition figure, one of the principal protagonists of the Democratic Alliance (Alianza Democrática).[12]

In 1987 he helped found a new political party, the Party for Democracy (Partido por la Democracia, PPD) and became its first party president. The PPD was designed to be a vehicle for Lagos's presidential aspirations, because he did not believe the PS had the organizational capacity or unity to help him achieve that goal. He nonetheless continued to be a member of the PS, although his influence within it was clearly weakened.

Lagos's performance during the 1988 plebiscite campaign, and in particular a memorable appearance on a TV program, gave a strong boost to his political career. As he recognized in his memoirs (Lagos, 2013) that appearance was the result of several days' careful preparation, undertaken in the knowledge that the result could be crucial for his career. Towards the end of the program Lagos addressed Pinochet directly, questioning the general's thirst for power while brandishing an accusatory finger directly into the camera lens. The gesture and his words were a carefully crafted spectacle that caused a great impact. The incident, widely referred to simply as 'Lagos's finger,' made him the principal personality of the left and opened the door for him to advance towards the presidency. It did, however, damage his image on the right, as it tapped into the right's atavistic fears of a radicalized left wing that would seek revenge were it ever to take power. The mainstream press of the day, sympathetic to the dictatorship, reported it in this vein. Lagos later explicitly moderated his discourse and views, declaring himself to be in favor of the market economy, part of the institutional framework inherited from the dictatorship that he was ready to respect.

In parliamentary elections held alongside the presidential contest of 1989, Lagos was defeated for a Senate seat by then-president of the DC, Andrés Zaldívar. The result, while not expected by Lagos, may be explained by his tendency to overstate his own popularity and ability to rally popular support. His years in academia and inexperience at running for elected office—this was his first attempt—contrasted with the trajectory of Zaldívar, who had first been elected senator in 1973 and had previously been a deputy minister and minister in the Frei Montalva administration.

Lagos served as education minister under Aylwin, but he resigned in 1992 to stand in 1993 for nomination as the Coalition's presidential candidate. He was, however, defeated in primaries by the DC's candidate, senator Eduardo Frei Ruiz-Tagle, whose personal support was boosted by the memory of his father.[13]

During the Frei Ruiz-Tagle administration, Lagos was Minister of Public Works. He took an energetic approach to the role, pressing ahead with an ambitious program of infrastructure development. Public-private sector partnerships were created by opening up public works contracts to private bidding, a practice that had been introduced under Aylwin. Lagos saw this as his opportunity to overcome the lack of trust between the left and business sectors, a legacy of the latter's traumatic memory of the Allende government. He launched a policy of privatization of public works through concessions to private enterprise, without having first established a regulatory framework to govern the process, which continued throughout his presidency.

Although Lagos had not been a minister under Allende, he suffered by association with the latter's poor economic management, which had led in turn to hyperinflation, shortages, and a full economic crisis—accentuated, naturally, by a predictably hostile US foreign policy towards Chile under Nixon. Lagos set himself the task of demonstrating that the left could be responsible in government, and effective in ministries and in the presidency.

Lagos achieved high visibility ratings in polls carried out a few months into the Frei Ruiz-Tagle government and won a comfortable victory in the Coalition primaries of 1999. However, in the first round of the subsequent presidential elections he led the right-wing candidate by the slimmest of margins—only 31,140 votes. The election duly went to a second round, which Lagos won. However, the narrow electoral victory marked him psychologically, and he took possession of the La Moneda presidential palace with a sense of being 'on the back foot'. He felt particularly weak in the eyes of the right and business sectors, and he drew on the media to shore up his power. He sought agreements with business associations and proved receptive to the public policy agenda and representations of Sofofa (Confederation of Industry Association), the foremost industry alliance.

Lagos was more an academic than a politician. He appealed to rationality rather than to the electorate's feelings or emotions, and his lack of active militancy in the Socialist Party meant he did not have much first-hand knowledge of the internal party machine, or of the concerns and preoccupations of grassroots party activists or its mid-level leadership. All of this had consequences during his administration. Although he did maintain direct contact with the left-wing parties, he adopted a strong presidential style in which decision-making was centralized in his hands and leadership was exercised in a personalist way, with frequent use of TV as a resource to influence public opinion in favor of his policies.

His dual training as a lawyer and an economist led him to believe that he could operate as an active head of government who was in command of the main policies. He put together a team of high-level professionals headed by a longtime advisor of his, a sociologist and former undersecretary general of Cepal (Economic Commission for Latin America, belonging to the United Nations). The group operated as an 'inner circle,' with direct access to Lagos, and became colloquially known as the 'second floor' ('segundo piso').[14]

The group was entrusted with a wide range of tasks, amongst them the monitoring of public policy success and implementation. This implied a loss of protagonism for the ministry of the presidency (Segpres) which was effectively sidelined or bypassed. The group also undertook much of Lagos's speech-writing and briefing, defining strategic priorities, and preparation of flagship policy innovations including the creation of new cultural institutions and an ambitious reform of the public health system (known as the 'Plan Auge'). A dozen members of this team of close collaborators were professionals from left-wing political parties, PS or PPD.

Lagos aimed to carve out a place for himself in Chile's democratic history, not only as the first left-wing president in Chile and Latin America to have presided over a successful administration, but also as the proponent of a constitutional reform that would effectively alter the 1980 Constitution, eliminating its authoritarian enclaves.

In his speech during the ceremony at which this reform was promulgated, Lagos declared: 'This is a great day for Chile. We have reasons for celebration: today we finally have a democratic Constitution, one that is in harmony with our national spirit . . .' It was an erroneous interpretation because some significant authoritarian enclaves had been preserved. These included the requirement of 'supermajorities,' high voting thresholds required for legislative action in certain sensitive areas. These in effect gave the political right veto power, allowing it to block legal and other changes aimed at modifying the still strongly neoliberal economic system.

Constraints on Presidential Power: The Increasing Role of the Senate

One of the most striking institutional continuities of the Chilean presidential system is the enormous power of congress, an important arena for negotiation between the government and the opposition. The legislature has strengthened its power since the early decades of the period under the 1833 Constitution, and this was achieved by diminishing the authority of the president, which provoked the comment that Chile had a parliamentary regime since the 1860s and not after the civil war of 1891 (Heise, 1974: 67).[15] Although formally bicameral, congress is in fact asymmetrical due to the fundamental lawmaking role played by the Senate. Every president democratically elected since 1931 has been a senator, even Gen. Ibañez, who had become a senator in 1949 before he was elected president in 1952. The tradition was revived in 1989: Aylwin had been a senator between 1965 and 1973, and Frei Ruiz-Tagle was a senator (from 1990–1994), as was Sebastián Piñera (1990–1998). Ricardo Lagos sought election to the Senate in the 1989 elections, but he was unsuccessful, largely because of the binomial election system. The only exception has been Michelle Bachelet, who was never a legislator.

The Senate's power can be seen also in the leadership of the parties, in that the majority of their presidents were senators when elected to this office; this enabled them to intervene directly in legislative negotiations underway in the upper chamber.

The role of congress is very important in the Chilean presidential system in that, since the re-establishment of democracy in 1931 (after the dictatorship of Ibañez), and from 1990 (after Pinochet), and until the government of Piñera, no president held a majority in the legislature, because none was able to control the Senate. During the period of the 1925 Constitution this was due to the Senate's method of election. Senators were elected for eight years, and half the members of the upper chamber were renewed every four years in elections that were not simultaneous with presidential elections. This prevented a president elected with broad popular support from benefiting from this support in the parliamentary elections, as these were held later, when the other half of the Senate was up for renewal, thus occurring after the president's popularity had waned. After 1990, the Senate retained the eight-year period and its renewal by halves every four years, but the presence of appointed senators, who supported the opposition, obliged the presidents to negotiate their principal policies and important decisions with the legislature. Under the Constitution of 1925, the Senate approved the appointment of ambassadors and top officials of the armed forces. The 1980 Constitution eliminated the first Senate attribution and gave it to the president, whereas the second was given to the commander-in-chief of the respective institution, to reinforce military autonomy from civilian control.

Later constitutional reforms limiting the authority of the president by allowing the Senate to intervene in the appointment of top state and executive branch officials strengthened the Senate even more. Until 1990, the Senate only participated in the election of the five councillors of the Central Bank, which enjoys constitutional autonomy, and the comptroller general of the republic, the main institution of horizontal accountability. The 1992 legal reform of the National Television Council established that the Senate would elect its ten members. The Senate also intervenes in the appointment of the board of Televisión Nacional, Chile's public television channel; in the election of the attorney general (who heads the public ministry, an institution created by the reform of the criminal procedure code of that year); and in the appointment of Supreme Court justices. The 2005 constitutional reform gave the Senate power to nominate four of the ten ministers of the Constitutional Court, two of whom are required to have been previously nominated by the Chamber of Deputies.

Conclusions

The re-establishment of the presidential system after the Pinochet dictatorship created difficulties that both presidents were able to resolve relatively successfully. The starting point was to break with Pinochet's authoritarian style, resume Chile's democratic continuity and learning the lessons of past errors that had led to the 1973 military coup. As first president of the new democratic era, and a politician whose long experience was recognized by the population and the Concertación leaders, Aylwin was able to reconcile this troubled and traumatic history with the demands of a country recovering from dictatorship. As a jurist, Aylwin saw with greater clarity than others the need to find truth and justice for the crimes of the dictatorship, despite warnings from left-wing leaders and ministers that this policy could lead to acts of provocation by Pinochet and threaten the continuity of the democratic process.

Lagos represented a different generation of left-wing politicians. He had neither participated in the Allende government nor been a parliamentarian, and this allowed him to adopt a modern left leadership profile that he carried on into his presidency. As a successor of Frei Ruiz-Tagle, who had led an opaque presidency, his strong leadership style was effective and he was responsible for some important policy innovations, particularly in public health and foreign policy. Differences in the leadership styles of the two presidents—a coalition government with broad ministerial autonomy in the case of Aylwin, and a more organized system, centralized around the president, in the case of Lagos—show the flexibility of the presidential system and the importance of the incumbent's leadership qualities. Both presidents faced continuities that complicated their administrations such as the increasing power of the Senate at the expense of the presidential office.

Chile's presidential government—a coalition of center and left parties in the four Concertación administrations and of two right-wing parties under Piñera—has been very successful both in consolidating democracy in a very difficult political context, and in implementing policies that have improved living standards for the great majority of the population.

No other democracy of the 'third wave' has enjoyed the continuity of four governments; others were unable to confront effectively the difficult political and economic agenda of democratization without losing popular support and having to surrender power to the opposition, in many cases in the midst of a grave economic crisis.

This performance has confounded pessimistic predictions about the presidential system's incapacity to ensure governability in democracy and, moreover, that a multiparty and presidential system would be incompatible with one another (Valenzuela, 1994).

Chile's success story is due to many institutional factors that demonstrate the flexibility of the presidential system in confronting situations of high political tension, as well as the leadership of presidents who had the political skills required to take controversial and unpopular decisions, and who could count on the support of the governing coalition parties in doing so. The country's long democratic tradition helped in this positive result, a tradition that led Sartori (1976: 173) to declare that 'Chile was the most significant (Latin American) country in terms of democratic tradition and structural consolidation of the party system.' The enormous value of this political capital was evident in the organizational capacity and leadership of the parties when they defeated Pinochet in the 1988 plebiscite that triggered the return to democracy.

Chile's leaders drew lessons from the past, from the dramatic collapse of democracy, the 1973 military coup and the repressive Pinochet dictatorship. Their capacity for negotiation and compromise avoided the escalation of conflicts that would have placed the advance of democratization at risk.

Institutions matter, but leadership matters too. Presidentialism can be found in many shapes and forms; its institutional resources leave open different options for presidents to decide how to tackle the past with its lights and shadows, how to deal with the short-term demands of the moment and have the vision to take long-term decisions that aid progress toward a more robust democratic system. Each with his own style and in different contexts, as analyzed in this chapter, both Aylwin and Lagos strove to accomplish these objectives. However, it is beyond the scope of this work to evaluate how successful they were in taking the best decisions for deepening democracy and improving its quality.

Notes

1. The possible re-election of president Patricio Aylwin was considered by some of his advisors but rejected due to minority support in the population. In a CERC survey (October 1992), a broad majority (58%) opposed his re-election. Furthermore, he did not have the support of party leaders and parliamentarians. Eduardo Frei Ruiz-Tagle was the Coalition's candidate in 2009 but was beaten by Piñera. As a condition of accepting the candidacy in 2009, Lagos asked for the power to select the list of candidates for congress before Frei Ruiz-Tagle announced his candidacy, a condition that leaders of the PS and PPD rejected.
2. The negotiations are carefully described by Cavallo (1998) and Otano (2006), two distinguished journalists.
3. I developed these ideas in Huneeus (2012 and 2014, chapter 5).
4. Pinochet did not establish the autonomous Central Bank during the dictatorship, precisely because it would have limited his power. He issued the organic constitutional law that created it, Law No. 18840, on October 10, 1989, two months before the first democratic elections.
5. Law No. 18993, of August 21, 1990.
6. I am grateful to Francisco Javier Díaz for this information.
7. Aylwin (1998) has writen his memoirs, but they cover only the years of the Pinochet regime.
8. I discuss this in depth in my book (Huneeus, 2014).
9. Michelle Bachelet, the Coalition's fourth successive successful presidential candidate, was not selected through primaries for her first period; however, she was for her second (non-consecutive) period. She won with 70% of the vote.
10. A senior managerial position, just below that of university rector and vice-rector, akin to an executive directorship.
11. The two tendencies came together in 1989 to form the Socialist Party of Chile.
12. A coalition of several parties, from the right, center, including the PDC, and the left, among which was the moderate socialist party, under the leadership of Ricardo Núñez (PS-Núñez).
13. In an open question posed in a CERC poll of December 1992 on the subject 'who is Eduardo Frei,' at a time when Frei had already been named as the DC's choice for the presidential nomination, 36% of respondents identified him as the son of ex-president Frei Montalva, 16% as a senator and 11% as the DC's presidential candidate.
14. Literally, the allusion was simply to the location, within the presidential palace, of the office of the head of the team.
15. The most important study of the 1833 Constitution recognizes the important function of congress even in its title, 'The Constitution before the Congress,' omitting mention of the presidency (Huneeus, 1981).

References

Aylwin, P. (1943). *El juicio arbitral*. Santiago: Editorial Nacimento.
Aylwin, P. (1998). *El reencuentro de los demócratas*. Santiago: Ediciones B.
Boylan, D.M. (2001). *Defusing Democracy. Central Bank Autonomy and the Transition from Authoritarian Rule*. Ann Arbor: The University of Michigan Press.
Cavallo, A. (1998). *La historia oculta de la transición. Chile 1990–1998*. Santiago: Grijalbo.

Couso, J. (2003). The politics of judicial review in Chile in the era of democratic transition, 1990–2002. *Democratization*, 10(4), 70–91.
Ffrench-Davis, R. (2002). *Economic Reforms in Chile: From Dictatorship to Democracy*. Ann Arbor: University of Michigan Press.
Garreton, M.A. (1995). *Hacia una nueva era política. Estudio sobre las democratizaciones*. Santiago: Fondo de Cultura Económica.
Greenstein, F.I. (2000). *The Presidential Difference. Leadership Style from FDR to Clinton*. Princeton: Princeton University Press.
Heise, J. (1974). *Historia de Chile. El período parlamentario 1861–1925*. Santiago: Editorial Andrés Bello.
Huneeus, C. (1981). *Der Zusammenbruch der Demokratie in Chile. Eine vergleichende Analyse*. Heidelberg: Esprint Verlag,
Huneeus, C. (2005). ¿Por qué ha funcionado el presidencialismo en Chile? *Persona y Sociedad*, 19(2), 11–53.
Huneeus, C. (2007). *The Pinochet Regime*. Boulder & London: Lynne Rienner.
Huneeus, C. (2012). Presidencialismo semisoberano. *Revista Uruguaya de Ciencia Política*, 21(2), 31–54.
Huneeus, C. (2014). *La democracia semisoberana. Chile después de Pinochet*. Santiago: Taurus.
Huneeus, C. and Maldonado, L. (2003). Demócratas y nostálgicos del antiguo régimen. Los apoyos a la democracia en Chile. *Revista Española de Investigaciones Sociológicas*, 103, 9–49.
Huneeus, C., Rodrigo Cuevas, J. and Hernández, F. (2014). Los centros de investigación privados (*think tanks*) y la oposición al regimen autoritario chileno. *Revista Uruguaya de Ciencia Política*, 23(2), 19–37.
Lagos, R. (1962). *La concentración del poder económico*. Santiago: Editorial del Pacífico.
Lagos, R. (2013). *Mi vida. De la infancia a la lucha contra la dictadura*. Santiago: Debate.
Lanzaro, J. (2003). *Tipos de presidencialismo y coaliciones política en América Latina*. Buenos Aires: CLACSO.
Mainwaring, S. and Shugart, M.S. (1997). Juan Linz, presidentialism, and democracy. *Comparative Politics*, 29(4), 449–471.
Otano, R. (2006). *Nueva crónica de la transición*. Santiago: Lom.
Pribble, J. (2013). *Welfare and Party Politics in Latin America*. Cambridge: Cambridge University Press.
Sartori, G. (1976). *Parties and Party Systems. A Framework for Analysis*. Cambridge: Cambridge University Press.
Shugart, M.S. and Carey, J.M. (1992). *Presidents and Assemblies. Constitutional Design and Electoral Dynamics*. Cambridge: Cambridge University Press.
Siavelis, P.M. (2000). *The President and Congress in Postauthoritarian Chile. Institutional Constraints to Democratic Consolidation*. Pennsylvania: The Pennsylvania State University Press.
Valenzuela, A. (1978). *The Breakdown of Democratic Regimes: Chile*. Baltimore: The Johns Hopkins University Press.
Valenzuela, A. (1994). "Party Politics and the Crisis of Presidentialism in Chile: A Proposal for a Parliamentary Form of Government", in: Linz, Juan J. Y Valenzuela, Arturo (eds.) *The Failure of Presidential Democracy. The case of Latin America*. (Baltimore: Ther Johns Hopkins University Press, vol. II, 91–150.

11 Conclusion

The 'coming of age' of Latin American presidentialism did not take place until the end of the twentieth century—almost two centuries after the idea of presidentialism was first raised by Bolívar in the early decades of the nineteenth century. Yet, however belatedly, it is important to note that presidentialism in Latin America is now a success, as the various chapters of this volume clearly suggest, despite long travails and especially despite pessimistic comments directed at this form of government.

There are indeed manifest reasons, well documented throughout this volume, why the Latin American presidential government should be considered a success. In particular, only one forced displacement of regularly elected presidents has taken place in the course of the twenty-first century, and indeed since the last decades of the twentieth: this was in Honduras, in 2009, when President Zelaya was forced out of office by the military; yet that action resulted from pressure by the legislature, and civilian rule was maintained immediately after Zelaya was dismissed.

Indeed, Latin American presidentialism had already gradually begun to function more smoothly in the last decades of the nineteenth century, as H. Davies pointed out in his *Government and Politics in Latin America* (1958):

> The North American student may be permitted to observe that the Latin American experience demonstrated that presidents can govern constitutionally, that legislatures can be responsible forums for the discussion and resolution of national issues, and that elections can be demonstrably free and can be accepted by the nation as a legitimate expression of the general will.
> (Davies, 1958: 511)

However, in particular from the 1930s to the 1980s, first as a consequence of the great depression which initially affected North America and Western Europe and then due to the Cold War, another long period of turbulence in Latin American political systems, with nearly two decades of military rule in Brazil and Chile. It seems permissible to conclude that Latin American countries have since overcome the fundamental dangers to which they were exposed. Although difficulties continue in a number of countries, presidential government in the region is no longer interrupted as it so frequently was in the past.

I

Latin American presidential government was initiated in particular by Iturbide in Mexico and by Bolívar in South America, especially in the northern part of that region. The key point is that, as a result of the French invasion of Spain and the fact that the Spanish king was taken prisoner by the occupying forces in 1808, the region was faced with having to decide what its political structure would be.[1] The situation was unlike what had occurred in the United States, where immigrants, overwhelmingly from Britain decided to secede the 'Thirteen Colonies' in the second half of the eighteenth century, having already enjoyed a form of 'representative government' fostered by the British government. Moreover, the question of the status of other inhabitants of the area—namely those who belonged to the 'native' population—was not considered at all.

Contrarily, early in the nineteenth century, the inhabitants of the Spanish American territories were totally unprepared for independence: the one major exception was Brazil, which became independent as a single 'empire' led by the son of the Portuguese king, first in the name of his father but subsequently in his own name through the simple act of superseding his father and becoming emperor himself.

Not surprisingly, in Spanish Latin America, a new political structure was difficult to elaborate and implement in the first decades following the independence of the newly created states, except, somewhat paradoxically, in Paraguay, where a strong president came to power without major problems and remained president for the subsequent two decades. Elsewhere, on the other hand, violence even the extreme of to civil war occurred in many parts of the region. The new leaders, and Bolívar in particular, failed even to see the need for leaders to be solidly implanted in these new states to be able to build a firm presidential and representative regime in any new countries being established. Chile was the country where, although not until the middle of the 1830s only, a stable presidential political system came to be established and to last (at least for several decades).

Meanwhile, outright wars took place throughout the region: in the north, Mexico lost almost half of its territory to the United States. In Central America, a 'quasi-federal' arrangement set up in the early 1830s among the five countries then belonging to the isthmus was quickly broken up, while, in South America, a number of major wars were waged between the 1830s to the 1870s. This was not the kind of background in which presidential government could be given a satisfactory fresh start. Thus, perhaps not surprisingly, the social and economic problems resulting from the great depression in the 'developed world' were to have also major political repercussions on the Latin American presidential republics from the 1930s, given the ties which many of these countries had had with the European countries since their independence.

II

While the difficulties experienced by Latin American governments were marked and prolonged, these countries did in practice forge an instrument, inherited from the United States but not tried elsewhere (except in France, after the monarchy was finally overthrown in 1848: but that experiment in presidential government quickly ended in disgrace, when the president of the country elected in 1848 by universal suffrage took full power to replace the presidential republic with a dictatorial 'empire' similar to that of Napoleon). It is easy therefore to forget how 'new' the Latin American 'nations' had been not only from the 1820s but by the end of the nineteenth century as well.

On the other hand, one must not forget the sheer size and number of the contingent of 'new' countries set up in the twentieth century, especially in the second half. Presidential republics were thus established in Asia and particularly in Africa, as most parts of that continent had theretofore been arbitrarily divided among European countries, Britain and France especially, but also Germany (up to 1918), Belgium, Portugal, and to a lesser extent Spain.

In a sense, Latin America was to bear the brunt, so to speak, of 'testing' presidentialism as 'the' form of government for 'new' countries, in the sense that their existing institutions could not rely on any previous national legitimacy. If these countries were to survive as units, or at least to avoid major political and social disruption, at least certain aspects of their new institutions needed to provide such legitimacy. What may not have been clear at the time, understandably, was that the presidency was (or could be) that legitimizing institution.[2] This meant that, by the 1950s and 1960s, the only political system which could embody such an 'instantaneous' personalized legitimizing principle was the presidential system.

In the United States, political conditions were such that 'representative government' had come to develop 'naturally,' so to speak, by generations of immigrants in what became the 'Thirteen Colonies': elsewhere, the only countries where such a development might have occurred (and indeed did occasionally occur) before the 1950s were the Latin American countries.

This is why the gradual buildup of legitimacy of many modern governments, at least in terms of linkage between leaders and citizens, referred to Latin American countries as a basis, however imperfect. Latin American presidential systems were the first to provide elements of such and they did so in a part of the world insulated from the immediate influence of other forms of government. The only intervention which could truly affect the ideology and behavior of these countries was from their one large neighbor, the United States.

Americans did indeed play a very large part in Latin American economic and social life: they were often markedly blamed for that behavior. On the political front, however, Americans could not blame Latin Americans for following their example: they could not say that Latin Americans did not practice presidentialism, but only that they did not practice it well. In contrast to the Europeans, they did not praise and attempt to promote the idea of another form of modern government, such as Britain had invented and had spread across (at least Western) Europe and large parts of the Commonwealth, but which was typically monarchical, parliamentary government.

Latin American countries thus undeniably had to demonstrate that presidential government was applicable beyond the United States, and indeed that it was applicable where it was particularly needed, in countries where the level of legitimacy of the national state was very weak, perhaps even non-existent. Such nations came to constitute, by the end of the twentieth century, the majority of the countries of the world (mostly in Africa, but also, in Asia, including the countries of Central Asia that were previously part of the Soviet Union—Russia itself having likewise adopted a presidential mode of government). Admittedly, some of these developments have taken place in the context of substantial variations from the American model, with a distinct presidential formula and even 'semi-presidential' regimes.

Still, with variations or without, and with changes large or small, all of these 'institutional systems' issued to some degree from the American model together with the difficulties that came to characterize the Latin American tradition and experience over nearly two centuries, during which countries gradually learned to adjust to the peculiarities of presidential government. In this way, other (later) 'new' countries were able to acquire a form of 'popular legitimacy.' The outstanding part which Latin America played in the development of the theory and the practice of 'modern' government in the contemporary world needs to be significant as having been large and even fundamental.

However difficult the process by which presidentialism in Latin America may have proved to be the emergence of presidentialism must be seen as having constituted the key institutional development without which, almost certainly, the 'new type of world' which emerged the nineteenth and twentieth centuries would not have had the proper 'tools' at their disposal to manage this 'new' world.

III

In the context of the 'progress' of presidentialism in Latin America occurring since the later decades of the twentieth century, three general points need to be recorded. One of these is positive, while the other two are not. The positive point relates to what appears to be the decline in the extent to which Latin American presidentialism is personalized, compared to earlier experience. The major part originally played by personalization unquestionably had the effect of rendering presidential rule more chaotic, and less based on rules adopted beforehand. The fact that, on the whole, presidencies have tended to follow previously adopted rules during recent decades has surely resulted in the eclipsing of personalization. Although presidents often enjoy high levels of popularity, these vary from president to president as well as over time in the case of each; perhaps more importantly, popularity seems no longer to exceed levels where pre-existing rules become inapplicable.

Meanwhile, as has been clearly pointed out in this volume, the fact that the presidential system had become 'established' in Latin America by the second half of the twentieth century does not mean that the countries have not suffered serious problems in the process of development of their presidential systems. The fact that we have here analyzed only two recent presidencies from six countries does not imply that the problems encountered in the other fourteen countries (all much smaller in population) were not also serious. What is clear is that, in the context of Colombia and Brazil in particular, two very serious problems have identified and discussed at some length here, although neither is regarded as having affected the contemporary development of the presidential system in those two countries.

One of the problems is violence: the amount of violence affecting Colombia has been catastrophic, to the extent that it is truly remarkable that the regular conduct of the electoral process has not been prevented from taking place. It was noted that the policies of the two Colombian presidents studied in Part II of this volume, Gaviria and Uribe, were fundamentally different, the first having pursued a 'war effort' against the rebels, the second attempting (unsuccessfully) to find a peaceful solution. Fortunately, their successor has apparently been able to make substantial progress in that direction.

In Colombia it has thus been possible, rather surprisingly, to maintain the main electoral rules of the liberal democratic process, although, at least in a substantial part of the country, confrontation has taken in effect the character of a civil war: the number of victims has not only been very large, but it has been so large as to ostensibly render almost impossible the emergence of the minimum conditions required for the maintenance of democratic politics.

It does therefore seem that violence (also much more widespread in the United States than in Western European countries) has been able to vary markedly in extent without preventing the politics of the country from remaining within a 'liberal democratic' framework: yet there would nonetheless seem to be a limit to governmental 'variations,' where a certain point, the level of violence must more brutally affect the practices to still be followed for the political process to still be regarded as liberal democratic. This 'level' has been affected by government policies; the article on Peru in this volume suggests that the level of violence was markedly diminished as the head of the national executive cleverly succeeded in promoting policies which were to have an impact on the origin of the phenomenon.

Yet, at this stage, and on the basis of this analysis of a minority of the Latin American countries, though not a minority of the Latin American population, it is not permissible to claim that the level of violence has never been able to profoundly disrupt the democratic system. Only a systematic study of the relationship between violence and (liberal) democratic forms of governance across the twenty states of the region can be expected to fully clarify the nature and character of the relationship between violence and liberal democratic modes of behavior.

The second major problem that appears to continually trouble and yet has not affect, directly or even markedly, the liberal democratic character of the countries is that of prevailing corruption. In general, one might expect a relationship to exist between the level of economic development of a given polity and the extent of corruption therin; perhaps more specifically, it seems that a general relationship does exist between the level of corruption in a country and the proportion of the population of that country which is living in poverty.

The most obvious case encountered among the six countries analyzed here in detail is that of Brazil, not only under Rousseff after the departure of Lula, but under Lula as well, despite the fact that Lula unlike his successor was highly popular. In the Brazilian case, in view of the fragmentation of the party system, the president has to rely on clientelistic practices that in turn lead to corruption. A very large public company, in particular, has thus been, directly or indirectly, involved in such a process.

The difficulty with respect to the assessment of the impact of corruption on the nature of political systems, in contrast with the level of violence, is that it is of course impossible to obtain truly reliable information and therefore to assess the precise extent of the phenomenon, since that phenomenon takes place in a context of secrecy, or at least of serious attempts at concealment. This is why the extent of corruption is often provided by means of judgments given by 'experts' rather than on the basis of data: only long and patient efforts undertaken to obtain evidence of the extent of corruption are likely to provide the reliable indicators required.

Yet, in the Brazilian case, it does seem that the general recognition of the phenomenon justifies the conclusion that corruption is rife in that country. As this is so, and like in the context of violence, one must aim at discovering whether 'variations' in the level of corruption are likely to affect the broad character of political systems, and in particular the extent to which these liberal democratic characteristics can be maintained.

Meanwhile, there are also significant differences among Latin American presidential systems with respect to the use of political structures and arrangements. Concretely, Latin American political systems vary in the extent to which governmental structures are closely dependent on the part played by parties on the nature of particular 'governments' in terms of the presidential administration of the region. In parliamentary systems, there is a well-known and vast literature about the extent to which parties form a key aspect of the building of cabinets: consequently, one is confronted by coalitions that may be considered 'small' or 'large,' or even 'grand.' The fact that this problem has not arisen in the United States, where there have been historically only two parties, and the fact that, in Latin America, parties are often lacking a solid 'structure', is surely among the reasons accounting for their role in presidential administrations not having been systematically examined. This matter is now being gradually redressed.

As a matter of fact, the role of parties in Latin American governments has markedly increased. In Chile, especially after the return of democratic government in the 1990s, the government of that country has constituted perhaps the most clear-cut example of a well-defined coalition system, and one that has functioned most efficiently. Other coalition arrangements have been more loosely structured, and less well defined, but some of these have emerged only since the early years of the twenty-first century. There is no doubt that a systematic analysis needs to be undertaken in this respect at the level of all the countries of Latin America—despite the fact that the very nature of presidentialism tends to render the relationship between the parties forming or supporting the 'government' less precise than is the case in parliamentary systems. Even in semi-presidential systems, let alone in 'pure' presidential systems, the position of the president is such that the extent of 'inequality' between a president and his or her ministers is much more pronounced than in parliamentary systems.

The study of governments, of the executive, and of the relationship between a president and other members of the government is only at an early stage in Latin American presidential countries, as well as in other presidential systems. The aim of this volume has therefore been to begin to open a debate around these matters, now that it has become clear that the presidential system in Latin America and elsewhere is truly a 'reality.' It is hoped that this volume will contribute significantly to the development of analyses and empirical theory within this domain, its aim having been to show that the character and behavior of the composition of the executive branch is a major topic requiring analysis in presidential systems, but one which had not been carefully and systematically considered until now.

Notes

1 See Blondel (2015: 97 and foll.).
2 A point which was to be most vividly stated by Jackson and Rosberg (1982).

References

Blondel, J. (2015). *The Presidential Republic*. London: Palgrave.
Davies, H. (1958). *Government and Politics in Latin America*. New York: Ronald Press.
Jackson, R.H. and Rosberg, C.G. (1982). *Personal Rule in Black Africa*. Berkeley: University of California Press.

Index

abstention, 18, 19, 124, 129
accountability, 7, 14, 15, 130, 249
activism, 95, 97, 98, 171, 175, 212
agenda, 5, 7, 8, 9, 11, 28, 42, 43, 100, 173, 177, 179, 180, 182, 183, 187, 188, 189, 192, 195, 197198, 199, 212, 213, 2226, 236, 237, 247, 251
ambition, 43, 102, 123, 151, 152, 153, 154, 193, 210
anti-politics, 81
approval, 38, 44, 46, 49, 60, 106, 137, 139, 150, 156, 159, 160, 170, 174, 175, 176, 180, 214, 224, 237, 238
attitude, 109, 131, 139, 242
attributes, 117, 129, 167, 168, 173, 174, 197
authoritarianism, 6, 7, 9, 18, 148, 156, 162

behavior, 10, 23, 24, 47, 57, 63, 93, 98, 109, 129, 137, 146, 147149, 152, 193, 210, 219, 225, 258, 260, 261
breakdown, 19, 26, 35, 97, 239, 240
bureaucracy, 70, 108, 120, 128, 185, 219, 222

campaigns, 15, 29, 48, 95, 102, 126, 127, 129, 139, 174, 210, 213
candidates, 1, 9, 15, 16, 26, 34, 36, 41, 46, 56, 64, 67, 75, 90, 98, 102, 120, 121, 122, 123, 124, 128, 131154, 155, 162, 170, 172, 178, 179, 181, 190, 199, 209, 211, 213, 222, 225, 236, 251
capitalism, 137, 148, 151
caudillismo, 5, 23
challenges, 33, 37, 40, 87, 93, 103, 127, 169, 198
charismatic, 11, 39, 80, 101, 169, 173, 198, 220, 221

citizens, 2, 7, 9, 37, 57, 59, 81, 83, 84, 98, 104, 127, 209, 258
cohesion, 45, 169
commodities, 2, 39, 44
communication, 15, 40, 90, 91, 105, 106, 110, 129, 135, 136, 139, 140, 173, 176, 177, 178, 212
competition, 6, 32, 36, 67, 74, 83, 93, 98, 100, 102, 111, 118, 119, 177, 179, 190, 192, 193, 197, 198, 220
confidence, 36, 85, 86, 125, 131, 135, 136, 158, 170, 172, 175, 176, 236, 239, 245
constitutional reforms, 9, 12, 16, 19, 20, 45, 47, 109, 249
coup, 2, 8, 11, 18, 19, 33, 34, 35, 55, 81, 147, 156, 161, 207, 208, 212, 217, 219, 231, 234, 235, 240, 243, 245, 246, 250, 251
Cuba, 2, 6, 13, 16, 19
cycle, 6, 13, 16, 17, 27, 159, 170, 171, 174, 198, 245

democracy, 2, 5, 6, 7, 8, 12, 14, 15, 16, 19, 20, 25, 26, 28, 29, 32, 33, 39, 45, 70, 75, 76, 80, 86, 87, 89, 90, 94, 130, 131, 134, 136, 141, 146, 147, 156, 157, 159, 162, 190, 191, 205, 208, 219, 231, 233, 234, 235, 238, 239, 240, 241, 242, 243, 244, 245, 246, 249, 250, 251
democratic consolidation, 2, 7, 8, 81
democratization, 6, 7, 25, 87, 98, 100, 103, 148, 162, 170, 174, 182, 192, 197, 245, 251
deputies, 30, 98, 99, 100, 110, 151, 180, 183, 191, 192, 193, 194, 195, 196, 198, 199, 200, 203, 213, 221, 224, 232, 233, 250

dictatorship, 5, 25, 32, 45, 46, 64, 150, 151, 159, 168, 170, 208, 212, 231, 232, 233, 234, 235, 239, 241, 242, 244, 245, 246, 247, 249, 250, 251
discipline, 15, 31, 192, 193, 194, 195, 196, 219, 222, 223, 226
discontent, 158, 234
discourse, 26, 27, 38, 39, 81, 95, 125, 145, 146, 147, 151, 156, 157, 158, 160, 162, 172, 173, 214, 247

economic crisis, 6, 18, 44, 47, 106, 124, 147, 205, 222, 234, 247, 251
economy, 5, 8, 9, 10, 20, 39, 44, 48, 122, 124, 134, 137, 146, 149, 151, 152, 153, 160, 169, 175179, 206, 207, 213, 215, 216, 219, 234, 239, 245, 247
education, 2, 3, 18, 29, 57, 73, 74, 76, 77, 78, 79, 83, 95, 96, 97, 107, 108, 135, 137, 151, 159, 173, 199, 209, 234, 247
efficiency, 9, 26, 112, 171, 172, 183
electoral defeat, 85, 86, 220
electoral system, 31, 93, 98, 104
elites, 5, 30, 149, 160, 161, 170
environment, 8, 23, 40, 41, 75, 117, 138, 140, 167, 168, 175, 190, 198
expertise, 84, 96, 171

family, 3, 17, 73, 74, 76, 87, 137, 150, 154, 168, 182, 199, 241, 245
foreign affairs, 27, 108, 170, 171
freedom, 6, 11, 18, 23, 105, 122, 134, 135, 233
fujimorismo, 147, 148, 149, 157, 161, 162

GDP, 21, 94, 96, 100, 122, 124, 206
governing, 37, 42, 46, 93, 108, 118, 124, 148, 158, 160, 182, 190, 192, 193, 194, 195, 198, 199, 221, 226, 243, 251
growth, 2, 12, 21, 29, 38, 39, 45, 46, 48, 96, 107, 122, 124, 148, 153, 159, 161, 180, 182, 192, 239

hyperinflation, 18, 28, 48, 147, 153, 155, 156, 161, 171, 221, 247

identification, 27, 169, 171, 198
ideology, 20, 39, 90, 98, 151, 215, 221, 222, 258
impeachment, 19, 35, 85, 170, 191, 218, 225

income, 2, 39, 104, 135, 182, 199, 206, 213, 215
incumbent, 12, 16, 25, 28, 34, 102, 108, 172, 176, 180, 250
indigenous, 15, 18, 94, 122, 130, 134
inequality, 8, 12, 14, 15, 17, 39, 46, 78, 141, 200, 206, 261
instability, 11, 19, 26, 55, 101, 112, 121, 155, 160, 170, 172, 173, 174, 177, 198, 226
institutional crisis, 81, 226
institutions, 1, 2, 5, 7, 8, 15, 19, 23, 30, 34, 36, 40, 75, 81, 100, 107, 112, 130, 137, 148, 150, 157, 161, 167, 168, 173, 177, 191, 199, 205, 223, 227, 233, 235, 239, 248, 250, 257
interest in politics, 95, 168

justice, 2, 100, 111, 112, 114, 122, 128, 162, 225, 227, 231, 239, 241, 250

leadership capabilities, 78, 81, 239
left turn, 145, 146, 148, 158, 161, 162
left-wing, 11, 25, 28, 29, 39, 45, 47, 89, 110, 207, 215, 231, 240, 242, 244, 246, 247, 248, 250
legacy, 7, 29, 101, 239, 247
legislative, 9, 17, 18, 26, 30, 31, 32, 33, 35, 36, 41, 46, 81, 82, 87, 89, 104, 109, 110, 111, 113, 157, 171, 174, 182, 183, 185, 187, 192, 193, 195, 196, 198, 199, 200, 209, 214, 217, 218, 223, 226, 235, 237, 238, 248, 249
legitimacy, 9, 19, 40, 43, 93, 94, 98, 99, 104, 129, 131, 136, 147, 148, 149, 150, 154, 156, 241, 257, 258
loyalty, 38, 75, 107, 122

middle class, 2, 17, 45, 95, 119, 120, 133, 135, 169, 239, 245
ministerial portfolios, 32, 43, 185, 193
mobilization, 128, 169, 180, 188, 212, 237, 7, 10, 11, 12, 27, 29, 38

neoliberalism, 13, 14, 46, 97, 211, 215
networks, 15, 73, 77, 102, 118, 124, 167, 222

opposition, 15, 24, 25, 26, 32, 34, 36, 40, 41, 45, 90, 98, 99, 100, 101, 102, 110, 113, 130, 131, 132, 137, 138, 140, 141, 146, 149, 151, 152, 155, 157, 162, 168, 169, 172, 174, 180, 183, 191,

Index 265

192, 193, 196, 211, 212, 213, 214, 217, 219, 222, 223, 226, 232, 233, 235, 236, 237, 242, 243, 244, 245, 246, 248, 249, 251
outsider, 5, 25, 26, 40, 48, 64, 75, 79, 80, 81, 89, 147, 153, 154, 160

partisanship, 185, 186, 189, 197
party control, 75, 187, 220
party system, 14, 15, 25, 33, 36, 37, 40, 75, 81, 82, 90, 122, 145, 150, 156, 161, 174, 251, 260
perceptions, 117, 126, 213
performance, 6, 7, 14, 16, 23, 27, 33, 38, 41, 43, 44, 45, 47, 87, 106, 153, 154, 157, 168, 170, 173, 174, 175, 176, 181, 197, 200, 220, 246, 251
Peronism, 39, 40, 205, 207, 209, 210, 212, 213, 214, 215, 220, 221, 222, 223, 224, 225, 226, 227
personalism, 7, 10, 14, 23, 39, 117, 152
personalization, 1, 2, 7, 10, 15, 40, 48, 75, 89, 90, 174, 180, 198, 226
polarization, 2, 6, 11, 13, 31, 147, 154, 155, 172, 179, 180, 185, 198, 233, 240, 243
political capital, 1, 2, 3, 73, 74, 75, 76, 77, 78, 82, 85, 86, 251
political career, 3, 26, 73, 74, 75, 77, 78, 80, 81, 82, 86, 90, 93, 94, 95, 97, 99, 109, 112, 113, 118, 119, 120, 121, 123, 125, 129, 167, 168, 170, 208, 209, 210, 222, 240, 242, 244, 246
political crisis, 44, 93, 106, 145, 205, 234
political dynasties, 77
political regime, 1, 5, 7, 19, 147, 148, 205, 211
political skills, 13, 169, 238, 251
political system, 5, 9, 15, 29, 38, 39, 41, 58, 73, 74, 75, 76, 78, 81, 84, 86, 87, 93, 107, 112, 114, 148, 207, 217, 226, 239, 256, 257, 260, 261
popularity, 34, 36, 37, 38, 39, 40, 45, 46, 48, 49, 90, 91, 93, 99, 102, 106, 107, 130, 131, 132, 152, 170, 174, 175, 176, 179, 180, 209, 211, 213, 214, 237, 247, 249, 259
populism, 5, 9, 10, 11, 26, 38, 39, 132, 147, 159
poverty, 2, 8, 17, 29, 45, 46, 122, 124, 134, 135, 141, 146, 173, 206, 215, 234, 239, 260

presidential office, 2, 71, 185, 187, 188, 199, 250
presidentialism, 1, 2, 3, 5, 12, 15, 16, 18, 26, 31, 33, 36, 55, 57, 68, 70, 74, 80, 81, 86, 93, 156, 162, 217, 218, 231, 232, 233, 235, 250, 255, 257, 258, 259, 261
professionalization, 14, 15, 37, 74, 99, 108, 112, 192, 209
protest, 25, 35, 95, 103, 130, 153, 156, 157, 215, 216

quality of democracy, 14, 26, 75, 87

re-election, 9, 156, 162, 172, 208
referendum, 7, 20, 34, 45, 49, 55, 123, 125, 136, 137
religion, 95, 136
representation, 6, 30, 31, 32, 42, 81, 129, 142, 147, 149, 154, 156, 160, 161, 193, 209, 213, 247
revolution, 8, 11, 25, 57, 94, 147, 152, 153, 159, 161, 162, 207, 208, 234, 243, 257
right-wing, 12, 14, 27, 28, 29, 35, 46, 89, 90, 124, 135, 147, 207, 234, 245, 246, 247, 250

satisfaction, 37, 40, 146
scandals, 35, 37, 45, 105, 106, 124, 174, 180, 182, 198, 200, 212, 214, 220
second term, 34, 38, 44, 49, 84, 136, 158, 173, 174, 175, 177, 182, 185, 193, 197, 207, 212, 214, 215, 222, 226
security, 2, 8, 14, 17, 28, 38, 44, 104, 105, 106, 107, 112, 127, 131, 135, 136, 139, 169, 188, 199, 233
social background, 73, 75, 167, 197, 205
social capital, 85
socialism, 8, 11, 13, 151, 242
socialization, 73, 76, 77, 161, 168
spheres, 6, 114, 117, 137, 139, 145, 146, 237
strategy, 30, 37, 38, 40, 44, 45, 48, 74, 90, 102, 104, 105, 106, 110, 113, 125, 126, 128, 136, 153, 154, 156, 158, 162, 180, 185, 187, 199, 213, 222, 224, 238, 241

technocrats, 27, 28, 43, 89, 96, 107, 120, 127, 197

trajectories, 73, 74, 75, 76, 79, 81, 85, 86, 87, 96, 140, 240
transition to democracy, 5, 15, 19, 45, 76, 233
transparency, 15, 94, 212, 222
trust, 81, 101, 108, 113, 226

United States, 1, 3, 8, 10, 11, 55, 56, 57, 58, 59, 60, 61, 62, 64, 66, 68, 69, 94, 97, 109, 139, 149, 154, 207

values, 10, 28, 77, 97, 109, 136, 147, 151, 215
violence, 2, 9, 14, 17, 18, 101, 104, 107, 118, 121, 122, 123, 124, 125, 126, 127, 131, 140, 256, 259, 260, 261
voting, 19, 30, 31, 32, 162, 175, 180, 183, 193, 195, 199, 249

Washington Consensus, 207
way out, 84, 85